THE IMAGE OF THE BUDDHA

THE IMAGE OF

JEAN BOISSELIER
AHMAD HASAN DANI
SU-YOUNG HWANG
NIHARRANJAN RAY
DIETRICH SECKEL
ALEXANDER C. SOPER
MAURIZIO TADDEI
OSAMU TAKATA

GENERAL EDITOR: DAVID L. SNELLGROVE

THE BUDDHA

KODANSHA INTERNATIONAL/UNESCO

First published 1978 by the United Nations Educational, Scientific and Cultural Organization, 7 Place de Fontenoy, 75700 Paris, France and Kodansha International Ltd., 2-12-21 Otowa, Bunkyo-ku, Tokyo 112, Japan and Kodansha International/USA, Ltd., 10 East 53rd Street, New York, New York 10022 and 44 Montgomery Street, San Francisco, California 94104. Printed in Japan.

(Kodansha International) ISBN 0-87011-302-x
LCC 77-75964
JBC 1071-785822-2361

First edition, 1978

CONTENTS

PREFACE

Our intention is to illustrate the various forms of expression of the ideal of Buddhahood, which for two thousand five hundred years has been a source of profound inspiration to many peoples of Asia and more recently to other parts of the world as well. By the term 'image of the Buddha' we mean any valid traditional expression, whether symbolic or anthropomorphic, which has served as a presentation of the Buddha ideal.

To cover so wide a field demands the co-operation of several scholars, each of whom is proficient in the traditions of a limited area. At the same time we have tried to produce a work which is a genuine attempt at international co-operation and which is not simply a collection of articles by individual authors. This has required an unusual amount of mutual accommodation and a readiness to submit the earlier contributions to such re-editing as has been necessary in order to produce a single coherent work on our agreed theme.

Since Buddhism has been in the first place an Indian religion, flourishing through a great variety of phases in the land of its origin during a period of about one thousand seven hundred years (even longer than this in the south), and since these various phases have had their repercussions on Buddhist developments elsewhere in Asia, special attention has been given to relating the original and useful contributions of Professors Ray and Dani to those of their fellow contributors. As editor I have accepted responsibility for the introductory sections to the chapters and for most of the additions, especially in so far as these relate to Buddhism in Kashmir, Nepal and Tibet, for which sections I was in any case personally responsible. Professor Boisselier, who has covered the whole of South-East Asia, has similarly added material relevant to contacts between South-East Asia and South India. Likewise, while Professor Seckel has been exclusively responsible for the chapter on early Buddhist symbols, others of us have added to his material in the last chapter, in so far as this relates to our special areas. No such adjustment seemed necessary in the case of East Asian Buddhism, where we have relied upon the individual contributions of Professors Hwang, Soper and Takata. Finally Professor Taddei has written for us the important chapter on Central Asia, which links the Indian world with that of the Far East.

The chapters are arranged according to four general periods and at the same time according to different geographical and cultural areas. Chapter 1 covers the period of approximately third century B.C. to first century A.D.; Chapter 2, approximately first century to fourth century A.D.; Chapter 3, approximately fourth century to eighth century A.D. These first three chapters are concerned with developments in the Indian subcontinent.

Chapter 4 covers the rest of Asia from various times, depending upon when Buddhism first arrived in the various cultural areas, during the first millennium A.D. Chapter 5 covers the whole of Asia, including India, from the eighth to the fifteenth century and in some cases rather later.

The periods can be only approximate because convenient divisions are not necessarily the same for all cultural areas. It must also be emphasized that the various cultural areas as defined by us cannot necessarily be understood in terms of modern political frontiers, many of which have only been fixed in recent times.

It is hoped that while remaining a scholarly work throughout, this book will have widespread appeal. Despite the number of books published on Buddhism, this great Asian religion still remains foreign to modern ways of thought. It may be easy to simplify the approach by forcing Buddhist ideas and teachings into the historical, social and moral moulds of the modern world, but believing that this falsifies the very essence of the religion, we have deliberately refrained from this. The reader is therefore asked to accept a more philosophical and mythological approach, which accords better with traditional Asian attitudes. So long as one thinks of the Buddha in a modern historical sense as a purely human teacher, who lived once and for all about 500 B.C., the expressions of his image as portrayed in this book will remain largely incomprehensible. For generations of millions of Buddhists, the Buddha is a religious ideal, a supernatural manifestation, who at various times and places has assumed a human form on earth. While this earthly character is never entirely forgotten, much of the time it recedes into the background, while the self-manifesting Buddha ideal of supramundane tranquillity and bliss remains clearly to the fore.

Just as Christian theology required several centuries for its development and formulation, so 'Buddhology', the theory of the Buddha-nature, gradually developed in India over a period of a thousand years and more. Various movements took place in Buddhism just as in Christianity, and important philosophical and doctrinal differences soon appeared. I have drawn attention to these in the introductory sections to Chapters 1 to 5, and the interested reader can conveniently go through these sections consecutively in order to gain a grasp of those Buddhological developments that alone can explain the wealth of expression of the Buddha image. Just as one cannot understand the symbolism of early Christian art and its rich mediaeval development without some knowledge of Christology as expressed in terms of Hebrew and Greek teaching and some knowledge of the history of Christianity itself, so it is impossible to understand Buddhist art without some knowledge of Indian religious concepts and Buddhist religious history, as interpreted in all those Asian countries where Buddhism became a major religion. Thus while we can try to explain such developments in clear terms, we cannot simplify the presentation to the extent of pretending that there are no complications at all. This is a traditional religious Asian world with which we are dealing, an Asian world that still remains meaningful for those many Asian peoples who are scarcely touched in their religious sensibilities by the enquiring scepticism and materialistic concepts of the present century.

The modern world is largely concerned with realities in a material sense. The higher religions, of which Buddhism is certainly one, are concerned with reality in a supramundane or transcendental sense. It was certainly important to early Christians that Jesus of Nazareth lived and taught and died in Palestine, and his historicity has never seriously been put in doubt. But what was important for the earliest Christians and has been essential to Christianity ever since is that this same Jesus, to use an early biblical phrase, was raised to God's right hand and thus became identifiable as supramundane and divine in his essential nature. The elaboration of this realization is precisely the substance of all Christology. Similarly those who compiled the earliest Buddhist scripture never doubted that Śākyamuni, 'the Sage (*muni*) of the Śākya people', who occupied a small territory on what is now the borderland of India and Nepal, was a human teacher and in every sense a man of flesh and blood. But they also believed that he had achieved Final Enlightenment (*bodhi*), and thus the physical elements of which his human body was composed disintegrated into the transcendental condition, known as *parinirvāṇa*, the 'ultimate extinction', defined as the final extinction of all worldly aspiration and craving. As such he was regarded as higher than all the gods and as representing, just as Buddhas of the past had represented, the supramundane aspect of existence, distinguished in its simplest philosophical formulation as *saṃsāra*, the round of existence, and *nirvāṇa*, the peace deriving from the cessation of *saṃsāra*. The goal of Enlightenment (*bodhi*) exercised the minds of Indian philosophers for over a millennium, and thus it is not surprising that the historic as well as the symbolic presentations of this supramundane ideal assumed a large variety of forms here on earth. Indian conceptions of 'rebirth', or to use the more familiar Western term 'transmigration', are certainly earlier than Śākyamuni and thus were taken for granted by him and his followers. The acceptance of such a belief results in one great difference between Indian religions and the great monotheistic religions, Israel, Christianity and Islam. According to Indian theories, phenomenal existence manifests itself in time-cycles. Thus any dogma of a one and only Buddha, through whose teachings one may be saved, is ruled out from the start. Since Buddhas may appear in different world-ages and different time-cycles, the goal of Buddhahood is essentially a unitary ideal with a plural expression.

In their very different ways, the great religions are a subtle combination of previous cosmological, philosophical and ethical ideas prevalent in a particular society, which are then given a new force and sense of direction by an extraordinary human being, who speaks with such authority that not only do his immediate disciples listen to him (there have been many such religious teachers in the history of the world) but also an ever-widening circle of converts, who continue to accept on faith his authority for the new interpretation of old doctrines that characterizes his teaching. His personality becomes thereby identified with his teaching as its supreme living representative, and in so far as his teaching aims at the realization of superhuman realities normally beyond the reach of ordinary mortals, he comes to be regarded as a specially ordained manifestation of those superhuman realities. Thus while on the one hand Śākyamuni could be regarded as a mortal man who had gained Enlightenment in the course of a rather special human life, it was also believed by his followers that his actual birth was a predestined event, and that having descended from the 'Heavens known as Joyful' (*Tuṣita*) into his mother's body, he was born miraculously from her right side, thus avoiding the physical impurity of a normal human birth. Not only his birth but all the great events of his life, especially his Enlightenment, his First Preaching and his Death, are heavy with mythological significance, and they are thus presented in the earliest available canonical accounts.

Since the nineteenth-century rationalized accounts of the life of Śākyamuni have been produced, and for some modern Buddhists, Śākyamuni is a mere human being, certainly a remarkable one, but no more than that. Whatever value or interest such modern interpretations may have, they are manifestly in conflict with all the traditional presentations of Buddhism as available to us in Buddhist literature and Buddhist art. They are produced by accepting the canonical records where Śākyamuni appears as just a human being, and by rejecting as spurious those records where his superhuman nature is affirmed. The first are readily accepted as historical and the second are assumed to be the superstitious beliefs of simple folk, supposedly added later in order to attract a larger circle of supporters. It is even sometimes argued that Śākyamuni himself and his more intelligent disciples were just like rational liberal-minded men of the twentieth century.[1] As it happens there is very little history indeed in early Buddhist writings and it is precisely the apparently factual matter, for example, the details of Śākyamuni's life and the account of the first Buddhist congress, supposedly held at the Magadhan capital soon after Śākyamuni's death, which responsible scholarship tends to regard as spurious.[2] Certainly the earliest Buddhism known to us from Buddhist art is highly mythological, and it is the progress of this art which it is our task to follow here.

This book provides an historical survey of the ways in which the ideals of Buddhahood have been expressed through the centuries, and it will be seen that the earliest expressions were mythological and symbolic and that attempts at a more realistic representation came several centuries later, only to be submerged almost at once in more elaborate forms of symbolism. In this process the history of Buddhist art accords with that of Buddhist literature. To follow this process as editor of so comprehensive a work and to see it to its conclusion have been for me matters of great satisfaction, and I express my sincere thanks to all who have co-operated in the task, not only my collaborators but also those members of UNESCO who have been involved in the work, especially Monsieur N. Bammate and Mme. Noriko Aikawa. Finally we are all very much indebted to Mr. Jules Young, who has done so much work of painstaking checking in order to ensure that this book will appear in print with as few errors as are humanly possible. The maps have been drawn by Mr. A. F. de Souza, and the index prepared by Mr. Tadeusz Skorupski, who has helped me much in the latter stages.

David L. Snellgrove

[1] For such a presentation, see Trevor Ling, *The Buddha* (London, 1975), noting perhaps my review article, 'In search of the historical Śākyamuni', *South East Asian Review*, 7 (January, 1975), pp. 151–58.

[2] In this respect one should see especially the works of André Bareau, *Les premiers conciles bouddhiques* (Paris, 1955) and his *Recherches sur la biographie du Buddha* (Paris, 1963, 1970 and 1971). Full references are given in the Bibliography. The best book available in English remains that by E. J. Thomas, *The Life of the Buddha as Legend and History*, first published in 1927. This is based almost entirely on the Pāli and Sanskrit sources available to him, while André Bareau draws also upon other early canonical material, lost in its Indian original but available in Chinese translations. Another excellent and very readable work in French is that of Alfred Foucher, *La vie du Bouddha d'après les textes et les monuments de l'Inde* (Paris, 1949).

THE IMAGE OF THE BUDDHA

I. THE FIRST SYMBOLS OF THE BUDDHA

1. THE ESSENTIAL NATURE OF A BUDDHA

The name 'Buddha', 'the Enlightened One', represents one of the highest—and certainly the most widely acknowledged—aspirations of the religious and philosophical thought of Asia. It is a name of numinous implications, transcending altogether the temporal human personality of Śākyamuni, namely Gautama, the Sage of the Śākya clan, the most renowned of Buddha manifestations, who lived and taught in India round about 500 B.C. Certain misleading comparisons have been made between the central figures of the main world-religions, as though they were all founders in much the same kind of way of the religions that sprang forth from their teachings and from the personal inspiration that they gave. Thus in order to clarify the significance of the name 'Buddha', certain distinctions must first be made in order to remove any false assumptions. For the adherents of Islam, Mohammed is the last of the Prophets and the greatest of the Prophets, promulgating through his revealed word, the Koran, all that is necessary for the salvation of his followers. For Christians, Christ represents in human form the fullness of the supreme Godhead, and such a divine revelation is regarded as ultimate for all time, however varied may be its expressed form in differing languages and cultures. In the case of both these great religions the historical person of one human founder remains central. By contrast, there is nothing unique or ultimate in the historical person of Śākyamuni, and by referring exclusively to him as the Buddha, in the same manner as one may refer to Jesus of Nazareth as the Christ, there results a fundamental misunderstanding. Certainly Śākyamuni is the most renowned of Buddhas in our present world-age, and thus many of the images presented in this book represent him in particular, but the traditional teachings and the living faith and devotion of practising Buddhists throughout Asia have never limited the concept of Buddha to a single human personality, and thus many Buddha figures besides Śākyamuni have been represented in symbolic as well as in human and divinized human form.

The Recognition of Śākyamuni as Buddha

Since the latter part of the last century, when sufficient scholarly information about the teachings and general history of Buddhism became known in the Western world, many European writers, captivated by the gentleness, the detachment and the tolerance of Buddhist teachings, have produced many and varied accounts of the life of Śākyamuni, whom all without exception treat as the founder of this religion, in precise analogy with the founders of other great religions. They have also noted that in the earlier Buddhist literature, preserved in greatest bulk in the Pāli canon of Theravādin Buddhism, Śākyamuni, while certainly recognized as Buddha and 'Lord' (Sanskrit: *bhagavān*), appears as a human teacher surrounded by a following of devoted disciples, like many other religious teachers in India at that time, and in fact ever since.[1] This earlier Buddhist literature, in the first place transmitted orally from the fifth century B.C. onwards, arranged in ordered sections by specially qualified groups of monk-reciters, and finally committed to writing by the first century B.C., contains the most varied as well as the most voluminous materials, but the general presentation of the various sets of teachings is certainly intended to be historical. Śākyamuni wanders with his disciples throughout a well-defined geographical area, the central Ganges Valley, and care is taken to fix the actual locality of every discourse attributed to him. Throughout he is credited with omniscience, miraculous powers and clairvoyance, the normal attributes of a Buddha, but at the same time he remains a human being.

What European writers have often known, but with few exceptions have failed to take full account of, is that Śākyamuni was recognized as Buddha and, according to the earliest available texts, claimed himself to be Buddha as a result of his experience of Enlightenment (*bodhi*) under the pipal tree at Gayā (south of modern Patna) in his thirty-fifth year, and that up to this great event he is more properly referred to as Bodhisattva (*bodhisattva*), that is, as a 'living being' (*sattva*) who is striving towards Enlightenment (*bodhi*). Here we must note at once a significant difference between the great Semitic religions, which are concerned with the salvation of mankind, and Indian religions, which are concerned with the salvation of all 'living beings' (*sattva*) throughout the universe (in the special way in which they conceive it). In the early Buddhist texts these 'beings' include gods, men, animals, wandering spirits (*preta*) and the creatures in hell. Since belief in rebirth is fundamental to Buddhist teachings, a Bodhisattva—a 'living being' on his long progress towards Enlightenment—may be born in any of the five categories of possible rebirth. Later a sixth category, that of the 'titans' or 'anti-gods' (*asura*) was added. Once again, the earliest Buddhist literature contains many references to Śākyamuni's previous births as a Bodhisattva, and later on, large collections of such stories were made, known as *jātaka* ('birth stories'). Western scholars tend to overlook such traditions in their presentation of Śākyamuni as Buddha because these stories are manifestly drawn from a large fund of early Indian folklore and thus may be simply dismissed as pure legend. However, we must ask the question whether such an imposition of a modern rationalizing viewpoint does justice to the idea of a Buddha developed and elaborated in India more than two thousand years ago.While we ourselves

[1] The earliest Buddhist teachings seem to have been transmitted in various dialects by the different groups and 'schools' that gradually spread over the whole of India, reaching Sri Lanka in the south and the far north-west parts of India during the third century B.C. Every school possessed its own approved canon. Apart from substantial parts preserved in Chinese and Tibetan translation and a large part of a rather late Sanskrit canon (viz., the *Vinaya* of the Mūlasarvāstivādins) re-discovered this century, the only really substantial representative texts of early Buddhism are formed by the canon of the Theravādin school, transmitted orally from South India to Sri Lanka and finally written down in its Indian dialectical form, possibly a western Indian dialect, in the first century B.C. Known as Pāli, 'the (sacred) book', this term is now commonly used as a name for this particular form of Indian dialect.

may try to distinguish in the whole Buddha complex of traditions and stories that which might reasonably be accepted as historical and that which must be judged pure legend, it would seem that the generations of monk-reciters who compiled the first Buddhist canons clearly did not make such distinctions. From their point of view, history, legends, mythological conceptions, and philosophical theories are all intricately linked together, and we have absolutely no reason for assuming that Śākyamuni was a rationalizing moralistic philosopher, holding beliefs that might be acceptable to liberal theorizers of the nineteenth and twentieth centuries but that are clearly in conflict with the earliest recorded Buddhist traditions.

Fortunately this present work on the image of the Buddha is not concerned with attempting to answer the intractable questions of what Śākyamuni thought of himself and what the form of his own self-consciousness was. From a traditional Buddhist viewpoint, this might even seem to be a nonsensical question, for it is a fundamental teaching that there is no such entity as a person (*puruṣa*) or a self (*ātman*), and what we recognize as a person is merely a fluctuating stream of variable mental and physical elements (*dharmas*). All Buddhist schools in all periods have believed that Buddha appeared on earth as a human being and as a man. His humanity as Gautama of the Śākya clan has never been in doubt. One must note, however, that the Indian view of the world and of history as essentially unreal, as a succession of fleeting appearances, renders any statement about Śākyamuni's humanity very different in implication from any corresponding statement about the humanity of Jesus of Nazareth. According to Christian belief, Jesus is at once God and man in an entirely inseparable manner, appearing once and for all on earth during one short human lifetime. According to the traditions of all Buddhist schools from the earliest times onwards Śākyamuni, this great sage of the Śākyas, lived on earth as a man and as a religious teacher, but this human form of his has no greater reality than that of any other 'living being', whether god, man, animal, or whatever else. What was judged really important about Śākyamuni was that during a particular human life, he finally achieved Enlightenment (*bodhi*) and thus became recognizable as a Buddha, just like the Buddhas of the past.

Belief in the Buddhas of the past and, by implication, in Buddhas of the future belongs to the earliest known Buddhist traditions. Such accounts of the events of Śākyamuni's life as are included in the early canonical material are linked with similar supposed events that occurred during the lives of previous Buddhas. Moreover, archaeology confirms such early traditions, for the great Indian emperor Aśoka (3rd century B.C.) repaired and erected stupas (Sanskrit: *stūpa*, 'reliquary mounds') in honour of previous Buddhas as well as of the latest Buddha, Śākyamuni himself. One of Aśoka's inscriptions refers specifically to his arranging for the enlargement of the stupa of the previous Buddha Kanakamuni. Whether we as modern research scholars can find any historical evidence for the actual existence of such previous Buddhas affects in no way traditional Buddhist beliefs on the subject, and in this present work on the image of the Buddha we are properly concerned with Buddhist traditions and not with modern rationalist interpretations of them.

The recognition of Śākyamuni as a Buddha meant that all the traditional qualities of Buddhahood were attributed to him—knowledge of all his own previous states of birth, knowledge of the previous states of birth of all other living beings, miraculous powers and superhuman wisdom, expressed in concepts and instructions suitable for any particular audience. He is the supreme guide, the Lord, of such incomparable standing that at first it was felt and taught that in the whole universe there could never be more than one such Buddha at once. At the same time it is not denied that he lived on earth as a man, usually appearing simply as a religious teacher. Modern writers often present Śākyamuni precisely as an exceptional religious teacher, who only later on, perhaps long after his death, was given some kind of divine honours. Such an interpretation is manifestly in conflict with the earliest known Buddhist traditions, which present him both as man and as Buddha, together with all the special connotations that the title Buddha implies.

Speaking of himself, Śākyamuni is often represented in the early texts as using the title Tathāgata in the third person. Tathāgata is usually interpreted as the one who has come in such a way, that is to say, the Predestined One, the one who after an infinite series of previous states of birth has now reached, as predestined, his last state on earth in human form and achieves recognition as the Enlightened One, the Buddha. Many other subtle meanings are given to this title Tathāgata, which thus becomes a synonym for Buddha.

In the Pāli canon of the Theravādins, there are many discourses attributed to Śākyamuni that describe his special attributes as Tathāgata or Buddha.

> In regard to things that are past, future and present, the Tathāgata is a speaker at a suitable time, a speaker of fact, of what is relevant, of the Doctrine (*Dharma*), of Monastic Rule (*Vinaya*). Therefore he is called Tathāgata.
>
> In so far as what is seen, heard, felt, cognized, achieved, sought, pondered by ascetics and Brahmans, by gods and by men, in so far as the Tathāgata is fully aware of all this, he is therefore called Tathāgata. From the time when the Tathāgata became fully enlightened in the state of Supreme Enlightenment to the time when he attained final nirvana in the state of nirvana where nothing subsists,[2] during that period of time whatever he spoke, declared and explained, all that is just so (=*tathā*) and not otherwise. Therefore he is called Tathāgata.
>
> (*Dīgha-nikāya*, III: 135)

As a non-Buddhist one is quite free to doubt whether Śākyamuni was recognized as a Buddha, with all that this title implies, during the actual course of his life, or whether such an identification was made only by some of his followers after his physical death. It would seem to be inevitable, however, that during his lifetime reactions to him were of various kinds. It is certain that some, especially rival teachers and their disciples, rejected his authority altogether. Many layfolk would also have regarded him as a revered religious teacher, perhaps more gentle and approachable but not essentially different from other teachers of the time. The claim that he was Buddha, whether or not first asserted by Śākyamuni himself as the earliest traditions inform us, can only have been fostered and elaborated by some, if not all, of his own monk-disciples, who are the ultimate source and authority for the

[2] Concerning his Enlightenment as a realization of Nirvana and his passing from this world as the Final Nirvana, see p. 18.

first oral recitations concerning his teachings and the more important events of his life, as preserved for us in the early canonical writings, notably the Pāli canon of the Theravādins.

It is often quite wrongly assumed that because Śākyamuni usually appears as a human religious teacher in this canonical material, he was therefore regarded as a mere human being. The events of his miraculous birth, the notion of predestination that infuses the main events of his life, his claims to the supernatural power and omniscience of a Buddha, all this is overlooked. In fairness to a quite universal Buddhist tradition, we must assert that he is clearly represented throughout both as man and as Buddha.

The Concept of a Buddha

In non-Buddhist usage the term '*buddha*', meaning 'awakened' or 'enlightened', may be applied to any learned man or sage, or to an ascetic of profound intuitive insight. In Buddhist usage, with which we are exclusively concerned in this book, a Buddha is the very acme of all conceivable forms of existence, thus transcending altogether this impermanent fluctuating world of mere appearances. In his absolute perfection a Buddha also transcends all philosophical concepts of being and non-being.

> Since a Tathāgata, even when actually present, is incomprehensible, it is inept to say of him—of the Uttermost Person, the Supernal Person, the Attainer of the Supernal—that after dying the Tathāgata is, or is not, or both is and is not, or neither is nor is not.
>
> (*Saṃyutta-nikāya*, III: 118)

In the course of the first few Buddhist centuries much philosophical thought was expended on the problem of to what extent it might be arguable that a Buddha is or is not, and there was considerable disagreement between the various schools. All, however, are agreed on the ineffable nature of the Buddha-state in whatever terms one may attempt to express it. The Theravādins, like the other early schools, asserted the reality of all the elements (*dharmas*), physical and mental, of which all phenomenal manifestations, including 'living beings' (*sattva*) as listed above, were assumed to be components. By contrast the Buddha-state was achieved through Nirvana (*nirvāṇa*), that is to say the extinguishing or the effacing of all the elements of phenomenal manifestation. The absolute calm that resulted from their non-manifestation might thus be defined as 'non-existence', but only in relationship to the assumption that the basic elements of the everyday world really existed. The relativity of such assertions has often been overlooked, by some Buddhists as well as non-Buddhists, who assume that Nirvana is absolute nothingness in a nihilistic Western sense. Such an interpretation clearly conflicts with the more positive aspects of a Buddha's attributes, and other philosophical schools restored a better balance of viewpoint more in accordance with the non-committal statement as given in the brief quotation above.

A Buddha's passage on earth involves four main acts: his miraculous birth without the agency of a male parent, his Enlightenment (*bodhi*) at Gayā, where all Buddhas gain Enlightenment, his decision to preach the Doctrine, which he alone can now make available once more for the good of many, and finally his passing from this world, leaving his Doctrine (*dharma*) to replace him, until it finally comes to nothing and it is time for the next

Buddha to appear. It is in a framework such as this that are set Śākyamuni's birth at Lumbinī, his realization of Nirvana at Gayā, his first preaching in the Deer Park of Sārnāth near Vārānasi and his Final Nirvana on passing from this world at Kuśinagara (modern Kasia, just east of Gorakhpur). These events are all attested in the early canonical material, and the four sites rapidly became important places of pilgrimage for Śākyamuni's followers.

During his previous rebirths and up to the time of his Enlightenment, that is, his realization of Nirvana at Gayā, Śākyamuni is properly referred to not as Buddha but as Bodhisattva, as a 'being' who is intent on 'Enlightenment'. Thereafter he is known as the Buddha, the Lord (*bhagavān*). It is interesting to note that certain philosophizing purists amongst the Theravādins found a logical difficulty in admitting that, as Buddha, Śākyamuni could have any effective contact with the world during the forty-five years that elapsed between his 'Enlightenment' or first Nirvana at Gayā and his Final Nirvana at Kuśinagara. They claimed that throughout this period he had not spoken a single syllable, although he was present in bodily form, and that it was Ānanda, his favourite disciple, who actually preached.[3] This extreme view emphasizes the state of a Buddha as ineffable and transcendent, and is in marked contrast with modern rationalizing views, where a Buddha is assumed to be a mere human being.

An important canonical text for understanding the nature of a Buddha is the 'Great Discourse on the Final Nirvana' (*Mahāparinirvāṇa-sūtra*), which exists in similar versions in the Pāli canon of the Theravādins, in the Sanskrit canon of the Mūlasarvāstivādins, who flourished in the far north-west of India, as well as in Tibetan and Chinese translation. This great discourse describes in detail Śākyamuni's last journey from Rājagṛha, the capital of Magadha, where he had spent much of his teaching life, via Pāṭaliputra (modern Patna) and Vaiśālī on the Pāva, and lastly to Kuśinagara, where he lay down and finally expired under two *śāla* trees (*Shorea robusta*). It appears to be a compilation of various materials, part historical, part tendencious fabrication, part doctrinal, part mythical, but it was probably compiled within the first hundred years of Śākyamuni's decease, thus becoming with slight variations the common property of the various Buddhist schools, which soon began to separate geographically. It is the earliest account available to us of these particular events, and it records indisputably the beliefs of the first generations of his followers, as learned and recited by the monk-recorders (*bhāṇaka*). Like all early canonical material it represents Śākyamuni under the dual aspect of a human religious teacher, who knows that his end is near, and of an omniscient Buddha, whose imminent Nirvana is announced by signs and wonders. It is announced by the appearance of the Evil One, Māra, the 'Satan' of Buddhism, who had appeared in an even more provocative way on the occasion of the Enlightenment at Gayā. It is announced by a succession of earthquakes, and it is announced especially by a kind of 'transfiguration' of Śākyamuni. As he approaches Kuśinagara, accompanied by his faithful attendant Ānanda, a devout layman named Mukkusa offers him a pair of

[3] See the *Kathāvatthu*, VIII: 1–4; *Aṅguttara-nikāya*, II: 24; and for further references, Louis de la Vallée Poussin, *Bouddhisme* (Paris, 1925), pp. 251–55. Some went so far as to maintain that as Buddha he was so absolutely detached from everything that 'the Lord Buddha has no compassion' (*natthi buddhassa bhagavato karuṇā*; *Kathāvatthu*, XVIII: 3).

garments of golden hue. He puts them on, and the splendour of the cloth is eclipsed by the sudden brilliance of his own corporeal form. On Ānanda's asking the reason for this miraculous transfiguration, he explains that it is the sign of his imminent passing into Final Nirvana.

This 'Great Discourse on the Final Nirvana' is also important in that it announces the cult that is due to a Buddha. After the death of Śākyamuni under the two trees just outside Kuśinagara, the village folk ask Ānanda about the funeral ceremonies, and he replies that they should do things as for a great king (*cakravartin*).

> 'O, most worthy Ānanda,' they reply, 'how should things be done for a great king?' 'People, the body of a great king should be wrapped in muslin. Having been wrapped in muslin, it should be wrapped in five hundred pairs of garments. Having been wrapped in five hundred pairs of garments, it should be placed in an iron coffer. When this has been filled with vegetable oil, it should be closed with a double iron lid. Then heaping up all kinds of scented woods and having burned it, one extinguishes the fire with milk, and having placed the bones in a golden vase, one constructs a tumulus (*stūpa*) for the bones at a cross-roads, and honours it with parasols, banners of victory, flags, scents and garlands, perfumes, powder and music. One has a great festival, honouring, venerating and worshipping it.'[4]

Śākyamuni's remains were supposedly dealt with in this way, but following upon a dispute by eight contestants representing various nearby towns and villages, including of course Kuśinagara, who all claimed a share of the bone relics, these were eventually divided into eight. The vase that had contained the relics was taken by the Brahman who arranged for the peaceful sharing out, and a Brahman youth from yet another village took the ashes. Thus ten original stupas or reliquary mounds are said to have been constructed in honour of this particular Buddha, and we really have no reason for doubting that such stupas were indeed built and that they were soon being honoured and worshipped in the way described in the extract quoted above. In any case, this is the only available account of Śākyamuni's decease, and if one rejects it as altogether unhistorical, one simply has to invent something else. There is no historical doubt whatever that by the time of Aśoka (3rd century B.C.) stupas were already in existence, constructed in an earlier period in honour of Śākyamuni as well as of previous Buddhas. It is also certain that funeral mounds were constructed in a very early period as tombs for the great, and thus there is no reason whatsoever why Śākyamuni's relics should not have been enshrined in this way.

[4] Translated by the Editor from the Sanskrit and Tibetan versions, for which see E. Waldschmidt, *Das Mahāparinirvāṇa-sutrā* (Berlin, 1950), p. 411; for the Pāli version, see the *Mahāparinirvāṇa-sutrā*, VI:33. A complete translation of these events will be found in *The Sacred Books of the East*, vol. 11 (London, 1881), republished as *Buddhist Suttas*, (Dover Publications, New York, 1969). One should also see the recent article by André Bareau, 'Les récits canoniques des funérailles du Bouddha et leurs anomalies: nouvel essai d'interprétation', *Bulletin de l'École Française d'Extrême-Orient*, 20 (1975), pp. 151–89, and the short article on the same theme by D. L. Snellgrove, 'Śākyamuni's final *nirvāna*', *Bulletin of the School of Oriental and African Studies*, 36 (1973), pp. 399–411.

THE STUPA AS AN IMAGE OF THE BUDDHA

There are no firm dates in Indian history before the third century B.C., and by that time the religion of Śākyamuni was beginning to spread over the whole of India. Its success was greatly assisted by the profoundly religious attitude of the Emperor Aśoka, as well as by the peace and prosperity that characterized the later part of his reign. Merchants travelled safely along established trade routes linking the various parts of India, and with the merchants also travelled many wandering religious. It is significant that the merchant class was one of the main supporters of the growing Buddhist order, and Buddhist monastic settlements, which had first been founded close to towns and villages whose interested support was necessary for the material requirements of the monks, now began to grow up close to important trade routes, where simple lodging might be available for travellers and where gifts might be expected in return.

We learn from the early canonical literature that parks were placed at the disposal of Śākyamuni and his followers by wealthy supporters. Thus on the outskirts of Rājagṛha, the capital of Magadha, they seem to have had two such parks at their exclusive disposal, one given by the ruler himself, King Bimbisāra, and one by a rich physician named Jīvaka. On the outskirts of Śrāvastī they owned another, given by a wealthy merchant, and near Vaiśālī yet another, given by a royal courtesan. During the early period such residences were used mainly during the monsoon period, June to September, when travel was generally difficult, and it was already the established custom of wandering mendicants and ascetics to stay together in groups wherever suitable provisions could be found. These parks were fitted out with simple dwellings, a hut for each monk and general meeting-halls, and so good were their provisions thanks to the support of pious layfolk, that they gradually came into use for longer and longer periods, until they became in effect quite regular monastic establishments. Śākyamuni was certainly responsible for establishing the tradition of a fixed monastic rule, and this code of discipline (*vinaya*) was later enlarged and developed to suit new and more complex needs.

It also happened that the sites associated with the main events of his life gradually became places of pilgrimage, and we may safely deduce from the inscriptions of Aśoka that refer specifically to such sites, that the centre of interest at each such place was a stupa containing relics, which was honoured as the symbol of the departed Lord and of the ultimate state of Nirvana into which he had disappeared. It is sometimes suggested that the stupa-cult was reserved for pious laymen, while the monks attended to the more serious business of gaining Nirvana by means of strict moral, contemplative and ascetic practices. But that the monks were equally interested in stupas is proved not only by inscriptions recording donations by monks but also by the rapidity with which the stupa became a necessary object, indeed the central cult-object, in every Buddhist monastic establishment. In the rock-cut monasteries of West India dating from the second century B.C. onwards, a specially large shrine or temple, often resembling a Christian church of Romanesque style, is an essential feature. The nave of such a shrine is flanked by rows of pillars with ornamented capitals and at the far end there is the equivalent of a Christian sanctuary, containing the stupa, with space around it for the necessary ceremonial circumambulation.

1. Five of the seven Buddhas

Relief on the upper beam of a gateway (toraṇa) *of Stupa No. 1; from Sāñcī, Madhya Pradesh, India; 1st century* A.D.; *yellowish-white sandstone; in situ.*

On the uppermost beam there are alternating trees and stupas, each of them flanked by worshippers; they represent symbolically six Buddhas of past aeons and, as the seventh, Śākyamuni (see p. 24). The central part of the beam shows five of them; two more are shown on the ends of the crosspiece projecting beyond the pillars to the right and left. Other symbolic representations are found in the panel below: the Nativity scene, symbolized by the goddess Lakṣmī being sprinkled with water by elephants; the Wheel of the Doctrine on a throne, representing the preaching Buddha, etc.

It is not Śākyamuni who is worshipped in the stupa. His life on earth is at an end, and his person is no more durable than that of any other living being. It is the idea of Buddha that is worshipped, the great idea that had manifested itself previously in former Buddhas and then in recent times had manifested itself in him. This is the *dharmakāya*, the Body of the very Buddhist Doctrine itself, which is somehow felt to be manifest in this tomb-like symbol of a departed manifestation of Buddha. This *dharmakāya*, the very essence of Buddha, can never depart, for it is never really present in any tangible sense, transcending as it does all notions of being and non-being. In contrast with this ineffable *dharmakāya*, the manifestation of a Buddha on earth was known first as *rūpakāya*, the Body of Physical Form, and later as *nirmāṇakāya*, a Created Body or Manifested Body.

To remind the worshipper of such a 'Manifested Body', without the appearance of which the Doctrine could not be revealed to men, these stupas came to be decorated with carvings illustrating important scenes from the life of Śākyamuni on earth. It is interesting to note that even in such scenes, where Śākyamuni had not yet achieved Enlightenment and was therefore still a Bodhisattva, a being intent on Enlightenment, he is never depicted in these early carvings. There is either an empty space or a stereotyped symbol, such as a tree to indicate his Enlightenment or the image of a stupa to indicate his final decease. The lesson is clear. Since Śākyamuni was recognized as Buddha, he possessed no physical form in which he might be suitably portrayed. Thus early Buddhist art insists firmly upon the ineffable and indescribable state of Buddhahood.

The early stupas also teach us that from the start Buddhahood was inevitably associated with the idea of the long career of the Bodhisattva through different conditions of rebirth, for popular scenes from his previous lives corresponding to the stories already being recited as traditional teachings are likewise depicted on the surroundings of these great shrines. The best preserved are the stupas of Sāñcī, which survived for many centuries as a monastic settlement close to an important trade route, and of which the fallen stones, with their many carvings intact, were happily rediscovered during the nineteenth century. Also, just as the oral traditions often described local divinities in attendance upon Śākyamuni, so these, too, appear in attitudes of devotion on the stone railings and gateways.

Throughout the whole history of Buddhism in the countries of Asia where it became an established religion, the stupa has never lost its primary importance as the supreme symbol of Buddhahood. Later on, other ways of portraying the serenity of the Supreme Enlightenment of a Buddha were devised—Buddhas carved of wood or stone, cast in bronze or other metals, painted as frescoes or as hanging banners—but the stupa was never displaced from its central position, and thus has remained as essential to Buddhist faith and devotion as has the cross for Christians. Its external appearance and its subsidiary symbolic designs have certainly changed in accordance with those cosmic and philosophical conceptions that mark the later periods of all Indian religions, Buddhism included, but as an expression of the unutterable truth of Buddhahood as the goal of all worthwhile effort, its meaning has never changed.

2. EARLY BUDDHA SYMBOLS

The Non-Image as Image

Our account of the Buddha image must begin with the non-image, for those craftsmen who first portrayed in stone the wonderful events of Śākyamuni's last and previous lives remained well aware of the teachings recorded concerning them. Thus they might recall the instruction given by their Lord to an enquiring Brahman named Upasīva, as recounted in a section of the *Suttanipāta* (verses 1069–76). Here we quote just some of the replies:

> 'He who is passionless regarding all desires,
> Resorts to nothingness, abandoning all other,
> And so released in perfect freedom from conceptual thought,
> Abides just there, free of all further questing.'
>
> 'As flame is blown by the force of wind goes out and is no longer reckoned', so said the Lord to Upasīva,
> 'Even so the sage, released from name and form, goes out and is no longer reckoned.'
>
> 'For him who gains the goal there is no measurement,
> By means of which one tells of him; for him this just is not.
> When all the elements are removed, all terms of reference are likewise non-existent.'[5]

When all the elements of existence (*dharmas*) through which the apparent human being and any kind of being assume 'name and form' (a Buddhist term conveying perhaps much the same idea as our word 'personality') are brought to rest, as in the case of a perfected sage, then he can only be described as being in a state of 'nothingness' (*akiñcana*).[6] It was thus felt to be quite unsuitable at first to form a human image of him, and so where he might be in the early sculptures, we see an empty space, made meaningful by the use of symbols. These symbols contain far more of the highest truth that he has realized, and so express far better his true nature, which is identical with that same truth (literally, the state of being 'just so' as on p. 16 above), than any image might. Later, certainly, various legends concerning a First Image were created and certain works were acknowledged as authentic portraits of the Buddha; but until his personal representation became a generally accepted practice around A.D. 100 and in the course of the second century, Buddhist art confined itself to substituting aniconic symbols for his holy person.

This attitude, it has to be recalled, was in accordance with contemporary thought and practice: the earliest Buddhists, between the lifetime of Śākyamuni and the first century A.D., did not try to represent the central personalities of their religion in human images,

[5]The Pāli version of the whole passage can be found in the *Suttanipāta* as recently re-edited by Andersen and Smith (Luzac, London, 1965), pp. 202–7. The English translation is by the Editor, who expresses his thanks for much help received from Miss I. B. Horner. Miss Horner's translation of the Pāli passages quoted on pp. 16 and 17, there reworded with her kind consent by the Editor, can be found in *Buddhist Texts through the Ages* by Conze, Horner, Snellgrove and Waley (Oxford, 1954), pp. 106 and 108.

[6]Heinrich Zimmer, in *The Art of Indian Asia*, has made use of some of the terms from the passage quoted above, especially this term, which he translates or rather interprets as 'not being anything definite any more'. See his vol. 1, pp. 61–62, where he refers to the *Suttanipāta*, and misleadingly to verses 5,7,8. See also his p. 79.

but neither did the Brahmans nor the Jains. The earliest images of such a kind were created simultaneously with the first Buddha figures, due to parallel changes in religious and philosophical thought, as well as in the devotional attitudes of believers towards holy beings in general. Early Brahmanism concentrated on a highly developed ritual of sacrifices, using a complicated system of signs and symbols, an 'iconography without icons'.[7] This preference for symbols was inherited by the Buddhists, and in several cases—e.g., on coins of the latter half of the first millennium B.C.—we find a generally accepted body of symbols not clearly to be divided into Buddhist and non-Buddhist ones. Even in one of the most famous instances, the column at Sārnāth crowned with a lion capital and originally surmounted by a huge, many-spoked wheel, it is highly probable that this symbol was primarily meant to express the idea of imperial rule rather than the preaching of the Buddha, which it came to signify in later times.

On the other hand, in those same centuries preceding the Christian era there did exist some religious images in human form. On a popular level, images of serpent divinities (*nāga*, *nāginī*) and tree-spirits (*yakṣa*, *yakṣinī*) had been venerated since olden times, as indeed they still are now, and numerous early terracotta figurines may certainly be interpreted as mother-goddesses and fertility idols. Even in the earliest reliefs illustrating scenes from the Buddha's life or from his former lives (*jātaka*s) dating between the second century B.C. and the first century A.D., we encounter iconic representation of subsidiary figures—men, gods, demigods and genii—while the Buddha himself was still represented by non-personal symbols. The reluctance to depict the Buddha in human form, therefore, is not simply the outcome of a universally valid principle of aniconism or of a law forbidding image-making, but finds its explanation in the philosophically radical doctrine concerning his true Nirvana essence, inconceivable in visual form and human shape.

The Biographical Use of Symbols

However, it may come as a surprise to find that in early illustrations of biographical scenes preceding Śākyamuni's Enlightenment and his Entry into Nirvana, he is never represented in personal form although in these phases of his life he certainly moved amongst men as one of them. One might expect that during his first thirty-five years, before he actually attained the transcendental state of Nirvana, he might logically have been represented as a human individual. But probably the concept of a Buddha's nature had already developed at this early date, and so he was regarded not simply as teacher and founder of the community but—according to the doctrine that later was to be termed Mahāyāna—as a manifestation of the superhuman and supermundane Buddha essence (*buddhatā*). There is clear literary evidence that already in Aśoka's time (3rd century B.C.) it was believed that Śākyamuni had six predecessors in former aeons, who in the illustrations were likewise represented by symbols and not in human form (Pl. 1). Śākyamuni, in consequence, was conceived as of the same nature as the other Buddhas and so it seemed unsuitable to portray him as a person involved in this ephemeral life of ours.

[7] A. K. Coomaraswamy, 'The origins of the Buddha image', *Art Bulletin*, vol. 9, no. 4 (1926–27); reprint (New Delhi, 1972), p. 7.

2. The Bodhisattva incarnated as a golden deer (*Ruru-jātaka*)

Medallion on a pillar of a stupa railing; from Bhārhut, Madhya Pradesh, India; 2nd century B.C.*; red sandstone; Indian Museum, Calcutta.*

This is an illustration of a famous *jātaka*, one of the many stories that tell of the incarnations of the future Buddha (called 'Bodhisattva' until he attains Buddhahood) in his previous lives. Here he appears as a golden deer who has rescued a drowning man. This man, however, ungratefully reports to his king the place where he may hunt the deer. The animal informs the king of his retainer's misdeed and thereupon receives the veneration of the king. In an archaic but naively charming way the deer is shown twice, once in the water carrying the man to safety, then being shot at by the king, and simultaneously in a third phase of the story, receiving veneration. The king appears twice, in the latter two phases.

3. Sujāta feeding a dead cow (*Jātaka No. 352*)

Relief on the coping of a stupa railing; from Bhārhut, Madhya Pradesh, India; 2nd century B.C.*; red sandstone; H. 43 cm.; Indian Museum, Calcutta.*

In this *jātaka* story the future Buddha appears as a young boy, Sujāta, whose father incessantly mourns the grandfather's death and neglects his work and his family. In order to demonstrate to his father the instability and futility of life and all existence, Sujāta feeds a dead cow, imploring her to eat and enjoy life. Thus the father becomes aware of his own equally nonsensical behaviour, learning from his son the basic truth of the vanity of all things.

4. The Nativity of the Buddha Śākyamuni, symbolized by the goddess Lakṣmī

Medallion on a pillar of a stupa railing; from Bhārhut, Madhya Pradesh, India; 2nd century B.C.*; red sandstone; Indian Museum, Calcutta.*

The goddess of fertility and good luck, Lakṣmī, is in the centre axis of an heraldic group, being sprinkled with water from jars held by two elephants in their trunks. This rite, known as *abhiṣeka*, 'consecration', forms part of regal enthronement ceremonies. Here primarily the fertility aspect is emphasized, the group symbolizing the birth of Śākyamuni in an aniconic and non-narrative form basically different from the usual representation of the birth scene as shown in Pl. 5. The fertility symbolism is further stressed by the 'vase of abundance' (*pūrṇaghaṭa*) placed at the bottom of the composition and resembling the jars held by the elephants. From this vase rise several lotus stalks with leaves, buds and flowers, with Lakṣmī standing on the central flower. The strictly symmetrical group with its central axis rising from the sphere of the life-giving waters up to the heaven of the gods has a cosmological significance.

In the illustrations of his former incarnations, the Bodhisattva, or Buddha-to-be, is usually shown in his various mundane personifications as described in the *jākata* texts: as an animal sacrificing his life for the benefit of others (Pl. 2), or as a human being (Pl. 3) inspired by wisdom and compassion, depicted in the same way as all other figures appearing in the particular scenes. The Buddha-to-be could be represented in human shape but not the Tathāgata, who appears in this world and as a perfected being (see p. 16) enters Final Nirvana. Even in the earlier phases of his last life on earth he appears as a temporal manifestation of the timeless, transcendental and absolute 'Buddha Body' (*dharmakāya*). Only by symbols can this body be mentally evoked; such a symbol is a 'non-manifest image' (*avyaktamūrti*).

The symbols used in the early monuments, which are mainly illustrative reliefs decorating the railings and gateways of the stupas at Bodhgayā, Bhārhut and Sāñcī (2nd century B.C. onwards) and to a certain extent those of Amarāvatī and Nāgārjunakonda (1st–3rd century A.D.), are strictly related to biographical or legendary scenes of Śākyamuni's life and religious career. The symbols form the focus of interest within these narrative pictures, which often vibrate with life and are graced by a charming naiveté. The first of these scenes, the entry of the Bodhisattva (the future Buddha) into his mother's womb in the guise of a white elephant, is very literally illustrated in a medallion of one of the Bhārhut pillars, while the next scene, the birth of the holy child from the right side of his mother's body during her visit to Lumbinī grove, was given a highly symbolistic form (Pl. 4). Instead of showing

5. The Buddha's Nativity

Relief from a stupa; from Nāgārjunakonda, Andhra Pradesh, India; 3rd century A.D.*; greenish-white limestone; W. approximately 90 cm.; National Museum of India, New Delhi.*

The panel combines three clearly differentiated phases of the birth story. On the left we see the birth under the tree during Queen Māyā's visit to the Lumbinī grove; the child, being born from the right side of his mother's body, is invisible, while in later illustrations he is shown, frequently as a miniature Buddha, i.e., in his transhistorical timeless essence. On the extreme left, a whisk-bearing heavenly maiden is in attendance. The second scene represents the First Bath by the simple device of a ewer standing on a pedestal; the child's presence is indicated by the tree decorated with an umbrella and two fly-whisks, symbols of honour, respect and veneration. Whether the adoring female figure belongs to this scene or to the third is not clear, but presumably she is part of both. The last scene, on the right, shows the First Seven Steps by which the future Buddha proclaimed his universal rulership; we see seven tiny footprints impressed on a piece of cloth held by four gods (only three are shown). This cloth, however, at the same time belongs to the bathing scene, so that the several phases of the biographical sequence merge into each other. They are further united by a lively rhythm pervading the well-arranged groups of joyfully animated figures. In the background rises a columned building, presumably the palace of the new-born prince's father.

the garden scene with Queen Māyā and her entourage, as was done in most later illustrations and even as early as in the Amarāvatī and Nāgārjunakonda reliefs of the third century A.D., Śrī Lakṣmī, the goddess of fertility and good luck, is substituted, but without a child. She is being sprinkled with water by two elephants as a kind of *abhiṣeka* ('consecration'). Thus the Nativity scene is represented by fertility and life symbols: the goddess and the elephants, sometimes with a lotus and a 'vase of abundance' (*pūrṇaghaṭa*) added. Although this interpretation has been disputed, it seems convincing because these old Indian fertility and felicity symbols lend themselves very well to the representation of a birth scene, and also because this episode would be altogether missing from the biographical sequence as it is illustrated in the early reliefs if the Lakṣmī group were to be discarded.

In the two subsequent scenes entirely different symbols are used; in the First Bath (Pl. 5), exemplified by a relief from Nāgārjunakonda, the presence of the child is suggested by an umbrella and fly-whisks suspended in a tree (these are signs of respect due to a venerable person), while the ensuing First Seven Steps are symbolized, in the adjoining group within the same relief, by seven little footprints that, as we shall see, are one of the most widely used devices for indicating the personal presence of the Buddha.

From among the numerous episodes of the Buddha's life, we can pick out only the more important ones. In the First Meditation under the rose-apple tree (*jambu*) during his boyhood, we see an empty throne on which the invisible prince is supposed to sit. When he makes his Great Departure, escaping by night from his family and his harem in order to become an ascetic, just the horse is shown, while above the invisible rider a god holds a royal umbrella. The feet of the horse are suspended above the ground by four other gods so that the noiseless flight may go unnoticed. In the forest Śākyamuni removes his turban and severs his princely coiffure; both are seized by gods and triumphantly taken to the Heaven of the Thirty-three Gods, where they are venerated as the first relics (Pl. 6).

The central event of Śākyamuni's career, the Enlightenment under the bodhi tree (*aśvattha* or *pippala*; *Ficus religiosa*) at Bodhgayā, is represented by the tree itself, with its characteristic heart-shaped, long, pointed leaves. Frequently an empty throne, the Diamond Seat (*vajrāsana*), is placed under it, indicating the unshakeable centre of the universe (Pl. 7). The seat can be a simple block of stone or an elaborate throne with richly decorated back, sometimes even provided with cushions. In front of it we often see a footstool with two footprints (Pl. 19) suggesting Śākyamuni's presence; they may be stamped with two wheels, which symbolize the teaching of the doctrine and the spiritual rulership of the Buddha over the universe (Pls. 8, 23). The ensemble formed by the tree, the throne and the footprints, often adorned by various symbolic animals such as the royal lion, is called the Place of Enlightenment (*bodhimaṇḍa*); its prototype at Bodhgayā has been the main centre of veneration for Buddhist believers from all parts of Asia. That the tree is meant to suggest the Buddha himself is proved by inscriptions that actually name it '*bhagavato*' ('the Exalted One'), and in the *Divyāvadāna* the Buddha is quoted as having described the tree 'as my permanent abode' (*mano nibaddhavāso viya*). But we should note that not every tree appearing in early iconography signifies Śākyamuni and his Enlightenment. Other trees of different botanical varieties symbolize his six predecessors, and certain other trees, such as the mango, may play a role in one of the legends told of Śākyamuni or some other Buddha. Thus in order to identify a given illustration correctly, a careful analysis of the picture in relation to the underlying story is indispensable. In some cases the tree is meant to be an object of veneration in pious memory of the Buddha and his Enlightenment but not actually taken as representing his holy person. Thus a symbol that had its origin and proper place in one of the biographical scenes may acquire a broader significance and, isolated from the original narrative context, may be used anachronistically—or rather trans-historically—in contexts where it seems to be out of place; e.g., in a scene involving the new-born Śākyamuni where he is represented as the Enlightened One by the empty throne with the umbrella above and

6. Veneration of the Bodhisattva's turban by the gods

Relief on the Ajātaśatru Pillar of the stupa; from Bhārhut, Madhya Pradesh, India; 2nd century B.C.*; red sandstone; Indian Museum, Calcutta.*

After leaving his palace, family and secular life, Prince Siddhārtha cuts off his coiffure and turban, tossing them into the air. They are seized by the god Indra, carried to the Heaven of the Thirty-three Gods, enshrined in their assembly hall and venerated there. The first step taken by the future Buddha on his way to Enlightenment is joyfully celebrated by the gods; in the lower panel we see them dancing and making music. The coiffure and turban may be regarded as the first relics left behind by the Buddha.

7. The Buddha seated under the bodhi tree while Sujātā offers him food (*below*); (*above*) the Buddha crossing the Nairañjanā River

Reliefs on a railing pillar from a stupa; from Amarāvatī, Andhra Pradesh, India; 2nd century A.D.*; greenish-white limestone; D. approximately 85 cm.; British Museum, London.*

The medallion shows the bodhi tree (*Ficus religiosa*) with its characteristic pointed leaves, and in front of it the block-shaped Diamond Seat (or Throne) (*vajrāsana*) on which the Buddha is supposed to be seated. After six years of the most ascetic practices by which he almost starved, he has realized that this is not the right method to attain Enlightenment. Before sitting down under the bodhi tree he takes food that is prepared and offered to him by a pious maiden called Sujātā. We see her on the left with a bowl in her hands; other girls surround her, either assisting her or venerating the Buddha. Above, we see the Buddha, represented by his footprints, crossing the Nairañjanā River in order to reach the place where he is to gain Enlightenment. He is venerated by a *nāga* king (on the right, with a cobra's hood around his head) and other divine beings. The time sequence of the events as told in the texts is not strictly observed in these illustrations.

8. Veneration of the new-born Bodhisattva by gods

Relief on the Ajātaśatru Pillar of the stupa; from Bhārhut, Madhya Pradesh, India; 2nd century B.C.*; H. approximately 60 cm.; Indian Museum, Calcutta.*

An inscription gives as the theme of this panel the announcement made by a god to the other gods of the last rebirth of this Bodhisattva, at news of which they rejoice. Actually, however, the illustration shows how the god Maheśvara, accompanied by a host of gods, venerates the new-born, who is represented by his footprints in front of a richly decorated throne on which, anachronistically, he is supposed to be seated, or else by an altar carrying votive offerings; it is surmounted by a canopy as a sign of honour. The whole group—footprints, seat or altar, and canopy—may represent the spiritual body of the Buddha in a cosmological sense (according to Coomaraswamy), provided that this concept and iconographical scheme was current at the time of the Bhārhut monument.

9. Descent of the Buddha from heaven

Relief on the Ajātaśatru Pillar of the stupa; from Bhārhut, Madhya Pradesh, India; 2nd century B.C.*; red sandstone; H. approximately 60 cm.; Indian Museum, Calcutta.*

After having preached for three months to his deceased mother in the Heaven of the Thirty-three Gods, the Buddha descended on a triple staircase built for him by Indra. His movement is suggested by two footprints, one on the first and one on the last step; gods are venerating him. On the left, we see a tree with a throne or altar in front of it, surmounted by a canopy, probably suggesting the Buddha's presence at the town he visited after his return from heaven.

10. The Buddha walking over the waters of the Nairañjanā River

Relief on a pillar of the Eastern Gateway (toraṇa) *of Stupa No. 1; from Sāñcī, Madhya Pradesh, India; 1st century* A.D.*; yellowish-white sandstone; in situ.*

By walking over the water's surface the Buddha convinced the sceptical Uruvilvā-Kāśyapa of his superhuman wisdom and power. The river has inundated the land so that only the tree-tops show above the waters; Kāśyapa and two of his disciples are drifting in a boat. Below we see the *caṅkrama*, the Walking Path, a simple symbolic device to indicate the miraculous act performed by the Buddha. In the lower right corner he is again represented by a tree and a throne, being venerated by Kāśyapa and his disciples.

11. The Malla nobles rejoicing on receiving their share of Śākyamuni's relics

Relief on a pillar of the Northern Gateway (toraṇa) *of Stupa No. 1; from Sāñcī, Madhya Pradesh, India; 1st century* A.D.*; yellowish-white sandstone; in situ.*

After the Buddha's decease (his Entry into Perfect Nirvana), a dispute arose about his relics that was settled by distributing them evenly among the contenders. Here the Mallas of Kuśinagara, the town where the Buddha had passed away, are shown rejoicing over their share of the relics and holding a feast with music and dancing. Some of them are venerating, by circumambulation, the magnificent stupa that was erected over the relics and symbolizes Nirvana. In the air some *kinnaras*—heavenly beings half birds, half men—are bringing garlands for the adornment of the stupa, which represents a simplified form of the Sāñcī stupa. See Pl. 21 for the complete pillar.

12. Veneration of a stupa

Relief on the Prasenajit Pillar of the stupa; from Bhārhut, Madhya Pradesh, India; 2nd century B.C.*; red sandstone; H. approximately 90 cm.; Indian Museum, Calcutta.*

The stupa, of primeval type, simple in structure but richly adorned with garlands, is being venerated as the symbol of the Buddha's Entry into Perfect Nirvana. Evidently it is the very stupa that was erected over his relics at Kuśinagara, as is indicated by the two *śāla* trees with their characteristic leaves flanking the panel on either side. A king with his consort is shown three times: first, approaching the stupa in an adoring attitude on the right, then kneeling down in veneration, and finally, after the circumambulation has been performed, again worshipping the stupa and the Buddha. It seems that he is standing beside or behind a column crowned by a four-lion capital such as we know from the so-called Aśoka columns. Above the stupa, heavenly beings in flight are offering flowers and garlands.

13. Stupa venerated by elephants

Relief block from a stupa gate, crowning a pillar and supporting a lion figure; from Amarāvatī, Andhra Pradesh, India; 2nd century A.D.*; greenish-white limestone; H. 32 cm.; British Museum, London.*

Around the stupa dome are coiled two intertwined snakes, probably *nāga*s venerating the stupa. Their hoods are shown on either side below the groups of umbrellas that adorn the stupa as signs of honour. Two elephants are approaching, kneeling in adoration and holding large flowers(?) in their trunks. This is one of the many examples of animals venerating the Buddha, transcendently present in this symbol of his Nirvana.

the footprints before it (Pl. 8). Even in the early iconography with its overriding concern for 'biographical' narration, a tendency is noticeable to liberate from the bonds of time and space the Buddha and the symbols representing him and his actions; so the symbols become freely available and applicable in various contexts for new religious purposes.

The most unequivocal signs indicating the Buddha's personal presence are the footprints (*buddhapāda*); they appear in front of his throne (Pl. 8), on the water of the Nairañjanā River while he crosses it (Pl. 7), or when he descends, on a ladder built for him by Indra, from the Heaven of the Thirty-three Gods where he had preached to Māyā, his long-deceased mother (Pl. 9). In the later history of Buddhist cult and symbolism, the footprints acquired, as we shall see, great popularity and additional meanings.

Next to the Nativity and the Enlightenment, the third great event of the Buddha's career is the First Sermon held in the Deer Park at Sārnāth near Vārānasi. As the act of preaching is called the 'Turning of the Wheel of the Law' (*dharmacakra*), the symbol employed here is the wheel, normally six-spoked, which originally was the emblem of the world-ruler, the *cakravartin* ('he who sets the wheel in motion'), and by analogy was associated with the Buddha as the spiritual world-ruler. Frequently it is placed on or above the empty throne and surrounded by worshippers, gods, men and even animals, prominently two or more gazelles suggesting the place of the Deer Park. Isolated from the original context in the Buddha's biography, from the story of his first preaching and from the locality, the wheel has come to represent the actual teaching as such, the Buddhist doctrine in a most general sense, and thus has acquired, throughout Asia, universal validity (see p. 417). In the early iconography it is often seen on top of a pillar or column (*cakrastambha*), sometimes combined with a throne; the column, associated with the wheel of universal rule and doctrine, suggests the world-axis, exemplifying the remote origin of some of the Buddhist emblems in ancient, pre-Buddhist cosmological and imperial symbolism.

In some of the numerous events during the Buddha's long life of wandering and teaching he is represented by a curious device, the Walking Path (*caṅkrama*), a sort of beam suspended in the air, e.g., when the Buddha walks over the waters of the Nairañjanā River in order to convert non-believers by a display of his superhuman power (Pl. 10). This symbol differs from most of the others in two respects: it is an abstract sign, not taken from among real objects, and it serves to indicate neither the Buddha's person nor a locality but an action that would have been difficult to illustrate by other aniconic signs.

The last and crowning event in Śākyamuni's career, the Entry into Final Nirvana—i.e., his passing away at Kuśinagara—is depicted by the stupa (Pls. 11, 12). Not only Śākyamuni, but all of his predecessors, the Buddhas of previous ages, can be represented in this way (Pl. 1). Originally a grave mound or tumulus of rulers and saints, the stupa had acquired the function and meaning of a receptacle for relics, and it is in the form of a reliquary that it has been used ever since in Buddhist ritual, though undergoing many metamorphoses. In these relics the Buddha's bodily and spiritual essence is thought to be present; they are also called 'seeds' (*bīja*) contained in the 'egg' (*aṇḍa*) or 'womb' (*garbha*) of the hemispherical stupa. Therefore, the stupa can be identified with the Buddha's holy person, but at the same time it stands for the event of his Entry into Nirvana and, by implication, for the final goal

14. Stupa in the *caitya* hall of Kārlī

From Kārlī, Mahārāshtra, India; early 2nd century A.D.*; stone (cut from the rock); H. of hall approximately 15 m., W. approximately 14 m.; in situ.*

Rock-cut grottos are the oldest preserved form of Buddhist monasteries that consist, typically, of groups of cells with a large *caitya* hall as their ritual centre. The cathedral-like hall of Kārlī, hollowed out of the rock and provided with a sham vault of wooden ribs, has a broad nave and two narrow aisles separated by rows of columns. Opposite the entrance in a semicircular apse stands the solid, rock-cut stupa as the ritual focus of the entire monastery. It stands free so that it can be venerated by circumambulation (*pradakṣiṇā*) and is a miniature model of the contemporary type of independent stupa monuments; thus its surface shows imitated railings in relief, and above the dome, the box-like *harmikā*, surmounted by a canopy. Except for the sculptural decoration of the columns—pot-shaped bases and bell-like capitals crowned by animals, gods or genii—the interior of the early *caitya* halls and their stupas show no figural images; the Buddha is symbolized in aniconic form, suggesting his undefinable and unimaginable Nirvana state by the radical simplicity and austerity of the stupa. A later version of the same type of monument is shown in Pl. 15.

15. Stupa in a *caitya* hall of Ajantā

From Cave No. 26, Ajantā, Mahārāshtra, India; c. A.D. *600–40; stone (cut from the rock); in situ.*

After the representation of the Buddha in human form had become a generally accepted practice, his figure—and even those of numerous other Buddhas—appear in front and along the walls of the stupa base. This and parts of the dome itself are further decorated with reliefs and figures of venerating gods, and above the richly adorned columns of the *caitya* hall is a row of relief panels with groups centered around a Buddha. The Buddha in front of the stupa, seated in 'European' fashion on a richly decorated throne under a palace-like pavilion, is shown in the attitude of preaching, forming with his hands the *mudrā* of 'Turning the Wheel' (*dharmacakra-mudrā*); the right hand is missing. His figure is here to be understood as a manifestation of the intrinsically invisible and unimaginable Buddha in his true essence, issuing from the Nirvana sphere symbolized by the stupa so that he and his message may be visualized and understood in terms of the phenomenal world. The rich imagery and decoration of this monument combined with the relative smallness of the slightly deformed stupa dome is characteristic of a later period, and is a long way from the pristine purity and simplicity of the Kārlī stupa chapel (Pl. 14).

16. The Great Stupa of Amarāvatī

Relief slab originally encasing a stupa; from Amarāvatī, Andhra Pradesh, India; late 2nd century A.D.*; greenish-white limestone; H. 188 cm.; Government Museum, Madras.*

This relief slab gives a complete impression of what a stupa looked like in the transitional period between the aniconic and the iconic phase of representing the Buddha. While in the centre of the upper part of the relief we see a seated Buddha in human form surrounded by attacking forces and by the daughters of Māra, who are attempting to seduce him, in the immediately adjoining scenes to the right and left he is still symbolized by the empty throne. This dualism is repeated in the main panel, which shows a richly decorated stupa such as the one this slab once helped to cover. In front of the stupa we see the Buddha represented aniconically by the typical combination of throne, column and wheel, while immediately above in a small panel belonging to the stupa decoration, he is shown in human form. The other parts of the stupa decoration include narrative reliefs, railings adorned with lotus rosettes and relief bands, portals opening in the four directions and crowned by lion figures, and groups of pillars. Above the stupa, heavenly beings are hovering in adoration. To the right and left rise two tall columns that represent the imaginary body of the Buddha composed of a throne, a slender column with superimposed 'storeys' symbolizing heavenly spheres, and a wheel crowning the lion capitals.

of Enlightenment in the general Buddhist sense. Thus it became a monument embodying the absolute truth, venerated by pious acts and embellished with ornaments and lavish decoration (Pls. 12). The earliest types, as at Bhārhut and Sāñcī or in the *caitya* hall of Kārlī (Pl. 14), where the stupa forms the ritual centre, show an austerely simple, immensely impressive monumental form, while rather later stupas, like those of Amarāvatī or Nāgārjunakonda, are covered with relief slabs illustrating legendary scenes and depicting whole stupas with all their original decoration (Pl. 16). These slabs provide us with indispensable details concerning the authentic appearance of these monuments. In the course of a few decades, the personal image of the Buddha in human shape begins to appear in these stupa reliefs (Pl. 16, upper register), gradually replacing his symbolic representation by the empty throne and the wheel; probably the Buddha is meant here as showing his invisible essence in visible form from within the stupa, symbol of his perennial abode (Pl. 15).

This brief survey of the most important symbols used in the early iconography has shown that there did not exist one exclusive and universally valid symbol for the Buddha's person, but that a number of them stood side by side almost equal in importance and frequency, mainly the footprints, the tree, the wheel and the stupa. They are differently associated, either with a part of his body or with some place in his spiritual career, with an established object of imperial symbolism or with a sacred monument; others, such as the Walking Path, seem to have been freely invented. This multiplicity is due to the close connection of each symbol with a specific biographical event or the locality where it took place, as well as to the strong predilection of early Buddhist art for scenic narration; and it is also due to the disinclination of early Buddhism to establish fixed dogmas and rules. Only secondarily were the symbols isolated from their original context and used independently to indicate the Buddha and the main tenets of his teachings. Later, after the Buddha image had been created, a limited number of canonical types of the Buddha figure were endowed with universal validity, and from among them the meditating Buddha, sitting in the unshakeable, eternal attitude of *samādhi* on the Diamond Seat (*vajrāsana*), became the most generally accepted type in that it shows the Buddha in an archetypal form. It should be emphasized that the highly idealized, almost schematic figure of this basic Buddha type, being entirely liberated from all biographical and other bonds of the phenomenal world, is again a symbol that comes very near to transcending any visual image by passing into the realm of invisibility, i.e., the absolute Nirvana state.

The non-personal, aniconic representation of the Buddha in the early illustrations enabled the artists to visualize the Enlightened One and his teaching in a purely spiritual way, without involving him in the sphere of *saṃsāra* and degrading him to the same level of existence as that of all other living beings. Thus they succeeded in creating, in the midst of a teeming crowd of figures, a centre of quiet emptiness suggesting the Buddha's Nirvana state much more convincingly than any human figure among a multitude of other human figures could have done. In the same way the simple, austere dome of the early stupas, such as at Sāñcī, speaks silently of the ultimate truth transcending the phenomenal world of *saṃsāra*, which, as represented on the gateways and railings in all its infinite multiplicity, is confined to the periphery.

17. The Enlightenment, First Sermon and Entry into Nirvana

Relief slab originally encasing a stupa; from Amarāvatī, Andhra Pradesh, India; 2nd century A.D.; greenish-white limestone; H. approximately 236 cm.; British Museum, London.

The three main events of Buddha's career are represented by the tree, the wheel and the stupa, arranged in ascending order.

18. The Enlightenment, First Sermon and Entry into Nirvana

Fragment of a relief slab originally encasing a stupa; from Nāgārjunakonda, Andhra Pradesh, India; 3rd century A.D.; limestone; Nāgārjunakonda Archaeological Museum.

Here the central place of honour is devoted to a reliquary representing Nirvana, flanked by the symbolic tree and wheel.

19. Rāhula being presented to his father, Śākyamuni

Relief medallion from a stupa railing; from Amarāvatī, Andhra Pradesh, India; 2nd century A.D.; greenish-white limestone; D. 86 cm.; Archaeological Museum, Amarāvatī.

When the Buddha visited his family, his wife, Yaśodharā, presented to him their son, Rāhula, so that he might receive his father's heritage. But the Buddha persuaded him to enter the monastic community, thus gaining a much greater treasure, namely, Nirvana. In the midst of a lively scene the Buddha is represented by symbols: the empty throne with footprints in front of it, the pillar surrounded by flames and crowned by a wheel and a trident (*triśūla*, representing the Three Treasures—the Buddha, the Doctrine, and the Community). The boy on the left, being encouraged by his mother, greets his father by raising his hands while women and other members of the household are surrounding the central group in various attitudes of veneration. The palace is in the background.

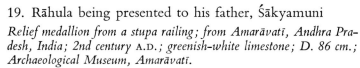

The Cosmological Use of Symbols

Although originating in the narrative contexts of the Buddha's biography, most of the symbols indicating his person or a locality relevant to the stages of his spiritual career were not only used separately but were also assembled in certain combinations. Thus two, three, or more symbols, selected from the biographical sequence, may be arranged side by side or vertically, one above the other. At Amarāvatī, for example, the Buddha's career is reduced to the three main events, the Enlightenment, the First Sermon, and the Entry into Nirvana, represented by the tree, the wheel and the stupa arranged in ascending order (Pl. 17). Evidently all three are to be interpreted as individual cult-objects since groups of divine worshippers are seen surrounding them. In another type of combination, several symbols, usually three, are placed side by side so that they form something like a triad. A relief from Nāgārjunakonda (Pl. 18) reserves the central place of honour to a reliquary representing Nirvana, flanked by the tree and the wheel; the latter two have thrones and footprints in front of them, indicating the Buddha's personal presence, while logically these elements are missing from the central panel. This is specifically distinguished not only by its central position but also by a temple-like design transforming the mere reliquary into a sanctuary. The symmetrical, heraldic arrangement of these groups is another indication of their having been separated from the context of historical narration and elevated to the rank of solemn monuments embodying the essence of the Buddha person and doctrine in powerful concentration.

An altogether different method of grouping several symbols is represented by the composition of an imaginary body of the Buddha. Frequently we see a column crowned with a wheel; in front of it, a throne and a stool with footprints are placed so that the whole arrangement clearly represents the Buddha's body with head, trunk and feet, sitting on the throne (Pls. 16, 17, 18). The flames that are often seen flaring around the column give a precise definition of the underlying scene—the miracle of Śrāvastī, when the Buddha's supernatural power manifested itself in flames issuing from his shoulders and in water streaming from his feet; but here, of course, it was not really intended to illustrate this scene. As in so many other instances, this symbol could be transferred to various contexts, e.g., to the biographical scene in which Śākyamuni's son, Rāhula, is presented to his father and persuaded by him to enter the monastic community (Pl. 19). With an entirely different intention and meaning the imaginary composite body appears in other reliefs at Sāñcī, Amarāvatī and other places; there rises, between the throne with footprints below and the wheel above, a slender column built up by many superimposed layers or 'storeys' (Pls. 16, 21), symbolizing heavenly spheres.

Evidently, even in the early phase the image of the Buddha was understood in a universal cosmological sense. This accords not only with ancient Indian concepts but also with the later philosophical ideas of the Buddha as conceived in Mahāyāna thought. This universalization implied also imperial authority, since the Buddha, being the spiritual ruler of the universe, was taken as a counterpart of the world-ruler (*cakravartin*) and was therefore endowed with royal emblems. Furthermore, the Buddha was equated with the Brahmanic *mahāpuruṣa*, the Primordial Man or personified cosmos, whose body is identical with the

20. Rāhula being presented to his father, Śākyamuni

Relief medallion from a stupa railing; from Amarāvatī, Andhra Pradesh, India; 3rd century A.D.*; greenish-white limestone; D. approximately 85 cm.; British Museum, London.*

This is an illustration of the same scene as in Pl. 19, but with the Buddha shown in human form. Here he is provided with a halo and with lotus flowers springing up under his feet as he is walking. This type, which was to become one of the basic Buddha types throughout Asia and in all periods, appears here in an early example during the later phase of the transitional period, when aniconic and iconic representation often appeared side by side.

world-body that originated from him. This development of religious thought gave an additional dimension of meaning to the symbols used in the scenes of Śākyamuni's biography, but it has to be kept in mind that the symbols themselves had a much older history reaching back far before the rise of Buddhism to remote antiquity. Thus the tree was already a very ancient image of the world-axis and of the idea of fertility (the Tree of Life) with a function in regal enthronement rites; the throne was connected with the world's centre, the occupation of which gave true authority and legality to the ruler; the wheel, long before becoming the sign of the Buddha's teaching, had been a disk-like weapon and, as such, a regal emblem, at the same time being identified with the sun's disk and its world-controlling revolution. The solar wheel crowns the pillar or column representing the *axis mundi*; the symbolic body of the Buddha, composed of throne, column and wheel has to be understood beyond any limited meaning derived from specific Buddhist doctrine as a universal and imperial symbol. Equally, the stupa, primarily a tumulus, then a re-

21. The pillars of the Northern Gateway of Stupa No. 1

From Sāñcī, Madhya Pradesh, India; 1st century A.D.*; yellowish-white sandstone; in situ.*

On the eastern (nearest) pillar we see the symbolic body of the Buddha, which may be compared with the pillars shown in Pl. 16 on either side of the stupa. Here, however, the wheel has the form of a lotus rosette and supports a *triśūla* symbol (see Pl. 19). On the western pillar we see the scene already shown in detail in Pl. 11.

liquary, acquires the quality of a world symbol by virtue of its spherical shape, its orientation towards the directions of the compass, and its having a vertical axis indicating the centre of the universe. In the stupa, the Buddha in his Nirvana state and in his universal essence embracing and pervading all existence is thought to be bodily present in his relics, so that we may speak of a consubstantiality of the stupa, the Buddha and the universe. In this homogenous system of cosmological and universal concepts, many of the symbols, having completely divergent origins, converge and, in spite of their diverse origins, acquire a high degree of ideological unification.

The Interchangeability of Symbols

Notwithstanding their remote origin in ancient Indian thought and their subsequent interpretation in a universal sense, the symbols primarily derive their meaning from the biographical scenes, indicating the presence of Śākyamuni's person or even identified with

22. Enlightenment represented by a tree sanctuary

Relief on the Prasenajit Pillar of the stupa; from Bhārhut, Madhya Pradesh, India; 2nd century B.C.*; H. approximately 80 cm.; Indian Museum, Calcutta.*

The inscription on the roof of the sanctuary reads '*bhagavato Sakamunio bodho*', 'The Enlightenment of the Lord Śākyamuni'. This means that the bodhi tree—with its characteristic pointed leaves and rich decoration of parasols and garlands—and the throne symbolically represent the Buddha, but at the same time a later stage is introduced in an anachronistic way when the sanctuary was built around the sacred tree. The depiction of the shrine shows many typical features of early Indian temple and palace architecture. On the right side, outside the fence, a column crowned by an elephant has been erected, recalling King Aśoka's columns or the ones that we see today at the entrance of the Kārlī *caitya* hall (most of them carrying lions). The gods above, bringing garlands or expressing their astonishment at the great event by raising their fingers to their lips, venerate the Buddha immediately after he has gained Enlightenment. But the four noble persons below evidently worship the sacred object and the sanctuary by adoring gestures and by placing flowers on the altar-like Diamond Seat (*vajrāsana*) at some later time when a bodhi tree cult had developed. In early art such 'continuous narration', assembling several phases into one picture frame, is common practice; for the Buddhists, however, the Buddha and his Enlightenment are timeless, 'without beginning', and therefore 'present' even long after the historical event took place.

23. Footprints of the Buddha

Relief from Amarāvatī, Andhra Pradesh, India; 2nd century A.D.*; limestone; Government Museum, Madras.*

The footprints of the Buddha (*buddhapāda*), originally used as a symbolic sign indicating his personal presence in a biographical or legendary scene, soon became independent cult-objects. As such they are depicted here, venerated by four princely figures. They carry the Wheel of the Doctrine with a lotus flower as its hub and *triśūla* signs on toes and heels—in the latter case flanked by two swastikas—some of them originally of cosmological significance.

him (the tree 'as my permanent abode'). In many illustrations, however, such a personal symbol does not represent the Buddha himself but the locality where an important event of his career took place, such as when King Aśoka, who reigned 273–232 B.C., is shown visiting the site of the Buddha's First Sermon at Sārnāth, or when he looks after the withered bodhi tree at Gayā in order to revive it. Here the symbol acquires an historical dimension as a monument with a specific place not only in the sacred story but also in the later development of Buddhist religion and cult. The tree, like the other symbols, was already in pre-Buddhist times an object of miraculous efficacy, and therefore worthy of worship (*pūjā*). The simple tree, as soon as it received in the Buddhist cult this new function, was thus turned into an enclosed sanctuary and later into a temple-like edifice (Pl. 22). Thus the 'Place of Enlightenment' (*bodhimaṇḍa*) developed into the 'House of Enlightenment' (*bodhighara*). The throne and the stupa are frequently shown lavishly decorated with flowers and garlands and impressed with hand-prints (*pañcāṅgagulika*, 'five-finger signs'). Besides its specific ritual function, the tree was still used to indicate Enlightenment as such; correspondingly, the wheel can stand for the Law or Doctrine, and the stupa for Nirvana, as the ultimate goal and highest consummation of the Noble Eightfold Path. Holy person, holy place, holy object—these three are the main variant meanings of those symbols. Seen *sub specie aeternitatis* they are identical because their ultimate truth is one and the same. The various meanings and functions are therefore not always clearly discernible, since several meanings may overlap or fuse. Sometimes careful analysis may reveal anachronisms and discrepancies, but these are resolvable if we understand that in an early phase the Buddha and all events of his career were thought of as transcending historical time and space. He represented a mere temporal manifestation, for the benefit of the suffering world of living beings, of absolute truth and transcendental Buddhahood.

These few instances may illustrate the important fact that there exists, among the numerous symbols and the various ways in which they are used in early Buddhist art, a broad spectrum of meanings, functions and dimensions. They may represent the person of the Buddha, an object belonging to him or associated with his person, one of his actions or experiences, a sacred place with biographical associations and venerated by later generations, a sacred object as the centre of ritual observances, a representation of a fundamental idea of Buddhist philosophical thought, and, last but not least, even a symbolic image of the world. To decide which of these variant meanings is the correct one in a particular case calls for carefully differentiating analysis with constant regard to the texts or other traditions that the reliefs serve to illustrate. One must also bear in mind that the symbols may overlap or interchange with one another, and that several meanings may be intended.

The Indian terminology distinguishes three categories of venerable objects. The first is called *sārīraka*: 'bodily, corporeal', and comprises relics of a holy person or parts of his body, such as hair or footprints (Pl. 23), or again the famous tooth of the Buddha at Kandy in Sri Lanka (Ceylon). The second is called *paribhogika*: 'for use, serving a purpose', including things belonging to the holy person such as garments, alms-bowls, seats or thrones (*āsana*); even the bodhi tree is counted among them. The third is called *uddeśika*: 'indicating, illustrating, explaining, signifying'; to this group belong some of the most important symbols, as the wheel, the *triśūla* (Pls. 19, 21), a trident-like emblem signifying the Three Jewels or Treasures (*triratna*); the Buddha, the Doctrine (*dharma*), and the Community (*saṅgha*); and finally the stupa. Among the stupas, which in their turn may have different meanings and functions, the same three types are distinguished: *sārīraka-stūpa*, containing bodily remains as relics; *paribhogika-stūpa*, in which an object having belonged to a holy person is deposited; and *uddeśika-stūpa*, indicating or commemorating a sacred spot and an event having occurred there. All of them, of course, can receive worship and ritual offerings (*pūjā*). A given symbol may belong to more than one of these categories; we mentioned the tree as a typical example. But behind the multiplicity of these symbols and their various meanings, we have to recognize the ultimate unity of the fundamental ideas of Buddhism unfolding and diversifying themselves in a spectrum of considerable range.

II. THE BUDDHA IN HUMAN FORM

1. CULTURAL AND HISTORICAL BACKGROUND

The early conception of the Buddha as represented by the stupa and its external decoration corresponds remarkably well with the ideas expressed in the early canonical literature. Although Śākyamuni appears clearly in these texts as an historical person, no sustained interest is yet shown in him by the compilers of the canon as a distinctive historical person in any biographical sense. The only sections of his life-story that are treated coherently are the events from his leaving home to his gaining of Enlightenment and his first preaching, and then his last journey and final passing into Nirvana. These events are explicitly related to the normal course of actions and events, as exemplified in the lives of previous Buddhas, with the result that Śākyamuni's life in this world becomes a kind of special act or show. He is the Tathāgata, the Predestined One who has come in just such a way in order to achieve just such an objective. As has been shown in the previous chapter, the image of the Buddha, as reflected in the symbols, especially those of the stupa and of the tree, corresponds to exactly the same ideas of transcendence and universality. Much as they revered Śākyamuni as Teacher, Lord and Buddha, the first Buddhists were clearly more interested in the ideal that he embodied than in his transient human person. Everything that we know about him has either been recorded incidentally in relationship to his teachings or has been deliberately told in order to prove his Buddha-nature. Such events deliberately told with this intention were arranged very early into two sets of four, namely, the four stages of his progress—Birth, Enlightenment, First Preaching, and Final Nirvana associated respectively with Lumbinī near Kapilavastu, with Bodhgayā, with the Deer Park near Vārānasi, and with Kuśinagara—and secondly, the four special miracles, associated with the towns of Śrāvastī, Rājagṛha, Vaiśālī and Sāṅkāśya. These eight places are all in the Ganges-Jumna (Gangā-Yamunā) Valley, the 'heart-land' of his wandering and teaching, and they all became important places of pilgrimage. It is quite possible that a deliberate collection of the stories and legends connected with these places provided the first incentive towards the production of a full-scale biography of Śākyamuni.[1] Several such extra-canonical biographies were produced, concocted from the stories of his previous lives as well as from the material

[1] See A. Foucher, *La vie du Bouddha d'après les textes et les monuments de l'Inde* (Paris, 1949). This presents the life of Śākyamuni within the framework of the eight main places of pilgrimage, and thus illustrates how the various legends came together in groups.

already available in the canonical writings. In the case of two such early productions that have survived in Sanskrit, the *Lalitavistara* ('An Extended Version of the Display') and especially the *Mahāvastu* ('The Great Matter'), interest in previous lives tends to predominate, and Śākyamuni's final life on earth is taken only as far as the First Sermon in the one, and as far as the famous story of the conversion of three Brahman brothers named Kāśyapa in the other. It was not until the second century A.D. that the first coherent 'lives' of Śākyamuni were produced, covering all the main events as recorded in well-established legendary accounts, from his Birth until his Final Nirvana and the subsequent division of the relics. The first of these *Buddhacarita* ('Acts of the Buddha') was composed by Saṅgharakṣa in Gandhāra during the reign of Kaniṣka; this survives in Chinese. The second, by Aśvaghoṣa, also a contemporary of Kaniṣka, survives in Sanskrit and Tibetan, and has been translated into English by E. H. Johnstone.[2]

It is interesting to note that the production of the first anthropomorphic images of the Buddha and the first attempts at a kind of quasi-historical account of his actual life on earth seem to have been contemporary with one another, and that the first successes both of an artistic and of a literary kind must be referred to the reign of the Kuṣāṇa emperor Kaniṣka. The empire of the great Aśoka, the enthusiastic religious benefactor of the third century B.C., broke up within some fifty years of his death in 232 B.C. His capital of Pāṭaliputra (modern Patna), as well as the whole 'heart-land' of Buddhism, became subject to the kings of the Śuṅga dynasty who ruled from a capital at Vidiśā, much further to the south. Although never regarded as special protectors of Buddhism, they seem to have encouraged the development of magnificent Buddhist settlements, such as Bhārhut and Sāñcī, which have provided so many illustrations for the present book. It was impossible for the Śuṅgas to hold the far north-west provinces of the Indian subcontinent, where Aśoka had encouraged the first Buddhist missions, and Gandhāra (corresponding nowadays to eastern Afghanistan and north-western Pakistan) was taken over by a Greek dynasty from Bactria on the other side of the Hindu Kush. The eclectic interests of these Greek intruders are well illustrated by the case of Menander, known in Buddhist tradition as Milinda, the Yavana (Old Persian *Iaunā*, meaning 'Greek') ruler of Śākala (modern Sialkot), whose discussions with the Buddhist monk Nāgasena were supposedly recorded in an early apologetic work on Buddhist beliefs, the *Milindapañha*, or 'The Questions of Milinda'.[3] Although this work is a deliberate literary production, its rather unusual form, perhaps in imitation of the conversations attributed to kings and specially favoured Brahmans in Upanishadic literature, is presumably based upon a real interest of this particular king in Buddhist teachings.

These Greek rulers of the north-west were ejected by a barbarian people who had slowly pressed in from the north, becoming gradually more civilized as they advanced. These are the Scythians, known perhaps more precisely as the Indo-Scythians, the Śakas of

[2] The available Sanskrit text (up to chapter XIV) is published with English translation in two volumes (Calcutta, 1936). The final section is available in Tibetan with an English translation in *Acta Orientalia*, 15 (1937), pp. 1–128.

[3] Available in English translation (*Questions of King Milinda*) by T. W. Rhys Davids, recently republished by Dover Publications (New York, 1963).

Indian tradition. These Śakas were in constant strife with the Pahlavas (Parthians), and all of them, Yavanas (Greeks), Śakas and Pahlavas succumbed round about the beginning of the Christian era before the advance of another barbarian race, known as the Yueh-chi by the Chinese who first had trouble with them on their western borders, and as the Kuṣāṇas according to Indian tradition. The vast empire of the Kuṣāṇas included a great variety of religions—Greek, Zoroastrian, Buddhist, Jain and Hindu—and their eclecticism is shown by the freedom with which they employed religious symbols of all kinds on their coins. Their greatest king is Kaniṣka I, who was probably ruling during the first half of the second century A.D., when the first coherent life-stories of Śākyamuni were produced.

Whereas the western provinces of the Kuṣāṇa empire had belonged previously to a whole variety of peoples with different cultural heritages, amongst which Persian, Greek and Indian influences certainly predominated, the eastern parts, extending into the upper valleys of the Ganges and Jumna, remained largely Indian in culture. The most important city in the eastern parts was Mathurā, capital of the Śurasenas, a famous Indian aristocratic (*kṣatriya*) lineage. Ptolemy (*Treatise on Geography*, vii, I, 50) knows it as a sacred city, and Hinduism, Buddhism and Jainism all flourished there. It was within these wide Kuṣāṇa domains that the first anthropomorphic images of major Hindu divinities, as well as of the Buddha and the Jina ('conqueror'; see Glossary), were first produced. It is no more easy to explain precisely why the Buddhists should feel the need for such an image, having already done without it for four centuries or more, than to explain why there should be a demand for a complete literary biography. It cannot have been caused simply by an upsurge of popular devotional religion, for the stupa itself was already providing a suitable cult-object. Maybe there is a swing in higher Indian religion at this time from devotion to a transcendent ideal to a more personal kind of devotion directed at the manifested god, or the manifested Buddha or Jina. A special kind of 'personality cult' emerges, and it is expressed both in art and in literature. In the present chapter we are concerned with the varying forms of expression of the Buddha image as conceived in the Indian setting of the upper Ganges-Jumna Valley, in the eclectic setting of Gandhāra in the far north-west and in the Āndhra region to the south. These three areas all interacted upon one another, but each has certain distinct characteristics, and each is important so far as subsequent developments are concerned throughout Central Asia, throughout India, Nepal and Tibet, and throughout South-East Asia. It is therefore convenient to consider them separately.

2. THE GANGES-JUMNA (GANGĀ-YAMUNĀ) VALLEY

About the beginning of the Christian era certain groups within the ever-extending Buddhist community felt the need for an anthropomorphic representation of their Lord (*bhagavān*) that they might approach with adoration (*bhakti*) and worship (*pūjā*). According to the archaeological evidence a similar cult of gods and great beings in human form seems to have developed in Brahmanism and Jainism about the same time. There had already existed for many centuries a cult of tree-spirits (*yakṣa*, male, and *yakṣinī*, female), water-spirits (*nāga* and *nāginī*) and other local divinities, and there was never any inhibition about representing them iconographically. As has been illustrated above (p. 24), their cult as protective and subsidiary deities had been associated from the earliest times with the Buddhist cult of the stupa. They were popular local divinities and no higher religion ever neglected them. Presumably it was under the impact of their cult that the worship of such higher Hindu divinities as Śiva, Skandha, Viśākha, Saṅkarṣana and Vāsudeva came into vogue about the second century B.C. The start of the making and of the cult of the image of Śākyamuni Buddha and of Mahāvīra Jina seem to relate to the same cultural background, namely that of a widespread movement of devotion to the higher personal divinities.

When an artisan or a group of artisans was asked for the first time to produce an image in human form of the Buddha, it was necessary to create something new by drawing upon traditional material available locally. It is in and around Mathurā that the greatest number of very early Buddha images has been found, and on the basis of this evidence this ancient city-state, an eastern province of the much larger Kuṣāṇa empire, has come to be regarded as one of the first creative centres of the Buddha image in human form. It is clear that in this area the stone-workers drew upon two main traditional sources: firstly, their own experience in the making of the images of superhuman figures, whether gods or royal heroes; and secondly, upon the indications given in literary tradition concerning Śākyamuni's special characteristics (*lakṣaṇa*) as Buddha and 'Superman' (literally 'Great Man', *mahāpuruṣa*).

The most important local gods, of which images were already being made, seem to have been the *yakṣa*s and *yakṣinī*s. Their cult must have been widespread throughout the Ganges-Jumna Valley and the whole of central India. Their popularity is certainly indicated by their ubiquitous presence on the reliefs of the stupas of Bhārhut and Sāñcī, as well as by their frequent appearance in stories preserved in the Buddhist canon itself. Such divinities as these, each with his or her local name and habitat, were regarded as beings of superhuman size and power, sometimes benevolent, sometimes malevolent, but often willing to act as protectors of individuals or communities. They were very much concerned, or rather supposed to be concerned, with the affairs of this world, and their representation was usually solid and this-worldly. A number of free-standing and seated images of these local divinities has been found around Mathurā, Gwalior, Pratapgarh, Besnagar (ancient Vidiśā, capital of the Śuṅgas) and Patna (ancient Pāṭaliputra). An inscription on the pedestal of an image of the Yakṣa Maṇibhadra from Gwalior confirms that these divinities were specifically named and that their devotees were referred to as *bhakta*s ('devoted ones'). A glance at Plates 24 and 25 will show how the artisans treated these more-than-life-size images with their superhuman proportions and the impression that they give of massive earthly power. They are shown frontally with heavy roundness of form. From the Mathurā region there have also survived some portrait statues of Kuṣāṇa emperors. These give the same massive this-worldly impression, for they are conceived in much the same way as the images of *yakṣa*s. The best known, both identified by inscriptions, are Wima Kadphises, seated on a throne (Pl. 26) and Kaniṣka, standing.

Thus when the members of the Buddhist community of Mathurā first wanted an image of the Buddha in stone, the same artisans who produced images of local gods and kings

24. A *yakṣa*

From Parkham, near Mathurā, Uttar Pradesh, India; 2nd century B.C.*; sandstone; H. 264 cm.; Archaeological Museum, Mathurā.*

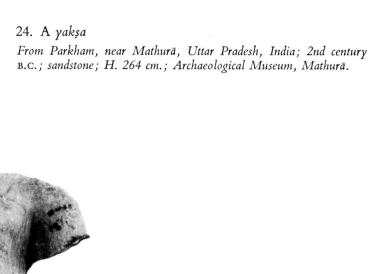

25. Torso of a standing *yakṣa*, illustrating the mode of dress

From Pratapgarh, Uttar Pradesh, India; 2nd century B.C.*; buff sandstone; H. 115 cm.; Municipal Museum, Allahabad.*

26. Headless statue of the Kuṣaṇa emperor Wima Kadphises, illustrating a lion throne and lay dress, especially the tunic and boots.

From Mathurā, Uttar Pradesh, India; 2nd century A.D. *(dated to the 6th year of Kaniṣka's reign, which, however, remains of uncertain dates); sandstone; H. 208 cm.; Archaeological Museum, Mathurā.*

27. Standing Bodhisattva

From Sārnāth, Uttar Pradesh, India; 2nd century A.D.*; red sandstone; H. 208 cm.; Sārnāth Museum.*

Though this piece was set up at Sārnāth, it is presumably a Mathurā production. Note the lion between the feet and the close-fitting religious robe; and also the girdle that is the same as on the *yakṣa* figures.

were the ones commissioned for the task. Since the Buddha was Lord (*bhagavān*) and World-ruler (*cakravartin*) in a supreme religious sense, it was to be expected that the earliest image of him produced in this region should bear an obvious relationship to those of the other 'lords', whom they had previously fashioned.[4] However, since they were also used to producing a whole variety of human and divine figures, as illustrated by the many subsidiary images of gods, goddesses, demons and men that adorn the stupas in the earlier aniconic days of the actual Buddha, they had no problem in introducing sufficient characteristics from a well-established oral and literary tradition concerning Śākyamuni, so that his particular image might be clearly differentiated (Pl. 27). Thus as a religious leader he was portrayed in religious garb that clings closely to the body and leaves the right arm free. In the very early images the head is shaven as befits a monk, but sometimes there is a kind of thick top-knot (*uṣṇīṣa*) of a spiral shape. This may relate to the canonical account of how Śākyamuni, having escaped from his palace to the forest in order to commence the religious quest, pulled his bejewelled and braided hair together on the top of his head and cut it off. The figure either stands free in the round or in very high relief, always frontal, or he may be seated in the regular cross-legged religious posture, known as *yogāsana* ('yoga-posture'), or as *padmāsana* ('lotus-posture') in later tradition. However, in these early Mathurā images, he is seated not on a lotus but on a lion throne (*siṃhāsana*), and when he is standing there is sometimes a seated lion between his feet. This motif relates to his well-established title of Śākyasiṃha, 'Lion of the Śākyas'. A special characteristic is the spoked disc, the 'Wheel of the Dharma' (*dharmacakra*), which is often shown on the palms of his hands and the soles of his feet. In canonical accounts he is said to have been born with these marks of a *cakravartin*, 'world-ruler'.

There is a story in the Pāli canon (*Nālaka-sūtra*, *Suttanipāta*, 679–98), admirably translated by E. J. Thomas, describing the visit of the sage Asita to the remarkable infant:

> When in his arms he received the illustrious Sakya,
> Eager to take him, versed in the lore of bodily signs,
> He raised his voice with believing heart, and said:
> 'Unrivalled of all mankind is he, supreme.'
> But when he brought to mind his own departure,
> Sad was his countenance; then burst he into tears.
> The Sakyas, seeing the sage lamenting, said:
> 'Surely upon the boy will fall no danger?'
> Beholding the Sakyas sorrowful, the sage addressed them:
> 'Nought that will harm the boy do I remember;
> Moreover upon him will alight no danger.
> No lowly person is he, be confident.
> The summit of enlightenment the boy will reach,

[4] The title 'Lord' (*bhagavān*) suggests supreme overlordship when applied by believers to Śākyamuni, although the same title was used of kings, rulers, gods of various kinds and in normal polite address. Thus the *yakṣa* was regarded as a *bhagavata*, a *lokapāla devatā*. See Coomaraswamy, 'The origins of the Buddha image' in *Art Bulletin*, vol. 9, no. 4, pp. 13–15; *Yaksha*, part 1, pp. 4–14.

And with the highest purest insight will set going
The Wheel of the Doctrine, anxious for the good of many,
And far and wide his religious life shall spread.
Here in this world of my life remaineth little,
But meanwhile the close of my life shall come upon me;
I shall not hear the Doctrine of the Incomparable,
Hence am I pained and wretched and afflicted.'[5]

Texts such as these would have been familiar to the monks who commissioned the image, and at the time of the efforts to produce one, they can be imagined giving precise indications. 'He was once a prince,' they might have said, 'so let the fact that he once wore heavy precious ear-rings be indicated by long stretched lobes to his ears.' Thus long ear-lobes became one of the characteristics of the Buddha icon. Sometimes artistic tradition held its own against literary tradition, and in conformity with the kind of Buddha produced in Gandhāra, of which more will be written below, the later Mathurā images have short curly hair, although of a special type of their own (Pl. 28).

Images were commissioned in Mathurā for communities in quite distant places. Three such are especially well known. One was set up at Kauśāmbī at the instance of a nun named Buddhamitra in the second year of Kaniṣka's reign, therefore towards the end of the first century A.D. Another one was set up at Sārnāth in the third year of his reign on the order of a monk named Bala, who like the nun named above, was responsible for the dedicatory inscription. A third one was commissioned and dedicated by the same monk Bala, and was set up at Vārānasi during the reign of Kaniṣka, although the actual date on the inscription is now illegible.

It has often been noted that some early images, including the two set up at Śrāvastī and Vārānasi, are designated in the inscriptions as 'Bodhisattvas', while other similar ones are referred to as the Lord Buddha (*bhagavato buddha*). It is clear that no iconographic distinction was made at this early stage between Śākyamuni as Bodhisattva and as Buddha. Maybe the use of the term Bodhisattva in this context indicates the existence of a lingering suspicion that it was somehow more suitable to portray him in human form as Bodhisattva (potential Buddha) than as Buddha. It may be noted too that the title Bodhisattva draws attention to his saving activities on behalf of others.

All these early images from Mathurā and the surrounding areas are closely related with the local *yakṣa* figures and with the images of Kuṣāṇa emperors. They belong to the same world, where the concepts of overlordship, of fame and of fortune (*bhāga*) predominate. They reveal as yet no expression of the notions of tranquil repose, of worldly detachment and of all-transcending compassion, all so typical of the later 'classical' period. It is interesting to recall that according to a legend in the Pāli canon (in the *Nidānakathā*) the maiden Sujātā, who brought Śākyamuni curds when he was seated in meditation under the sprawling banyan tree, mistook him for a *yakṣa*, or tree-spirit.[6] However, such a tale can

[5] See E. J. Thomas, *Early Buddhist Texts* (London, 1935), pp. 3–4. In the quotation we follow his reading 'Sakya' for Śākya.
[6] See E. J. Thomas, *The Life of the Buddha as Legend and History* (London, 1949), pp. 70–71.

28. Bodhisattva in the meditation posture (*yogāsana*)

From Bodhgayā, Bihār, India, but in the typical red sandstone of Mathurā; 2nd century A.D. *(?) (inscribed and dated in the 64th year of Mahārāja Trikamaladeva, whose dates are unknown); H. 118 cm.; Indian Museum, Calcutta.*

scarcely have influenced the craftsmen, who were merely working within the limits of their actual experience in producing an image of a superhuman being. They could not suddenly be expected to visualize and reproduce spontaneously in artistic form the higher concepts of Enlightenment (*bodhi*), Transcendent Wisdom (*prajñā*) and Compassion (*karuṇā*). Even if they were already conscious of such concepts themselves, it would inevitably take time for them to acquire the skill necessary for their artistic expression.

It has been pointed out by some scholars that the standing Buddha image is really a replica of the earlier standing *yakṣa* or royal image but lacking the regalia and insignia of royalty. This helps to explain why the Buddha, who should have been shaven-headed just like ordinary Buddhist monks in the early sculptures, is soon shown with a top-knot (*uṣṇīṣa*) and also with hair on his head. The term *uṣṇīṣa* refers originally to a turban or jewelled head-dress of just the kind worn by royal figures and *yakṣas*. The argument has been stated quite clearly by Professor J. E. van Lohuizen-de Leeuw:

> When the figure of the Buddha had to be represented in human form, the sculptors met with the difficulty that it was explicitly known of the Master, that he having become a mendicant friar had laid aside all his regalia. Consequently all those royal characteristics of the Yakṣa images, like ornaments and turban, could not be reproduced. So the Buddha figure is, as it were, a Yakṣas or rather a monarch, without regalia. The bracelets, necklaces and other ornaments were simply omitted, and the head, now uncovered, was given the hair-dressing, occasionally shown by the Yakṣas and kings as well, when not wearing a turban; that is to say that the Buddha was represented with a top-knot of hair, the so-called kaparda.[7]

But there is another aspect of this matter. An '*uṣṇīṣa*-like head' (see below p. 76) is one of the signs of a 'superman' (*mahāpuruṣa*) and a Buddha is supposed to show these signs. Thus the top-knot of hair on the head came to be considered part of a specially shaped Buddha-head, and the *uṣṇīṣa* came to mean in normal Buddhist usage a kind of wisdom-bump. Another distinctive 'superman' sign applied to the Buddha-image is the *ūrṇā* or small circular mark between the eyebrows, indicating originally a special wisp of hair as a kind of 'beauty-spot'.[8] Reverting to the other major element in the production of the first Buddha images, namely, the already established patterns for divine and superhuman beings, we may note that the halo of the early Mathurā images has a decoration of little semicircular laps, which seem to correspond to the tips of the open cobra-hood of sculptured serpent-divinities (Pl. 32).[9] Thus the early sculptors seem to have been influenced by this motif. Unravelling the disparate elements included more or less spontaneously in the first Buddha images is clearly a very complex matter.

It is possible that the Jains were first in the field with a seated cross-legged effigy of their master. Representations of Mahāvīra in a seated meditating posture occur on dedicatory plaques (*āyāgapaṭa*) predating the Christian era. As is probably well known, the Jina image

[7] See J. E. van Lohuizen-de Leeuw, *The 'Scythian' Period* (Leiden, 1949), p. 166.
[8] See A. Foucher, *L'art gréco-bouddhique du Gandhāra*, vol. 2 (Paris, 1922), pp. 288–304. A complete list of the thirty-two special signs (*lakṣaṇa*) is given by E. J. Thomas, *op. cit.*, pp. 220–21.
[9] See Heinrich Zimmer, *The Art of Indian Asia*, vol. 1 (New York, 1955), p. 62.

is distinguishable from the Buddha image by its total nakedness, for Jain monks, unlike Buddhist monks, went naked.[10] It is possible that the first Buddha effigies are contemporary with the Jain ones, but they were so scarce that none has been found. Mathurā was certainly known as a flourishing Jain centre, and thus one may equally well allow for the possibility of their taking the first initiatives in the production of a seated Jina type. In this case the seated Buddha image, of which all surviving examples are certainly later than the Jina effigies, may be a deliberate adaptation of the Jina.[11] Such a question of priority has no essential importance, for it must be emphasized that artistic craftsmanship was never a sectarian pursuit. The sculptor fraternity of those days merely strove to satisfy their different clients with the arts and techniques at their disposal, simply making such innovations from time to time as might be suggested to them. It has often been observed that apart from the use of specific symbols, as described in the previous chapter, there is nothing specifically Buddhist about the rather erotic female figures that adorn the early Buddhist stupas. They simply spring from the available repertoire of the Indian sculptors who were commissioned to do the decorations. Thus when asked to produce for the first time a seated Buddha image, they would draw, as they always did, on their previous experience and this might well be any seated religious teacher or even the Jina, if, as seems likely, he was indeed produced before the Buddha in human form.

As well as furnishing dates and the names of donors, the inscriptions on the images also sometimes record to whom an image was given and for what particular end. One such inscription occurs on the image commissioned by the monk Bala for the community at Śrāvastī (it is now in the Indian Museum); another occurs on the fragment of a seated Bodhisattva image found at Mathurā and now in the Archaeological Museum there.[12] These inscriptions state that the gifts were made for the benefit of the *sarvāstivādi ācārya*s (teachers) or simply for the Sarvāstivādins, one of the better-known monastic communities of early times that certainly flourished in the north-west part of the Indian subcontinent. Such gifts were regularly made also 'for the welfare and happiness of all sentient beings' (*sarvasattvānāṃ hitasukhārthaṃ*), an aspiration associated with the Sarvāstivādins and later with the followers of the Mahāyāna. The fact that the language of these inscriptions is more Sanskrit than local dialect may be significant in that this was the language used by the Sarvāstivādins, but one must remember that the use of Sanskrit seems to have been on the increase in all Buddhist schools in India from the beginning of the Christian era onwards, and so it might be rash to associate the popularity of the newly created anthropomorphic images with any one particular school. In the case of later Mathurā images of the fifth and sixth centuries, it is stated clearly that these were made 'for the attaining of supreme

[10] Jina, meaning 'conqueror', although sometimes used of Śākyamuni, is the normal term used by Jains for their world-teachers, of whom the last one in the series was Mahāvīra. Thus to the Buddhist belief in a series of Buddhas who have manifested themselves in the past, there corresponded a similar Jain belief in a series of previous Jinas. The name Jain (Sanskrit: *jaina*) is simply an adjectival form of Jina.

[11] The arguments for this view are well stated by van Lohuizen-de Leeuw in *The 'Scythian' Period*, p. 154 ff. For a good example of a Jain dedicatory plaque (*āyāgapaṭa*), see the frontispiece of that book.

[12] See J. P. Vogel, *Catalogue of the Archaeological Museum at Mathurā* (Allahabad, 1910), p. 63, Museum acc. no. A 66.

knowledge by parents, teachers and all sentient beings', an aspiration that is typical of the Mahāyāna.[13]

A votive inscription in early Kuṣāṇa Brāhmī script places early in the second century A.D. a red sandstone Bodhisattva image that was recovered originally from the village of Katra near Mathurā (Pl. 29). To about the same date there probably also belongs a smaller but similar image of which a fragment found at Mathurā is now in the Museum of Fine Arts, Boston. Of the same period are presumably many other similarly seated Buddha/Bodhisattva images, now housed in various museums in India and elsewhere. Yet another statue from Anyor, a village near Mathurā, may be about a century later. It is inscribed on the upper rim of its pedestal as a *buddha-pratimā*, 'Buddha image'. Iconographically, no distinction may be drawn between this example and that of the Katra Bodhisattva mentioned above. This suggests that even as late as the third century A.D. the titles Buddha and Bodhisattva were still being used in some circles in an indiscriminate way when referring to Śākyamuni himself. It is certain, however, that by this time they had much wider application when referring to other 'great beings' (*mahāsattva*) apart from him. Of this more will be written below (pp. 84–89).

All the Mathurā images mentioned above were produced according to the same vision and the same traditional source, namely, the *yakṣa*-like Buddha/Bodhisattva images of the first century with their sturdy and expansive physical frame and their firm stance. The Katra statue, the similar one to it now at Boston, another from Ahicchatrā (Pl. 30) and the Anyor image, all conform to the same general pattern. The last-mentioned, being rather later in date, perhaps reveals a more advanced technique and a maturer vision, as expressed in the softer plastic treatment of the whole. We may also mention a statue of Buddha seated, found in the Sitalghati locality of Mathurā (Pl. 31). Enough remains of the broken right arm to indicate that it was held raised palm outwards, making the sign of fearlessness (*abhaya-mudrā*). This is the most typical gesture of early Mathurā images, whether standing or seated. It corresponds to what Westerners would regard as a sign of bestowing a blessing, and this is probably the implication of the Indian gesture, which is understood as evoking fearlessness (*abhaya*) or confidence in the beholder. This image from Sitalghati is especially interesting because it resembles in certain other respects the style of Gandhāran images, which we shall be considering below. Thus the figure is draped with the regular monastic outer-garment (*saṅghāṭi*), normally absent on Mathurā images, and the way in which the robes are draped over the body represents the rather looser fold arrangement of Gandhāran images, quite distinct from the close-fitting manner of the garments on Mathurā images. Such differences are striking during the earlier period now under consideration, but the mutual influences of one region upon the other resulted eventually in certain composite styles, while the elaboration of postures and symbolic hand-gestures gradually became stereotyped for the whole Buddhist world. All this, however, is rather a long way ahead.

[13] *Ibid.*, p. 50, Museum acc. no. A 5; p. 59, Museum acc. no. A 48, as examples.

29. A famous Buddha/Bodhisattva image

From Katra, near Mathurā, Uttar Pradesh, India; 2nd century A.D.*; black sandstone; H. 69 cm.; Archaeological Museum, Mathurā.*

The all but transparent robe that leaves the right shoulder bare is typical of Mathurā images. As on other early images from this region, no actual hair is shown on the head except for a hair-line and the snail-shell(*kaparda*)-like coil, which represents the traditional *uṣṇīṣa* (see pp. 75–76). The halo has on its edge semicircular indentations suggestive of the hood of a serpent (*nāga*). On either side is a divine attendant dressed in the normal Indian style of the period. The lion throne is also typical of early Mathurā images. The inscription in Brāhmī letters of the Kuṣāṇa period reads: 'Buddharakṣita's mother Amohasi has set up this Bodhisattva [image] in association with her parents in her own religious house for the welfare and happiness of all living beings.' The right hand is raised in a gesture of blessing (lit., fearlessness, *abhaya*).

30. An early Buddha image

From Ahicchatrā, Uttar Pradesh, India.

This image, similar to that in Pl. 29, is apparently also of Mathurā craftsmanship. Note, however, that the two attendant divinities are here identifiable as Vajrapāṇi, who grasps the sacred thunderbolt (*vajra*) in his right hand, and Padmapāṇi, who holds aloft a bunch of lotus buds. Vajrapāṇi, who often accompanies Śākyamuni on Gandhāran sculptures as a kind of personal bodyguard, is dressed in blouse and short kilt, a Hellenistic form of dress, exactly as in the Gandhāran models.

31. Buddha in the meditation posture on a lion throne, with a robe of heavy 'Gandhāran' type

From Sitalghati, Mathurā, Uttar Pradesh, India; probably 3rd century A.D.*; buff stone; H. 45 cm.; Archaeological Museum, Mathurā.*

32. An early Buddha image

From Mathurā, Uttar Pradesh, India; red sandstone; H. 81 cm.; Archaeological Museum, Mathurā.

The robe is full and covers both shoulders in the Gandhāran style. The bare head and the halo with indentations suggesting a serpent's hood are typical of Mathurā. Thus we see here a mingling of the two styles, which were never far apart geographically and which developed within the same Kuṣāṇa kingdom.

3. GANDHĀRA

Ancient Gandhāra, comprising modern North-West Pakistan and eastern Afghanistan, was the centre of great Kuṣāṇa empire, of which Mathurā and the upper Ganges-Jumna Valley represented the outlying eastern areas. While local Indian cultural influences were predominant in those eastern areas, Gandhāra had already been open for several centuries to Persian and Greek influences as well as to barbarian influxes from the north. One must not imagine the existence of any well-defined cultural barrier between the Ganges-Jumna Valley and the more central parts of the Kuṣāṇa empire, for it is certain that Persian and Greek influences had already penetrated, at least to some extent, into the very heart-land of India.[14] But whereas such influences are slight and so less clearly definable in India, they were predominant in Gandhāra. However, here again one must note that Gandhāra was as much open to influence from the Indian side as from the Persian and Greek side. The whole Buddhist religion, the cult of the stupa and its carved decorations, the aniconic symbols of the Buddha and even probably the very idea of creating an anthropomorphic image of the Buddha, not to mention the vast literature on which the whole religion was based, all this was of Indian provenance. By the time the first Buddha images in human form were produced, Gandhāra was quite as much a Buddhist land as the Ganges-Jumna Valley, and not only Buddhist but also Jain and Hindu in so far as all these religions represented variant forms of Indian culture. Mathurā was quite as much part of the Kuṣāṇa empire as Gandhāra, and the same incentives for the production of Buddha images would have been equally active in both areas. Various attempts have been made to give priority to one area over the other, but nothing would be gained by following the arguments here.[15] For present purposes a satisfactory conclusion is that of Ananda K. Coomaraswamy, namely, 'that the Buddha image must have been produced simultaneously, probably in the middle or near the beginning of the first century A.D. in Gandhāra and in Mathurā, in response to a demand created by the internal development of the Buddhism which was common ground in both areas; in each case, by local craftsmen, working in the local tradition'.[16]

Buddhism is believed to have reached the far north-western regions of the Indian subcontinent during the reign of Aśoka in the third century B.C. Certainly his inscriptions bear witness to his personal aspirations in this regard. During the following century a king of

[14] See, for example, Zimmer, *The Art of Indian Asia*, ch. 4, p. 42 ff., 'Mesopotamian patterns in Indian art'. Also Foucher, *L'art gréco-bouddhique du Gandhāra*, vol. 2, p. 742 ff., 'L'influence classique dans l'art de l'Inde'.

[15] The chief protagonist of the Greek origin of the Buddha image was Foucher. His brilliant work quoted above all leads to this conclusion. His arguments are given briefly in an article 'The Greek origin of the image of Buddha', in *The Beginnings of Buddhist Art and Other Essays in Indian and Central Asian Archaeology* (London, 1917). This view has been consistently opposed by Indian scholars, of whom we may regard Coomaraswamy as one of the chief representatives, and their arguments are sustained by van Lohuizen-de Leeuw in *The 'Scythian' Period*, pp. 169–71. She argues that, 'we find the Buddha image at least half a century, if not a whole century, earlier at Mathurā than at Gandhāra. And this, we think, proves what HAVELL and COOMARASWAMY —be it often on intuitive and emotional grounds—have maintained, viz., that the Buddha image originated on Indian soil, conceived as a supply for Indian need. The credit for this idea is always given to the two just-mentioned scholars, but it was VICTOR GOLOUBEW (in a review of Foucher's *L'art gréco-bouddhique* in *Bulletin de l'École Française d'Extrême-Orient*, vol. 23 [1924], pp. 438–54) who propounded this thought for the first time'.

[16] A. K. Coomaraswamy, *History of Indian and Indonesian Art* (London, 1972), p. 60.

(a)

(b)

(c)

(d)

33. Coins (in the British Museum, London)

(a) The Greek (Yavana) king Menander (the Milinda of Buddhist tradition, see p. 46); 2nd century B.C.; copper. Note the wheel, already a Buddhist symbol in India, and perhaps with intended Buddhist associations on this coin.

(b) The Indo-Scythian (Śaka) king Maues; 1st century A.D.; copper. The meditating figure may be intended as a Buddha image.

(c) The great Kuṣāṇa emperor Kaniṣka; 1st–2nd century A.D.; gold. The standing Buddha figure is clearly named 'Boddo'.

(d) Kaniṣka; 1st–2nd century A.D.; copper. The seated Buddha figure is identified as 'Go Boydo'.

34. The gift of the Jetavana

Stone plaque from Gandhāra, exact provenance unknown; schist; H. 20.3 cm.; Archaeological Museum, Peshawar.

This illustrates the gift of the Jetavana, the royal park on the outskirts of Śrāvastī, by the merchant Anāthapiṇḍaka, who bought it for the Buddhist order. He holds a water-pot used in the ceremony of formal gift-giving. Note his Indian-style costume and those of his three companions. Śākyamuni conforms to the Gandhāran type with his hair-style and toga-like robes.

Greek extraction who ruled at Śākala in the upper Indus Valley, known as Menander according to his coins and as Milinda in Buddhist tradition, seems to have taken an interest in the new religion. A Buddhist work, preserved in Pāli and known as 'The Questions of Milinda' (*Milindapañha*), records his discussions with the Buddhist monk Nāgasena. Also he may have deliberately copied the Buddhist Wheel of the Doctrine (*dharmacakra*) on one of his coins. More to our immediate purpose are the coins of the Śaka kings Maues and Azes of the first century B.C. and of the Kuṣāṇa king Kadapha, all of which show figures in relief that may be Buddha images.[17] However, it is not until the reign of Kaniṣka that we reach any certainty in the matter of coins with Buddhist implications and these take us to the second century A.D. or possibly to the end of the first (see Pl. 33).

One of these Kaniṣka coins shows a standing Buddha image, clearly identified by the legend 'Boddo' in Greek letters. He wears a monastic robe over both shoulders and the right hand seems to be raised in the conventional gesture of blessing, or more exactly of instilling fearlessness (*abhaya*), while the left hand grasps the edge of the robe. Another such coin shows a seated Buddha image, identified by the legend 'Go (i.e., Gautama) Boydo (i.e., Buddha)'. The standing figure is similar to that represented on schist and slate stone reliefs, as well as to other Gandhāran Buddha figures (Pl. 34). Special mention must also be made of the magnificent gold relic casket from Bimran in Afghanistan, preserved in the British Museum. This is adorned with figures in relief of the Buddha and his worshippers, all standing in niches (Pl. 36). There is also the equally well-known relic casket of Kaniṣka, on the lid of which there is a seated image of the Buddha flanked by two Bodhisattvas (Pl. 35). The Bimran casket has been regarded as one of the earliest pieces from Gandhāra, one of the reasons being that it was found together with coins of the pre-Kuṣāṇa period, but there are good stylistic arguments against so early a dating.[18]

We noted above (p. 46) that the production of the first anthropomorphic images of the Buddha seemed to coincide with the first attempts at a quasi-historical account of Śākyamuni's life on earth. In this respect it is significant that Gandhāran sculpture depicts primarily just this in a newly realistic way. One may compare the two birth scenes in Plates 37 and 38, one stylized and suggestive, the other completely realistic. The earlier Indian art, as described in the previous chapter, was concerned with a mythical conception of Buddhahood, as represented by symbols and by scenes referring to previous lives of the Bodhisattva (*jātakas*). One may note the stark realism of the scene of the Bodhisattva abandoning his sleeping wife on earth (Pl. 39), or the scene of his quelling a dangerous snake (Pl. 40). It is likely that Gandhāra led the way in introducing such realism into Buddhist art, while Hellenistic influences were the motivating force. The stylized representation of the birth scene mentioned above (Pl. 37) could well be inspired in its production by the Gandhāran counterpart (Pl. 38). In this case we witness a deliberate 'Indianization' of Hellenistic suggestion.

[17] Coomaraswamy, 'The origins of the Buddha image', *Art Bulletin*, vol. 9, no. 4 (1926–27), figs. 6–12. Kadapha may be the same as Kadphises I; Wima Kadphises mentioned on p. 48 is Kadphises II.

[18] See Coomaraswamy, *History of Indian and Indonesian Art*, pp. 51–52; and for more detail, van Lohuizen-de Leeuw, *The 'Scythian' Period*, pp. 83–94.

35. Relic casket

From Shāh-Jī-Kī-Dherī, Peshawar, Pakistan; bronze; H. 19.3 cm.; Archaeological Museum, Peshawar.

This casket was found at the site where Kaniṣka is known to have built one of his most famous stupas, and this very casket, containing Buddha relics, was presumably once enshrined within it. On the lid the Buddha is seated on a lotus pedestal. He makes the typical *abhaya* gesture, instilling 'fearlessness' or confidence. His hair-style and his robe conform to the Gandhāran pattern (see p. 67). He is worshipped by the gods Brahmā and Indra, who are often associated with him in the early canonical accounts. The top of the lid has an incised lotus design and around the edge there is a frieze of flying geese. The goose (*haṃsa*) is a bird sacred to Brahmā and its early spontaneous appearance here is interesting, for it was not absorbed into Buddhist iconography. On the body of the casket a Kuṣāṇa monarch, probably intended as Kaniṣka himself, appears on one side, flanked by the sun-god and moon-god, while on the other three sides there is a Buddha image in each case similar to the main one on the lid and being worshipped by a royal figure. The four 'scenes' are held together by a garland, which is supported by *patti* (cherubs).

36. Relic casket

Found at Bimran, Afghanistan; date uncertain; gold repoussé decorated with jewels; H. 7 cm.; British Museum, London.

This casket is decorated with a series of arched niches with figures of the Buddha flanked by Indra and Brahmā. The full robes of the figures correspond to Western styles, but the arches are in the Indian style as seen, for instance, on the front of Buddhist cave temples. The flying eagles between the pointed arches are again Western in inspiration. Altogether it is an extraordinarily composite piece, maybe from the second or even the third century A.D. (see p. 61).

37. Three scenes related to the birth of Śākyamuni

From Sārnāth, Uttar Pradesh, India; c. 5th century A.D.*; National Museum of India, New Delhi.*

The three interrelated scenes referring to the birth of Śākyamuni are: to the left of the plaque, his conception, where his mother, Queen Māyā, dreams that the child is entering her womb in the form of a white elephant; to the right of the plaque, the actual birth from his mother's side; and in the centre, the child standing on a lotus throne in the process of making his seven steps to the four directional quarters (see p. 27). This item comes from Sārnāth and the figures are all quite Indian in appearance, but such didactic 'biographical' productions are comparatively rare in the Ganges-Jumna Valley and the overall inspiration for its production may be regarded as Gandhāran. Hence it is probably rather late, about fifth century.

39. The Bodhisattva abandoning his sleeping wife ▷

Stone plaque from Gandhāra; H. 62.6 cm.; Lahore Museum.

The Bodhisattva abandons his sleeping wife and escapes from the palace in order to adopt the religious life. The horse, which is going to carry him away and which subsequently became a god, awaits above on a balcony with other divine beings. The extraordinary 'realism' of the main scene, so typical of these Gandhāran sculptures, may be usefully contrasted with the more 'mythological symbolic' representation of the birth scene in Pl. 37.

38. The birth of Śākyamuni

Stone plaque from Gandhāra; Victoria and Albert Museum, London. This plaque illustrates the birth of the infant Śākyamuni from the right side of his mother and also shows the child on the ground, presumably about to take the seven steps (see Pl. 37). The greater realism of this Gandhāran scene is in marked contrast with the more symbolic representation, as illustrated in Pl. 37.

40. Śākyamuni quelling a snake

From Ranigat, Pakistan; H. 34.2 cm.; Lahore Museum.

In this scene, Śākyamuni is quelling a terrifying snake that was the reincarnation of an avaricious man of Rājagṛha. He undertakes this action at the request of King Bimbisāra, who is concerned for the welfare of the townsfolk. Following close behind Śākyamuni is Vajrapāṇi in the role of his special guardian (see Pl. 30), and all the other figures are presumably members of Bimbisāra's entourage. He himself is probably facing the Buddha with hands raised in adoration. Note the simple halo, a kind of 'solar disk', which is typical of all these Gandhāran Buddha/Bodhisattva figures (Pls. 39–45).

The dating of the Gandhāran sculptures is an intractable problem. Attempts have been made to establish some kind of sequence for the countless pieces recovered in this region by arguments based on changes in style. It has been argued that the more obvious the Hellenistic influence, the earlier the piece, and the greater the Indian stylistic influence, the later the piece, and this argument has easily been associated with the idea that the Hellenistic influence was an ennobling one, while the Indian influence represented a deterioration. Not only has the basic argument been disproved by the discovery of Hellenistic Buddha images of known late date, but the very variety of the finds confounds altogether such a simple rule of thumb. The reliefs illustrating scenes of Śākyamuni's life, with the movement and action that they often depict, may indeed represent a form of Greek influence, but the more stereotyped Buddha images, already mentioned above, which bear resemblance to the effigies on coins, are certainly just as early, if not earlier, as indicated by the approximate dates of the coins. It certainly seems that the strongest impetus was given to Buddhist architecture and art by the interest of Kaniṣka and his immediate successors. His reign must have ushered in a new burst of popularity for the religion, and thus it seems unlikely that we possess any Buddha image earlier than the end of the first century A.D., and the various types—the more Hellenistic ones and the more stylized ones—could all have been produced at more or less the same time in a variety of different circumstances.

We may now consider the basic characteristics of these Buddha images from Gandhāra. Seated or standing, the Buddha is conceived as a short, rather stocky figure, and the position of the body is invariably frontal wherever he appears independently (Pl. 41). His hair is arranged in waves gathered together on the top of his head. The eyes are open and there is a little circle (the *ūrṇā*, or 'beauty-spot') between the brows. He often wears a moustache, and it has been suggested that even in cases where the sculpturing does not suggest the presence of one nowadays, one may have been painted on.[19] The ear-lobes are distended. The body is covered in a heavy monastic cloak that hangs in deep folds and covers the standing figure to just above the feet, while the seated cross-legged figure may be covered completely (Pl. 35). The hands may be held in the gesture of blessing (fearlessness, *abhaya*), or together on the lap in the gesture of repose and meditation (*dhyāna*), or together in front of the body in the gesture of teaching (Turning the Wheel of the Doctrine, *dharmacakra-pravartana*), or touching the earth with the right hand to call the earth-goddess to witness (*bhūmisparśa*). This last gesture refers to the legend of the attack of Māra, the Evil One, upon Śākyamuni, as he sat under the tree at Bodhgayā. Challenged by Māra concerning his fitness to realize Nirvana, he called the earth-goddess to witness.

All these gestures clearly belong to early Indian Buddhist tradition and, except possibly the gesture of blessing, have no association with Western ideas. The mound of hair on the head, corresponding to the *uṣṇīṣa*, already discussed above, as well as the circle between the brows and the extended ear-lobes, all relate to Indian tradition. Of these the mound of hair requires special consideration, for it may plausibly be compared with the hair-style of Greek divinities, and the adoption of this style by the first sculptors of Buddha images in Gandhāra has been one of the main arguments in support of the Greek origin of the

19 van Lohuizen-de Leeuw, *The 'Scythian' Period*, pp. 105–6.

41. Sākyamuni with an ascetic

From Gandhāra; National Museum of Pakistan, Karachi.

Śākyamuni with a moustache is certainly very common though not universal in his Gandhāran representation. It is certainly not typical of normal Indian representation, but from Gandhāra his moustache found its way across Central Asia to the Far East. Śākyamuni's vast superiority to other ascetic leaders, with whom he is shown in the canonical accounts to be often in conflict, is indicated by his very much greater size here. There are not enough indications in this sculpture to identify any particular scene. Concerning the *uṣṇīṣa* represented by a Greek hair-style, see p. 75.

42. Preaching Buddha

From Sahr-i-Bahlol; H. 74.5 cm.; Archaeological Museum, Peshawar.

The facial features and hair-style are almost identical with those of the preceding illustration and one wonders if the same master craftsman was involved. The robe hangs in the rather heavy Gandhāran manner, but it is arranged to leave the right shoulder bare in the Mathurā way, which is also in accord with canonical practice. Note, too, the lion motif on the throne, also typical of Mathurā images. The small figure inset on the throne is a meditating Bodhisattva, flanked by worshippers. One may observe once again how closely associated are the Buddha and Bodhisattva ideals (see p. 52).

43. Standing Buddha

Black calcareous marble; National Museum of India, New Delhi.

This is a fine example of the typical Gandhāran Buddha, described on p. 67. The popularity of this Buddha figure is indicated by the many examples included in H. Ingholt, *Gandhāran Art in Pakistan* (New York, 1957), Pls. 195–228.

Buddha image, as maintained by Alfred Foucher. It is argued that the sculptors preferred to follow a Greek tradition of a divine image with a comely hair-style rather than produce a bald-headed monk as would have been in keeping with the scriptural accounts. This argument may be accepted, especially when one regards the full and radiant face with its sharply chiselled and refined proportions, which have called forth some of the more ecstatic lines of this great French archaeologist scholar (see Pl. 43):

> Is it not as though the Hellenizing master-craftsman, whose skilful chisel-cuts produced this Buddha image from a block of blue schist, had left his own thoughts imprinted on the stone? Standing before his finished work, we think we understand how he conceived it and why he executed it in such a way. For one matter, had he not something of us in him, with the result that it is easier for us to read his thoughts? For another matter, do we not know in advance what those who ordered the images would have suggested to him? When they encountered the figure of the Buddha, he was not just fading in the mists of the past; he was rather beginning to lose his clear outlines in the clouds of incense that everywhere arose towards his divine nature now being realized. So after all, what one needed to represent was someone like a young prince, a descendent of the solar dynasty and more glorious than the day, who in former times, filled with loathing for the world and compassion for living creatures, had assumed the garb of a monk and had become by the power of his intellect a kind of saviour god. . . . .
>
> 'Apollo, Saviour God, God of mysteries so learned,
> God of Life and God of all salutary plants,
> Divine conqueror of Python. God triumphant and youthful. . . .'
>
> Remembering these fine ancient verses of André Chénier (*Bucoliques*, VI), no one would be surprised that our artist should have thought at once of using as his model in such circumstances the most intellectual of his own youthful Olympian gods.[20]

Probably no one would dispute the plausibility of such reactions on the part of a sensitive Western scholar imbued with a sympathetic understanding for all that is best in the Greek classical tradition. However, from the Indian viewpoint this Hellenized Buddha is a kind of accident on the soil of the subcontinent, which may have left certain lasting effects, but degenerates and disappears as a style in its own right. Moreover, it is easily brought into a kind of logical relationship with the Buddhas that were being produced in Mathurā at about the same time. It was suggested above (p. 54) that there the Buddha image may be regarded simply as a royal or divine figure deprived of his glorious insignia and decorations. In exactly the same way the Buddha image of Gandhāra has been described by Foucher himself as the Gandhāran type of Bodhisattva deprived of his ornaments, and thus this type of Bodhisattva is nothing other than a specialized version of the local royal or divine figure.

The type of Buddha—one can no longer doubt this after seeing it arise—is in the end

[20] From Foucher, *L'art gréco-bouddhique du Gandhāra*, vol. 2, p. 283; passage translated by the Editor.

> nothing other than the royal and divine type that we have already seen serve for the Bodhisattva; only it has been deprived of the lay indications of temporal power and wealth. It is there that resides the whole secret of the transformation. Given an image of Siddhārtha, just remove the turban from his head, the rings from his ears, the necklaces from his neck, and you obtain quite naturally a head of Śākyamuni. In a last resort, you could even overlook the delicate moustache that plays on his upper lip and that you will find at the limits of the Far East, where having traversed Central Asia, it is still marked by a brushstroke on the golden background of Japanese images.[21]

We have quoted this short passage for, quite apart from its extraordinary perspicacity, it is essentially in agreement with the views of other scholars, who in disagreement with Foucher have insisted upon the independent origins of the Mathurā image and whose views we feel bound now to accept. The interesting point is that in both places the Buddha image was conceived, not as that of a simple monk, but as a royal and divine figure deprived simply of his lay ornaments (Pls. 43, 44). The Buddha was nowhere conceived of as a simple mortal. He was a 'superman' (*mahāpuruṣa*), and although as a religious he could not wear lay accoutrements, all were agreed that he should bear on his body the marks of his superhuman associations. In Gandhāra, as would be expected, these divine marks show Hellenized influence, often to a remarkable extent. Further east, in the upper Ganges-Jumna Valley, such influence is much less or is altogether lacking. But wherever the Buddha image was produced, there was no essential difference in the spirit and the intention of the production. It was a divine, or more accurately expressed, a superhuman and super-divine figure in all respects worthy of devotion and worship.

A few other special points must be made before we leave the subject of origins. It was noted above that the early Buddha images of Mathurā were often referred to on the inscriptions as 'Bodhisattva', and after all that has been written above, this may not seem so surprising. The Buddha retains in popular imagination all the spiritual attributes of the Bodhisattva, and thus from one point of view there can be no essential difference between the two types. Professor J. E. van Lohuizen has pointed out that we nowadays tend to understand the term 'Bodhisattva' in a rather specialized Mahāyāna sense of a being, usually a human being, who is striving towards Enlightenment and who is not yet a Buddha, and for that reason alone certain scholars have detected illogicality in the use of the term for the early Mathurā images.[22] But for the early Buddhists themselves Śākyamuni was already the Tathāgata, the Predestined One, and the term 'Bodhisattva', literally 'the being whose nature is Enlightenment', refers to his whole glorious career throughout previous lives and the last one. It has its own numinous quality just like the term 'Buddha' itself, but whereas 'Buddha' suggests absolute transcendence that is best indicated by means of symbols, the Bodhisattva is manifest in this world, and therefore immanent as well as transcendent, for he belongs to the realm of the gods as well as that of men. Despite the interest that the

[21] *Ibid.*, vol. 2, p. 302.
[22] See van Lohuizen-de Leeuw, *The 'Scythian' Period*, pp. 177–79.

44. Standing Bodhisattva

Black calcareous marble; National Museum of Pakistan, Karachi.

This is the typical princely Bodhisattva of Gandhāran inspiration. Such a figure is usually identified as Maitreya, the future Buddha, because of his Brahmanical associations and hence the water-pot that he holds in his left hand. Śākyamuni himself was known to be of princely *kṣatriya* caste, but tradition claimed that the student Megha who had taken the vow to become Buddha himself one day at the feet of the then Buddha Dīpaṅkara was a Brahman youth (see p. 187). The Buddhists were quite as sensible as everyone else to the importance of social status.

many Gandhāran friezes show in the last life of the Buddha Śākyamuni, the conception of Buddhahood itself remains essentially transcendent and mythical just as in the earlier aniconic period. In illustration of this one may refer to the interesting image of the previous Buddha Dīpaṅkara with the Brahman student Megha, who is the future Śākyamuni, worshipping at his feet (see p. 187). This is doubtless a later image, as the wavy hair gathered up into a tuft already has the appearance of a cranial bump, but it illustrates the fact that as a transcendent being the Buddha figure is necessarily stereotyped, while as the Buddha Śākyamuni operating in this world and thus depicted on the illustrative friezes, greater freedom in the posturing of the body is inevitable and quite natural. It is clearly in this latter form of the Buddha figure that experience in Hellenistic craftsmanship was invaluable to the sculptor.

As a Bodhisattva living a worldly palace life, Siddhārtha, the future Śākyamuni, is portrayed with royal accoutrements, and the same type of figure serves also to represent the Bodhisattva Maitreya, the Buddha of a future age. Interesting in this regard is the frieze from Takht-i-Bahi, now in the Peshawar Museum, which shows the six previous Buddhas, the seventh Buddha Śākyamuni, and next to him the Bodhisattva Maitreya in regal attire.[23] This type of royal Bodhisattva becomes increasingly popular and increasingly differentiated according to name and function throughout the early Mahāyāna period, to be considered below.

It has been suggested that the main impetus for the production of a human image of the Buddha was this whole new movement, the Mahāyāna, with its increasing emphasis on devotion and also with its changed philosophical conceptions. It has even been argued that the philosophical school, known as the Mādhyamika (the 'Middle Way'), which based its arguments on the 'Perfection of Wisdom' literature (*Prajñāpāramitā*), prepared the way by teaching that not only the phenomenal world (*saṃsāra*) but also Nirvana and the very ideal of Enlightenment (*bodhi*) are all empty (*śūnya*) in a relative sense. Thus 'the illusory historical Buddha, who through *bodhi* entered into Nirvana, yet until his *parinirvāṇa* ('final disappearance') continued to live for the eyes of the world, may consequently be represented as though alive in the illusory world'.[24] This may be a fine piece of philosophical justification after the event, but it probably has little to do with the real reasons for the production of a Buddha image. One might as well argue that the first complete life-stories of Śākyamuni, which were produced during the Kuṣāṇa period, were likewise provoked by 'Perfection of Wisdom' teachings of universal relativity. However, it takes some time for philosophical theories to have a social and a more general religious impact, and the later impact of 'Perfection of Wisdom' teachings on later Buddhist art we must mention below. It would seem clear that in its early stages the Buddha image serves two purposes: to express a stereotyped and rather static conception of Buddhahood in a transcendent sense (although the art of expressing this adequately was only gradually acquired); and secondly to illustrate events in the actual life of Śākyamuni on earth, corresponding perhaps to a need felt by foreign converts of Hellenistic background. Who is this person Śākyamuni, they might

23 See Foucher, *L'art gréco-bouddhique du Gandhāra*, vol. 2, p. 323
24 See Zimmer, *The Art of Indian Asia*, p. 340

45. Bodhisattva Maitreya
Stone plaque; Kabul Museum.
The Bodhisattva Maitreya is attended by dignitaries of the Kuṣāṇa kingdom. Note the hair-styles and costumes of these 'barbarian' converts.

have asked, whose doctrines we are asked to follow?[25] The answer to this question could ultimately only be an Indian one, whatever incidental Hellenistic motifs played a part in the production of the first images.

The case of the Buddha's hair, which he is not supposed to have had in so far as he was a shaven-headed monk, is interesting. One might argue that the presence of hair, imitated from other divine figures as mentioned above, suggests in itself his superhuman nature. The early Gandhāra hair-style is indisputably of Greek origin, but an indigenous Indian justification was easily found for hair of another kind. The second of the thirty-two signs of a 'superman' (*mahāpuruṣa*) specifies that his hair curls to the right (*pradakṣiṇāvarta-keśa*). Thus it came about that in conformity with this injunction the head of a Buddha was covered and has ever since been covered with small curls twisting to the right. This style was rapidly adopted in Mathurā in preference to the bare head of the very earliest images as well as to the foreign, wavy hair-style. Finally, the *uṣṇīṣa*, which might still be regarded as a special hair arrangement on the more Hellenistic heads, becomes a cranial bump when covered

[25] It is interesting to observe as some kind of parallel that the Christian gospels were compiled from earlier traditional materials and produced in Greek for Greek-speaking converts, who perhaps similarly wanted to know more of the person of this Christ Jesus, to whose teachings they had turned. What had been accepted on trust in a Judeo-Christian setting required re-statement in a kind of consecutive historical form when transported into an inquiring Greek setting. Similarly, the foreign converts of the far north-west of the Indian subcontinent would pose the question: 'What is a Buddha?', a question that was simply taken for granted in the Ganges Valley.

with short curls in the acceptable Indian manner. It is interesting to note that the meaning of the epithet 'turban-headed' (*uṣṇīṣa-śiraska*), the first of the thirty-two signs of a 'super-man', may thus have gone full circle in meaning. Foucher is probably right in arguing that originally this whole list represented a set of prognostications for foretelling the degree of future greatness of an infant, precisely in fact as they were used by the sage Asita when he visited the infant Siddhārtha. In such a context the epithet 'turban-headed' could only mean possessing a head that bulged like a head-dress because of the super-intelligence that it contained.[26] This is precisely what the term came to mean in accepted Buddhist practice, namely a wisdom-bump.

4. ĀNDHRADEŚA (KRISHNĀ VALLEY)

In Āndhradeśa and particularly in the low valleys of the Krishnā and Godāvari rivers, the appearance of anthropomorphic images of the Buddha in the second and third centuries did not result immediately in a rejection of the firmly established aniconic tradition. It was as if the 'human' portrait of the Buddha served new purposes and so could not entirely replace the earlier symbolic images, which disappeared only slowly. Among a large number of sects, the existence of which is proved by inscriptions around Amarāvatī (former Dhānyakataka) and Nāgārjunakonda (former Vijayapurī, the capital of the Ikṣvākus in the third and fourth centuries), it would seem that some remained especially faithful to tradition and were somewhat reluctant to accept portrayal of the Buddha as a human being. But it is even more important to note that on some monuments, and sometimes even on the same relief, in particular on the *vedikā* ('balustrades') of the Great Stupa of Amarāvatī (*mahācaitya*), symbols and human images often appear side by side. The explanation for the obvious co-existence of the two iconographies lies equally in the slow evolution from aniconic to iconic forms and in a kind of routine attachment to earlier artistic formulas. The choice made by Amarāvatī art is certainly more a matter of doctrine than of craft traditions. Perhaps the symbols were retained for so long just because they possessed a profound significance; for instance, the 'Wheel on a Pillar' (*cakrastambha*) and, above all, the 'Pillar of Fire' have a universal character that no representational scene can claim.

Whatever the reason, the so-called Amarāvatī school portrait of the Buddha in the round, as in bas-reliefs, presents a completely original group of characteristics. It was to have a strong and lasting influence, not only in southern India and Sri Lanka but also throughout most of South-East Asia. All the statues known are standing figures, but the evidence of the bas-reliefs (in particular in compositions representing stupas) leads one to assume the existence of a considerable number of seated figures, in particular of the Buddha protected by the *nāga* Mucalinda (Pl. 46).

After an initial period marked by a certain heaviness of the features (as in the case of images found at Allūru), the Buddha of the Amarāvatī school rapidly acquired a truly classic beauty (Pl. 47), owing nothing to the aesthetics of Mathurā or of Gandhāra. This fact has led a number of writers to raise the possibility of the influence of Roman art. Without at-

[26] See Foucher, *L'art gréco-bouddhique du Gandhāra*, vol. 2, p. 284 ff.

46. Decorated stupa, showing the Buddha protected by the *nāga* Mucalinda

From Amarāvatī, Andhra Pradesh, India; c. 3rd century A.D.*; marble; H. 150 cm.; British Museum, London.*

This is a representation of one of the great stupas (with its richly carved panels and platforms) of Āndhradeśa, of which only ruins now remain. The scenes depicted with such amazing delicacy on the panels and medallions are taken from the life of the Buddha. In front of the platform, framed by the porch of the balustrade, is an image of the Buddha protected by the *nāga* Mucalinda. Concerning the gesture of the right hand raised in blessing (*abhaya-mudrā*), see p. 56. The gathering of draperies on the left shoulder is one of the characteristics of seated figures of the Āndhra school.

47. Buddha head

From Vijiaderpuram, India; c. 2nd–3rd century A.D.*; marble; H. 21 cm.; Musée Guimet, Paris.*

This head, as remarkable for its expressiveness as for its iconography, is perhaps one of the best examples of the Āndhra school. The face recalls traditional Roman portraiture and may well be further evidence of flourishing contacts between the Roman world and South India in the early centuries of the Christian era. Unlike the schools of Gandhāra and Mathurā, the hair is shown here neatly coiled around the head in curls that cover the whole cranium and the small *uṣṇīṣa*. This treatment of the hair would seem to be the point of departure for a stylization that was adopted by all schools of Buddhist art. The *ūrṇā*, clearly marked between the eyebrows, would seem to distinguish the Āndhra school from that of Sri Lanka, which, although adopting the same iconography, does not represent an *ūrṇā*.

48. Standing Buddha

From Amarāvatī, Andhra Pradesh, India; c. 2nd–3rd century A.D.*; marble; H. approximately 180 cm.; Government Museum, Madras.*

A characteristic product of the Āndhra school, the neatly and finely pleated robe reveals the shoulder and the right side of the chest and is held in position over the bent left forearm. The pose, frontal without being stiff, is that adopted by the school of Sri Lanka (see Pls. 94, 95). The contours are rounded and the proportions are rather heavy. Although it is based on the same iconographic assumptions, the face does not achieve the serenity of the image from Vijiaderpuram (above).

49. The pacification of the wicked elephant Nālāgiri

A transverse medallion from a balustrade; from Amarāvatī, Andhra Pradesh, India; c. 3rd century A.D.*; marble; D. approximately 80 cm.; Government Museum, Madras.*

This is a well-known episode in which Devadatta, first cousin of the Buddha, is so consumed by pride and jealousy that he attempts an assault on the person of the Enlightened One himself, provoking against him the elephant Nālāgiri, 'a wicked animal, killer of men'. But the mere presence of the Buddha is sufficient to tame the wild creature, for, as we read in one verse: 'Men tame them with sticks, hooks, and whips, but the Enlightened One needed neither stick nor weapon to tame the wild elephant.' This scene shows Nālāgiri twice and portrays with great eloquence the serenity of the Buddha, the delight of his disciples, and the dismay of most of the spectators. The frightened gesture of the young woman represented in the centre of the composition is no doubt one of the high points of Amarāvatī art.

tempting to resolve the problem, we can certainly point out that there is solid evidence for Roman trade at various places, in particular at Ghaṇṭaśāla, the Kontakossylum of Ptolemy. In the very earliest examples, the hair of the Amarāvatī Buddha is already treated in a quite specific manner and one that was finally adopted by all schools of Buddhist art: namely, very short curls twisting in regular spirals cover the head and the *uṣṇīṣa*, which is reduced to a low conical protuberance. The robe has fine, even pleats suggesting pre-pleated fabric and it is usual to leave the right shoulder completely uncovered. In the standing statues (Pl. 48), the over-garment (*uttarāsaṅga*) is very long and is held in the crook of the left arm, which is bent back towards the shoulder; it falls in a broad pouch to ankle level, leaving visible the bottom edge of the lower garment (*antaravāsaka*), and the end is thrown over the back and hangs free. Thus, while the style of the garment appears to derive from that of Mathurā, there are quite important differences: the fabric never has the transparency characteristic of Mathurā, nor does the robe cling so closely to the body thus clearly marking the private parts, nor is the belt visible in the manner so typical of the Mathurā school. In the rare portrayals where both shoulders are covered—and this is more often seen in bas-reliefs than in the round—a portion of the edge of the robe is held in the left hand,

50. The descent and conception of the Bodhisattva

Stone slab from the dome (aṇḍa) *of a stupa; from Nāgārjunakonda, Andhra Pradesh, India; 3rd–4th century* A.D.*; marble; Nāgārjunakonda Archaeological Museum.*

This and the two following illustrations represent scenes from the legend of Śākyamuni Buddha. In the upper scene here the Bodhisattva (i.e., the future Buddha) takes the decision to be born on earth. Here he is shown in the heaven known as 'Joyful' (Tuṣita), surrounded by admiring gods. In the lower scene he descends to earth in the form of a white elephant. This motif was originally simply his mother's dream of how the wonderful child was conceived. Here the Bodhisattva is shown actually descending as an elephant amidst a concourse of gods.

51. The Bodhisattva's escape from the palace

Stone slab from the dome of a stupa; from Nāgārjunakonda, Andhra Pradesh, India; 3rd–4th century A.D.*; marble; Nāgārjunakonda Archaeological Museum.*

In the lower scene the Bodhisattva, now a prince amidst his harem, decides to escape from so worldly a life, taking advantage of the opportunity provided while the women are asleep. In the upper scene he escapes on his faithful horse, led by his groom. He is surrounded by happy gods, some of whom hold the horse's hooves in order to ensure silence so that the escape should not be detected. On these Āndhra carvings (Pls. 50–52) the halo is of the simple Gandhāran kind (p. 66).

52. The first meal after Buddha's Enlightenment

Stone slab from the aṇḍa *(dome) of a stupa; from Nāgārjunakonda, Andhra Pradesh, India; 3rd–4th century* A.D.*; marble; Nāgārjunakonda Archaeological Museum.*

These two scenes, one following immediately after the other, relate to the Buddha's first meal taken seven weeks after attaining Supreme Enlightenment. In the scene shown on the left he sits in the 'European' fashion on a throne in front of the bodhi tree and receives the four alms bowls that the Four Great Kings who guard the points of the compass have brought. In the scene on the right, having pressed the four bowls into one, he receives the food offered by the rich merchants Tapussa and Bhallika. Note that to receive the gods the Buddha bares his right shoulder, but that he keeps both shoulders covered to receive the merchants.

which is raised to the level of the chest. This is a gesture that was to become popular in the somewhat later statues, which have the right shoulder bare, and spread to Sri Lanka (for example, Badullā, Pl. 98) and South-East Asia (for example, Dong-duong, Pl. 119).

The hand-gesture almost always represents a kind of benediction, implying the absence of fear (*abhaya*). It would thus seem reminiscent of the oldest pose shown on the Mathurā images, except that the gesture of the left hand is never the same. The differences in iconography that we have noted are greater in the seated bas-relief figures. In contrast to other schools, the art of Āndhra and South India never portrayed human beings sitting in *vajrāsana*, with the legs tightly crossed and the soles of the feet showing. The position shown, which was the one later adopted by the majority of the schools of South-East Asia, is *vīrāsana*, the legs simply folded one above the other. In this first period the knees are always very far apart and the ankles touch each other. Figures sitting in the 'European' fashion are fairly rare (as an example from Nāgārjunakonda, see Pl. 52); they also seem to appear in Āndhra art before becoming generally seen in the schools of the fifth to eighth centuries.

In the case of the standing figures, the style of the robe is more evocative of Mathurā art. Most of the right side of the chest is uncovered; the robe is usually draped over the left shoulder from front to back; one arm is free and the long ends of the garment are brought forward over the forearm. The same style of drapery is used for figures seated in the 'European' fashion. In general the pose and the manner of wearing the robe gradually tend to vary, and the fourth-century reliefs of Nāgārjunakonda and Goli, executed at the time of the school's apogée, provide good examples of this evolution.

The bas-relief scenes are remarkably faithful to the narrative style of the aniconic period and may be regarded as distant heirs of the Sāñcī tradition. While giving the same importance to portrayals of Śākyamuni's previous lives (*jātaka*), sculptors of the Āndhra school gradually integrated the human image of the Buddha into scenes containing a large number of subsidiary characters. Many such remarkable compositions occur as panels and friezes around the stupas and the copings of *vedikā*, and also as round medallions decorating the posts and crossbars of *vedikā*. Fairly often, as in depicting the Great Departure, artists limited themselves to introducing the human figure of the Buddha into a composition with an already established iconography (Pls. 49–52). In friezes, several episodes of the same event are sometimes presented side by side. On the Great Amarāvatī Stupa (interior and exterior *vedikā*), symbols (such as the 'Pillar of Fire' and footprints) appear in association with human figures of the Buddha. But it was in the medallions that Amarāvatī sculpture truly became great art. After the already remarkable compositions of the aniconic period came ensembles that on the Great Amarāvatī Stupa achieve true classical equilibrium and attest a consummate skill in handling composition, movement and volumes (Pl. 46). It is interesting to note an apparent tendency to avoid using the human figure of the Buddha for the great miracles. Thus there is no iconic representation of the First Sermon, although this is a favourite theme of the aniconic style, nor is there one of the scene of the Victory over the Evil One (*māravijaya*), although there is a very fine portrayal at Ghaṇṭaśāla (now in the Musée Guimet, Paris) according to aniconic conventions.

It seems as if certain scenes were so sublime that no one dared to depict them in the usual figurative manner nor carve them on the stone balustrades (*vedikā*). On the other hand, Āndhra art accords special importance to certain miracles ignored by the contemporary schools of Mathurā and Gandhāra; the best example of this is the scene of the Buddha protected by the *nāga-rāja* Mucalinda. Often portrayed on stone slabs representing miniature stupas (Pl. 46), which lead one to infer the existence of real statues of a similar kind, the theme was to become extraordinarily popular first in Sri Lanka and then in South-East Asia, particularly in Cambodia in the Angkor period (see p. 323).

Developed during the reigns of the last Sātavāhana rulers and at its best during the time of the Ikṣvākus (end of the second century to about the mid-fourth century), when it also benefitted from close ties with Sri Lanka, Āndhradeśa art suffered as a result of the fall of the Ikṣvākus and the expansion of Brahmanism encouraged by the new Pallava dynasty. As early as the second half of the fourth century, the decline of Buddhism led to the abandonment of a number of sites, of which Nāgārjunakonda is certainly the most important. However, other sites were to remain more or less active. In the sixth century Amarāvatī again became important and remained so until at least the fourteenth century, much affected however by the growing influence of the Mahāyāna.

III. MATURITY AND EFFLORESCENCE IN INDIA

1. CULTURAL AND HISTORICAL BACKGROUND

The history of the Indian subcontinent is not different from the rest of the civilized world in that it comprises periods of relative peace and prosperity under established dynasties alternating with periods of political division and devastating warfare. Often peace in one area corresponded with war in another, and the great empires that rose and fell were usually engaged in battle on their frontiers. The most disturbed region was the far north-west, which was always liable to disruption from a hinterland that was itself often in a state of turmoil and change. Thus the Kuṣāṇa empire, established by foreign barbarians who had gradually learned civilized arts, was always under threat from later barbarian arrivals. It was further weakened when, from the third century A.D. onwards, it had to confront a more effectively aggressive Persian empire united under the new Sassanid dynasty. Thus it split up into petty states, which were quite unable to withstand the ruinous onslaught of the Ephthalite Huns, who poured down into Indian territory during the last quarter of the fifth century, destroying all before them.

But, meanwhile, another empire had been founded in the Ganges Valley during the fourth century by the Guptas, who seem to have come originally from the old Magadhan capital of Pāṭaliputra. Excepting the far north-west (corresponding more or less to modern Pakistan), they won and held together until the end of the fifth century an enormous Indian empire that was almost as extensive as Aśoka's had been during the third century B.C. But they too succumbed to the relentless attacks of the Huns, and it was not until a century later that order was restored in northern India by the Vardhanas, a branch of the Guptas, who found their strength by bearing the brunt of the barbarian attacks, eventually defeating them and then bringing into subjection their neighbouring Indian rivals. The most renowned emperor of this second Gupta régime was Harṣa Vardhana, who ruled from 606 to 647. He is well known from both contemporary Indian literature and the glowing accounts of the famous Chinese pilgrim-scholar Hsüan-tsang, who was in India from 631 to 643.

This period of relative stability lasting from the fourth to the seventh centuries and even later represents the 'classical' period of Indian art. This idea has been well expressed by A. K. Coomaraswamy:

> In the Gupta period the image has taken its place in architecture; becoming necessary, it loses its importance and enters into the general decorative scheme, and in this inte-

> gration acquires delicacy and repose. At the same time technique is perfected, and used as a language without conscious effort, it becomes the medium of conscious and explicit statement of spiritual conceptions; this is equally true of sculpture, painting and the dance. With a new beauty of expression, it establishes the classical phase of Indian art, at once serene and energetic, spiritual and voluptuous. The formulae of Indian taste are now definitely crystallised and universally accepted; iconographic types and compositions, still variable in the Kuṣāna [sic] period, are now standardized in forms whose influence extended far beyond the Ganges valley, and of which the influence was felt, not only throughout India and Ceylon, but far beyond the confines of India proper, surviving to the present day.[1]

Like Aśoka's empire, the Gupta domains never included southern India. Here the Āndhra dynasty seems to have been replaced in the first century B.C. by the Śātakarṇi or Sātavāhana, although the exact extent of their domains is uncertain. During the third century A.D., they in turn were expelled from their position of supremacy by Śaka invaders from the north, who had been expelled from their former territories by the Kuṣāṇas. Two dynasties, the Traikūtaka, which flourished around Nāsik towards the west coast, and the Vākātaka, which flourished in central India, seem to have predominated up to about A.D. 500. Thereafter the Cālukyas established themselves as the main power for several centuries. Against them Harṣa waged ineffective war during much of his reign.

Buddhism certainly prospered under the Āndhras and the Sātavāhanas. It may have been to the last king of the Sātavāhana dynasty that Nāgārjuna, the great philosopher of the early Mahāyāna, dedicated a short moral work, known as 'A Letter to a Friend' (*Suhṛllekha*), but the new theistic Hinduism with its cult of the great gods, Śiva and Viṣṇu, seems to have prevailed more easily against Buddhism in the south than in the north. It should be observed that Indian rulers were very seldom confessed Buddhists, but with few exceptions Hindu monarchs protected Buddhism as one of the acknowledged state religions. Harṣa, whose eclectic sympathies are well known from contemporary accounts, was presumably typical in this regard.

Throughout the Kuṣāṇa and the following Gupta period, great changes took place in basic Buddhist philosophical theory, as well as often in the actual practice of the religion. The multiplication of Buddha images with their gradual differentiation according to fixed gestures and special names corresponded to philosophical theories of a plurality and indeed an infinity of possible Buddha manifestations. During the early period, as represented by the Theravādin canon, preserved in Pāli, and other such fragmentary canons as have survived in Sanskrit and in Tibetan and Chinese translations, it was certainly taught that there could be only one Buddha in the universe at a time. As has been noted above, a plurality of Buddhas in a time sequence was taken for granted, for belief in former Buddhas is part of the earliest recorded Buddhist teachings. Gradually, however, the dogma of only one Buddha at a time was disputed, for in so far as Buddhahood is an ineffable and entirely non-personal state, number does not enter into it. One may surmise that this particular dogma arose

[1] A. K. Coomaraswamy, *History of Indian and Indonesian Art* (London, 1972), pp. 71–72.

as a result of the immense respect in which Śākyamuni was held by his followers. It was explicitly taught that no one could equal him as teacher and guide. Thus for those of his followers who gained Nirvana just as he himself had gained it, a different title from Buddha was used, namely that of Arhat, 'worthy one'. The qualities of an Arhat are often listed in early Buddhist literature, and there is no apparent difference between them and those of a Buddha, except that a Buddha is the original shower of the way to salvation. After Śākyamuni's decease the great Arhats taught and passed into Nirvana just as he had done. Nevertheless, the theory was propounded that in contradiction to a Buddha who sought salvation for the good of all living beings, an Arhat merely achieved Nirvana for his own consummation. Feeling turned against a terminology and an ideal that seemed to suggest selfishness, and some Buddhist schools began to propound Buddhahood and not Arhatship as the universal goal for all striving 'living beings'. Since Śākyamuni was referred to as Bodhisattva, 'a being whose essence is Enlightenment', throughout all his previous lives of heroic striving as well as during his last life on earth, it was logical that any monk or layman (for Śākyamuni had often been a layman as well as a god or an animal in previous lives) who vowed to achieve Buddhahood, as he had done, merited already the title of Bodhisattva. Clearly, therefore, there could be many Bodhisattvas in existence at the same time, and those who in the course of their long career through various states of rebirth, became manifest as gods, always on their way to Buddhahood, be it understood, could assist human beings who prayed to them in the way that gods had always been able to assist men. It is this new practical ideal of the career of the Bodhisattva as open to all men of determination, as well as the cult of Bodhisattvas as divine beings, that differentiates early Buddhism, the Way of the *Śrāvakas* (early disciples), from the Great Way, the Mahāyāna.

The cult of Bodhisattvas admits at once into Buddhist practice attitudes of faith and devotion that the cult of a transcendent impersonal Buddha-ideal renders altogether illogical. It was during his previous lives as Bodhisattva that Śākyamuni had repeatedly sacrificed himself for others, and it was as a consummated Bodhisattva that he had entered upon Buddhahood for the ultimate salvation not only of himself but of all other living beings as well. In the serene equanimity of his all-transcending wisdom a Buddha might seem remote from the crying needs of ordinary mortals, but as Bodhisattva his primary objective appeared to be the satisfying of their necessary requirements. Śākyamuni had now disappeared into Buddhahood, but already a future Buddha, intent on the salvation of future generations, was making his way towards the ultimate goal. Thus there developed, by a logic that accords with fundamental Buddhist principles, the cult of the Bodhisattva Maitreya, the next Buddha-to-be. We must note also that by the beginning of the Christian era, Buddhism was well established in North-West India, where many of its converts were Scythians and Greeks, or at least people of Hellenistic culture. The significance of this for the styles of Buddhist sculpture in this area will be considered in more detail below (see pp. 102–3), but now we may observe that one of the main reasons for the success of Buddhism as a pan-Asian religion was the ease with which it was accommodated to the beliefs and aspirations of different peoples. Thus for the people of North-West India, already accustomed to synchronistic religious notions and familiar with the cult of the saviour-god Mithra, the cult of a celestial Bodhisattva, such as Maitreya, might seem to provide an easily accepted equivalent for an already popular divinity. It must be emphasized that the whole philosophical theory of the nature of Maitreya as a future Buddha was totally different from the nature of Mithra, a kind of divine son in his own right of Ahura Mazda, the great god of transcendent light, the supreme lord of Zoroastrian religion. As always, Buddhism accommodated itself by accepting the existence of other gods, but also by fitting them into a traditional Buddhist setting. Since there was very little that was rigid about the Buddhist setting itself, the process was never very difficult (Pl. 53).

The greatest change in the history of Buddhist thought was occasioned by the general shift in Indian philosophical and cosmic theory, noticeable from about the beginning of the Christian era, perhaps about five hundred years after Śākyamuni's Final Nirvana. All Indian religious and philosophical schools were affected by it, and it could be argued that Buddhists initiated it. Its most famous Buddhist representative is Nāgārjuna, certainly an historical person who probably lived about the first century A.D., although the accounts of his life appear to be almost entirely legendary. From this time onwards, the universe of continual states of becoming and the ineffable state of Enlightenment that altogether transcends it are not necessarily envisaged as two separate and opposing entities, but rather as different sides of the same coin, as different aspects of a single reality, or to use a terminology closer to that of Nāgārjuna, as different aspects of a non-dual non-reality. Here we are not concerned with philosophical terminology, but it may be sufficient to note in passing that Buddhist negations are never absolute, but always represent a doctrine of relativity and are designed to confute false assertions. The early Buddhists and also all later Buddhists denied the real existence of a human person or of any other existential being whatsoever, as we have already noted above. Such an existence is relative to time and place, and since neither is constant, such an existence, the Buddhists argue, can never be absolute. But for practical purposes, or as we may say, existentially, the person is accepted as a willing agent, and throughout his successive rebirths, he has an apparent or conventional existence. Thus the denial is not absolute. Nāgārjuna and his followers went further by denying the existence of the basic mental and physical elements (*dharmas*), which the early Buddhist schools in common with other contemporary philosophical schools had accepted as the real stuff of the universe. If existential beings were essentially unreal because of their inherent impermanence, then obviously one could argue for precisely the same reason the unreality of the elements of which they were thought to be composed. Some of the early Buddhists had also insisted upon the non-reality of Nirvana, arguing that it could not be experienced except by the extinction of all the supposedly real basic elements. But if these basic elements are themselves essentially non-existent, then Nirvana would be the extinction of the essentially non-existent.

> There is no difference at all between Nirvana and the world.
> There is no difference at all between the world and Nirvana.
> What makes the limit of Nirvana is also the limit of the world.
>
> (Nāgārjuna's *Mādhyamikakārikā*, XXV: 19–20)

53. Śākyamuni and Maitreya

Stone relief from Gandhāra; Lahore Museum.

To the right of Śākyamuni, the Buddha of the present world-age, is Maitreya Bodhisattva, the next Buddha-to-be. This might be the end fragment of a long plaque showing also the Buddhas of previous world-ages, as illustrated, for example, in A. Foucher, *L'art gréco-bouddhique* (Paris, 1922), 2, p. 323.

Nāgārjuna's chief disciple, Āryadeva, mocks the realists who are supposed to be terrified by such a doctrine: 'What shall I do? Nothing at all exists!' With these words he feigns their supposed fear, and then adds his answer: 'If there were anything to be done, then this world could never be stopped.' (*Catuḥśataka*, 184)

Thus while both this world and salvation from it are accepted existentially, both are denied in philosophical terms. Yet this philosophical denial is felt to detract in no way from the validity of the religious life, especially that of the Bodhisattva who progresses through series of rebirths consisting of unreal appearances in order to achieve a state of Buddhahood that is also unreal. These teachings, expounded at great length in the later canonical works with the authority of the Buddha's word and argued and justified in the treatises and commentaries of Nāgārjuna, Asaṅga and those who succeeded them, are known as the 'Perfection of Wisdom' (*Prajñāpāramitā*), and they represent not only the philosophical basis of all later Buddhism throughout the whole of Asia but also the underlying meaning of almost all Buddhist art, which entered upon its most prolific expansion precisely in association with this transcendent ideal.

Such teachings contradict all notions of time-sequence. Thus the earlier belief in a series of Buddhas, of whom Śākyamuni was the last to appear on earth, becomes altogether meaningless and is easily forgotten. Buddhahood is now conceived of as a kind of timeless absolute, manifesting itself as Buddha figures throughout a timeless space. The stupa, already from the earlier period the primary symbol of the 'Ineffable Body' (*dharmakāya*) of Buddhahood, lent itself admirably as the chief symbol of a new cosmic conception of Buddhahood. It was thereby dissociated from any essential connection with Śākyamuni, except in so far as Śākyamuni was still remembered as a comparatively recent historical figure. But since the historical process was essentially meaningless, the ideal of Buddhahood was now expressed in entirely symbolic terms and with new symbolic names that bore no relationship to historical events. A cosmic pattern, already suggested by the circular shape of the stupa, enclosed by railings with entrance-archways facing each of the four cosmic quarters, was now adopted as the symbolic expression of Buddahood, which was now envisaged as one and as fivefold, as a transcendent absolute, the centre of the universe or rather of all that becomes manifest in the sphere of eternal becoming, and as an emanation from this centre to the four cosmic directions of east and west, south and north.

So long as Buddhism survived in India, Śākyamuni was never forgotten as a kind of local manifestation, the latest to appear in human form on earth, but to what extent he was felt to be historical in a strictly modern sense we may justifiably have doubts. Many parts of India, especially the central Ganges Valley, which had certainly been the original homeland of his teachings, and also the north-west part of India where he had never been, boasted shrines and stupas associated directly with him. The best accounts that we have of these Buddhist centres, certainly up to the eighth century A.D., are provided by Chinese pilgrim-scholars, who made the long journey across Central Asia, across the Pamirs and the Hindu Kush into what is now eastern Afghanistan and northern Pakistan, but was then known as Gandhāra, and thence by well-trodden routes to the holy places of the Ganges Valley. These pilgrim-scholars accept and record with equal interest and faith all the stories connected with these Buddhist shrines, whether they concerned Śākyamuni's last life on earth in any way, his visit to the Heaven of the Thirty-three Gods in order to preach to his mother there (commemorated at the great shrine of Sāṅkāśya, where he had re-descended to earth), his former lives, or whether they are associated with previous Buddhas, whose cult certainly continued in India, where it is still being mentioned in the seventh-century travellogue of the Chinese scholar-pilgrim, Hsüan-tsang. Thus it would seem, despite the philosophical changes described above, that the majority of Indian Buddhists remained faithful to the earlier traditions concerning Śākyamuni, his former births as Bodhisattva, and the original traditions concerning the Buddhas who had preceded him. Under the new influences, however, stupas were constructed, of which the decoration expressed not so much a new idea of Buddhahood, but rather a changed attitude towards this world and indeed towards the whole cosmos.

The earlier manner of decorating stupas included, as has been already noted, sculptured scenes from Śākyamuni's last life and from his previous lives, symbolic representations of him as Buddha and also symbolic representations, usually stupas or trees, of previous Buddhas, and even carvings of local divinities and the higher Indian gods in attendance on the shrine or on Śākyamuni himself. The everyday contemporary world of gods and men is clearly depicted on these ancient monuments. On many of the later stupas all this rich imagery has disappeared, and is often replaced by inset shrines on the four directional sides of the stupa, containing images of the Buddhas of the four quarters, while the whole stupa itself represents the central Buddha, who comprehends the other four, symbolizing his cosmic manifestation. Each of these Buddha figures may be attended by Bodhisattvas, conceived of as divine manifestations of their respective Buddha forms. This new symbolism, typical of the later Mahāyāna, might seem to detach the idea of Buddhahood altogether from this world. One may say at least that it shows no historical or quasi-historical associations. There is no direct reference to Śākyamuni or to any of the previous Buddhas who were believed to have appeared in this world, and there is no representation of local divinities or other Indian gods, except where they were relegated to the role of guardian spirits.

This new cosmic symbolism was achieved by the addition to the stupa of stereotyped Buddha statues, representing Buddhahood in its fivefold cosmic form. Before they could be produced, a long and highly complex iconographic development was first necessary for the Buddha statue itself. This aspect of the matter will be considered below, but it may be helpful to observe in advance that the iconographic development of the Buddha statue was to a large extent conditioned by the later cosmic 'non-historical' conception of Buddhahood. Like the stupa itself, the Buddha statue progressed from the earlier stage of representing Śākyamuni as Buddha to the later stage of symbolizing the idea of Buddhahood without any specific reference to Śākyamuni. Thus Buddhas are known by symbolic or mythical names, as well as by historical or quasi-historical ones.

54. Buddha head

From Mathurā, Uttar Pradesh, India; 5th century A.D.; red sandstone; Archaeological Museum, Mathurā.

For description, see text p. 94.

2. THE GANGES-JUMNA (GANGĀ-YAMUNĀ) VALLEY

Not far from Allahabad is the village of Mankuwar where at one time there seems to have been a Buddhist monastery, for this village has yielded a largish icon of the Buddha seated in *yogāsana* with his right hand held in *abhaya-mudrā* (Pl. 55). An inscription on the pedestal indicates that it was installed by a Buddhist monk named Buddhamitra in the year 120 Gupta era, corresponding to A.D. 448–49. Its shaven head (Pl. 55–a) appears as though covered by a tight-fitting cap, exactly in the manner of the shaven head of the seated statue of the Bodhisattva Śākyamuni from Katra, Mathurā (Pl. 29). Also like the Katra statue, this figure has a round face, broad shoulders, a heroic mien and a warm, fleshy appearance. That it is very much of the Mathurā type no one would question; but that nearly three centuries of maturation have also produced a significant change not only in the aesthetic vision and perception but also in the execution of the Buddha image is also equally clear from this figure. Firstly, the trunk of the body suggests the type of a hero with a broad chest tapering to a narrow waist, the type of a 'lion of a man' (*puruṣasiṃha*). Secondly, the chastened and disciplined treatment of the plastic surface not only controls the warm fleshiness of the figure but also gives to its facial expression a textureless smoothness and abstract softness. Thirdly, and this is very significant, the robe is not indicated at all as a separate entity except for the hanging ends and even these are in thin and light folds; in fact, the robe is treated like a fine sheet of gossamer and thus seems to be a part of the body surface itself. Aesthetically, this kind of treatment of the robe, witnessed here for the first time, reveals the plastic purity of the body and, ideologically, its immaculate character. The effect is heightened by the utter bareness of the stele at the back of the figure. The facial expression and even more so the character of the plastic treatment have imbued this ponderous and fleshy figure with an abstract softness. The inwardness of the half-closed eyes, the steady curves of the eyes and the eyebrows, the full and warm lips and the smooth roundness of form, all these seem to emphasize that here is an image that expresses an inner experience of purity and compassion, the supreme attributes of Enlightenment (*bodhi*). Here is just the beginning of the articulation of the inner experience, which will reach its fulfilment less than a century later at Sārnāth. Many things will have to happen in the meantime before such fulfilment is achieved, and one of the first things necessary is the shedding of the weightiness of the ponderous Mankuwar physical frame.

That this was not easy is proved by what was happening in contemporary Mathurā, where a somewhat different aesthetic vision and experience seem to have been simultaneously at work. Here the standing Buddha figures are still relatively massive in size and heavy in proportion, but this heaviness is far removed from the solid earthiness of the earlier tradition. The clumsy and expansive frame of the Kuṣāṇa/Mathurā Buddha-Bodhisattva of the second and third centuries has been surpassed. In fact, these standing Buddha figures reveal a new experience and register an advanced perception of form and an equally advanced knowledge and experience of technique, and yet the stamp of traditional Mathurā is unmistakable, not merely in its typical mark of the red, mottled sandstone of Sikri but also in the size and proportion of the figures.

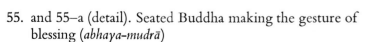

55. and 55–a (detail). Seated Buddha making the gesture of blessing (*abhaya-mudrā*)

From Mankuwar, Allahabad, Uttar Pradesh, India; dated to A.D. *448–49; sandstone; State Museum, Lucknow.*

Note the symbol of the Wheel of the Doctrine on the lion-supported throne. For description, see text p. 91.

56. Standing Buddha

From Jamalpur, Mathurā, Uttar Pradesh, India; 5th century A.D.*; sandstone; H. 220 cm; Archaeological Museum, Mathurā.*

Inscribed in Gupta letters on the base is: 'This is the pious gift of the Buddhist monk Yasadinna. The merit of this gift, whatever it may be, let it be for the attaining of supreme knowledge by his parents, teachers, preceptors and all living beings.' Note the appearance of the very ornamental halo with its flower and leaf patternings. Compare the floral wheel in Pl. 21. See also text p. 94.

The physical frame, despite its heavy proportions, is more elongated and so keeps harmony with the oval face and the head, which had been given a spherical shape. The face is treated with a simplified abstraction that gives a textureless but somewhat hard smoothness, heightened by the sharp outline of the face, by the chiselled lines of the eyes, eyebrows and the lips, and by the sharpness of the 'snail-shell' curls of the hair (Pl. 54). As if to mitigate this metallic sharpness, the head has been set off against a huge halo (*prabhāmaṇḍala*) worked out elaborately in a characteristically classical vegetal pattern set in concentric circles. But there, too, the chisel cuts are sharp and perceptually hard. The Gandhāran robe that is supposed to cover the figure falls from the shoulders in schematic loops or ridges down the central vertical line of the body in a manner that shows the natural body through a network of lines. In the kind of experience a Buddha image is supposed to reveal, a robe of this kind is perhaps a distraction (Pl. 56).

Yet this is the farthest reach of the classical Buddha image from Mathurā, a centre that has yielded a fairly good number of Buddha heads and torsos, which are smaller in size and are now housed not only in the Mathurā Museum but also in many other museums at home and abroad. One of such images, formally and stylistically at a much lower level than those two huge figures that were recovered from the ruins of Jamalpur at Mathurā, one of which is reproduced in this album (Pl. 56), is now housed in the Indian Museum, Calcutta (Pl. 57). All these images belong to the fifth and sixth centuries and in all of them the plastic theme of the articulation of the idea of disciplining the body and conquering the mind is perfectly clear; that the physical frame has been brought under control is also equally clear. What is not yet perfectly registered is the conquest of the mind and the senses. These images do not seem to have experienced the Supreme Enlightenment of wisdom, the bliss and the glow of weightless existence and the melting quality of compassion. A certain heaviness of form, toughness of plastic treatment and conventionality in treatment of the folds of the robe, the eyes and eyebrows are a few of the elements that seem to obstruct the realization of the final meaningful experience. That even in the sixth century the Buddha images of Mathurā could not forget their formal lineal descent from the heavy *yakṣa*-like predecessors of the first, second and third centuries is amply proved by an inscribed standing Buddha icon dated 230 G.E., i.e., A.D. 549–50 (Pl. 58). Although aesthetically less impressive than the images from Jamalpur, Mathurā, this icon is a reminder of the persistence of tradition even under changed social and ideological situations.

Much lighter and thinner body and limbs, treated more softly and sensitively, a more mellow and compassionate oval face, and a monastic robe covering both shoulders, these are the characteristics of the terracotta Buddha figure seated in *dhyāna-mudrā* on a conventional lotus seat, recovered from the ruins of Mirpur Khas in Sind, where there seems to have stood a Buddhist establishment at one time (Pl. 59). Set in bold round relief against the background of a decorated rectangular frame and a decorated *prabhāmaṇḍala*, all worked out somewhat clumsily, in its simplified abstraction the figure marks a significant contrast. Equally significant is the treatment of the monastic robe, which here has certainly not the textureless, wet silk-like transparency of the Mankuwar image, but belongs nevertheless to a similar kind of vision, although it is of poorer execution. Except at the edges, the

57. Standing Buddha

From Mathurā, Uttar Pradesh, India; 5th century A.D.*; red sandstone; H. 144 cm.; Indian Museum, Calcutta.*

While still a classical Buddha image, this statue is less impressive than those discovered at Jamalpur (Pl. 56).

58. Standing Buddha

From Mathurā, Uttar Pradesh, India; dated to A.D. *549–50; red sandstone; life-size; State Museum, Lucknow.*

The date of installation of 230 in the Gupta era (i.e., A.D. 549–50) is given in an inscription. There seems to be a lion between the feet as in the case of early Mathurā images. The halo seems to be a combination of 'solar disk' and floral patterns. See also text p. 94.

59. Buddha in the posture of meditation (*vīrāsana*)

From Mirpur Khas, Sind; 5th century A.D.*; terracotta relief; Prince of Wales Museum of Western India, Bombay.*

For description, see text p. 94.

60. Buddha head

From Sārnāth, Uttar Pradesh, India; 6th century A.D.*; sandstone; Sārnāth Museum.*

For description, see text p. 97.

robe is treated integrally as a part of the body-modelling itself, the schematic folds being etched very thinly and softly. It is clear that the artist intended to reveal the soft smoothness of a lightened and disciplined body surface. But it is the face on which the artist seems to have bestowed most attention. Its plastic treatment is soft, simple and abstract, and this has given it a graceful mellowness. The half-closed eyes and softly closed lips imply a delicate smile. The fourth-century images of Bodhgayā and Devnimori, and the fifth-century ones of Mankuwar, Mathurā and Mirpur Khas show clearly how a new understanding and aesthetic vision were being articulated at different centres of India, Bodhgayā and Mankuwar, emphasizing perhaps rather the ideological vision of yoga, while Devnimori, Mathurā and Mirpur Khas suggest compassion (*karuṇā*) and wisdom (*prajñā*).

It would appear that during all these formative centuries a new concept and vision of the human figure itself was slowly emerging. It is therefore essential that we should try to understand what it was.

The pivot of Indian plastic art after third century A.D. is the human figure. Already in the earlier centuries at Mathurā and Amarāvatī, for instance, human figures were becoming independent of the animal and vegetal world that used to surround them at Bhārhut and Sāñcī. Now all animal and vegetal figures are removed from the narrative and restricted to the borders, panels and halos (*prabhāmaṇḍala*). Formed by deep oblique cuts, the rich floral and vegetal scrolls twist exuberantly in playful contrasts of light and shade; but such rich patterns of decoration serve now to emphasize the importance of the human figure. Thus the human figure itself becomes the conveyor of the unceasing flowing movement that used to reside in every vegetal device, especially in the lotus stalks and the winding creepers; the latter, while moving away from the world of human beings, seem to have bequeathed their rhythm and ceaseless flow to the human figure itself.

Since it is in youth that this inner movement of life finds its fullest and most vital expression, it is invariably youthfulness in men and women that captures the imagination and engrosses the vision of the artist of this period. The young human frame seems to shine with a soft smoothness and an almost transparent luminosity of texture. For such an experience of existence there is no need for elaborate robes and decorations. Indeed, in the art of this period they are used very sparingly; in the Buddha images, not at all. Even when sparingly used in the case of Bodhisattvas, this is done with a keen eye on the sensitiveness of the plastic surface, since any decoration is but a superfluity that clouds and weighs on the body, which is itself the receptacle of wisdom, joy and bliss. Nor in an experience of this kind is there any scope for agitated physical or emotional action.

Sārnāth, where Śākyamuni preached his first sermon and which later became a great monastic complex, has yielded to the archaeologist's spade numerous seated and standing images of Buddhas and Bodhisattvas, as well as a great quantity of severed heads and torsos (Pl. 60). Most of these are stylistically assignable to the fifth and sixth centuries, and now at last one finds the perfection of a process of which all the earlier stages have not been revealed to us. When the anthropomorphic figure of the Buddha was first evolved, Sārnāth, we have seen, used to import such figures from Mathurā. The large figure of the standing Bodhisattva-Buddha installed by the *bhikṣu* ('monk') Bala in the third regnal year

61. Headless Buddha statue

From Sārnāth, Uttar Pradesh, India; 4th century A.D.*; sandstone; H. (of surviving body) 230 cm.; Sārnāth Museum.*

For description, see text p. 101.

62. Standing Buddha

From Sulṭāngañj, Bihār, India; 5th century A.D.*; copper over an earth core; H. 228 cm.; Birmingham Museum and Art Gallery.*

With his right hand he makes the gesture of blessing (*abhaya-mudrā*), while in his left he holds his cloak. See also text p. 101.

63. Seated Buddha

From Sārnāth, Uttar Pradesh, India; late 5th–early 6th century A.D.*; Chunar sandstone; H. 160 cm; Sārnāth Museum.*

The hands make the preaching gesture, i.e., 'Turning the Wheel of the Doctrine' (*dharmacakra-pravartana*). The wheel is shown on the front of the throne with figures worshipping it.

64. Standing Buddha

From Sārnāth, Uttar Pradesh, India; 6th century A.D.*; sandstone; Sārnāth Museum.*

This is our first example of the gesture of generosity (*varada-mudrā*). Also the halo is replaced by a larger almond-shaped back piece, sometimes known in Western terminology as a mandorla (from the Italian *mandorla*—stress on the first syllable—meaning 'almond'). This is to become slightly more elaborate in India (Pl. 215) and Nepal (Pls. 127, 263) and very much more so in the Far East (Pls. 154–202) and Tibet (Pls. 282–84).

of King Kaniṣka was probably just one of such imported figures. Half a century later or thereabouts, when the craftsmen of Sārnāth attempted to fashion an icon of the Master in the Chunar sandstone, which became the standard material for all Sārnāth sculptures, they adopted as a model the Mathurā image that was available to them. Even two centuries or so later, the same Mathurā-like form seems to have been an important source of inspiration for these artists, but gradually they were evolving their own form and style. This is illustrated by the figure of a headless Buddha made of Chunar sandstone, standing 2.3 metres high, with his right hand in *abhaya-mudrā* and the left with fist clenched, supporting the heavy and conventional folds of the outer robe (*saṅghāṭi*), very much in the well-known idiom of Mathurā Buddha-Bodhisattvas (Pl. 61). But the physiognomical form of this Sārnāth icon, which is perhaps assignable to the fourth century, has shed much of the heavy and clumsy weight of its Mathurā lineage and has grown taller; the limbs, too, are lighter in comparison, while the monastic robe has been treated integrally with the plastic treatment of the body surface except at the folded ends. Doubtless, this marks an intermediate stage before the fifth-century transformation.

A standing image of the Buddha in bronze from Sulṭāngañj in Bihār, now in the Birmingham Museum, tries to capture the vision and style of the Sārnāth Buddha and Bodhisattvas (Pl. 62). It nearly succeeds, but it qualifies the subtle delicacy and spiritual refinement of Sārnāth with a warmth of emotion and a sensuous appeal marked by the deep cuts that cast shadows round the more-than-half-closed eyes. The Sulṭāngañj image does not stand alone in this regard, for it is closely akin to a huge metal image of the standing Buddha now in the Nālandā Museum, and a similar stone image from Biharail in Rājshāhi, Bangladesh.[2] The Sulṭāngañj and Nālandā examples prefer the Mathurā treatment of the robe in conventional loops and curly ends, though not quite in such a pronounced manner, while the Biharail image closely follows the vision and idiom of Sārnāth. Nevertheless, everywhere the unearthly sublimation of Sārnāth is subtly touched by a charm and emotion that are essentially human. This is achieved by very slight variations in the form of the eyes and the lips and in the plastic treatment of the body.

The perfection of the Sārnāth images has been achieved by very simple means, but this simplicity was attained as the result of a long and difficult quest through the realm of ideas as well as of iconographic forms (Pl. 64). Chunar sandstone itself was certainly a great help in the rendering of the smooth and shining textureless face and body of these figures, but the transparent purity of the form has been mostly due to the utter simplification and abstraction of the different planes and their rendering in soft, gracefully gliding lines and rhythmic plastic surfaces. An immaculately perfect body results, which shines through the robe that is treated like wet silk as though a part of the body itself. On the body rests the head with an oval face, which is equally immaculately pure and perfect, but to which has been added the soft charm and lyrical tenderness of a water-lily in full bloom (Pl. 63).

[2] *History of Bengal*, ed. R. C. Majumdar, vol. 1 (Dacca University), section on 'Sculpture' by Niharranjan Ray, pl. 46, fig. 112.

3. GANDHĀRA

The main difficulty in treating the later Gandhāra period coherently and succinctly is caused by the vast amount of material available and by the absence of firm dates. Alfred Foucher published in 1951 some critical comments and amendments to his enormous work, *L'art gréco-bouddhique du Gandhāra*, of which the first volume appeared as long ago as 1905. While observing that these two large volumes could be much abbreviated, he adds that the preliminary condition to a complete retreatment of the subject would be the methodical and exhaustive excavation of one of the great ruined sites that still remain more or less intact.[3] It seems now to be very difficult indeed to find sites that have not been disturbed by treasure-hunters and purveyors of antiques, but attempts have been made to excavate thoroughly in the Swat Valley, and on the basis of this useful work, some generalizing statements are possible.[4] Dani's observations are made in terms of three periods, namely the first and second centuries A.D. (Period I), and the third and fourth (Period II), and the fourth to the seventh centuries (Period III). It is noted that no independent figures of Buddhas and Bodhisattvas were found in the first period. They are found from the second period onwards, while in the third period they are normally required for placing in niches around the stupa and perhaps in temple walls (Pl. 134). Apart from these figures the art is used for decorative purposes, and thus panel scenes are very popular. The scenes depicted relate to the last life of Śākyamuni, and only one scene relating to his previous lives was found, namely the exceptional event of his taking the vow of a Bodhisattva at the feet of the previous Buddha Dīpaṅkara (Pl. 137) Each scene is separated by a pillar ornamentation, and the panel representation follows the same pattern from beginning to end. The pillars are of Persepolitan or Corinthian type. In the third period the architectural style is completely changed. There was now a greater demand for niches so as to fit Buddha images into them, and thus new niches were added onto the upper parts of old stupas.

It seems clear that the changes in the application of the Buddha image are the same in Gandhāra as in the Ganges-Jumna Valley. It is only in the original application that some difference appears, for whereas Gandhāra seems to have shown a primary interest in the last life on earth of Śākyamuni, elsewhere the primary interest was in the mythical aspects of Buddhahood, as typified by the use of symbols and the portrayal of previous lives (*jātaka*). Thereafter the Buddha image was developed as an independent figure, but even here it is interesting to note its close association with the stupa. In a later period the image is multiplied and becomes itself a decorative motif, thus replacing the earlier motifs that were of non-Buddhist inspiration. In Indian tradition these were represented by pre-Buddhist divinities and symbols, and in the early tradition of Gandhāra by Hellenistic motifs,

[3] See A. Foucher, *L'art gréco-bouddhique du Gandhāra*, vol. 2, fasc. 2, *Additions et corrections* (École Française d'Extrême-Orient, 1951), p. 811.

[4] See, in particular, *Ancient Pakistan*, ed. A. H. Dani, vol. 4 (1968–69), 'Chakdara Fort and Gandhāra Art', pp. 17, 72–73, 75 and *passim*. For a vast collection of invaluable material, see also the publication of the Istituto del Medio ed Estremo Oriente, Rome, *Reports on the Campaigns in Swat (Pakistan)*, ed. Domenico Faccenna, vol. 1 (1962), vol. 2, no. 2 (1962), vol. 2, no. 3 (1964), photographs by Francesca Bonardi and descriptive catalogue by Maurizio Taddei.

pillars, garlands, angelic figures and so on. But everywhere the Buddha and Bodhisattva image triumphs over the earlier decorations. To multiply the figure of the Buddha is clearly more meritorious than multiplying anything else.

As for the Gandhāran Buddha figure itself, this tends to conform more and more to a general Indian type, although the process was a complex and uneven one. The reason for this has been well expressed by Dietrich Seckel: 'The prototype itself was already a late hybrid phenomenon, a blend of many different elements: Greek, Hellenistic, classical Roman, provincial Roman and Near Eastern (principally Mesopotamian and Iranian). It followed that the orientation of this style, once it had become imbued with Indian and Buddhist thought, could only occasionally bring forth really great works of art. This process was influenced to a considerable degree by the native Indian style of the Mathurā school, from the 3rd century onwards, and later still by Gupta art. Gandhāran figures show only too obviously that they are derived from a prototype that was itself derivative, in which a large number of historical influences overlaid one another.'[5] (See Pl. 65.)

The break-up of the Kuṣāṇa empire from the third century onwards, when it was confronted with the might of Sassanid Persia, also led to a noticeable division in the type of cultural influence that affected Gandhāra workmanship. The Hindu Kush became a kind of cultural watershed. On the western side of it, Persian influence began to insinuate itself more strongly into Buddhist art, while on the eastern side, that is to say, the Kabul Valley and what is now generally northern Pakistan, the influence of Indian styles, scarcely ever absent from the beginning, began to predominate. On the western side we may refer in passing to Bāmiyān, the most famous of the sites, and Fondukistān. Here Persian influence appears especially in the dress and decorative ornaments, of which the most distinctive are perhaps long flying ribbons, which were a sign of royal dignity. But even so, one must assert that Buddhist art remains basically Indian in inspiration, just as the whole religion was of Indian origin (Pl. 66). Bāmiyān seems to have been by-passed by the destructive Ephthalite Huns, who laid waste the rest of Gandhāra towards the end of the fifth century, and since it lay on one of the main routes from India and Gandhāra to the lands beyond the Oxus and the Pamirs, its styles of craftmanship were carried into Central Asia along the routes that lay north and south of the Takla Makan.[6] For a living description of these far northern and western reaches of Buddhist civilization we depend primarily upon the eyewitness accounts of the Chinese pilgrim-scholar Hsüan-tsang, who traversed these routes round about A.D. 630. He passed through Balkh (Bactria), where there were about a hundred Buddhist monasteries with three thousand religious, all belonging to the earlier sects (Hīnayāna, or more accurately Śrāvakayāna), then to Bāmiyān, where there were some twelve monasteries of the same persuasion. From there he crossed the Hindu Kush to the Kabul Valley (Kāpiśa), where the earlier sects and the Mahāyāna flourished side by side, and which had recovered from the onslaught of the Huns in the previous century. Only when he travelled further eastwards to Peshawar and the region that now forms part of Pakistan was he still confronted with the devastating effects of their vandalism.

[5] D. Seckel, *The Art of Buddhism* (London, 1964), p. 34.
[6] See Madelaine Hallade, *The Gandhāra Style* (London, 1968), p. 64 ff. and p. 165 ff.

65. Preaching Buddha on a lotus throne

From Mohammed Nari, Pakistan; c. last quarter of 2nd century A.D.*; H. 116.8 cm.; Lahore Museum.*

The Buddha's manifest power is suggested by reference to the famous miracle at Śrāvastī, when Śākyamuni is said to have multiplied his form on countless lotus thrones. Here this motif is turned into a glorification of the Buddha ideal, expressable in various Buddha-bodies and Bodhisattva manifestations. The *nāga* divinities under the lotus and the layfolk in the bottom row of figures refer to the motif of the Śrāvastī miracle, but the whole scene nonetheless represents a universal statement of the utter supremacy of Buddhahood.

66. Preaching Buddha

Kabul Museum.

The Buddha is here surrounded by devotees in elegant Sassanian-style costumes. If we identify the larger male figures, which stand in graceful attendance on either side, as Bodhisattvas, then we have a new style of Bodhisattva adapted to the farthest west area to which Buddhism spread. Such an identification is plausible. Note, however, the Indian-style arch under which the Buddha figure is seated. In this late setting, the preaching Buddha may be identified as Vairocana (the Resplendent One), whose cult spread from Gandhāra across Central Asia.

67. Buddha head
From Taxila, Pakistan; 2nd century A.D.; *terracotta; National Museum of Pakistan, Karachi.*

The testimony of Hsüan-tsang is important, for not only does it confute the easy way in which Buddhist art is often labelled Hīnayānist when it appears relatively simple and Mahāyānist when the decoration and symbolism appear more complex, usually with complete disregard of what may be known of the Buddhism of the area from other sources, but it also confirms the flourishing state, at least in some districts, of Gandhāran styles, even after the Hun invasions.[7] Also, as much as Gandhāran art at all times, and especially

[7] Coomaraswamy, *History of Indian and Indonesian Art*, pp. 73–74: 'Most of the Gandhāra sites seem to have been wrecked by the White Huns under Mihiragula in the latter part of the fifth century, and this practically ended the activity of the school. The original influence nevertheless continues to be apparent in the architecture and sculpture of Kāśmīr, and that of a few related monuments, such as that of Malot, dating from the time of the Kāśmīri domination in the Pañjāb.' This scarcely does justice to the effective limits of Gandhāran art-forms.

68. Śākyamuni practising austerities

From Sikri, Pakistan; 2nd–3rd century A.D.*; H. 83.8 cm.; Lahore Museum.*

After leaving his religious teachers because they could teach him no more, the Bodhisattva attempted to discover truth by the practice of austerities of the most extreme kind, as described in detail in the canonical literature supposedly in Śākyamuni's own words: 'My body became extremely lean. . . . The bones of my spine when bent and straightened were like a row of spindles through the little food. As the beams of an old shed stick out, so did my ribs stick out through the little food. . . . When I thought I would touch the skin of my stomach, I actually took hold of my spine. . . . Some human beings seeing me then said, "The ascetic Gotama is black." Some said, "Not black is the ascetic Gotama. He is brown." . . . So much had the pure clean colour of my skin been destroyed by lack of food. Then I thought, those ascetics and brahmans in the past, who have suffered sudden, sharp, keen, severe pains, at the most have not suffered more than this. . . . But by this severe mortification I do not attain superhuman, truly noble knowledge and insight.' (See E. J. Thomas, *The Life of the Buddha as Legend and History* [London, 1949], pp. 66–67). Once again, one may note the extraordinary realism of Gandhāran art, at least so far as the body is concerned. The hair-style and robe arrangement are, however, immaculate. On the base of the throne, monks are seen worshipping at a fire altar, and the fire altar—normally a symbol of the supreme Zoroastrian god, Ahura Mazda—here indicates a transference of supreme power to the Buddha on the part of the converted Zoroastrians. It has a precise aptness in the present context as the Sanskrit *tapas* means 'fire' as well as 'bodily mortification for religious or magical purposes', and thus fire might symbolize this aspect of Buddha's activity, just as the lotus suggests his birth and the tree his Enlightenment.

in the later period, owed to Indian inspiration and influence, it is fair to note that Gandhāran styles were not without their reverse influence on the Ganges-Jumna Valley and indeed far beyond. Thus a series of Buddha images was produced at Mathurā with the Gandhāran style of a monastic cloak draped over both shoulders, while Persian influences that can only have penetrated through Gandhāra affect the dress styles in some of the frescoes of Ajantā. It could, however, be argued that while Gandhāran influences in India were incidental, the Indian influence in Gandhāra and indeed throughout the whole of Asia remained essential and fundamental. Indeed, in so far as Buddhism is an Indian religion rooted in Indian culture, no one would expect the situation to be otherwise.

Gandhāra certainly experimented in other materials than stone and wood. With the ever-growing demand for Buddha images there was a great increase in the use of cheaper and more easily worked materials, namely stucco, lime composition and terracotta (Pl. 67). An enormous number of heads made of these materials have survived buried in the sands after they were knocked off, while the bodies have simply disintegrated. These later Gandhāran heads reveal a rather different conception of the Buddha image from the one described in the earlier period. The typical features remain, such as the hair arranged in schematic waves of separate locks, the same type of *uṣṇīṣa* and *ūrṇā*, the sharp chiselling of the eyes, lips and nose, and even the serene inward look. But there is now a difference in the general treatment; the lines are softer and the chiselling more graduated. Thus despite the well-defined clarity of the features, the face with its half-closed eyes shows a mellow and spiritual disposition, almost as though emitting a soft light. This mellowness may be interpreted as the expression of a Bodhisattva's compassion (*karuṇā*), and the suggestion of subdued light implies sublime knowledge (*prajñā*), while the self-composed look that imbues the whole suggests the spirit of *yoga* as understood in Gandhāra. This may be taken as the farthest extent of the realization of the Buddha ideal as conceived in Gandhāra in concrete plastic terms. Two or three centuries later in Kashmir and the neighbouring Himalayan regions, the process is carried yet further, but all too easily degenerates into a kind of warm sentimentalism and decorative prettiness, as in the case of the seated Buddha figure from Fondukistān, now housed in the Kabul Museum (Pl. 141). It is possible that these later Gandhāran images fall short of the mature Indian aesthetic vision simply because the whole style was limited from the start by Greco-Roman human proportions and standards of beauty. The abstraction of an intellectually idealized vision, which transcends altogether the perception of physical form, was never a fundamental part of their tradition. Even though they were clearly aware of the ideal of Supreme Enlightenment (*bodhi*), as expressed in the Indian classical tradition of the Gupta period, the Gandhāra craftsmen were prevented by the traditions already received from elsewhere from rendering the idea perfectly in concrete plastic form. Their Buddha faces doubtless suggest compassion and sublime knowledge, as well as the serene inwardness of yogic experience, but all this is registered in terms of human proportions and human standards of beauty. But for a return to the stark realism of Gandhāran art, one should note the image of Śākyamuni as an ascetic (Pl. 68).

4. WESTERN INDIA

In the western Deccan, mainly at Kanheri, Ajantā and Ellora, the use of a new material, namely the granite rock of the Sahyadri hills, and the new technique of cutting into rock, led to the emergence of a new language of form in regard to the Buddha image. The later rock-cut Buddha-Bodhisattva figures of Kanheri, Ajantā and Ellora are more or less contemporary with the images of Sārnāth, since the former may be assigned generally to the fifth and sixth centuries. Yet the formal and stylistic character of the Buddha-Bodhisattvas of these rock-cut caves is very different from the sandstone images of Mathurā and Sārnāth.

In the verandah of Cave No. 3 at Kanheri (c. 575) a rock-cut Śiva-like Bodhisattva faces us, as still as the rock itself, sunk deep in meditation. His crown of matted locks, exhibiting a stupa in the centre, is in harmony with the strong and dignified oval face with its sharply chiselled half-closed eyes, its sharp nose, closed lips and shapely chin (Pl. 69). It is easy to recognize that here is a new interpretation of the Buddha-Bodhisattva image, in which one readily perceives what spiritual experience in depth can really mean, not so much in terms of luminosity in this case, but in terms of latent power and energy, of perfect stillness, of poise and grace. It lacks the textureless, shining smoothness of the Sārnāth images, without doubt; there is here no transubstantiation of the physical substance of the live rock. But this does not prevent the idea of compassion (*karuṇā*) being made manifest in the treatment of the eyes and the lips and in the total expression of the face. Sunk in deep and concentrated meditation, this Bodhisattva figure has much in common with the well-known Śiva relief from Parel near Bombay[8] and with some of the figures of the Elephanta caves, but at Kanheri the rock from which the figure has emerged has been allowed to retain the character of its substance, while at Parel and Elephanta that substance has been transformed by making the plastic surface smooth and shiny.

Images of the Buddha seated in various positions, standing or walking, abound at Ajantā (fifth and sixth centuries) (Pl. 70). In certain caves, as in No. 1, a large seated image of the Buddha making the preaching gesture (*dharmacakra-pravartana-mudrā*) occupies the main sanctum at the farthest end of the cave (Pl. 71). In others, the Master appears on the front of stupas or on the facades of the cave temples. In the last instance alone, as in Caves Nos. 9, 10 and 19, the figures seem to have served as edifying decorative pieces. Elsewhere they were installed in the sanctum and were intended for worship (Pl. 72). Somewhat condensed in height, the large seated images are characterized by a mute, heavy roundness of form. The treatment of the monastic robe and of the plastic surface, of the 'snail-shell' curls, etc., all follow the classical tradition, but there is apparently no articulation of the luminosity of sublime knowledge (*prajñā*).

Condensed in height, heavy and plump are also the images on the facade of Cave No. 19; the porous stone lends to these figures a spongy softness that is heightened by the soft and sensitive treatment of the plastic surface (Pl. 73). But, on the whole, despite a conscious attitudinal stance as in the relief representing the Buddha meeting a child while walking, a somewhat dumb insensitivity clings to the figures.

[8] Heinrich Zimmer, *The Art of Indian Asia*, vol. 1 (New York, 1955), p. 353, ill. opposite p. 247.

Aesthetically and from the point of view of the articulation of the Buddha idea, the Buddha images on the facade of Caves Nos. 9 and 10 are the best and most significant (Pl. 74). Here in a tall, rectangular niche there stands in a relaxed posture a rather elongated Buddha image, making the gesture of giving (*varada-mudrā*) with his right hand, while his left hand holds the ends of the outer robe (*saṅghāṭi*). In the wet silk-like treatment of the robe, in the very soft, abstract and sensitive treatment of the plastic mass and in the generalized and very simplified treatment of the oval face, one easily senses the influence of Sārnāth. Where it differs from Sārnāth is in its physiognomical form, which is heavier and sturdier. But in the soft mellowness of expression and tender and light treatment of the plastic surface the registration of compassion, of *karuṇā*, and the illumination of *prajñā* is unmistakable, though in a somewhat lower key.

But it is not in the sculptures and reliefs of Ajantā that the contemporary ideological vision of the Buddha-Bodhisattva idea finds its finest articulation. It achieves this in the wall paintings of caves Nos. 1 and 2 of Ajantā (Pls. 75–79) and in those of Cave No. 4 at Bagh (Gwalior, Madhya Pradesh). Nature and human callousness have been responsible for obliterating most of the Bagh paintings, but an idea of them can be gained from earlier reproductions.

The paintings of Cave No. 19 of Ajantā reveal already a complete mastery of compositional power and stylistic majesty (compare the scene of the story of the return to Kapilavastu), but the articulation of the numerous Buddhas on this cave's walls presages the perfection of the Bodhisattva paintings of Cave No. 1.

It is this tradition of painting Buddha-Bodhisattva figures that happily survived at Ajantā and Bagh, and that was continued in Bihār, Bengal and Nepal and thence in Tibet and Mongolia, each region interpreting the tradition in its own way.

In Cave No. 10 at Ellora (c. A.D. 600) the Buddha is shown inset against the stupa seated in the 'European' posture (*bhadrāsana*), making with his two hands the gesture of preaching (*dharmacakra-mudrā*); he is flanked by two Bodhisattvas (Pl. 84). Here the Buddha is not as condensed in height as in Cave No. 1 at Ajantā, but nevertheless is quite as mute and insensitive, an effect caused by the hard treatment of the plastic surface and by the heavy, round, log-like legs and arms. Despite its seemingly meditative or introspective attitude, the image fails to articulate the idea of what the Buddha was supposed to be.

The best Buddha figures of Ellora are, however, in Cave No. 12, which seems to have been planned and executed as a gallery of images (Pl. 82). On each side of this rectangular hall there is a row of seven Buddhas, arranged on a platform. On one side, the figures are seated in the posture of meditation and on the other, they are seated cross-legged making the gesture of elucidation (*vyākhyāna-* or *vitarka-mudrā*). At the farthest end of the gallery, on a raised platform, is the figure of a Buddha seated on a high lion pedestal in *yogāsana* and showing the *dhyāna-mudrā*; the central figure is flanked by two Bodhisattvas, one standing gracefully on either side. The rock lends to all these figures a somewhat sturdy physiognomical form, tall, heroic and dignified. The body and the limbs are full, round, warm and vibrant; they have been modelled firmly but with some amount of grace and sensitivity. There is no doubt that the aesthetic and ideological message of contemporary Mahāyāna as interpreted at Sārnāth has been heard here with attention. The nature of the

69. Upper part of a Buddha torso

Rock-cut relief in Cave No. 3, Kanheri, Mahārāshtra, India; 6th century A.D.; granite.

Note the stupa set in his crown. See also text p. 108.

70. A general view of Ajantā, Mahārāshtra, India

71. Preaching Buddha flanked by attendants

Rock-cut relief in Cave No. 1, Ajantā, Mahārāshtra, India; 6th century A.D.*; granite.*

At the foot of the throne is the Wheel of the Doctrine, flanked by deer and devout listeners.

72. Preaching Buddha enshrined within an inner sanctum and surrounded by subsidiary Buddha images

Rock-cut relief in Cave No. 19, Ajantā, Mahārāshtra, India; 6th century A.D.*; granite.*

73. Śākyamuni with a child

Rock-cut relief facade of Cave No. 19, Ajantā, Mahārāshtra, India; 6th century A.D.; granite.

74. Standing Buddha making the gesture of generosity (*varada-mudra*) and flanked by a Bodhisattva

Rock-cut relief facade of Caves Nos. 9 and 10, Ajantā, Mahārāshtra, India; granite.

75. Scene from the story of Prince Mahajanaka (Śākyamuni in a former life)

Wall painting in Cave No. 1, Ajantā, Maharashtra, India; 5th century A.D.

Here, as he receives lustration as the crown prince, he resolves to renounce the world.

76. Bodhisattva Avalokiteśvara Padmapāṇi
Wall painting in Cave No. 1, Ajantā, Mahārāshtra, India; 5th century A.D.

77. The Bodhisattva in the Tuṣita heaven prior to his descent to earth

Wall painting in Cave No. 2, Ajantā, Mahārāshtra, India; 5th century A.D.

Compare Pl. 50.

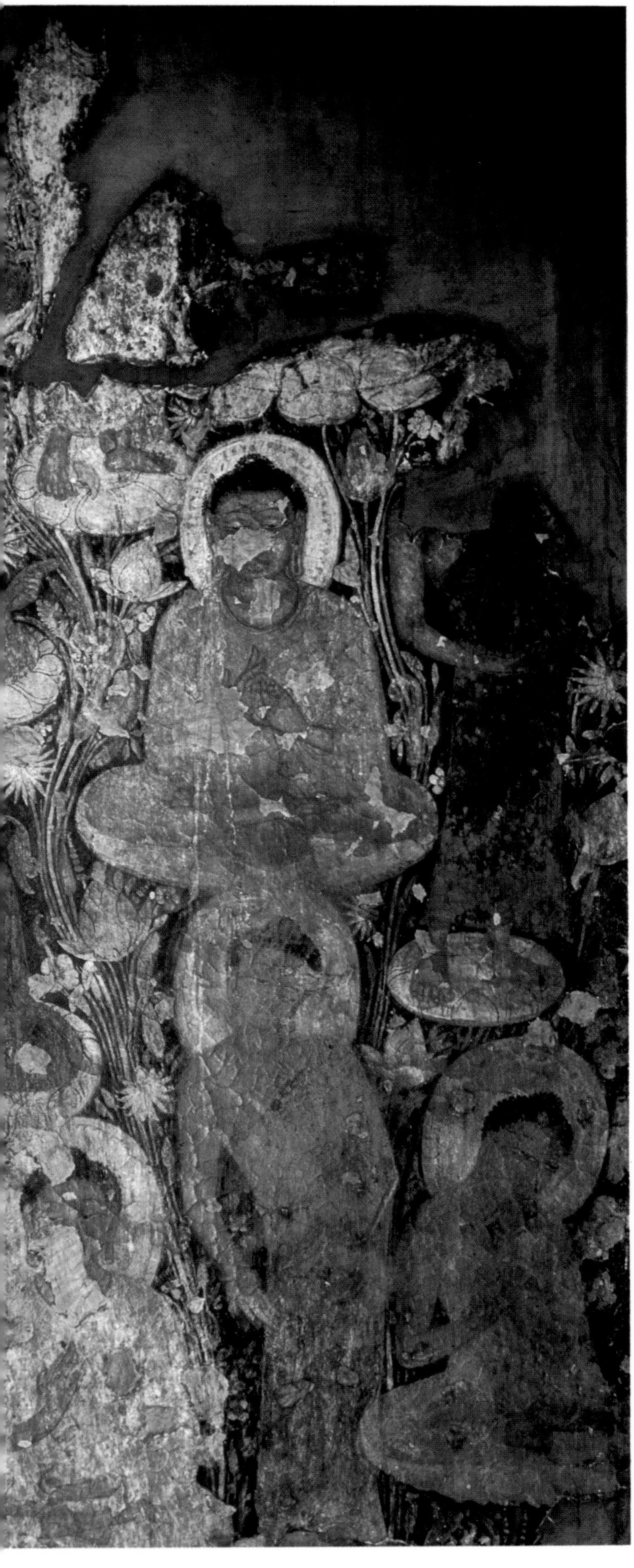

78. Buddhas making a variety of conventional gestures
Wall painting in Cave No. 1, Ajantā, Mahārāshtra, India; 5th century A.D.

79. Carved and painted pillar

In Cave No. 2, Ajantā, Mahārāshtra, India; 5th century A.D.

80. The Buddha's universal preaching

Wall painting in Cave No. 17, Ajantā, Mahārāshtra, India; 5th century A.D.

This is the lowest of three scenes; in the top scene he is preaching in heaven; in the centre scene he is descending to earth; and in the lowest scene, shown here, he is preaching to high dignitaries (on his right) and to monks (on his left).

81. Śākyamuni and a one-eyed monk
Wall painting in Cave No. 10, Ajantā, Mahārāshtra, India; 5th. century A.D.

82. Buddhas seated in meditation

Rock-cut relief in the eastern wall of the third floor, looking north, Cave No. 12, Ellora, Mahārāshtra, India; A.D. *625; granite.*

83. Preaching Buddha

Rock-cut relief in Cave No. 89, Kanheri, Mahārāshtra, India; 5th–6th century A.D. *(?); granite.*

The Buddha is raised on a lotus flower that is supported by gods and he is attended by two Bodhisattvas accompanied by goddesses.

84. Preaching Buddha flanked by Bodhisattvas

Set into a stupa of a rock-cut cave (No. 10), Ellora, Mahārāshtra, India; 6th century A.D.*; granite.*

85. Line of attendant monks
Rock-cut relief in Cave No. 26, Ajantā, Mahārāshtra, India; 6th century A.D.*; granite.*
Contrast the bald heads of the monks with the elaborately developed Buddha and Bodhisattva hair-styles.

articulation of the inwardness of being, of the still, meditative poise and of the heroic dignity of perfect wisdom are proof enough of this. But this articulation has been made in a different language, that is, in the language of the living rock and according to the technique of rock-carving. There is therefore no melting quality nor any suggestion of luminosity in the plastic treatment of the body and its rounded planes.

But this represents the highest point of perfection attained by the Buddha image makers of the Deccan. By the end of the seventh century, deterioration had begun, and if we are to judge by the style of the Buddha figures in the caves of Lonad near Bombay, the modelling has already become languorous and spongy and there is a noticeable loss of dignity and repose.[9] It must be emphasized, however, that our opinions and judgements can only be based upon the materials available to us now. As we know from the descriptions of pilgrim-scholars who travelled from China across the vast distances of Central Asia in order to visit the Holy Land of Buddhism, India was still covered in the seventh century with splendid Buddhist establishments. Nālandā, a great university and monastic centre, founded already in the fifth century in southern Bihār, as described by Hsüan-tsang, was certainly one of the glories of the civilized world. Yet now only the foundations, the ruined stumps of stupas

[9] For an aesthetic and ideological interpretation of the Buddha image, see Niharranjan Ray, 'The idea and image of *bodhi*', in *Idea and Image in Indian Art* (New Delhi, 1973), pp. 9–52.

86. Sākyamuni entering Final Nirvana
Rock-cut relief in Cave No. 26, Ajantā, Mahārāshtra, India; 6th century A.D.*; granite.*

and some salvaged images survive. We rightly praise the murals of Ajantā, which have survived by the happy chance of being totally buried in the jungle until rediscovered accidentally by a British officer in the nineteenth century, but these are now the only Buddhist paintings that survive in India. Thus here we have no comparative standards of judgement, such as are available in the case of archaeological remains, inadequate as these often are. Indian styles of painting as well as of sculpture certainly lie behind the later developments in other Buddhist lands, but all the links are missing, and apart from dilapidated survivals in Afghanistan, we leap from Ajantā to the twelfth-century murals of western Tibet, which must in any case be related more closely with Kashmir and a northwest Buddhist tradition, or to the fifteenth-century murals at Gyantse on the route to Lhasa. By then there have been such great changes in doctrines and in religious symbolism that we can only assume that these were paralleled by art-forms in India itself, of which we have little or no surviving material record. Later Sanskrit Buddhist literature bears witness to such traditions on Indian soil, but with the entry of Islam on the scene, little still remained intact after A.D. 1200, and that little could scarcely be expected to survive until our times when there were no organized Buddhist communities to care for it. In a short section below (p. 271 ff.), we summarize the little that can be known of Buddhism in India from the eighth to the twelfth centuries.

5. ĀNDHRADEŚA AND SOUTH INDIA

After the veritable golden age of Buddhist art as represented by the rise of the Āndhra school between the second and fourth centuries, its eclipse in the fifth century seems due to both the growing power of the Pallavas, who were supporters of Brahmanism, and the increasingly active opposition of the Brahman and Jain religions. While we may still wonder why remains should be so scarce from such important sites as Kaveripaṭṭiṇam, Kāñchīpuram or Nāgapaṭṭiṇam (to mention only a few of the most famous), a scarcity quite unrelated to the presumed activity of the workshops in those places, nevertheless we possess a clear account of the actual situation when Buddhism appears to be in a decline there. During his visit to South India some time after 642, Hsüan-tsang noted the ruins of many monasteries, more or less completely abandoned, but since he had observed the same situation in the north of India (Magadha, etc.), it seems unlikely that the decline of Buddhist communities in the seventh century can be regarded as limited to the south. Moreover, although it never recovered its strength of the first centuries, South Indian Buddhist art none the less retained an undeniable vitality, which it owed as much to the influence of the great local craftsmen as to the maintenance of contacts with other major centres in India and elsewhere. Even though few in number, the figures reveal the changes in orientation of an art transformed by new contributions and destined to spread widely.

Marked as early as the fourth century by the rise of the Mahāyāna, South Indian Buddhism experienced the effects of doctrinal change and the influence of the ties established with the principal centres of Indian Buddhism. Many of the South Indian craftsmen seem to have encouraged, at least indirectly, the evolution and spread of the southern schools. About 520, Bodhidharma, a prince of the southern kingdom of Kāñchī, became the founder of the school of Buddhism, known as Ch'an in China (the Zen Buddhism of Japan). At about the same time and also from the south, Diṅnāga, a pupil of Vasubandhu, became the teacher of Dharmapāla, one of the heads of the celebrated university of Nālandā. At the end of the seventh century and the beginning of the eighth century, Vajrabodhi, a native of Pāṇḍya, a Vajrayāna adept and a master of Amoghavajra, visited Nālandā, Kapilavastu, Sri Lanka, Śrīvijaya and China. Such examples as these tempt one to think that, while maintenance of contacts with Magadha and northern India generally served to reduce the diversity among schools of art, the development of maritime trade was meanwhile contributing to the implantation of the southern school in South-East Asia.

Since no bas-relief from this period is known, the study of Buddhist art is limited to the examination of statues, usually quite small. The evolution of the image of the Buddha is complex, but it is characterized by an astonishing and enduring fidelity to the poses and gestures of the early period (see Chapter 2:4). The innovations, which seem to be associated with the special interests of local communities, concern mainly the clothing. Images of the Bodhisattvas, being new creations, were not dependent on any earlier tradition; thus they evolved quite naturally along the same lines as contemporary Brahmanical images from Pallava art to that of Vijayanagar, while retaining virtually the same iconography as Buddhist images from Bihār (Nālandā, Kurkihar, etc.).

87. Standing Buddha

From Buddhapād, Tamil Nadu, India; c. 6th century A.D.*; bronze; British Museum, London.*

In about the sixth century, Buddha images in South India underwent a transformation apparently through the influence of Gupta art. Very few features of the primitive school survive: the pre-pleated cloths are abandoned in favour of loose draperies similar to those found on so many Ajantā rock-carvings. The only sign of continuity of style is the fact that the *uṣṇīṣa* continues to be as small as for the Amarāvatī school. The gesture of 'dispensing gifts' (*varada-mudrā*) has become very common. In the sixth and seventh centuries, this iconographic tradition spread along the sea route from the Malay Peninsula (Kedah) to Sarawak (Santubong), passing through Cambodia on the way (Pl. 118).

In contrast with the earlier period, bronze certainly predominates from the fifth century onwards. The oldest images of the Buddha (as from Amarāvatī, c. fifth century) keep to the great Āndhra tradition, preserving the type of 'pre-pleated' fabric, but showing already an evolution towards new styles of drapery. The pleats are more shallow (on later statues they are reduced to simple engraved lines) and they appear in conjunction with the appearance of broad ends of fabric crossing the left shoulder, a change that could only be obtained by modifying the original drape of the robe. Likewise the aesthetic forms move away from those of Amarāvatī and approach the Gupta ideal; this also seems to have inspired the large bulbous *uṣṇīṣa* that became almost immediately an indispensable element. In these rare early images everything seems to indicate the hesitations of a style in the full process of change and still in search of its own unique quality. Later, about the sixth and seventh centuries, the art of South India achieves a kind of equilibrium based on the union of traditional iconographic elements (figures seated in *vīrāsana*, with small *uṣṇīṣa*)

88. Torso of Avalokiteśvara

From Krishnā Valley, India; c. 6th century A.D.*; bronze; H. 15 cm.; Victoria amd Albert Museum, London.*

This small figure, thought to be one of the first Pallava bronzes, is doubtless also one of the oldest South Indian images of Avalokiteśvara known to us. This type of image seems to have influenced the beginnings of Mahāyāna art in South-East Asia, where the same kind of ornamental hair arrangement was first used, especially in Thailand. It will, however, be noted that the coiffure contains no image of the Buddha Amitābha; this peculiarity will recur at a much later date in South India (Nāgapaṭṭiṇam) and Sri Lanka.

and innovations in the robe, such as the abandoning of 'pre-pleated' fabric, and adaptation to post-Gupta styles. The few examples known, discovered a little over a century ago at Buddhapād, provide almost the only evidence for the new tendencies (Pl. 87). None the less, they reveal extremely well the evolution of the style and its later extension. The figures making the hand-gesture of generosity (*varada-mudrā*) and clothed in a manner reminiscent of post-Gupta art represent a move away from the South Indian tradition, and in gesture and clothing they might appear to be closely related to contemporary cave figures in West India. Strangely enough, it is this style, still so poorly represented in the place of its origin, that seems to have given rise to the majority of schools throughout South-East Asia. As faithful reflections of the art of South India and of its evolution, they all witness the disappearance of original elements and the appearance of the same new tendencies. In contrast, the art of Sri Lanka remained much more closely attached to the great tradition of Āndhradeśa and was in the end to be its sole guardian for many centuries (see Chapter 4:2).

89. Standing Buddha

From Nāgapaṭṭiṇam, Tamil Nadu, India; c. 10th century A.D.*; bronze; overall H. 89 cm.; Government Museum, Madras.*

This large and beautiful statue, thought to be one of the oldest of the figures discovered at Nāgapaṭṭiṇam, is an example of the conservatism that is so common in Buddhist art. It preserves most of the iconographic characteristics of the Amarāvatī school (Pl. 48)—the posture, the arrangement of the draperies and the smallness of the *uṣṇīṣa*. However, the unpleated robe, the loose end thrown over the left shoulder like a scarf and the stylized flame surmounting the *uṣṇīṣa* all bear witness to a stylistic evolution.

Few representations of Bodhisattvas are known from this period, although the rise of the Mahāyāna at this time is well attested. None the less the few that exist are very instructive. A small torso of Avalokiteśvara, found in the Krishnā Valley (Pl. 88) and attributed to the first period of Pallava art, is interesting in its style and the influence it appears to have had on South-East Asia, in particular on the iconography of the Thailand peninsula. A lovely gilt bronze statuette of Maitreya (Pl. 90) found at Melayur, Tanjore district, is usually attributed to the eighth or ninth century. It is richly dressed with its robe (*paridhāna*) draped in a very special manner, such as was to become characteristic of Mahāyāna images, in particular of Avalokiteśvara (Pl. 88), throughout South-East Asia as far as Yunnan and especially at Champa. Salihundam, north of Āndhradeśa, reveals the arrival of the Vajrayāna in the seventh and eighth centuries with the appearance of images of Tārā, Mañjuśrī, Mārīci, etc. Although directly influenced by the iconography and sculptural techniques of Orissa (e.g., Ratnagiri, Khiching), nevertheless, some figures remain faithful to the use of the cross-legged posture (*vīrāsana*) of the type that is so characteristic of South Indian art. This whole period is characterized by the gradual decline of the old Āndhradeśa centres and the increasing influence of Mahāyāna traditions from the north (Pl. 91). Still, the importance of the earlier South Indian Buddhist art should be emphasized, for its profound effect upon developments throughout South-East Asia is quite disproportionate to the small number of surviving examples (Pl. 89).

90. Standing Maitreya in royal attire ▷

From Tanjore, Tamil Nadu, India; c. 8th–9th century A.D.*; gilt bronze; H. 39.5 cm.; Government Museum, Madras.*

This beautiful statue of the Bodhisattva Maitreya standing on a lotus support is the work of a Pallava craftsman, and has been dated on the basis of its similarity to figures from Nālandā and Kurkihar. The size and heaviness of the regalia contrast with the sobriety of earlier figures. The garland over the right arm is a feature of Pallava art. The coiffure of 'ringlets' is covered by a high ornate crown that, on the back, has a small aureole and, in front, a small stupa, which is a distinctive feature of Maitreya Bodhisattva.

91. Standing four-armed Maitreya

From Nāgapaṭṭiṇam, Tamil Nadu, India; c. 13th century A.D.; bronze; overall H. 75 cm.; Government Museum, Madras.

This image, which was carried in processions, demonstrates the persistence of Mahāyāna cults in South India. The attire and pronounced flexion indicate the dominance, in style and iconography, of the Cōlas, who represented the main power in South India from the tenth to thirteenth centuries. The pose, the facial features, the composition and treatment of the ornaments and the way of holding the attributes (rosary and bouquet of flowers) between the index and second fingers are Cōla style. The arrangement of the hair in a high crown with locks rising like flames is unusual, but the addition of a stupa confirms the identification as the Buddha Maitreya.

IV. THE BUDDHA IMAGE IN THE REST OF ASIA

1. GEOGRAPHICAL AND CULTURAL CONSIDERATIONS

The Buddha image in India has been treated largely in accordance with three main areas, Gandhāra (i.e., present-day eastern Afghanistan and northern Pakistan), the Ganges-Jumna Valley and the Dekkan ('Southern Region') with special reference to Āndhra on the eastern side as well as the western Dekkan, where so many cave temples have preserved Buddhist sculptures. As Buddhism spread beyond the limits of the Indian subcontinent, geographical considerations began to play a very important part. When from the first century onwards, maybe even earlier, Buddhism began to spread through Central Asia on the long and difficult land route to China, and thence to Korea and Japan, the north-western parts of the subcontinent were clearly the starting-point, and whatever of Indian Buddhism passed in this direction inevitably filtered through Gandhāra. This process continued for many centuries, certainly until the eighth century, when the irruptions of Islam were beginning to cause an almost impenetrable barrier. However, during these eight centuries or so Buddhist doctrines, and perhaps to a lesser extent Buddhist art-forms, were not necessarily introduced into Central Asia and thence to China and beyond in the same historical sequence as they had gradually evolved in India. They tended to be introduced in a rather haphazard way, depending upon the interests and tastes and particular schools of the scholars and artisans who were actively concerned with introducing the new religion. Since the various phases of Buddhist doctrine and also to some extent Buddhist art-forms continued to exist in India, the older ones often side by side with the newer ones, it was quite possible, indeed quite usual, for a Chinese pilgrim-scholar to import from India to China scriptures that related to a much earlier period of Buddhist doctrine, and later, when the Tibetans began seriously to import Buddhism from the eighth century onwards, they imported *pêle-mêle* texts and traditions of all Buddhist periods, and only very much later sorted them out for themselves into some kind of doctrinal sequence. In art and architecture it may not always be so easy to detect such haphazard order, but one must always be prepared for it. Thus there were certainly many so-called 'Aśok-*caityas*', that is to say, Aśoka-style stupas that were popularly attributed to Aśoka himself but were probably constructed in a similar style many centuries later. Thus the four great 'Aśok-*caityas*' around Pātan in the Nepal Valley are likely to be quite as distant in time from the true Aśokan style of the third century B.C. as English 'neo-gothic' of the nineteenth century is from the true Gothic of the thirteenth and fourteenth. Similarly with images, styles might be perpetuated or even revived in certain Indian schools, and then copied abroad very much later, just because a particular image was exported and met with the favour of benefactors who wished to have more made like it. The long land route across Central Asia with its thriving Buddhist city-states provided almost unlimited scope for accidental delays and sudden revivals of certain traditions.

By contrast Sri Lanka and the lands of South-East Asia were connected to India by sea routes, so that to some extent they responded more readily as one Indian phase followed another, but even here transmission could be accidental, depending upon the passing enthusiasm of particular kings, scholars or artisans. It is well known that Sri Lanka adhered generally (although there were exceptions) to the Theravādin tradition, one of the earlier schools, but this did not prevent the introduction of styles of Buddha image that are more readily associated with the Mahāyāna period in our external judgement since they were produced later in time in India. Sri Lanka, and even more so those other countries of South-East Asia where Mahāyāna doctrines were welcomed, Sumatra and Java in particular, remained liable to Indian cultural influences from across the sea up to the time of the final Moslem take-over of northern India, when overseas trade became their preserve (approximately 1200 A.D. onwards). From then on, Sri Lanka, with its overriding Theravādin interests, replaced India as a missionary land, and thus those countries of South-East Asia that have remained Buddhist to this day have all adopted the same Theravādin tradition. This includes a conception of Buddhahood that continued to relate primarily to Śākyamuni Buddha as the one and only Buddha of our present world-age, a tradition that also continued to be followed in India by all those other schools, now long since disappeared, who, like the Theravādins, represented the Śrāvakayāna, the 'Way of the Disciples', contemptuously referred to by the followers of the Mahāyāna as an 'inferior way' (Hīnayāna).

It must be emphasized that some of the other early schools found a following in Central Asia and China, but the Mahāyāna soon tended to predominate, and the Buddha and Bodhisattva forms that we meet there, as well as in Korea and Japan, relate closely to Mahāyāna ways of thought, concerning which a few introductory words are necessary.

The Mahāyāna differs from the earlier schools on two main principles. Firstly, it asserts that Buddhahood is ultimately available to all 'living beings' who make the effort to seek it, and secondly, it asserts the essential identity of the phenomenal world of eternal becoming (*saṃsāra*) and of the calm of Buddhahood that transcends it (*nirvāṇa*). The earlier term, 'Enlightenment' (*bodhi*), once a mere synonym for Nirvana, becomes in Mahāyāna teachings the essential realization of the ultimate identity of the world (*saṃsāra*) and Nirvana. Thus it transcends them both in so far as they may still be regarded as distinct and mutually opposing, precisely as they are regarded by the early Buddhist schools. It follows from this that Nirvana, as understood in the earlier teachings, represents an inferior stage of ascetic training, certainly taught by Śākyamuni but taught, so it was argued, to those who were still not capable of comprehending the higher teachings:

> Of innumerable living beings, so varied in their inclinations, I know the dispositions

> and conduct, for I have a knowledge of the various deeds they have done in the past, and of the merit they then acquired. With manifold explanations and reasonings I cause these beings to reach a greater spirituality; with hundreds of arguments and illustrations I gratify all beings, some in this way, some in that. At one time I taught them the ninefold Scripture, which is composed of the "*Sūtras*", the "Verses", the section called 'Thus it was said', the "Birth-Stories", the "Marvels", the "Origins", the sections consisting of mingled prose and verse, the "Expositions", and hundreds of similes as well. Therein I exhibit Nirvana to those kinds of people who are content with inferior things, who are relatively ignorant, who have not for very long practised under the Buddhas of the past, and who have got stuck in the Samsaric world and suffer greatly from it. This is really only a skilful device by which the Self-Existent wishes to prepare them for the day when he can awaken them to the cognition of a Buddha.[1]

Here Śākyamuni is preaching in accordance with theories already taken for granted in the earlier period, namely, that a Buddha has the power of adapting his appearance and his teaching to different audiences (as at Sāṅkāśya). Thus the whole Mahāyāna, according to its self-understanding, is a more mature form of the Buddha Word, of no less 'historical' validity than the doctrines professed by the *śrāvaka*, or early disciples. In order to emphasize this, these later sutras, or 'discourses', are given a supposed historical setting, in the present case that of the Vulture Peak near Rājagṛha, and here, too, the promulgators of these teachings are following a tradition established by the producers of the early canonical material. The audience consists of representatives of the human and divine spheres, as generally accepted in the earlier period, namely Arhats (perfected disciples), disciples still under training, nuns, virtuous laymen, gods of the Heaven of the Thirty-three Gods, guardian divinities of the cardinal points, gods of Brahmā's heaven, and lesser divine beings. However, it differs from the earlier world-view in that it includes a vast concourse of Bodhisattvas, of whom the principle ones are named, such as Mañjuśrī, Avalokiteśvara, and Maitreya.

It differs also in its cosmic conceptions. A ray of light, issuing from between the eyebrows of Śākyamuni, illuminates 1,800,000 Buddha-fields in the eastern quarter, and in each of these realms there is a Buddha preaching, surrounded by devotees exactly as on this earth of ours. The living beings in all the six states of existence from the heavens to the hells become visible, just as they are said to have become visible to Śākyamuni himself at the moment of his Enlightenment beneath the pipal tree at Gayā. But here the vision is extended to cosmic proportions. The idea of so many Buddhas existing at the same time clearly evoked opposition from some of the followers of the early schools, and the followers of the Mahāyāna found it necessary to justify such a belief.

Thus a Sarvāstivādin, a follower of one such school related to the Theravādins, is presumed to have argued:

> The Buddha has said: 'Two Buddhas cannot arise simultaneously in one and the same

[1]'The Lotus of the Real Dharma' (*Saddharmapuṇḍarīka*), II: 42–46, as translated by Edward Conze, *Buddhist Scriptures* (Penguin Books), p. 200.

world-system, no more than two universal monarchs can co-exist at the same time.' It is therefore untrue to say that at present there are other Buddhas besides Śākyamuni.

The follower of the Mahāyāna replies:

> These are certainly the Buddha's words, but you do not understand their meaning. The Buddha wants to say that two Buddhas cannot appear simultaneously in one and the same great Tri-chiliocosm. But he does not exclude the possibility of the whole universe extending in all the ten directions.[2] Two universal monarchs cannot appear together in the same Four-Continent world system, because each would brook no rival. And so in one Four-Continent world system there is only one single universal monarch. Just so with a Buddha and a great Tri-chiliocosm. The Sutra here draws an analogy between Buddhas and universal monarchs. If you believe, as you do, that in other Four-Continent world systems there are other universal monarchs, why do you not believe in the existence of other Buddhas in other great Tri-chiliocosms? Moreover one Buddha alone cannot possibly save all beings. There must therefore also be others. In fact, beings are countless and their sufferings are measureless. Countless Buddhas are therefore necessary to lead all beings to salvation.[3]

This argument still allows Śākyamuni his position of primary importance in our known world, but the Mahāyāna takes so vast a view of infinite space with its innumerable systems of universes that other Buddhas are easily allowed for. However, the argument as here presented is probably just a theoretical justification of spontaneous faith in other Buddhas deriving from two different factors. Firstly, just as the cult of Bodhisattvas in the role of future Buddhas intent on the welfare of all living beings allowed under cover of different names the worship of great gods vaguely related to other Indian or even non-Indian gods, so likewise the cult of other Buddhas might allow the cult of even greater gods amongst people who were otherwise committed before their conversion to the new religion. Thus the most famous of the cosmic Buddhas is Amitābha, 'Boundless Light', the great Buddha of the western quarter, whose connection with Ahura Mazda, the supreme god of Zoroastrian religion, has often been noted. It is significant that the extraordinary cult of this Buddha seems to have started in North-West India, and spread across Central Asia to China, Korea and Japan. The same cult also entered Tibet from the west. In India itself, in Nepal, and during the period of the expansion of the Mahāyāna to South-East Asia from India, a special cult of Amitābha seems to be little known. His position as cosmic Buddha of the west in the set of the Five Buddhas, representing the centre and the four points of the compass, was certainly assured, but in these other lands Akṣobhya, the 'Imperturbable', the great Buddha of the eastern quarter, was the more popular.

This results from the second of the two factors mentioned above, and here the influence of iconography, of the stereotyped forms of the Buddha statue, seems to have been decisive. We have observed above how the main places associated with events in Śākyamuni's

[2]The ten directions are north, south, east and west, the intermediate points, and the zenith and nadir. 'Tri-chiliocosm' translates a Sanskrit term for a vast cosmic unit, literally, 'Three thousand times the great world thousands'.
[3]'The Great Treatise of the Perfection of Wisdom' (*Mahāprajñāpāramitā-śāstra*) of Nāgārjuna, 93 b–c, as translated by Edward Conze, *op. cit.*, pp. 212–13.

life very early became important places of pilgrimage, marked in the first instance by their stupas, and in the special case of Gayā, where he had achieved Enlightenment, by its famous pipal tree, under which he had sat in meditation. With the emergence of the Buddha statue, certain stereotyped postures and gestures also became associated with his activities as recorded in canonical literature, and thus in some cases there came about a direct correlation between a particular place and a particular activity. Of the various scenes recorded in connection with his achieving Enlightenment, the one that seems to have impressed popular imagination the most is the tradition of his trial of strength with Māra, the Evil One, who appeared before the tranquil Śākyamuni and with the assistance of his vile horde of monstrous followers attempted to move him from his set purpose. On this occasion Śākyamuni called the earth-goddess to witness his fitness for Enlightenment, summoning her by touching the earth with the fingers of his right hand. This gesture seems to have become typical of the Buddha image of Gayā, and in this particular manifestion Śākyamuni was nicknamed the 'Imperturbable' (Akṣobhya).

Similarly the Deer Park at Sārnāth near Vārānasi, where Śākyamuni had preached his first sermon, was inevitably associated with the statue of the preaching Buddha, shown with thumbs and index-fingers touching in a graceful circular gesture, thus indicating his turning of the Wheel of the Doctrine. In a late Mahāyāna sutra ('discourse'), such as 'The Compendium of Truth of all the Buddhas' (*Sarvatathāgatatattvasaṃgraha*), Śākyamuni, who is still the foremost preaching Buddha, is known as Vairocana, the 'Resplendent One', and he manifests his transcendence by appearing in a fivefold cosmic form, as Amitābha in the west, as Akṣobhya in the east, as Amoghasiddhi ('Infallible Success') in the north and as Ratnasambhava ('Jewel-Born') in the south. These last two are seemingly devised aspects of Śākyamuni, representing respectively his protective miraculous power and his unlimited generosity. It is clear from the texts and certain surviving traditions that Buddhology progressed through a stage of three great Buddhas (Vairocana, Amitābha and Akṣobhya) to the cosmic set of five.[4] There is no need to trace this progression here, but it is important to note the iconographic distinctions between the five great Buddha manifestations.

COSMIC DIRECTION	SANSKRIT NAME	TRANSLATION	SPECIAL GESTURE (*mudrā*)[5]
Centre	Vairocana (Pl. 217)	Resplendent	Preaching (*dharmacakra-pravartana*)
East	Akṣobhya (Pl. 214)	Imperturbable	Touching the earth (*bhūmisparśa*)
South	Ratnasambhava (Pl. 93)	Jewel-Born	Generosity (*dāna*)
West	Amitābha (Pl. 92)	Boundless Light	Meditation (*dhyāna*)
North	Amoghasiddhi	Infallible Success	Fearlessness (*abhaya*)

[4]For detailed references, see D. L. Snellgrove, *Buddhist Himālaya* (Oxford, 1957), pp. 56–66.

[5] It may be noted that all these gestures, being typical of Śākyamuni in the earlier period, continue to relate to him in those Buddhist schools that did not adopt Māhayana teachings. Thus often only an inscription or a still living Buddhist tradition in the places where archaeological pieces are found can distinguish a preaching Śākyamuni from Vairocana (e.g., Pl. 257), Śākyamuni in his victory over Māra (*māravijaya*) from Akṣobhya (e.g., Pl. 206), or a meditating Śākyamuni from Amitābha (e.g., Pls. 219, 220). Few, if any, images of Amoghasiddhi appear in this book (Pl. 177 may be one), but there are many earlier images of Śākyamuni in precisely this posture (e.g., Pl. 55). When found in sets of five, there is no problem, and in paintings the Five Buddhas are distinguished by their colours: white, blue, yellow, red, green, in the order as listed above.

92. The Buddha of the west, Amitābha

Image set into the western side of the great stupa south of Pātan, Nepal.

The snake motif is interesting. It relates to the story of the *nāga* king Mucalinda, who protected the meditating Śākyamuni from a storm just after his Enlightenment. It has nothing to do with the celestial Buddha Amitābha (Boundless Light), but even when this Buddha is clearly intended, the 'biographical' associations of a meditating Buddha figure with Śākyamuni himself can still be recalled.

93. The Buddha of the south, Ratnasambhava

Image set into the southern side of the great stupa south of Pātan, Nepal.

In accordance with the predilections of different schools, any member of this five-fold group may assume supremacy and thus appear as a form of primary Buddha. As we have already noticed, Amitābha assumes the primary place in many Mahāyāna works popular in Central Asia, China and Japan. By contrast, in India and Nepal Akṣobhya seems to have the pre-eminent place. In Tantric texts he assumes a terrifying form, suitable for one who repels the attacks of evil. In this form he is known as Heruka or Hevajra. This particular tradition is not exclusive to India and Nepal, for the fierce aspect of Akṣobhya is related to the fearful Japanese divinity, Acala Vidyārāja (cf. Pl. 306). The pre-eminence of Akṣobhya as the favourite Buddha of later Indian Buddhism (ninth to twelfth centuries) accounts for the large number of images found on archaeological sites there, which show the 'earth-witness' posture (*bhūmisparśa-mudrā*).

Whereas popular devotion might favour any particular Buddha, the Five Buddha complex with Vairocana in the centre became in later Buddhism an esoteric expression of Buddhahood, used by tantric practisers with Enlightenment as their goal. Geographical considerations would suggest North-West India and Kashmir as an original centre of this cult, for it certainly spread across Central Asia to China and Japan and later into western Tibet and Ladakh. It is interesting to compare the mandalas (*maṇḍala*) of Vairocana from very much the same period, which survive in early pictorial form in Japan and Ladakh, lands very widely separated indeed (see Pls. 202, 344).

The Buddha figures of the 'mystic circle' (*maṇḍala*) differ only in their circular arrangement, and thus the conventional numbers must fit a circle and the directional points in one way or another. Thus there may be a total of five (the fundamental group already mentioned so often), or of nine (centre, four cardinal points, four intermediate points), or of seventeen (as before plus eight more points arranged symmetrically), or indeed any vast number that permits neat arrangement on the painting. The use of 'mystic circles' in which supernatural power may be concentrated is well known in other civilizations besides that of India. Indian Buddhists adopted the symbolism as an extension of the significance of the stupa, which already in the early Mahāyāna period represented Supreme Enlightenment as a kind of centrifugal force. In this matter there was never any noticeable break with the ideas of the earlier schools, but rather a growth in realization of the more positive aspects of Buddhahood. We have already shown above (p. 22) how in the early period the stupa represented the 'transcendental form' (*dharmakāya*) of Śākyamuni. As Buddha manifestations, the previous Buddhas as well as Śākyamuni represented on earth in their physical forms (*rūpakāya* or *nirmāṇakāya*) the supreme essence of Buddhahood. As the idea of manifestation in time was gradually replaced by the cosmic idea of manifestation in space, it was natural that the stupa should come to symbolize the very centre of existence, as the absolute non-manifest point whence Buddhas and all else emerge, and whither they return. The 'mystic circle', aided by a complex symbolism that allows the representation within its compass of the main components of phenomenal existence, took over in meaning from the stupa, which was inevitably limited by its set architectural form.

At the same time Buddhological theories on the 'Bodies' of Buddhahood required restatement in order to accord with the ever-advancing ideas about Buddhahood. Whereas the early schools were content with enunciating a theory of two 'Bodies', an absolute one (*dharmakāya*) together with one in which a Buddha was manifest on earth (*rūpakāya*) (see p. 22), the Mahāyāna found it necessary to think in terms of three such 'Bodies', and later even a fourth was added. They may be listed in descending order thus:

SANSKRIT TERM	TRANSLATION	SIGNIFICANCE
svabhāvikakāya	Self-Existent Body	This is the last to be added to the set in an effort to transcend the already transcendent notion of the *dharmakāya*. It tends to emphasize the positive aspect of Supreme Buddhahood.
dharmakāya	The Absolute Body (The Body of the True Doctrine)	As already explained.
sambhogakāya	The Glorified Body (The Body of Bliss for those privileged to behold it)	This is the 'Body' in which a Buddha may be manifest to those of higher sensibilities, especially to Bodhisattvas in the heavens and to those on earth who have qualified themselves by the right processes of purification and meditation.
nirmāṇakāya	The Physical Body (for practical purposes usually a human body)	As already explained.

Iconographically the 'Self-Existent Body' can never be represented, just as in the earlier stages the whole idea of Buddhahood was felt to transcend any form of direct representation. Thus it is taught that even when Buddhas are shown in painting or sculpture, this remains a mere convention and their ultimate form, as represented by the ancient symbolism of the bare stupa, can never be grasped in this-worldly terms. One must urge that despite the ever-growing richness of the symbolism, the absolute transcendence of final Buddhahood is maintained throughout the whole history of Buddhism in all its varied forms.

The *dharmakāya* comes to be represented iconographically by the set of Five Buddhas or by anyone of them in particular. The different hand-gestures have already been listed above (see p. 135fn.) and the style of dress is usually that of an ordinary monk.

The *sambhogakāya*, or the 'Glorified Body', allows special scope for the imagination of religious artists. The whole idea relates to the very early tradition of Śākyamuni's 'transfiguration' before his Final Nirvana, when he dressed himself in the very special garments presented by the layman Mukkusa (see above p. 18). Thus it easily came about that the 'Glorified Body' was conceived in royal attire, complete with crown and jewelled ornaments. Throughout the literature of all periods, the Buddha is constantly compared with a universal monarch (*cakravartin*), and the opportunity of acclaiming his all-transcending kingship was accepted quite naturally and spontaneously. Thus for later Buddhist thought there is nothing surprising about a crowned Buddha image.

The physical body of Śākyamuni, his *nirmāṇakāya*, was the first to be represented when the Buddha statue was devised, probably in the first century A.D. Gradually, however, as this new Buddha image became the vehicle of transcendent notions, it became stylized and stereotyped so that the symbolic significance might be the more clearly expressed. Thus, as a representation of Śākyamuni, the Buddha image became increasing rare, although one may remain free to assert that it often relates closely to him. Once again, we note how the idea of Buddhahood has in one way or another transcended the person of Śākyamuni throughout the whole long history of the religion he represents.

2. SRI LANKA AND SOUTH-EAST ASIA UP TO THE 10TH CENTURY A.D.

Local Schools of Buddhist Art

While Buddhism was introduced into Sri Lanka—and perhaps even lower Burma—during the time of Aśoka, it appears that no image of the Buddha survives anywhere earlier than the third or fourth century A.D. A real problem is raised by the long period of time that apparently intervened between the introduction of Buddhist doctrine throughout these regions and the time when local workshops were set up, or even the time when images are assumed to have been imported. The present state of investigations suggests that the dissemination of images and of the doctrine were two separate aspects of the spread of Buddhism overseas. In any case, written and archaeological evidence alike indicates that by at least the fifth century Buddhism had taken root in South-East Asia sufficiently firmly for regular contact to have been established with the major centres in India and Sri Lanka, and for China to be seeking in the area canonical texts, translators, precious relics and images of the Buddha.

Both historical remains and archaeological evidence reveal that the spread of Buddhism through South-East Asia was the result not of a single current but of successive waves from different sources, which spread along the sea routes from Sri Lanka as far as Celebes. A first wave, in which the influence of iconographic works by the Amarāvatī school was preeminent, was followed by other waves, generally reaching a smaller area, and representing successively the Gupta and post-Gupta schools, followed by the Pāla (see p. 271). In all cases the oldest images discovered have obviously been imported. Only gradually did workshops appear that produced more or less faithful copies of early models—probably about the third or fourth century in Sri Lanka, and the sixth century at the earliest in South-East Asia. The result was that the various local schools of art, quite apart from developments reflecting their own ideals, tended to evolve particular types of images in which the different influences they had undergone were combined in varying proportions. Generally speaking, none of the schools of Buddhist art that grew up in the former kingdoms of South-East Asia seems to have been wholly or simply an offshoot of any one of the major schools of India. All are of a more or less hybrid character; and even when, particularly in

Java, the role played by imported images seems to be predominant, sculpture as such always regains its originality. So, after a period of about five centuries, the schools of Buddhist art that were henceforth to characterize the different states of South-East Asia came into being.

Sri Lanka

The Chronicles and inscriptions bear witness to the introduction of Buddhism into Sri Lanka by Mahinda, a nephew of Aśoka, during the reign of Devānaṃpiya Tissa (247–207 B.C.), his founding of the stupa intended to house the relic of the Buddha's collar-bone, and the planting in Anurādhapura of a cutting, brought by Saṅghamittā of the Bo tree (the *bodhivṛkṣa*, 'Tree of Enlightenment', growing at Gayā), a shoot of which is still alive today. Notwithstanding all this, the oldest known image of the Buddha does not appear to date from before the third century A.D. at the earliest, and is appreciably later than the oldest images in India. Some authors have drawn attention to the fact that various passages in the Chronicles from the third century onwards refer to images attributed to the reigns of Devānaṃpiya Tissa himself, Duṭṭhagāmaṇī (161–137 B.C.) and Vasabha (A.D. 65–109), but there is nothing at present to confirm the hypothesis that Sinhalese images predate Indian ones; and it seems more probable that for a long time, out of fidelity to the early tradition, the only objects of the devotion of the faithful in Sri Lanka were stupas housing the venerated relics (the tooth relic was brought over at the beginning of the fourth century) and the shoot of the Bo tree. It is possible that the cult of sacred footprints (*buddhapāda*) developed at a fairly early date, but nothing in the style of the examples that have been preserved enables us to ascribe an exact date. Lastly, it is remarkable that, with the possible exception of a few fragments of imported marble in the Āndhra style found in the Dakkhina-thūpa at Anurādhapura (the Dream of Māyādevī, Colombo Museum), no narrative bas-relief seems to correspond to the aniconic stage of Buddhism.[6] A statue of the Buddha from Maha Illupallama (in the district of Anurādhapura) may be one of the oldest Sinhalese images. Six feet high, of white marble probably imported from the Veṅgi region, it is undeniably an example of Amarāvatī art, the heir and direct descendant of which was the Anurādhapura school.

The Anurādhapura School. The Anurādhapura period came to an end only after the destruction of the capital by the Cōlas (A.D. 993), and falls into two stages. The first, ending with the Tamil occupation of Sri Lanka (432–59) seems to have left behind little except statues of the Buddha, mostly standing, all following very closely the Āndhra iconographic tradition. Narrative bas-relief is represented only by a few very small slabs, and its importance is not comparable with the part it plays in Amarāvatī and Nāgārjunakonda art. The Chronicles and Pāli texts mention paintings of which unfortunately no trace has been found.

The second stage, beginning with the reign of Dhātusena (459–77), is much richer, owing to its intense artistic activity as much as to its duration. The standing statues of the Buddha are faithful to tradition, the only departure from it being that a gesture suggestive of teach-

[6] The spelling *thūpa*, which we must preserve in these Sinhalese names, corresponds to Sanskrit *stūpa* (stupa).

94. Standing Buddha

From Medavacciya, Sri Lanka; c. 4th century A.D.*; bronze; H. 46 cm.; Archaeological Museum, Anurādhapura.*

Originally gilt, this statuette is directly reminiscent of a tradition of the Amarāvatī school, both in its attitude and in the way the robe is adjusted (the right hand raised in a gesture of blessing [*abhaya-mudra*], and a loose end of the robe caught up over the left forearm). While these different iconographic features are found in Sri Lanka over a long period (Pl. 95), it appears that this statuette may be regarded as one of the oldest of a well-represented series of stone statues; they are large and often defaced.

ing is sometimes replaced by the gesture known as 'benediction' (Pls. 94, 95). At the same time images seem to become more hieratic, and from the beginning of the seventh century onwards some of them have already acquired the colossal dimensions characteristic of the rock art of Sri Lanka for many centuries thereafter. What is probably more important is the appearance in Sri Lanka and most of the schools of South-East Asia of seated statues—cross-legged (in *vīrāsana* fashion), sometimes protected by the *nāga* Mucilinda (Pl. 97), usually in the *samādhi* attitude that subsequently became the most common in Sinhalese art or, more rarely, making an explanatory gesture (*vitarka-mudrā*).[7] These seated images represent a more advanced stage of development than standing ones. In the few cases in which the monastic robe still falls in regular folds (Pl. 98), it hangs in the distinc-

[7]The term *vīrāsana*, 'heroic posture', corresponds to what has been called elsewhere *yogāsana*, 'yoga posture'. For all such terms, see Glossary.

95. Colossal standing Buddha

From Avukana, Sri Lanka; c. 5th–8th century A.D.*; rock-cut sculpture; H. 11.85 m.; in situ.*

Around the fifth to eighth century colossal statues of the Buddha seem to have been particularly popular in Sri Lanka. This very famous example was carved in the rock-face of a cliff at the foot of which a monastery had been built. It is in a remarkable state of preservation, and may have been worshipped by King Dhātusena (A.D. 459–77), though its somewhat severe style suggests a considerably later date, perhaps eighth to ninth century. The right hand makes a gesture of benediction in the manner peculiar to Sinhalese iconography known as *āśīsa*, a variant form of the *abhaya-mudrā*. The flame representing the *uṣṇīṣa* (the *siraspota*) is a modern addition.

96. Buddha seated in the *samādhi* attitude

From Toluvila (Anurādhapura), Sri Lanka; c. 6th century A.D.*; stone; H. 176 cm.; National Museum, Colombo.*

Despite the erosion of the arms and legs, the great serenity and beauty of the proportions of the Toluvila image make it one of the best examples of the statuary of Anurādhapura, though it is not one of the oldest. It seems that the robe, which leaves the right shoulder bare, did not fall in folds, but there is no way of knowing how it was draped, the only fact that would allow an exact dating of the statue. A stone block behind the head suggests that originally a halo was affixed to it.

97. Buddha protected by the *nāga* Mucilinda

From Sri Lanka, exact provenance unknown; c. 6th–7th century A.D.*; schist, bas-relief; H. 21 cm.; private collection, Colombo; cast: Archaeological Museum, Anurādhapura.*

This small relief is probably one of the most ancient iconic works depicting a scene that subsequently enjoyed exceptional favour in South-East Asia, especially in Cambodia. The *nāga*s and *nāgini*s portrayed in human form, the former in adoration and the latter playing various musical instruments, may be intended, like the images of the aniconic Sāñcī period, as a reference to the epilogue of the miracle.

98. Seated Buddha teaching

From Badullā, Sri Lanka; 5th–6th century A.D.*; H. approximately 65 cm.; National Museum, Colombo.*

Apart from its aesthetic value, the Badullā image is of very special interest in that it belongs to the iconographic series that produced the most ancient tradition of which we have examples in South-East Asia: the seated *vīrāsana* attitude (right leg crossed over the left); the *vitarka-mudrā* denoting teaching; and above all, in the first period, the robe falling in regular folds, leaving the right shoulder bare, with the left hand holding up part of the border (see Pl. 119).

tive manner of the oldest statues found all along the sea route (Pl. 119). It is characteristic of most of these statues that the garment has no folds, as in the styles influenced by the Sārnāth tradition—a feature that tends to disappear with the Polonnaruwa period (twelfth century onwards). The Mahāyāna Buddhism practised in Sri Lanka concurrently with the Theravāda does not seem to have had any greater influence on the style of images than had the protracted rivalry between the devotees of the Abhayagirivihāra and the Mahāvihāra. Among wall paintings, well represented by first-rate works (Sīgiriya, end of the fifth century), there are few images of the Buddha. Some seventh-century fragments are preserved in the grotto at Hindagala near Peredeniya (the visit paid by Indra to the Buddha in the grotto at Indrasāla), whose masterly execution and genuine distinction foreshadow Sinhalese Buddhist aesthetics.

Burma

An unverifiable tradition recounts that two merchants, Tapussa and Bhallika, introduced Buddhism into lower Burma, their country of origin, during the lifetime of the Buddha. Another, based on the identification of Suvaṇṇabhūmi—the 'Golden Country'—with the Thaton region, of which there is evidence at an early date, ascribes the conversion of the Mon country to the mission carried out by Soṇa and Uttara, monks sent by Aśoka at the time that Mahinda was introducing Buddhism into Sri Lanka. No historical remains can be ascribed to such a remote period, and the oldest objects so far discovered—inscriptions and images—do not appear to go back further than the fifth century A.D. The oldest archaeological remains, though few in number, are nevertheless of great importance. While no statue has yet been discovered belonging to the series with regularly draped garments (Pls. 94, 119), which appears to have been the earliest introduced into South-East Asia, these remains show quite clearly that Buddhism spread outwards in successive waves from centres that had their own distinctive iconographic traditions.

In the ancient Pyu kingdom, excavations conducted on the oldest site, Beikthano, have brought to light vestiges of monasteries and stupas in brick reminiscent of Āndhra architecture, but no image of the Buddha has been found. On the other hand, Thayekhittaya (Śrīkṣetra, formerly Prome), which flourished from the fifth to the ninth centuries, has yielded some statuettes and carved paving-stones (the Bebe Temple, Lemyethna, Yahandagu, East Zegu), all of which are in the South Indian tradition: the Buddha is seated in the *vīrāsana* attitude and, above all, the garments are draped in a manner typical of the schools derived from Āndhra art (Pls. 99, 100). This early style is thought to have persisted till at least the seventh century, when a number of images seem to suggest affinities with Gupta art, revealing the appearance of new influences. In addition, inscriptions bear witness to the simultaneous use of Pāli and Sanskrit.

Soṇa and Uttara are believed to have settled in the Mon country, some 50 kilometres to the north of Thaton; and it is also at Thaton (Sudhammavatī)—where the Shwezayan Pagoda, subsequently enlarged on several occasions, is believed to have been constructed in the fifth century as a shrine for four tooth relics of the Buddha—that the Burmese Chronicles locate the birthplace of Buddhaghoṣa, the great commentator of the Pāli canon.

99. Buddha seated in meditation

From the mound at Khin Ba (formerly Prome, Thayekhittaya), Burma; c. 5th–6th century A.D.*; gold; Hmawza Museum.*

Found among a variety of precious objects in a reliquary chamber, this image shows that, as throughout South-East Asia, the most ancient Buddhist art of which examples are found in Burma derives from the iconographic tradition of southern India. Though the robe is no longer shown falling in regular folds as in the first series, the posture is unmistakably that of the southern schools, and the *uṣṇīṣa*, as in the art of Amarāvatī and Sri Lanka, is very rudimentary. The throne, though simplified, is suggested by the standing lions supporting the crosspiece of the back, which terminates in traditional *makara* heads. The halo is of the simple 'sun-disk' type.

While it is not possible to link anything in the former capital of Rāmaññadesa with any of these traditions, it should be noted that the town was the major centre of Theravādin culture in lower Burma throughout the period from the fifth century to 1057, the date of its capture by Aniruddha. Yet the region of Thaton has yielded no indication of the existence of local workshops or of images comparable in antiquity with the vestiges found on the site of the former Prome. This absence of any genuinely ancient evidence raises a problem that has been stressed by most authors. While we are unable to suggest a possible explanation, we would at least emphasize that a bronze statue (Pl. 101), undeniably in the Gupta style, is of very special interest. Beyond all doubt imported, it suggests that, in the region where the Theravāda school was the most firmly established, iconography underwent a regeneration that is comparable to that observed in the Pyu country and due to the same influences; the newly introduced Gupta style seems at first to have existed side by side with the original school in the Āndhra tradition, and then to have gradually ousted it. There is no doubt that such a regeneration prepared the way for the adoption, at a date that cannot be determined but is certainly before the arrival of Aniruddha, of Pāla iconography, which in Burma was later commissioned into service by the Theravādin school, though it derives from the late Mahāyāna period of Indian Buddhism.

100. Reliquary

From the mound at Khin Ba (formerly Prome, Thayekhittaya), Burma; c. 5th–6th century A.D.*; gilt silver; Hmawza Museum.*

Found in the same area as the preceding statuette, this reliquary bears an inscription in Pāli and Pyu, carved in southern Indian characters. It reveals that the four Buddhas shown in the *bhūmisparśa-mudrā* attitude are the three previous Buddhas—Kassapa, Kakusandha, Koṅgāmana—and then Gautama, Buddha of the present age. While the *āsana* in this case is still in the tradition of South India, it is most noticeable that the robes of the standing disciples are adjusted in the Amarāvatī and Anurādhapura fashion. On the lid of the reliquary there was originally a tree, recalling the site of the bodhi tree, of which only the trunk remains.

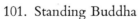

101. Standing Buddha

From the region of Thaton, Burma; c. 6th–8th century A.D.*; bronze; Saddhamma Jotika Monastery, Yanaung-taik, Thaton.*

With this statuette we come to an iconographic tradition entirely different from that previously illustrated. The drapery of the mantle covering both shoulders, the dissymmetry of its sides and the treatment of the *uṣṇīṣa* reveal a Gupta influence, the effects of which persisted for a long time in certain countries such as Burma and Indonesia; this makes it difficult to date images. Here, however, the membrane apparently linking the fingers of the right hand —one of the thirty-two signs of a *mahāpuruṣa* (see p. 48)—is a very rare feature in South-East Asia, and this suggests a fairly early date.

Thailand

Excavations carried out over the last ten years have considerably improved our knowledge of the early period of Buddhism in the regions that were later to become Thailand, and in particular in the western part of the Maenam Basin. The clearing of new sites and a number of largely accidental discoveries have had two important results. Firstly, it has been proved that there really was a Dvāravatī kingdom, to which a particular style of sculpture was ascribed for nearly half a century without its being identified in any way except by its name. This name was reconstituted from seventh-century Chinese texts that mention it as one of the kingdoms in the centre of the Indo-Chinese Peninsula at a time when Buddhism was flourishing there. Secondly, it has been shown that there was a genuine school of Buddhist art earlier than that of Dvāravatī and providing evidence of the earliest impact of Buddhism on the region. Some images belonging to a series with the garment falling in regular folds have long been familiar (see the Dong-duong Buddha, Pl. 119), and recent finds have not only revealed that they were widespread from the Korat Plateau to the Malay Peninsula, but also that locally executed copies existed (e.g., the Nakhon Pathom statuette, the U Thong relief, etc.). Thus there is clear evidence that workshops were already imitating imported models, and this at a period that the archaeological context suggests should be dated towards the fifth or sixth century at the latest. It is evident that at least two schools existed in the central and southern part of Thailand in the period before the appearance of images generally ascribed to Dvāravatī art; the earlier of the two continues the Amarāvatī tradition; the more recent, represented chiefly by a few large stone statues, is in the Gupta tradition, as at Thaton (the U Thong high relief, the fragments found in the Singhburi region, etc.). The Dvāravatī school, which was to succeed them, combined their heritage with fresh influence from India.

Dvāravatī Art. Nothing is known of either the geographical boundaries or the duration of the kingdom, but the art that characterized it, particularly sculpture, had considerable repercussions both in space and in time (Pls. 102–5). It also produced some original iconographic formulae—for example, the Wheel of the Law—which perpetuate one of the most ancient iconographic themes of Buddhism or the images of the Buddha, that of Buddha borne by a fabulous bird (Pl. 106), which raises a still unsolved problem of identification. Moreover, both these formulae seem to be unknown elsewhere in South-East Asia.

The image of the Buddha, particularly his clothing (especially in the case of standing figures), reveals a post-Gupta and in all likelihood Pāla influence, although we need not assume that this influence must inevitably have come from centres in North-East India. In any case, the merging of the new tradition with traditions already locally established produced a particular style in which the Buddha, portrayed in attitudes and making gestures that usually follow the tradition of southern India (*vīrāsana* and *vitarka-mudrā*), is shown in accordance with the Gupta aesthetic and wears a garment, of which the stylized draping seems reminiscent of the art of North-East India. Extremely rich and fertile, the Dvāravatī school has a widely varied iconographic repertory: standing images (with both hands usually in the same gesture of teaching); images seated in the *vīrāsana* attitude or in the

102. Standing Buddha

From the region of Songkhla, Thailand; Dvāravatī art, c. 6th–7th century A.D.*; bronze; H. approximately 30 cm.; private collection, Bangkok.*

This beautiful statuette, with the very supple movement of the hips, is related to an important series of bronze statues (Pl. 110) in the tradition of southern India (Buddhapād), but belonging to a later stage of development than the group of figures with the mantle in regular folds (Pls. 110, 119). There is no way of knowing whether this is the product of local workmanship or, as seems more likely, an imported work. The end of the robe is wrapped round the wrist and held in the left hand—a characteristic of this group—but note the gesture of the right hand which is a combination of the *abhaya-mudrā* and the *vitarka-mudrā*. The base is modern.

'European' fashion, protected by the *nāga*, borne by the fabulous bird; and narrative scenes. Every kind of material has been used: stone, metals (chiefly bronze, but also silver and gold), stucco, terracotta—the last two used only for decorating buildings with scenes in low-relief and isolated figures (Nakhon Pathom, U Thong, Ku Bua). There is the same diversity of techniques: in the round, in high and low relief, either carved directly or modelled. The art of bas-relief is represented by only a small number of works, but their dimensions range from the simple carved or modelled slab to the monumental rock carving (e.g., the cave near Sravuri); all bear witness to an art brought to perfection and a remarkable faculty for interpreting the texts (Pl. 107). Recent investigations have shown that towards the eighth or ninth century Dvāravatī art underwent the influence of the so-called Śrīvijaya school, which introduced Mahāyāna doctrines and iconography to the Theravādin world. This influence was to be of limited duration, but it brought about the decadence of Dvāravatī art as an indirect consequence.

103. Buddha head

From Thailand, exact provenance unknown; Dvāravatī art, c. 7th–8th century A.D.; limestone; H. 37 cm.; National Museum, Bangkok.

This head is a revealing example of the aesthetic trends of the so-called Dvāravatī school. The influence of Gupta and post-Gupta art can be seen in the size of the *uṣṇīṣa*, the large curls, and the unbroken, sinuous line of the eyebrows. The image does, however, bear the obvious imprint of local work; and the stylized treatment gave rise to a type that spread far and wide throughout the peninsula and is considered as specifically Mon.

104. Buddha teaching, seated in the 'European' fashion

From Ayutthaya and Nakhon Pathom, Thailand; Dvāravatī art, c. 7th–8th century A.D.; quartz; H. approximately 370 cm.; National Museum, Bangkok.

The fragments of this colossal statue come from Nakhon Pathom, where it was carved, and from Ayutthaya, where they were probably moved before the end of the sixteenth century. The seated 'European' attitude is not especially uncommon; there are examples of it in the iconographic traditions of both northern and southern India (though not Sri Lanka). On the other hand, the suggestion of teaching conveyed by both hands in the *vitarka-mudrā* gesture is peculiar to the south of India.

105. Buddha protected by the *nāga* Mucilinda

From Dong Si Maha Pot, Thailand; Dvāravatī art, c. 7th–8th century A.D.*; limestone relief; H. 75 cm.; National Museum, Bangkok.*

The miracle marking the sixth week following the Great Enlightenment is frequently illustrated in Dvāravatī art, and is probably a further indication of the influence of the Amarāvatī and Sri Lanka schools. Though the scene is treated in low relief, the restrained composition represents a stage on the way towards the severe presentation of the theme that later prevailed in the peninsula (Pls. 244, 245, etc.): votive stupas replace the figures of the early scenes (Pl. 97). The Mucilinda is here represented only by his sevenfold hood, as if the sculptor had given up trying to interpret the description of the *nāga* king surrounding the body of the Buddha with his coils.

106. Buddha standing on a fabulous bird

From Muang Pra Rot, Panasnikhom, Thailand; Dvāravatī art, c. 7th–9th century A.D.*; limestone, high relief; H. 47 cm.; private collection, Panasnikhom.*

Thailand has many reliefs portraying the Buddha, usually standing on a fabulous beast, with the hands in the *vitarka-mudrā*. In most cases he is accompanied by two bearers of fly-whisks. While it is often suggested, though without any certainty, that the latter should be identified as Indra and Brahmā, the hybrid character of the bird—a kind of *garuḍa* with horns and lion's feet, probably taken from the Amarāvatī bestiary—raises many problems as to the actual import of the scene. It should surely not be interpreted, as it is by some authors, as being the Descent from the Heaven of the Thirty-three Gods, a miracle described with such precise circumstantial details (see Pls. 227, 238) that it would have been difficult to depart from them so deliberately. We suggest that it is rather a representation of the Ascension to the Heaven of the Thirty-three Gods, since the silence of the texts on the subject gives sculptors considerable latitude.

107. The Great Miracle and the Teaching in the Heaven of the Thirty-three Gods

From Thailand, exact provenance unknown; Dvāravatī art, c. 7th–8th century A.D.*; stone, bas-relief; lacquered and gilt; H. 240 cm.; Wat Suthat, Bangkok.*

The large relief set into the rear of the pedestal of the main statue of the *vihāra* at Wat Suthat illustrates two separate scenes. Keeping very closely to the texts, the lower scene represents the great miracle of Śrāvastī (the miracle of the mango tree, the multiplication of the images of the Buddha) and the confusion of the Heterodox. The upper scene shows the teaching given by the Buddha to his mother and the gods in the Heaven of the Thirty-three Gods from the seat of Śakra (Indra), under the Pāricchattaka tree. The quality and the iconographic value of these compositions make us regret very much that so few reliefs of the Dvāravatī school have come down to us.

108. Standing four-armed Maitreya

From Prakon Chai, Thailand; end of 8th–beginning of 9th century A.D.*; bronze; H. 100 cm.; collection of Mr. and Mrs. J. D. Rockefeller 3rd, New York.*

This magnificent Maitreya with his delicate poise, discovered together with several hundred Mahāyāna images of all sizes, is a direct off-shoot of pre-Angkorian art (in the style of Kompong Prah), although very few Mahāyāna cult figures, particularly bronzes, have been found in Cambodia. The Bodhisattva is unadorned and wears a short and simple ascetic's garment. His young face has a small moustache and the very elaborate head-dress bears the stupa emblem. The hands with their delicate gesture would be made to hold movable attributes.

109. Eight-armed Avalokiteśvara

From Chaiya, Thailand; c. 9th century A.D.*; bronze; H. 72 cm.; National Museum, Bangkok.*

Although this very hieratic, large figure of Avalokiteśvara has been strongly influenced by Indonesian art, it cannot be regarded as an imported work. It is a product of the Śrīvijaya school of peninsular Thailand, and is one of its most remarkable achievements in spite of the rather dry treatment. It is regrettable that the various mutilations and the loss of the attributes make it impossible to identify the particular aspect of the Bodhisattva represented here.

Śrīvijaya Art. This name is traditionally used in Thailand to designate the art that developed in the Malay Peninsula (in the region of Nakhon Si Thammarat) in conjunction with the growth of the kingdom of Śrīvijaya from about the eighth century onwards. Initially subjected to the influence of the Mahāyāna, which came from Indonesia, it gradually returned to the Theravāda, while preserving some of its originality. The centres in the Malay Peninsula undoubtedly played an important role in the birth of Thai schools (Sukhothai), and succeeded in maintaining some of their traditions at least up till the fifteenth and sixteenth centuries. Early subjected to Indian influence, the Malay Peninsula produced both the oldest Hindu image in South-East Asia (the Viṣṇu of Chaiya) and a small Buddhist stele in the Gupta style belonging to the school of Sārnāth, which is comparable to examples found in the Maenam Basin. Śrīvijaya art is characterized to a greater extent by Bodhisattva statues, often admirably executed (for example the Avalokiteśvaras of Chaiya, Pl. 109), than by images of the Buddha, which are few in number, The latter bear witness to the direct influence of Pāla iconography and the Nālandā school, as in Indonesia (the same attitude for seated figures teaching expressed by the *dharmacakra-mudrā*). One of the most unexpected results of recent studies is that they have shown that the Śrīvijaya iconography, instead of keeping strictly to the Malay Peninsula, spread far and wide to all the centres belonging to the Dvāravatī tradition. But the achievements of the Śrīvijaya school, probably linked to the spread of the Mahāyāna, were short-lived and left no lasting trace in art.

Malaysia

The Federation of Malaysia, which comprises the countries marking the two extremities of the South-East Asian archipelago, Malaya and North Borneo (Sarawak and Sabah), has yielded only a very few images of the Buddha. Two of them, however, are of particular interest in view of their origin and iconographic features, even though they are certainly not anterior to the sixth or seventh century—a small bronze statue from Kedah and a stone statuette found at Santubong (Sarawak). Both images are of the same type, characterized by identical gestures and the way the dress hangs. As examples of this type are also to be found in Cambodia (Pl. 118), we have here obvious evidence of the dissemination of an image that appears at one time to have been the object of special veneration, and that may very possibly be Dīpaṅkara, the first of the Buddhas of the past.

Indonesia

The earliest information as to the presence of Buddhism in Indonesia is provided by the accounts of Chinese pilgrims. From Fa-hsien we learn that at Ye-p'o-t'i (Java or Borneo?), where he stayed for some months in 414, 'the Doctrine of the Buddha scarcely deserves mention' in a country where, on the contrary, 'heretics and Brahmans prosper'. Some ten years later, after spending some time in Sri Lanka, the learned Kashmir teacher Guṇavarman preached Buddhism in Java—converting first the mother of the king, then the king himself—and in Lin-i (i.e., Champa). It may have been due to royal patronage that in the seventh century the island of Java became a centre of Buddhist studies—probably beginning with Theravāda Buddhism—whose reputation attracted teachers such as Puṇyodana (who came from central India, and may have been responsible for introducing the Vajrayāna and the Mahāyāna) and Chinese monks such as I-tsing; the latter, incidentally, noted that the Mahāyāna had reached Sumatra.

Only very few items exist that can be ascribed to the period before the introduction of the Mahāyāna, but those we possess are particularly instructive. It is indeed remarkable that two bronze statues found in Java belong to a type of which examples are found in Sri Lanka (Pl. 94), Thailand and Champa (Pl. 119), and that one of them (Kuta Blater, South Jember, Museum van Aziatische Kunst, Amsterdam) even suggests the existence of a local workshop as noted above in the case of Thailand. The fine torso found in Celebes (Pl. 110) may predate this group; and the colossal statue at Mt. Seguntang (Palembang Museum) is further proof of the existence of local workshops at a date that can hardly be later than the end of the sixth century. Carved in granite from the island of Banka and 3.6 metres in height, it also belongs to the iconographic tradition of southern India. But it was only towards the middle of the eighth century, with the advent of the Buddhist dynasty of the Śailendra, that Java experienced its finest flourishing of Buddhist art, during the period known as that of 'Central Java'.

The Art of Central Java (*c.* A.D. 750–900). Two complementary influences marked Buddhist art in this period: one, of a doctrinal nature, led to the multiplication of Buddha and Bodhisattva images; the other, a stylistic influence, instituted a type of art in the Pāla tradition.

A distinction should probably be drawn between the two kinds of works commissioned by Buddhism: art as used in monuments and works of art in bronze. The former, particularly rich in inspiration, fully expresses the originality of the workshops of Central Java. The latter, represented for the most part by numerous statuettes, usually of excellent workmanship, is more indicative of the importance of Pāla influences, and is in itself enough to justify the designation of 'Indo-Javanese' often used for this type of art. While these influences appear to have extended from copying to the importing of images that seem to belong chiefly to the Nālandā school, it should be stressed that, as throughout South-East Asia, the Indonesian image of the Buddha is heir to several different traditions and by no means an imitation of any particular style. Whether in bronze or as monumental statues, the images of the Buddha in varying forms, whether representing Śākyamuni Buddha or a stereotyped transcendent Buddha (Jina),[8] conform with the post-Gupta and Pāla iconographies. The garment, which always falls straight without folds, follows the line of the body closely, but is draped in various ways (Pls. 111, 112); the figures are seated in 'European' fashion or cross-legged in 'Indian' fashion; the marked differences in the *mudrā*s make it possible to identify the particular Buddha (Jina). The aesthetic ideal is a search for gentle serenity, tranquillity and plenitude rather than a supramundane grandeur. Despite the great iconographic interest and technical excellence of the small bronze statues, which in fact more frequently represent the divinities of the Mahāyāna pantheon than the Buddha in one form or another, and seem to cover a period that is appreciably longer than that corresponding to the construction of the great groups of buildings by the Śailendra, they arrest our attention less than the large carved works (statues and bas-reliefs), which may be regarded as representative of one of the pinnacles of Buddhist art.

It is impossible to describe here all that gives such exceptional character to the great foundations of the plains of Kedu (Borobudur, Caṇḍi Mendut and C. Pawon) and Prambanan (C. Kalasan, C. Sari, C. Sewu and C. Plaosan), or to study the symbolical significance of the architecture commissioned by the later Mahāyāna Buddhism, which tended to convert certain groups of buildings into nothing less than three-dimensional mandalas, with a host of Bodhisattvas and divinities of all ranks around a Supreme Buddha. Special reference should be made, however, to Borobudur, a vast monument whose complexity and artistic wealth have given rise to so many masterly studies. Nowhere else does the Buddhist ideal of the Śailendra period appear to be expressed so perfectly, both in its essence and in its plastic interpretation: Borobudur is a combined stupa and mandala represented by a terraced pyramid supporting a central stupa surrounded by 72 perforated stupas with fretted walls laid out in three concentric circles on the rising levels of the topmost platform. Each terrace of the pyramid is an open gallery decorated with bas-relief panels. Those in the first gallery deal exclusively with the lives of Śākyamuni Buddha: the earlier lives (*jātaka*, *avadāna*) and the Last Existence, from the Birth to the First Preaching, according to the *Lalitavistara* (Pls. 113, 114). Inset along the upper part of each terrace and the platform, 432 niches contain images in the round of Jinas seated in 'Indian' fashion, placed according to the cardinal points of the cosmos they control, and recognizable by their *mudrā*s. On the plat-

[8]For Jina in the sense of one of the Five Buddhas, see Glossary, and for their different hand-gestures, see p. 135.

110. Torso of a standing Buddha.

From Sikendeng, Celebes; 3rd–5th century A.D.*; bronze; H. 75 cm.; Djakarta Museum.*

This fine large statue can probably be regarded as the most ancient in the extensive series to be found throughout South-East Asia and probably imported from Āndhra or Sri Lanka centres. It is the only one of the early examples of images that have been found along the sea route in which the corner of the mantle is held not in the left hand but simply in the bend of the arm, as in the oldest statues in the Amarāvatī tradition.

form an identical statue of a Buddha, making the *vitarka-mudrā*, stands in each of the 64 niches, while another Buddha, making the *dharmacakra-mudrā* gesture, is placed in each of the 72 perforated stupas. Lastly, in the central stupa, originally hidden from sight, an image making the *bhūmisparśa-mudra* gesture, which seems to have been left deliberately unfinished, represents Akṣobhya as the Supreme Buddha. While the portrayal of the cosmic Buddhas is of iconographic interest, it is chiefly the bas-reliefs in the first gallery that, with a remarkable feeling for composition emphasized by the balance of the uncluttered scenes and the subtle interplay of light and shade, reveal a consummate knowledge of the texts and a highly Buddhist vision of the world.

111. Preaching Buddha seated in the 'European' fashion

From Java, exact provenance unknown; Central Javanese art, c. 8th–9th century A.D.; *bronze; H. 37 cm.; Leiden Museum.*

This image, in which the presence of the wheel and the two gazelles recalls the First Sermon, is comparable in the attitude with the colossal statue in the Bangkok Museum (Pl. 104), but differs from it both by the way the mantle is adjusted and by the *dharmacakra-mudrā*; these belong to an iconographic tradition of which we have much evidence in northern India, particularly in the Nālandā school, and which seems to have influenced Indonesian art considerably at times. The throne, with its very elaborate symbolism, affirms the universal sovereignty of the Buddha and his teaching, just as ornaments do at a later period. Concerning the close relationship between the preaching Śākyamuni and Vairocana, see the following plate and p. 135.

112. Preaching Buddha seated in the 'European' fashion

From Caṇḍi Mendut, Java; Central Javanese art, c. 800 A.D.*; stone; H. approximately 3 m.; in situ.*

Accompanied by slightly smaller images of the Bodhisattvas Lokeśvara and Vajrapāṇi, this colossal statue at Caṇḍi Mendut immediately reminds us of the Leiden bronze statue (Pl. 111), and enables us to see more clearly the difference between the schools of Dvāravatī and Central Java. Dvāravatī follows the Theravāda tradition and portrays the teaching Śākyamuni. Central Java follows the Mahāyāna tradition, and here the Buddha represented is probably Vairocana. Iconographically the two become identical and the identification depends on the intentions, whether related to Mahāyāna interests or not, of those who set up the image.

113. The Cutting of the Hair

From Borobudur, Java; Central Javanese art, c. 8th–9th century A.D.*; andesite, bas-relief; H. approximately 80 cm.; in situ.*

Among the Borobudur bas-reliefs that deal, according to the *Lalitavistara*, with the last existence of Śākyamuni Buddha, from his birth to the First Sermon (first gallery), the scene of the Cutting of the Hair keeps particularly close to the text. Around the Bodhisattva, who is stripped of his princely robes and is in the process of cutting his hair, are grouped, on one side, his horse Kaṇṭaka and his equerry Chandaka, to whom he has just given his ornaments, and, on the other side, the gods, ready to receive the sacred hair and take it up to the Heaven of the Thirty-three Gods.

114. Śākyamuni receives *kuśa* grass from the herdsman Svastika

From Borobudur, Java; central Javanese art, 8th–9th century A.D.*; andesite, bas-relief; H. approximately 80 cm.; in situ.*

Before seating himself under the Bo tree at Bodhgayā, Śākyamuni received from a simple herdsman a bundle of grass with which to make a seat. This story belongs to early legend, and as in similar events in a Buddha's life, gods take part in the scene.

Cambodia

Up till the reign of Jayavarman VII (1181–c. 1218), on the whole Buddhism played only a minor role in ancient Cambodia, where the Brahmanic cults predominated. A genuine Khmer Buddhist style, therefore, did not evolve for some time. The oldest images reflect diverse traditions that reveal a variety of influences; thereafter, for several centuries, iconography remained directly influenced by contemporary Brahmanic art.

The earliest indications of the presence of Buddhism in Cambodia are provided by Chinese historians. They relate in the first place to Fu-nan, a vast territory whose heritage Cambodia in part acquired in the second half of the sixth century, at the same freeing itself from the bonds of servitude linking it to Fu-nan. Thus we learn that in 484 a monk from India, Nāgasena, who had been sent to the Chinese court by the king of Fu-nan, brought a present of two images, one of gold, the other of white sandalwood—though there are no grounds for stating that they were actually images of the Buddha. More exact information is not available until the beginning of the sixth century, when the different states of the Indo-Chinese Peninsula seem to have vied with one another in sending images and relics; a coral image of the Buddha was presented by the embassy sent in 503; two bonzes from Fu-nan went to translate texts in 503 and 506; and after the embassy sent in 539, the emperor of China asked that the hair relic of the Buddha should be sent there. It does not seem possible to relate any particular object with any of this information: no bronze statue has been found in Cambodia similar to those discovered on the sea route (Pls. 94, 119), though it should be emphasized that the works that appear to be the most ancient (the Wat Romlok head, Pl. 115) belong to the same tradition and already bear witness to the existence of local workshops, since they are carved from local sandstone. Nevertheless, the seventh- to eighth-century images chiefly reflect the diversity of the influences at work in Cambodia, some linked to the successive waves already noted throughout South-East Asia (Pls. 116, 118), others to the influence of schools firmly established in neighbouring countries (Dvāravatī, Śrīvijaya). The discovery at Oc-eo of a small Gandhāra head and a Chinese bronze statue confirms that the southern region served as a crossroads during the early centuries of the spread of Buddhism throughout the region of the southern seas. But the preponderance of Brahmanic cults, observed as early as the end of the fifth century, and historical developments did not favour either the growth of communities or the development of a unified style. I-tsing, who spent some time in Sumatra at the end of the seventh century, gives us this information about Cambodia: 'Buddhism flourished there, but a wicked king has now expelled and exterminated them all, and there are no members of the Buddhist fraternity at all, while adherents of other religions live intermingled. . . .' Even allowing for exaggeration, it was still the case that the political situation, with the secession that took place at the beginning of the eighth century and the threat from Indonesia leading up to the birth of the kingdom of Angkor in 802, could not possibly have created a climate favourable to Buddhism. Lastly, with the exception of small fragments of terracotta bas-reliefs (Angkor Borei), pre-Angkorian Buddhist art is represented only by statues of stone, bronze or even wood. Nearly always of a remarkable plastic quality, their diversity is due far less to chronology than to their stylistic affiliations.

115. Buddha head

From Wat Romlok (Prei Krabas), Cambodia; pre-Angkorian art, c. 5th–6th century A.D.*; sandstone; H. 25 cm.; National Museum, Phnom Penh.*

Cambodia has not yet yielded any bronze statues belonging to the Amarāvatī tradition. On the other hand, a sandstone statue, which is unfortunately very much damaged, and above all this remarkable head prove that the future Khmer kingdom did not remain outside the stream of the earliest dissemination of images. Works such as this even show that from a very early date what may properly be called local schools of sculpture, working from imported models, had achieved complete technical mastery of the subject.

116. Standing Buddha

From Wat Romlok (Prei Krabas), Cambodia; pre-Angkorian art, c. 6th–7th century A.D.*; sandstone; H. 90 cm.; National Museum, Phnom Penh.*

The mutilations suffered by this statue deprive us of valuable clues and make dating difficult. In particular, we should have liked to be able to see the hanging ends of the robe; the transparency of its treatment is very much in the post-Gupta style. In any case, the long, graceful proportions of the image and the supple lines of the hips are far removed from the hieratic style prevailing in Dvāravatī art. The two lotuses shown under the feet are a rare feature of images of the Buddha, though they are found in an Amarāvatī relief now in the British Museum (Pl. 20).

117. Buddha seated in meditation

From Phum Thmei (Kong Pisei), Cambodia; pre-Angkorian art, c. 7th century A.D.*; sandstone; H. 90 cm.; National Museum, Phnom Penh.*

The smiling serenity of this fine statue already foreshadows the basic trends of Khmer Buddhist statuary as they were to be developed at the end of the twelfth century (Pl. 249). Like the preceding image, it shows the originality and independence of certain Khmer workshops as compared with the Dvāravatī school, in spite of the latter's extensive spread and influence throughout the central part of the peninsula.

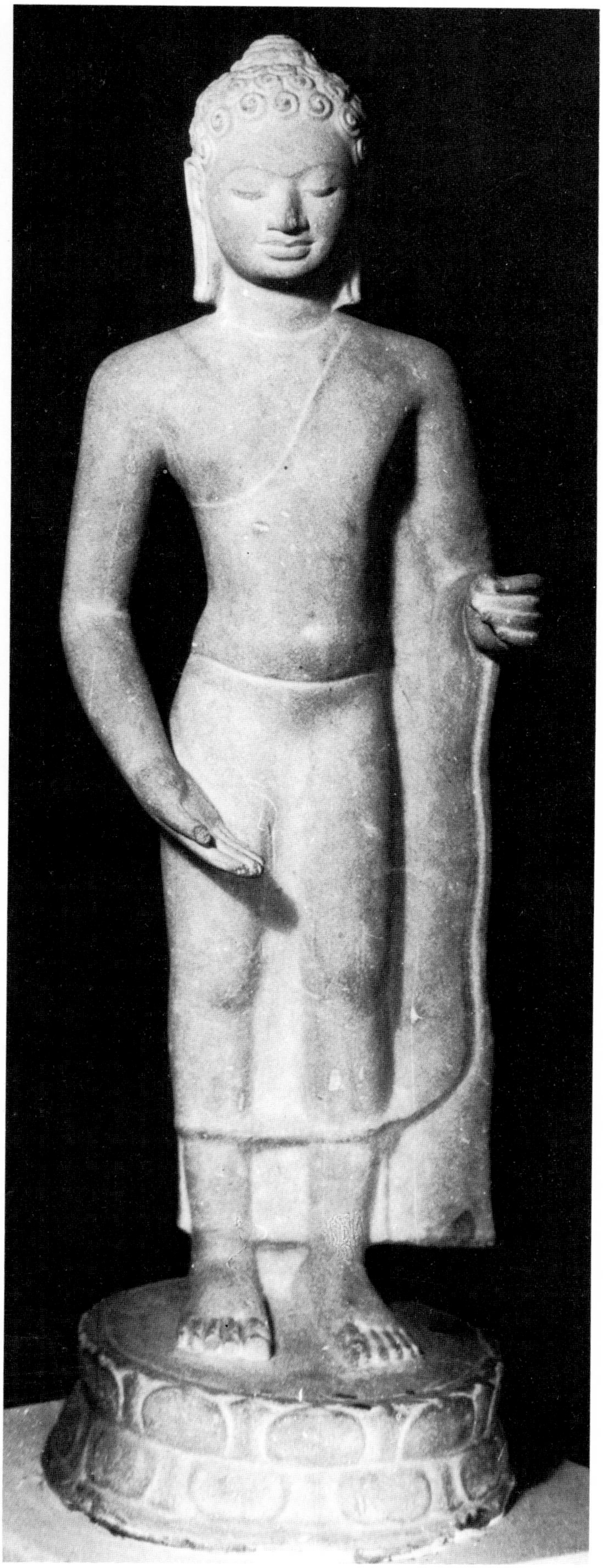

118. Standing Buddha

From Tuol Ta Hoy (Kompong Speu), Cambodia; pre-Angkorian art, c. 7th–8th century A.D.*; sandstone; H. 88 cm.; National Museum, Phnom Penh.*

This statue provides us with evidence of the popularity of certain types of image. The only reason for the closeness of the right hand to the body is the need to ensure solidity, due to the change from working in bronze to carving directly in stone. The strength of tradition should be noted: the left hand remains raised and closed, as it was when it held one end of the robe, which is not the case here.

Champa

Formerly an Indianized kingdom on the eastern coast of the peninsula, mentioned under the name of Lin-i by Chinese historians in the second century A.D., Champa was gradually absorbed into Vietnam, which having become independent of China in A.D. 939, began a steady advance southwards. As in Cambodia at that time, Brahmanism was predominant in Champa, and Buddhism played only a minor role. The most ancient images, a small bronze torso (Quang-Khe), and especially the Dong-duong statue (Pl. 119) (the most beautiful and outstanding of the series related to the Badullā Buddha, Pl. 98), are not adequate proof of either the importance of Buddhism or the existence of local workshops before the seventh century (Pl. 120). More instructive is the reference to '1350 Buddhist works in 564 bundles' as being part of the booty carried off by Liu-fang from the capital during his campaign in 605. Unfortunately there is no known image that can be ascribed to this period, and images of the Buddha are very rare up to the third quarter of the ninth century. A number of bronze statues found in the south (Dang-binh), associated with the cult of Bodhisattvas, are of the Śrīvijaya school, and thus bear witness, as in Thailand, to the dissemination of the Mahāyāna promoted by the expansionism of Indonesia from the end of the eighth century onwards, also borne out by Cham inscriptions. At all events it was the Mahāyāna that took root in Champa, together with a syncretistic Buddhism that was imposed for a time by the Indrapura dynasty with the foundation of the great temple of Dong-duong in 875. We cannot here analyze the different elements that give the art of Dong-duong its exceptional originality, but it should be noted that in varying proportions, it associates Indonesian and Chinese influences in a highly individual and absolutely unique interpretation of the supramundane beauty of the Buddha (Pl. 121). An art enamoured of power rather than classical beauty, and whose influence was rapidly to fade away, it may well represent the most astonishing aesthetic experience produced by Buddhism.

119. Standing Buddha ▷

From Dong-duong, Vietnam (Champa); c. 5th–6th century A.D.*; bronze; overall H. 122 cm.; Vietnam National Museum, Saigon.*

This statue, as remarkable for its plastic qualities as for its size and state of preservation, belongs to the oldest series of images found throughout South-East Asia. Representative of a tradition that is probably somewhat later than that of the Celebes torso (Pl. 110), it is comparable in the gesture and the adjustment of the robe with the Badullā Buddha (Pl. 98). However, we cannot be certain that it is of Sri Lanka origin; it will be noted in particular that the *ūrṇā*, or mark in the middle of the forehead, is never seen in Sri Lanka images.

120. The Great Departure and the Cutting of the Hair

From Dong-duong, Vietnam (Champa); after A.D. 875; sandstone, bas-relief; overall H. 67 cm.; Da-nang Museum.

The pedestal of the main sanctuary at Dong-duong was ornamented with a series of bas-relief panels in a powerful and somewhat crude style, illustrating the life of the Buddha and, probably, various *jātakas*. While some scenes are difficult to identify on account of their originality and economy of style, below we can make out the preparation for the Great Departure and, above, the Cutting of the Hair; the composition is slightly reminiscent of that of Borobudur (Pl. 113), except that the Bodhisattva is shown the other way round and the horse Kaṇṭaka is replaced by a hunter bearing his bow.

121. Colossal Buddha head

From Dong-duong, Vietnam (Champa); after A.D. 875; sandstone; H. 68 cm.; Musée Guimet, Paris.

Founded in A.D. 875, the great Mahāyāna temple at Dong-dương, where the preceding image was discovered, saw the flowering of what was the most original style not only in Champa but throughout the whole of South-East Asia, so free does it appear to be from any of the influences it has undergone, retaining only the essential iconographic data. This head, probably of Vairocana, seems to stand apart from all traditions: the flattened nose, powerful lips surmounted by a thick moustache, the curling hair falling in locks, and the *uṣṇīṣa* replaced by what is in fact a broad-petalled lotus bud.

3. KASHMIR AND NEPAL

Despite the differences that separate them, these two countries may be studied conveniently together, since there are several features that they have in common. Both exerted an influence in the spread of devotion to the Buddha and in the transmitting of iconographic forms, an influence that might seem to be rather out of proportion to their size. The chief beneficiary of this influence was Tibet, which is known to have been in contact with both countries from the seventh century onwards. Originally both were small kingdoms hidden away in remote Himalayan valleys. Kashmir was limited to the Valley of the Jhelum in the area of Srinagar, the present capital, but the title 'Srinagar', simply meaning 'Glorious City', has been applied to more than one such foundation. During certain periods the rulers of this small valley exercized a kind of hegemony over neighbouring areas, and in the eighth century during the reign of King Lalitāditya-Muktāpīḍa nearly all northern and western India was forced to accept the suzerainty of Kashmir, but this period of glory was short-lived.[9] Similarly, Nepal has been limited historically to what is now known as the Nepal Valley, comprising the ancient cities of Pātan and Bhadgaon, Kirtipur and Kathmandu, which was the last to grow in size and importance, when it was made the capital by the invading Gorkhas in the latter part of the eighteenth century. Under this new leadership Nepal embarked upon a period of conquest, and it was as a simple result of this that Śākyamuni's birthplace at Lumbinī on the edge of the Indian plain eventually fell within modern Nepalese territory. One often reads that he was born in Nepal, but while this is true in a modern geographical sense, historically it is a misleading statement. In the same way it may be said that while the Emperor Aśoka certainly visited Lumbinī, it is very unlikely that he ever visited Nepal, for Nepal might not have existed in the third century B.C. In fact the first reference to Nepal as a known land is found in an inscription on a pillar at Allahabad commemorating the conquests of the Gupta emperor, Samudragupta, in the fourth century A.D., and nothing has been found in the Nepal Valley so far to suggest that Indian influences reached this remote land before that time. Excavation of the four great so-called 'Aśok-*caitya*s' around Pātan might provide evidence of earlier contacts, but simply from their name and their shape nothing can be deduced with any certainty (Pl. 122). So far as Buddhist sculpture is concerned, nothing pre-Gupta has yet been discovered. Such was the fame of Aśoka in Buddhist tradition that foundations were ascribed to him far and wide. Thus the first 'Glorious City' (Srīnagarī) of Kashmir, of which archaeological remains are found at the village of Pandrenthan some five kilometres above the present capital, is also said to have been founded by him. Yet another city was established much further down the valley at the place known now as Ushkur, a modern form of Huviṣkapura, that is to say the 'City of Huviṣka', who was the successor of the great Kuṣāṇa emperor Kaniṣka. Here we may note a fundamental difference in the influences to which Kashmir on the one hand and Nepal on the other were subject. While Kashmir was

[9]See H. Goetz, 'The conquest of Northern and Western India by Lalitāditya-Muktāpīḍa of Kashmir', *Journal of the Bombay Branch, Royal Asiatic Society*, vol. 28 (1952), p. 43 ff. Now reprinted in a general volume, for which see note 12 below.

122. The eastern of four 'Aśok-*caityas*', Pātan, Nepal

These four great stupas are built one on each side of the old Buddhist city of Pātan, which was certainly founded before the fifth century A.D. It lies just south of Kathmandu. Apart from later legends, no indications have been discovered to suggest that Aśoka ever came here and had stupas constructed. The local name of this particular stupa is Teta-thur (*thur* is Newāri for *stūpa*).

primarily open to influences from Gandhāra and the north-west, Nepal was open to influences from the Ganges-Jumna Valley. Certainly from the Gupta period on, these same influences began to affect Kashmir until at last in the medieval period (eighth to thirteenth centuries) they predominate altogether. However, in the earlier period, from which unhappily so little remains, Kashmir experienced a rather different cultural history.

Kashmir

One of the earliest firm references to Kashmir as an important Buddhist land is found in the Sinhalese chronicle, the *Mahāvaṃsa*, which lists the monasteries (XXIX: 29–43) in India represented at the consecration in A.D. 104 of the Great Stupa of Anurādhapura in Sri Lanka. Here the second largest delegation is listed as having come from Kashmir. For references to Buddhism as a flourishing religion in these north-western regions we must refer to the travelogue of the Chinese pilgrim Fa-hsien, who passed through on his way to the Ganges-Jumna Valley about A.D. 400. He delights in recounting the legendary origin of the many stupas that he then saw. The main events of Śākyamuni's last life on earth were commemorated in the Ganges-Jumna Valley, but elsewhere the faithful were free to erect stupas in honour of his great acts in previous lives, for example, the giving of his flesh to save the life of a dove from a pursuing hawk, the giving of his body as food to a hungry tigress, or the giving of his eyes to a blind beggar. In Kashmir the foundations of such ruined stupas have been excavated, but very little of iconographic interest survives. The Huns, who first invaded Gandhāra in the mid-fifth century and who subsequently caused such havoc in north-western India, seem to have made Kashmir their base for raids on surrounding areas. Thus traces of the earlier Gandhāra art are very rare. The Archaeological Museum in Srinagar and museums abroad preserve a few items, interesting mainly for their rarity, which come from excavations on the sites of the two earlier cities at

123. Buddha head

From Ushkur, Kashmir; 7th–8th century A.D.; terracotta; H. 20.3 cm.; British Museum, London.

This is one of the rare non-metallic Buddhist pieces surviving from pre-Moslem Kashmir. The wavy hair is typical of the earlier Gandhāran style, which presumably persisted there.

124. Standing Buddha

From Kashmir; possibly 8th century A.D.; bronze; H. 26.7 cm.; Nelson Gallery of Art, Atkins Museum of Fine Arts, Kansas City, Missouri.

While not a particularly elegant figure, this statue may give some idea, on a very reduced scale, of the appearance of the enormous Buddha image set up by King Lalitāditya. The robe, while hanging in heavy folds as on Gandhāran images, none the less tends to cling to the body in a manner reminiscent of Gupta images. The hair-style with its little 'snail-like' curls is also Gupta.

Pandrenthan and at Ushkur (Pl. 123). Among such small plaques, broken heads and defaced images, one might mention a small seated Buddha clad in the typically heavy folded religious garments preferred by Gandhāran craftsmen, which has been preserved in high relief on a small plaque.[10] However, no sequence of styles or influences can be deduced from such scanty remains.

When Hsüan-tsang visited Kashmir (A.D. 631–33), the fortunes of Buddhism had been somewhat restored by a new local dynasty, the Kārkota, and he was well received by the reigning king at the capital, Pravarapura, named after its founder Pravarasena II (c. 409–69). This, the third important city of Kashmir, has survived on the same site as modern Srinagar, but scarcely anything Buddhist remains. It is well known that Buddhist monasteries were usually constructed on the outskirts of cities, and thus it is not surprising that at the village of Harwan, one and a half miles away, excavations have revealed the existence of just such a Buddhist monastery. Amongst the ruined foundations of stupas, chapels and dwellings, only broken fingers and toes and terracotta curls that once belonged to numerous Buddha images have been found.[11]

Yet a fourth city, Parihāsapura, was founded by the great conqueror Lalitāditya-Muktāpīḍa in the eighth century some twenty kilometres below Pravarapura (modern Srinagar), and during his reign he continued to embellish the former cities as well as his new capital with Hindu and Buddhist monuments. Professor Hermann Goetz in a number of articles, now conveniently gathered together in one volume, has revived the memories of the glorious times of Kashmir during this exceptional period.[12] Thus he reconstructs for us in imagination the enormous standing copper image of the Buddha, set up by Lalitāditya in his capital but of which now nothing remains except for the massive foundations of the shrine constructed to contain it.[13] Although none survive in India, such colossal Buddha images are known from elsewhere, especially from Bāmiyān in Afghanistan. This area was in any case subject to Lalitāditya, and the idea may have come from there. Goetz emphasizes the eclecticism of Kashmir art during the reign of a king who was able to import images and religious treasures of all kinds, as well as the actual craftsmen themselves, from regions as far distant as Central Asia on the one hand and central and western India on the other.[14] A Bodhisattva image, now preserved in the Archaeological Museum, Srinagar, but which once probably adorned a stupa erected by Lalitāditya's minister Cankuna, himself a Central Asian, certainly suggests Central Asian or even Chinese affinities.[15] A second such image, showing similar affinities and preserved in the same museum, was found at Pandrenthan.[16] It is likely, however, that a late Gupta style generally prevailed, although very little survives from this period (Pl. 124). After the death of

[10]See Ram Chandra Kak, *Handbook of the Archaeological and Numismatic Sections of the Sri Pratap Singh Museum, Srinagar* (Calcutta, 1923), p. 12.
[11]Ram Chandra Kak, *Ancient Monuments of Kashmir* (London, 1933), pp. 105–11.
[12]H. Goetz, *Studies in the History and Art of Kashmir and the Indian Himalaya* (Wiesbaden, 1969).
[13]*Ibid.*, pp. 51–52.
[14]*Ibid.*, pp. 33–34.
[15]Kak, *Handbook*, p. 43; and Goetz, *op. cit.*, pl. 18.
[16]Kak, *op. cit.*, p. 32; and Goetz, *op. cit.*, pl. 17.

Lalitāditya, his immense empire, so loosely held together, fell apart, and except for a brief period of stability and prosperity during the ninth century, internal strife and foreign invasion has totally wrecked Kashmir's Buddhist heritage.

Nepal

Nepal has suffered few invasions and unlike Kashmir it is covered with remains, both Hindu and Buddhist, from the fifth century A.D. onwards. Inscriptions from this century make it clear that Pātan already existed as a conglomeration of monastic houses and that for the upkeep of these, land was allocated by royal decree. Up to the beginning of the seventh century the valley was ruled by a strong line of kings belonging to the Licchavi dynasty. Like their Gupta counterparts in India, they were Hindus, with the possible exception of Vṛṣadeva, who ruled towards the end of the fourth century, but they were benefactors of Buddhist monasteries as well as of Hindu temples.[17] From this earlier period several Buddha and Bodhisattva images as well as small stupas have survived. As it was common practice to enlarge stupas by enshrining the earlier ones in later constructions, there are likely to be many more such without our knowledge. According to the national terminology, these early examples are known as Licchavi, but their close relationship with the neighbouring Gupta style of the Ganges-Jumna Valley is immediately apparent. A particularly fine early example is a small standing Buddha image, with both arms broken and the face rather spoiled, in the Cā-bāhī, three kilometres or so north of Kathmandu (Pl. 125).[18] Other early images are set into the sides of the main stupa there, while yet another fine example of a small standing Buddha is inset into the side of the great northern stupa of Pātan (Pl. 126). Other places where such early images are frequently found are the *praṇāli*, the picturesque watering-places, nowadays almost invariably below ground-level and some of them very deep indeed, where the villagers and townsfolk go to draw their water from elegant stone-carved water-spouts (Pl. 127). Thus another small Buddha image may be seen in the *praṇāli* in front of the Taṃgaḥ-bāhā in Pātan, side by side with a very fine early image of Śiva and his partner.[19] The gossamer-like drapery of these early Buddha figures, the fullness of their limbs and the rounded, finely moulded faces suggest the earlier Gupta period and the very best of Mathurā influences.

The Nepal Valley covers a very small area, some thirty kilometres from east to west and only twenty from north to south. Not only have stupas been rebuilt and refaced continually but temples also have been continually repaired and reconstructed. Thus earlier images had to make way for the later ones that were continually being produced. Many of the earlier ones must have disappeared, presumably underground where they await the excavator, and

[17]The evidence that Vṛṣadeva may have been a Buddhist derives from early inscriptions. See R. Gnoli, *Nepalese Inscriptions in Gupta Characters* (Rome, 1956), part 1, p. 2, lines 7–10, and especially p. 116, line 9. These references are interesting as providing the earliest firm references to the existence of Buddhism in Nepal. It may well have been there very much earlier, but evidence for this is still awaited.

[18]Cā-bāhī is said to be an abbreviation of Carumati-vihāra, that is to say the monastery (*vihāra*) of Carumati, supposedly Aśoka's daughter, who is said to have founded it. The normal local Newār form of *vihāra* is *bāhā*, which will be noticed in several names quoted in the text. The form *bāhi* seems to be a kind of diminutive, applied to smaller establishments. See also p. 411.

[19]See D. L. Snellgrove, 'Shrines and temples of Nepal', *Arts Asiatiques*, 8 (1961), p. 5.

125. Standing Buddha

From Nepal; c. 5th century A.D.*; limestone; the Cā-bāhī, Kathmandu.*

This image is of the Licchavi period, corresponding to the Gupta period of India. Note the typical 'snail-like' arrangement of the hair. The right hand was presumably held in the typical *abhaya-mudrā* (gesture of fearlessness), while the left hand held the robe. It could be fifth century or even earlier.

126. Standing Buddha

Another early image of the Licchavi period, preserved by being set into the revetted side of the northern stupa (Yampi-thur) of Pātan, Nepal.

127. An early Nepalese Buddha image

From Paśupatināth, Nepal; c. 5th–6th century A.D.

This image is in characteristic Gupta style. Many such early images survive in sacred places, inset or standing by stupas (see pp. 171, 177), or even let into the side-walls of watering-places typical of the towns of Nepal. The continual creativeness of Newār craftsmen, still uninterrupted after at least fourteen centuries of satisfying Buddhist clients, creates a surfeit of images, and the older ones are usually perforce replaced by the more recent. The older ones are not thrown away but are placed where they may receive some passing respect.

128. Stupa at the Dhvāka-bāhā, Kathmandu, Nepal

This small Licchavi stupa stands in the courtyard at the Dhvāka-bāhā on the old, northern side of Kathmandu. Apart from the style of the inset Buddha and Bodhisattva images, an early date is indicated (? fifth century) by the inscription in Gupta lettering on the base. This simply gives the well-known formula, 'The Tathāgata has told the cause of the elements that are causally produced, and of their stoppage, too, the Great Ascetic has spoken'. The small inset Buddha images are all identical figures in the posture of meditation (*dhyāna-mudrā*). Thus they precede the time when Buddha images were differentiated in accordance with the theory of cosmic directional Buddhas (see p. 135). Concerning the Bodhisattva images see Pls. 129, 130.

129. Śākyamuni as Bodhisattva

From the Dhvāka-bāhā, Kathmandu, Nepal.

This is another early image of Śakyamuni as Bodhisattva, for he appears here on the lower part of the little Licchavi stupa in the Dhvāka-bāhā in Kathmandu (see Pl. 128), side by side with Avalokiteśvara (Pl. 130). The connection with Gupta India is unmistakable.

130. Padmapāṇi (Avalokiteśvara)

From the Dhvāka-bāhā, Kathmandu, Nepal.

This Padmapāṇi (Avalokiteśvara) is inset into the side of the same stupa as Pl. 129. These two images of Śākyamuni and Padmapāṇi are duplicated on the other two sides. One may compare the enshrined Avalokiteśvara image in Pl. 268 for its basic similarity.

131. The birth of Śākyamuni

Relief sculpture; from the Sundara Fountain, Deo Pātan, Nepal; early Licchavi period; blue-grey limestone; H. 84 cm., W. 33 cm.; Nepal Museum, Kathmandu.

This relief shows Śākyamuni immediately after his miraculous birth from the right side of his mother, Queen Māyā. She conforms to the type of tree-spirit (*yakṣinī*) noted on the early stupas, and it was probably the typical stance of the *yakṣinī* that suggested the unusual manner of birth. For the account as given in the Theravādin canon, see E. J. Thomas, *The Life of the Buddha as Legend and History* (London, 1949), p. 31: 'As other women give birth sitting or lying down, not so does the Bodhisattva's mother give birth. The Bodhisattva's mother gives birth to the Bodhisattva standing. . . . When the Bodhisattva is born, two streams of water fall from the sky, one of cold and one of hot water, wherewith they perform the washing for the Bodhisattva and his mother. As soon as born, the Bodhisattva firmly standing with even feet goes towards the north with seven long steps, a white parasol being held over him. He surveys all the quarters, and in a lordly voice says: "I am the chief in the world. I am the best in the world. I am the first in the world. This is my last birth. There is now no existence again."' This sculpture has recently been transferred to the Nepal Museum. Compare Pls. 37, 38.

those that we find nowadays fixed into the sides of stupas or into the side-walls of watering-places represent just some of the displaced images whose shrines have been occupied by later models. All early stupas, small as well as large, may be referred to as 'Aśok-*caityas*', and it seems to be assumed popularly that they all go back to the time of Aśoka. They are mostly found in monastic courtyards, of which Pātan and the old parts of Bhadgaon and Kathmandu are veritable labyrinths, and the earliest of such foundations may be assigned more realistically to the fourth or rather the fifth century A.D. rather than the third century B.C. A particularly fine example of an early Gupta-style stupa with inset Buddha and Bodhisattva images stands in the courtyard of the Dhvāka-bāhā in Kathmandu (Pl. 128). A seated Buddha figure is inset into each of the four sides just under the dome, and in every case this figure is in a seated meditating posture (*dhyāna-mudrā*). The standing images set into the four sides below are Śākyamuni and Avalokiteśvara repeated on opposite sides (Pls. 129, 130). Not only is the period of production guaranteed by an inscription in Gupta letters on the base, but iconographically this piece represents the earliest Mahāyāna period before Buddhas and Bodhisattvas were arranged in stereotyped 'cosmic' sets of five. The later stupas of Nepal, representing religious traditions that were current from the eighth century onwards, if not earlier, usually have the four directional Buddhas, Akṣobhya, Ratnasambhava, Amitābha and Amoghasiddhi, as listed above on page 135, inset into each of the four sides, while Bodhisattvas, wherever present beneath the Buddhas, are distinguished accordingly: Vajrapāṇi beneath Akṣobhya to the east, Ratnapāṇi beneath Ratnasambhava to the south, Padmapāṇi (Avalokiteśvara) beneath Amitābha to the west, Viśvapāṇi beneath Amoghasiddhi to the north.

Within the monasteries the chief focal points for the cult of the Buddha are, as always, the stupa, with or without inset Buddha images, and the Buddha image itself. The stupa stands regularly in the centre of the monastic courtyard. It may be of modest proportions, some two metres high, or in a few special cases it may have been so enlarged as to tower above the highest surrounding buildings, as in the Sīghaḥ-bāhā at Kathmandu. However central to the cult and however varied in its forms the Buddha image later became, the stupa never ceased to be the primary Buddhist monument. The main Buddha image of the monastery resides within a special shrine, usually at the opposite side from the entrance of the main courtyard, and the shrine is surmounted by a tiered-roof temple in which the treasures of the monastery—manuscripts, small images and religious paintings—are preserved. The most popular Buddha images represent Śākyamuni or Akṣobhya (who, after all, is in origin a special manifestation of Śākyamuni at the moment of his calling the earth-goddess to witness his fitness for Buddhahood); of Bodhisattvas the most common are Maitreya, the Future Buddha, and the all-compassionate Avalokiteśvara. An early and unique Nepalese sculpture of Śākyamuni's birth can be seen in Pl. 131.

The great importance of the Nepal Valley in the history of the Buddha image derives from the fact that so many monasteries, however much they have been rebuilt over the centuries, still survive. The many Indian monasteries, of which nothing now remains but ruined stupas and foundations of various buildings, were often very much larger than the Nepalese establishments, but in Nepal it is still possible to see for oneself exactly how the many monasteries of Kashmir, now lost for ever, might have appeared in their prime, and we can certainly see how the many Buddha images that were produced in India and elsewhere were actually employed in the cult. The same usage was repeated in Tibet, but this subject will be treated in the next chapter together with later developments in Kashmir and Nepal.

4. AFGHANISTAN AND CENTRAL ASIA

The first representations of the various forms of the Buddha in present-day Afghanistan fall properly within the domain of Gandhāran art, which has already been discussed in detail. Yet the iconography of Gandhāran art in Afghanistan differs in certain points, though not in general, from that of the north-west; in order to understand these points of difference we must bear in mind certain evidence from art and history for which archaeology is now providing us with ever more abundant information.

Let us first consider Ai Khānum, the city in northern Afghanistan on the banks of the Oxus, which the French Archaeological Delegation began to investigate in 1964.[20] It was here that the presence of a centre of genuinely Greek artistic culture in Bactria was first revealed; some of the works found there (third century B.C.) could easily be thought to have been produced in Greece itself, but there are also heads—in stucco and in unbaked clay—that indicate a stylistic evolution towards distinctive new forms, although they are still definitely 'classical'. This implantation of Greek motifs in the distant regions of Bactria and the territory beyond the Oxus is also attested by the unbaked clay sculptures (first century B.C.?) of Khalchayan, which the Soviet archaeologist G. A. Pugachenkova considered to be one of the first manifestations of art commissioned by the Kuṣāṇas,[21] and also by those of Surkh Kotal, on which a work by G. Fussman is shortly to be published.

These works of art, which are quite distinct from Buddhist art, are related to others, of which we know more, whose style and subject-matter indicate that they belong to the Gandhāran tradition. This tradition has been well documented for some years now, thanks to the excavations of the French Archaeological Delegation at Haḍḍa (near Jalalabad, in eastern Afghanistan), which are yielding an abundant harvest of stucco sculptures, particularly of heads.[22] To these have recently been added the clay sculptures discovered by the Italian Archaeological Mission in the oldest strata at Tapa Sardār, near Ghazni[23] as well as those from the Afghan excavations at Haḍḍa, which are also of stucco and clay.

Definitive publications on these impressive groups of sculpture are still in preparation, and their dating is very uncertain, although they probably date from the third and fourth

[20] P. Bernard et al., 'Les fouilles d'Ai Khanoum', 1 (Campagnes 1965, 1966, 1967, 1968), *Mémoires de la Délégation Archéologique Française en Afghanistan*, 21 (Paris, 1973). For the succeeding expeditions, see the reports by Bernard in *Comptes Rendus de l'Académie des Inscriptions et Belles Lettres* (1970), pp. 301–49; (1971), pp. 385–452.

[21] G. A. Pugachenkova, *Skulptura Khalchajana* (Moscow, 1971).

[22] J. Barthoux, 'Les fouilles de Haḍḍa': 1. Stupas et sites', *Mémoires de la Délégation Archéologique Française en Afghanistan*, 4 (Paris, 1933); idem, 'Les fouilles de Haḍḍa: 3. Figures et figurines—Album photographique', *Mémoires de la Délégation Archéologique Française en Afghanistan*, 6 (Paris, 1930).

[23] M. Taddei, *Il Vetro*, 16, 5–6 (1972), pp. 549–61; also *East and West*, 21, 3–4 (1971), p. 442, figs. 3–4; 22, 3–4 (1972), p. 383, fig. 14; 23, 3–4 (1973), p. 420, figs. 17–18.

centuries A.D. What is certain is that there is a great divergence in style between the stucco sculptures from Haḍḍa, which are wholly Gandhāran, and the clay ones from Tapa Sardār and from Haḍḍa itself,[24] most of which have definitely classical, Hellenistic elements. One of the most surprising examples is the niche from the temple courtyard at Tapa Shotor (Haḍḍa), in which the Buddha is accompanied by Vajrapāṇi seated with his thunderbolt (*vajra*) leaning against his knee (Pl. 132).[25] We can see what a faithful transposition of a classical prototype the figure of Vajrapāni is—clearly a Heracles, sensitively executed by an artist accustomed to the Hellenistic style and fully master of a technique that enabled him to execute a male figure entirely classical in both form and iconography; the lion's skin that girdles the loins of this 'Heracles' and falls between his legs is really a skilful piece of Hellenistic drapery. By contrast the style of the figure of the Buddha, although classical in origin, is obviously modified by Gandhāran culture. The folds of the monastic garment —flat, regular and almost parallel—indicate not merely a difference of material or manner but an explicit qualitative difference that causes the figure of the Buddha to stand out from its surroundings.

The example that we have given was chosen as being a particularly clear case, but it is obvious that the phenomenon is not confined to Haḍḍa. We are dealing now with a period in which it was no longer acceptable in Gandhāran iconography for the Buddha Śākyamuni to be shown in the context of an episode in a narrative and on the same level of importance as the other characters, as was the case in the oldest reliefs of the school. The Buddha has now assumed greater proportions, his position is one of rigid centrality and the very style in which he is depicted, as we have just seen, differentiates him from the other figures; his 'divinization' is henceforth clearly reflected in the iconography, and this is all the more evident because here in Afghanistan more than elsewhere, the other figures continue to follow Hellenistic models.

Something very similar probably occurred further west in the areas around Ghazni: this seems evident from the sculptures in unbaked clay dating from the earliest phase at Tapa Sardār, which exhibit very close stylistic and iconographical similarities not only with the clay sculptures of Haḍḍa but also with some stucco pieces from Taxila in the Punjab (Kālawān, Jauliān, etc.). However, we cannot be definite on this point owing to the fragmentary state in which the sculptures of Tapa Sardār have come down to us.

Somewhat later perhaps, but in the same line of development, are the unbaked clay sculptures of Tapa Maranjān (Kabul), now housed in the Kabul Museum (Pl. 135).[26] In these we can discern even more clearly the characteristics that link these Afghan works in unbaked clay with the stucco sculpture of Gandhāra. The Buddha (or Bodhisattva) is depicted henceforth only in a purely architectural setting; his image is placed in a niche, so that it is isolated, or rather confined within its own space. This space may be a niche, or it may be the base panel of a stupa, with pilasters around it, as at Haḍḍa and in all the

[24]Various accounts in the reviews *Afghanistan* (in English) and *Āryānā* (in Persian); also S. and M. Mostamindi, *Arts Asiatiques*, 19 (1969), pp. 15–36.

[25]*Afghanistan*, 26, 1352, 4 (1974), back cover and pp. 75–77.

[26]On Tapa Maranjān, see J. Hackin et al., 'Diverses recherches archéologiques en Afghanistan (1933–1940)', *Mémoires de la Délégation Archéologique Française en Afghanistan*, 8 (Paris, 1959), pp. 7–12.

132. Buddha and disciples

From Haḍḍa, sacred ground of Tapa Shotor, Afghanistan; Gandhāran art, 3rd century A.D.*; clay.*

The architectonic and figurative context of this group, which was discovered in the course of excavations carried out recently by the Afghan Institute of Archaeology, has not yet been given the attention it deserves. Although even the image of the Buddha has a certain Hellenistic air about it, both in the ordering of the volumes and in the drapery, a comparison with the Vajrapāṇi in the form of Heracles at the Buddha's side remains surprising. Whereas the classicism of the Buddha actually seems to be mediated and rethought in terms of the Gandhāran experience, that of Vajrapāṇi suggests, on the contrary, direct contact with the Mediterranean world—one might almost say the intervention of an Hellenic artist. The central and frontal position of the Buddha and the fact that he is represented on a much larger scale than the other figures strengthen this impression.

133. Buddha head

From Tapa Kalān, Haḍḍa, Afghanistan; Gandhāran art, c. 4th century A.D.*; stucco; H. 30 cm.; Kabul Museum.*

One of the pieces of sculpture yielded by the old Barthoux diggings, this head is among the purest examples of the image of the Enlightened One produced by the late Gandhāran school. The Hellenistic model is tempered by the presence of representational conventions of Indian origin, as, for instance, the form of the eyes, clearly marked planes of the eyebrows, and the shape of the lips. Other specifically iconographical elements, such as the *ūrṇā*, the *uṣṇīṣa* and the elongated ear-lobes, are of course Indian.

134. Two Buddha figures in the meditation posture

From Stupa 11, Haḍḍa, sacred ground of Tapa Shotor, Afghanistan; Gandhāran art, c. 4th century A.D.; *images and architectonic elements moulded in stucco on stone.*

This is the base of one of the stupas brought to light by the excavations carried out by the Afghan Institute of Archaeology. The images of the Buddha, which are almost all alike, are set between plain-shafted pilasters that are topped with Corinthian capitals. Here the influence of classical models is much attenuated, as is apparent both in the considerable simplification of the drapery and in the architectonic elements, the relationship between which follows a different canon from the Hellenistic one. These images, which are reflections of the single central figure of the Buddha, as represented by the stupa itself, suggest his all-pervading presence.

135. A Bodhisattva in the meditation posture

From Tapa Maranjān, Kabul, Afghanistan; Gandhāran art, c. 4th century A.D.*; clay; H. (excluding head) 94 cm.; W. (at knee level) 95 cm.; H. of head 28.3 cm.; Kabul Museum.*

In 1933, the French Archaeological Delegation in Afghanistan carried out excavations on the hill known as Tapa Maranjān, near Kabul, bringing to light a religious building constructed over several periods. In a wall niche was found this Bodhisattva, a copy of a Gandhāran model that has been identified beyond doubt. The apparel consists of a *paridhāna*, or under-garment, tucked up at the waist, an *uttarīya*, or upper garment, which is a kind of wide shawl, and a turban. The same items of dress (and the same necklaces) are found in Gandharān art when members of the local Indian aristocracy are represented. In this period of the iconography of the north-west and Afghanistan, jewellery is one of the most obvious features distinguishing a Bodhisattva from a Buddha. Only later does the Buddha appear with necklaces.

Gandhāran temples in Pakistan from Taxila to Butkara (Swat). The scenes from the life of the Buddha and from the *jātaka*s then gradually disappear or become much reduced; they are no longer narrative accounts of an event but mere allusions to it. Yet within these limits the artists of Haḍḍa were capable of producing a masterpiece, very freely composed, such as the 'Preparation for the Great Renunciation'.[27] Most often, however, the elements that make the depicted scene comprehensible are extremely slight: the boy, who, with nothing else to offer, offers 'alms of dust', or the tiny lion that licks the foot of the Enlightened One.[28]

This development can hardly be explained in terms of religion. The appearance of a type of hieratic image, standing out in a narrative context, is not necessarily directly linked with the dominance of Mahāyāna attitudes; we are probably not even justified in seeing a parallel between the philosophical classifications of the schools and sects of Buddhism and the attitudes, even though religious, reflected in its artistic iconography. Undoubtedly, the view that the Buddha or the Bodhisattva was beyond the passage of time gained ground because of a profound social crisis affecting in particular the merchant class, which from its beginnings had supported 'heterodox' religious movements—first of all, Buddhism itself. Thus, whereas in the earliest Gandhāran reliefs the Buddha appeared as a man among men, he now only reveals himself to men as a constant source of salvation. It is difficult to say how far this is attributable to the reigning dynasty, that political power that at the time of the great Kuṣāṇas expressed its rarefied ideology in the frontal images—rigid, entirely non-Hellenistic and non-Indian—found at Surkh Kotal and Mathurā.[29] Yet we may get some light on the subject from the schist sculptures found at Kāpiśa (Begrām, Paitavā, Shotorak) (Pl. 136), and above all from those stelae that depict the *Dīpaṅkara-jātaka*, showing a Buddha of enormous proportions in contrast to the small figures below to the left (the same Buddha figure, in two different poses) (Pl. 137). These small figures execute the movements and so render the scene comprehensible. Similar clues may be found in other schist sculptures, for example, those in which the Buddha is shown with flames emerging from his shoulders (Pl. 136) and side by side with representations of the *Dīpaṅkara-jātaka* and the 'alms of dust'. Here a symbolic representation of light apparently links the figure of the Buddha with that of the sovereign, as has been frequently noted.[30]

We have seen how the tendency to depict the Buddha on a colossal scale is characteristic of the whole of this mature phase of Gandhāran art. In most cases, of course, this monumentality is relative to the other figures accompanying that of the Buddha on the same relief, but it is not exceptional to find instances in which the spectator himself is dwarfed by comparison with the effigy of the Enlightened One, and not only in Afghanistan.

[27] Barthoux, 'Les fouilles de Haḍḍa: 3', *op. cit.*, pl. 46.
[28] Mostamindi, *op. cit.*, figs. 11–12.
[29] On this question, see particularly J. M. Rosenfield, *The Dynastic Arts of the Kushans* (Berkeley and Los Angeles, 1967).
[30] On these aspects of Buddhist iconography, see particularly A. C. Soper, *Artibus Asiae*, 12 (1949), pp. 252–83, 314–30; 13 (1950), pp. 63–85; M. Bussagli, *Rivista dell'Istituto Nazionale d'Archeologia e Storia dell'Arte*, 5–6 (1956–57), pp. 198–205; Rosenfield, *op. cit.*, pp. 200–1; M. Taddei, *Gururājamañjarikā: Studi in onore di Giuseppe Tucci*, 2 (Naples, 1974), pp. 435–49.

Hsüan-tsang, the Chinese pilgrim who visited the Buddhist holy places in India in the seventh century, wrote of the city of Fan-yen-na (Bāmiyān, to the west of Kabul): 'To the east of the city 12 or 13 li there is a convent, in which there is a figure of Buddha lying in a sleeping position, as when he attained Nirvāna. The figure is in length about 1,000 feet or so' (trans. Beal). Nothing remains of this colossal figure, and it is difficult to say whether the text is corrupt or not, but the information is certainly not the fruit of Hsüan-tsang's imagination. We must remember that this same Hsüan-tsang tells us of two other colossal figures, not lying this time but standing, one 140–50 feet high, the other 100 feet high; these measurements are fairly accurate and can be verified,[31] for the two Buddhas still exist and bear witness to the religious zeal of the king of Bāmiyān. This king, according to Hsüan-tsang, used to summon an assembly every five years to the Monastery of the Nirvana, at which he was wont to give away to the monks all his possessions, even the queen, and afterwards his officials used to redeem all such the valuables from the monks. These two standing figures of the Buddha are hewn from rough mountain conglomerate and finished with a layer of moulded stucco. The smaller, 38 metres high, is usually assigned to the fourth or fifth century A.D., while the larger, some 53 metres high, is attributed with much hesitation to the fifth or sixth century A.D. (Pl. 146). These figures merely carry to extremes the tendency to monumentality that we have already encountered in the stelae of Kāpiśa; perhaps similar figures in China were inspired by them.

Of greater interest, perhaps, from the iconographical standpoint are the paintings at Bāmiyān, which decorate both the vast niches of the two Buddhas and other monastic structures hewn from the same rock-face (Pl. 140). Here the image of the Buddha shows stylistic traits that are Iranian and Sassanian in origin, both in the use of colour and in the presence of decorative elements, such as fluttering draperies and ribbons, which link Bāmiyān with certain stylistic trends in Central Asia.

The painting on the vault of the niche where the 38-metre Buddha stands, which portrays an astral divinity, is of great conceptual significance; the figure of the Enlightened One thus appears as a pillar linking the worlds and guaranteeing their continued existence, really the same notion as is expressed by the images in which flames shoot from the shoulders and water gushes from the feet. All this demonstrates most clearly the importance in Afghanistan of the symbol of light, itself of Iranian origin.

The seventh and eighth centuries saw the final surge of renewal of the stylistic and iconographical language of Buddhism in Afghanistan, before the Moslem invasion began to put an end to any religion other than Islam.

[31]For Bāmiyān the following are still of great importance; A. Godard et al., 'Les antiquités bouddhiques de Bāmiyān', *Mémoires de la Délégation Archéologique Française en Afghanistan*, 2 (Paris-Brussels, 1928); J. Hackin and J. Carl, 'Nouvelles recherches archéologiques à Bāmiyān', *Mémoires de la Délégation Archéologique Française en Afghanistan*, 3 (Paris, 1933). The height of the smaller of the two huge Buddhas is usually given as 35 m.; the most recent restoration work performed by an Indian expedition has shown that the exact measurement was 38 m. (cf. R. Sengupta, 'The Buddha in Afghanistan: India's aid to bring Bamiyan back to life', 2nd rev. ed. (1972); idem, in *Afghanistan*, 26, 1352, 3 (1973), pp. 23–25. For the travels of Hsüan-tsang, see *Si-yu-ki, Buddhist Records of the Western World, translated from the Chinese of Hiuen Tsiang (A.D. 629)*, by Samuel Beal (London, 1884; reprinted Delhi, 1969, 2 vols. in one) (concerning Bāmiyān, vol. 1, pp. 49–53), or Th. Watters, *On Yuan Chwang's Travels in India*, 2 vols. (London, 1904 and 1905).

136. Meditating Buddha with flames issuing from his shoulders

From Paitavā (Kāpiśa), Afghanistan; Gandhāran art; schist; H. 61 cm.; Kabul Museum.

The Buddha is seated on a lotus flower in the position of meditation (*dhyānāsana*), encircled by a great aureole of flames. Flames also issue from his shoulders. The significance of light probably relates to Iranian religion, where supreme divinity and kingship are symbolized by luminosity. It is possible that images of the Buddha with flames issuing from the shoulders were common in Kāpiśa, which was one of the centres of the dynastic power of the Kuṣāṇas. One notes the title 'Boundless Light' (Amitābha) of the Buddha of the west. The attitude of the two Brahman deities—Indra, on the left of the Buddha, and Brahmā—reduced to the rank of parasol bearers, emphasizes the indisputable supremacy of the Buddha over all other beings. The Bodhisattva Maitreya is shown on the base between two monks who are making offerings.

137. The *Dīpaṅkara-jātaka*

From Shotorak (Kāpiśa), Afghanistan; Gandhāran art; schist; H. 83.5 cm.; Kabul Museum.

The representation of the *Dīpaṅkara-jātaka* is often associated with the luminosity of the Buddha (flames issuing from the shoulders). Here, the Enlightened One, making the gesture of fearlessness (*abhaya*), is portrayed on a far larger scale than the other figures. The young ascetic, known as Megha or Sumegha, who is shown twice, once throwing flowers, and then again prostrating himself at the Buddha's feet, as well as the gods Indra and Brahmā shown in adoration above, and also the curious figure on the right, which stands on a base decorated with rosettes, all these appear tiny by comparison. The last figure must be a Bodhisattva, presumably the future Śākyamuni, Prince Siddhārtha, thus indicating the future state of the young ascetic on the left, who is destined to become Śākyamuni in a future reincarnation. On the lower part of the stele is the Bodhisattva Maitreya between figures making offerings. The proportions of the figures, their arrangement on the same plane, the fact that the narrative aspect of this scene is unimportant as compared with the principal image—all these show the originality of this work from Kāpiśa, viewed against the more Hellenistic Gandhāran art of the other centres in Afghanistan and Pakistan.

138. The Final Nirvana of the Buddha

From Kāpiśa, Afghanistan; Gandhāran art; schist; H. 27.5 cm., W. 51 cm.; Kabul Museum.

The scene of the passing of the Buddha Śākyamuni is depicted according to a plan that remains practically unchanged in Buddhist iconography. The figure of the Enlightened One lying on his right side, his head resting on the palm of his hand and his left arm stretched out, is exactly the same as in the later gigantic representations at Tapa Sardār and Adzhina-tepa. In the latter, however, the attendant figures, the mourners and those concerned with the funeral rites, are absent. The figure behind on the right is probably a donor. A peculiar feature of this relief is the representation of Vajrapāṇi (on the left) in Kuṣāṇa costume. The object shaped like a clepsydra that he is holding in his left hand is the thunderbolt (*vajra*) by which he is recognized.

139. Buddha venerated by the three Kāśyapa

From Shotorak (Kāpiśa), Afghanistan; Gandhāran art; schist; H. 58 cm., W. 89 cm.; Kabul Museum.

Another of the themes designed to illustrate the subordination of Brahmanism to the Buddha is represented in this relief from Shotorak, one of the most important finds made in that monastery by the French Archaeological Delegation in Afghanistan in 1937. The three Brahman Kāśyapa brothers, each accompanied by a disciple, devoutly approach the Buddha, who makes the gesture of fearlessness (*abhaya*). The strictly hierarchical proportions of the various figures in relation to one another should be noted. Not much larger than the Kāśyapa brothers and the other figures in the scene, but distinctly smaller than the Enlightened One, the two on the extreme right are undoubtedly donors. The man, although wearing garments of Kuṣāṇa style, has an Hellenistic cast of features, while the woman has adopted an entirely Greek costume. This shows the vitality of the classical tradition, which affects even the élite circles most closely related to the dynasty. The frieze at the top shows Maitreya with worshippers.

140. Rock-cut caves for monks and the defaced effigy of a Buddha image in its sanctuary, Bāmiyān, Afghanistan

Pictorial evidence for all this has been available for some years now, from the time in 1937 when the French Archaeological Delegation brought to light the remains of the monastery of Fondukistān, between Begrām and Bāmiyān; and to them have been added in recent years the sculptures discovered by the Italian Archaeological Mission in the buildings of the last phase of the monastery of Tapa Sardār, near Ghazni.[32]

The figures from Fondukistān and Tapa Sardār are technically similar, and this technical link extends to figures from Central Asia: they are made of clay mixed with straw, horsehair being added at Fondukistān, while at Tapa Sardār a fairly thin layer of tougher red clay, which took colour well, was applied on top; a solid wooden framework supported the figures, which often display considerable daring in structure. They also resemble each other in iconography and style, though in this respect Fondukistān shows greater freedom and a stronger inclination to innovate that evidently reflect a changed outlook. We are not thinking only of the figures of Bodhisattvas, *nāgas*, or *devatās*, with youthful, graceful, shapely limbs, but also of those of the Buddha himself, which underwent the same process of transformation, inspired by a somewhat feminine ideal of beauty and grace unquestionably aristocratic (Pl. 141). They are subtly equivocal in the inclination of the head, and the *mudrās* are no longer severe, as in the sculptures of the previous centuries, but are charming gestures of courtesy rather than symbolic attitudes heavy with religious significance.

[32]On Fondukistān, see Hackin, in 'Diverses recherches', *op. cit.*, pp. 49–58 (also *Journal of the Greater Indian Society*, 7 [1940], pp. 1–14 and 85–91). On Tapa Sardār, see particularly M. Taddei, in *East and West*, 18 (1968), pp. 109–24; idem, in *Il Vetro*, *op. cit.*

141. Buddha teaching

From Fondukistān, Afghanistan; 7th century A.D.*; clay mixed with straw and horsehair, with painted surface; H. 70 cm.; Kabul Museum.*

Of all the images of Buddha and Bodhisattva from the Fondukistān monastery, this is one of the most faithful to the Gandhāran iconographical tradition. However, the refined facial features and the restrained gestures clearly indicate a profound change in taste, certainly more aristocratic, and also a change in religious feeling, more consonant with the ideology of the new feudal class.

Who commissioned these refined and attractive works? It is not easy to say, but there may be a hint for us in another group of sculptures, which seems to be contemporary but is executed in marble or some other calcareous stone, and which is found throughout the north-west frontier areas of Pakistan and eastern Afghanistan. These are known as the Śāhi sculptures from the name of the dynasty (or dynasties) that reigned first at Kabul, then at Und (near Attock, at the confluence of the Kabul and the Indus), and was finally overthrown by the Ghaznavidi. They are characterized by two concomitant traits: the subjects were almost all Śaivite or Vaiṣṇavite at a time when Buddhism appeared to be dominant in the region; and it was virtually the only sculpture in marble or in any kind of calcareous stone at a time when sculpture in clay was undoubtedly the most widespread. It is true that the area of distribution of Śāhi marble sculpture was not identical with that of clay sculpture of the Fondukistān type, but there is undoubtedly a very wide area of overlap. This would suggest that two different social groups commissioned them, those for whom the Hindu marble sculptures were made being perhaps more closely linked to the Śāhi dynasty, which would not be a new phenomenon in the north-west of India and in Afghanistan. We should perhaps note that the two streams converged briefly at Tapa Sardār in one of the chapels of the sanctuary: there, confronting a jewelled figure of the Buddha, appears that of the Śaivite goddess Durgā,[33] one of the most frequent subjects of Śāhi marble sculpture.

The jewelled figure of the Buddha is a type found in various places; it has been explained as an expression of the Mahāyāna conception of the *sambhogakāya* (see p. 138), 'that Body of Bliss of transcendent form in which the Buddha reveals himself only to the host of the Bodhisattvas',[34] but according to some scholars such figures 'do not represent any particular school of Buddhism'[35] but are a consequence—and on this all scholars are agreed—of a desire to proclaim complete identification of the Buddha with the universal monarch. Nevertheless this would not be an innovation, as the more or less explicit identification of the sovereign with the divinity is a widespread phenomenon and one not confined to India. The problem to be solved is, in our opinion, rather that of understanding why the Buddha-sovereign should have been differently adorned in this case. It seems to us that a clue may be furnished by an analysis of this iconographical phenomenon over a wider area, including Central Asia.

In this vast region, extending from the Soviet Republics of Turkmenistan, Uzbekistan and Tadzhikistan to the Tarim basin, that is, as far as Chinese Turkestan (Sinkiang), we find, at a fairly early period, reflections of Gandhāran art, which to some extent gave rise to new developments. Thus the Buddha appears in a costume both stylistically and iconographically completely Gandhāran (of the Kuṣāṇa period) in a relief at Termez (Uzbekistan)[36] and in a painting recently discovered intact in a cave at Kara-tepe (Termez) (Pl. 142)[37] and

[33] M. Taddei, in 'South Asian Archaeology: papers from the first conference of South Asian archaeologists held in the University of Cambridge' (London, 1973), pp. 203–13.

[34] B. Rowland, in *Artibus Asiae*, 24 (1961), pp. 20–24.

[35] Y. Krishnan, in *East and West*, 21 (1971), pp. 91–96.

[36] G. A. Pugachenkova and L. I. Rempel', *Vydajushchiesja pamjatniki izobrazitel' nogo iskusstva Uzbekistana* (Tashkent, 1960), pp. 22–24, pl. 2.

[37] B. J. Staviskij, in *Buddijskij Kul'tovyj centr Kara-tepe v Starom Termeze* (Moscow, 1972), pl. 4.

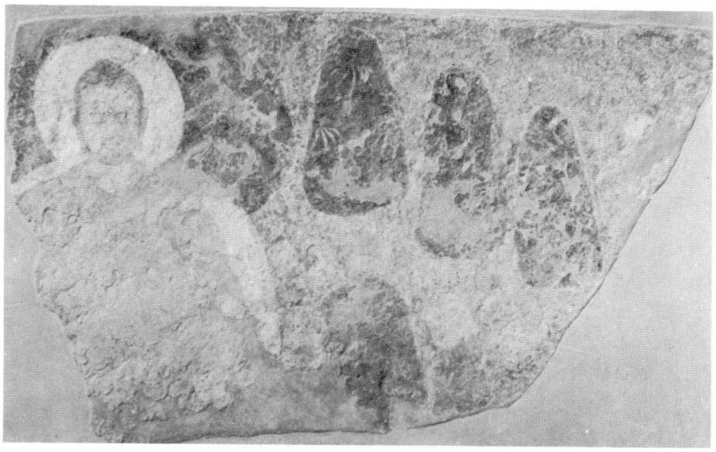

142. An early painting of the Buddha

Wall painting; from Kara-tepe, Termez; 2nd–3rd century A.D.*(?).*

This precious relic of Central Asian painting shows how closely this area was connected with Gandhāra as regards both style and iconography. It is one of the few fragments of painting found in the Buddhist complex of Kara-tepe in the old Termez during one of the recent campaigns of the archaeological expedition organized by the State Ermitazh, the Institute of Archaeology of the Academy of Sciences, and other scientific institutions of the U.S.S.R.

143. Stupa and thrones

From Tapa Sardār, Ghazni, Afghanistan; 8th century A.D.*; unbaked clay.*

Star-shaped stupas with four stairways were very common in this period and were often quite small, and sometimes miniature. This magnificent Tapa Sardār group comprises a series of votive stupas on lotus flowers, raised above the ground, and images on thrones that have backs. They are decorated with applied mouldings. The sides of one stupa are profusely decorated with small images of the Buddha, a decorative motif that suggests the principle of the irradiation of the Buddha to all points of the universe.

144. Buddha lying in the pose of the Final Nirvana

From Tapa Sardār, Ghazni, Afghanistan; 8th century A.D.; unbaked clay; L. approximately 17 m.

Typologically and stylistically this *parinirvāṇa* is closely related to that of Adzhina-tepa (Pl. 145). It resembles it also in its colossal size and in the technique. Both are of unbaked clay; that of Tapa Sardār is about 17 metres long, while that of Adzhina-tepa is about 12 metres. Both are badly damaged and incomplete. That of Tapa Sardār preserves only a part of the left (upper) side of the body, for one must remember that in the pose of *parinirvāṇa*, a Buddha always lies on his right side. Of particular interest is the position that the image occupies in its architectonic context, which gives the impression that an attempt has been made to ensure that it could be approached from all sides by means of an appropriate system of passages, despite the fact that it is placed against the wall of the shrine. A section of the wall consisting of baked bricks and the wooden rafters form part of a modern protective structure.

145. Buddha lying in the pose of the Final Nirvana

From Adzhina-tepa, Tadzhikistan; 8th century A.D.; painted unbaked clay; L. approximately 12 m.

Adzhina-tepa is a small mound that owes its present name ('devil's hill') to legends that associate it with evil spirits. A Buddhist monastery was functioning there between the second half of the seventh and the first half of the eighth centuries. The sculptural decoration of Adzhina-tepa seems to have been fairly similar to that of Tapa Sardār at Ghazni, from the point of view of both style and technique. In both sites, the cores for the larger figures were made of horizontally laid unbaked bricks; several layers of clay mixed with chopped straw gave the basic shape and sometimes the deeper features and folds; the small details were modelled in a surface layer of plastic clay (brown or green at Adzhina-tepa, reddish at Tapa Sardār) mixed with sand. The clay surface was painted (red on the *saṅghāṭi*), but the image underwent some repairs, while the pedestal was given a new stucco coat, covered with *ganch* (gypsum) and was then painted with different hues of red.

also in a famous painting at Mirān (Chinese Turkestan) (Pl. 151) that Bussagli, basing his suggestion on an interesting hypothesis, has compared on stylistic grounds with the reliefs in the old collection of the Corps of Guides at Mardān, now in the museum at Peshawar,[38] which are characteristic examples of Gandhāran art.

It is easy to see, too, that the unbaked clay sculptures of Adzhina-tepa (Tadzhikistan)[39] are in line with the development we have traced in Afghanistan; they are very close in style, iconography and technique to those of the late period of Tapa Sardār, which are almost contemporary. Although excavations have not yet been completed at either Tapa Sardār or Adzhina-tepa, it is nevertheless worth noting that in both sanctuaries colossal figures have been found of the Buddha in *parinirvāṇa* (original measurements: the figure at Adzhina-tepa, about 12 metres; that at Tapa Sardār, about 17 metres (Pls. 144, 145). There are other obvious similarities between Tapa Sardār (and hence Fondukistān) and Adzhina-tepa, but Adzhina-tepa gives us some additional information: fragments of paintings have been discovered there, with donors—kneeling figures dressed in white, with wide sleeves and wearing short swords at their sides—which B. Litvinskij and T. Zejmal have rightly compared to certain 'princely' figures from Bāmiyān and the fortress at Balalyk-tepe (Uzbekistan).[40] There are, of course, many other similarities between Balalyk-tepe and Fondukistān, and so on, till we come to Piandzhikent, so that we can see the essential cultural unity in this group of sculptures and paintings found in Uzbekistan, Tadzhikistan, and Afghanistan over a period that probably extends from the end of the sixth to the eighth century A.D. Balalyk-tepe is one of the most interesting of these centres from a socio-historical standpoint, for it is an example of a fortress-farm, the residence of a rural lord, that is to say, a member of the feudal class that—as we can also see from the excavations at Piandzhikent—in the artistic expression of their own aristocratic outlook showed a preference for themes such as banquets and battles, which we would call 'chivalric'[41] and which in a Buddhist context could well lend support to theories of donors: they are doing homage to the Buddha or to the stupa (as at Adzhina-tepa), but at the same time they bear witness to the power and refinement of their lord, the donor. It is therefore to the outlook of this feudal aristocracy that the notion of the jewelled Buddha can be attributed, a form represented at both Fondukistān and Tapa Sardār.

By contrast with Afghanistan, where Buddhism remained the dominant religion even though the reigning dynasty was Hindu, in Central Asia, crossed by the great caravan routes that linked the Mediterranean west with China, different religions co-existed: Buddhists, Christians, Zoroastrians, Manicheans and Śaivites frequently had their places of worship side by side. At Ak-Beshim, near Frunze (Kirghizia), for example, Soviet archaeologists have brought to light two Buddhist shrines and a Nestorian Christian church, which can be attributed to the seventh or eighth century A.D. This peaceful coexistence,

[38]M. Bussagli, *Painting of Central Asia* (Geneva, 1963), pp. 21–27, fig. p. 23.

[39]B. A. Litvinskij and T. I. Zejmal, '*Adzhina-tepa: Arkhitektura, Zhivopis', Skulptura* (Moscow, 1971).

[40]On the excavations at Balalyk-tepe, see L. I. Albaum, *Balalyk-tepe* (Tashkent, 1960); on the dating of the paintings, see the recent suggestions (end of the sixth to the beginning of the seventh century) made by C. Silvi Antonini, in *Annali dell'Istituto Orientale di Napoli*, 32 (1972), p. 71 ff.

[41]See A. Belenitsky, *Asie Centrale* (Geneva, 1968), pp. 140–41.

147. Circle of Buddhas

From a ceiling decoration of the sanctuary in the Kakrak Valley, Bāmiyān, Afghanistan; c. 7th century A.D.*; paint on dry plaster with a support of clay mixed with straw; Kabul Museum.*

This is part of a ceiling decoration that follows the lines of a mandala. The central medallion depicts the Buddha seated in meditation on a lotus flower, set in a polychrome halo, with his breast bearing the mark of the *śrīvatsa* (one of the marks of a Buddha as prescribed in the texts, but only seldom shown in images of the Buddha). Eleven other images of the Buddha, also in the meditation posture, encircle the central one, as though emanating from the centre.

◁ 146. The Great Buddha of Bāmiyān

From Bāmiyān, Afghanistan; 5th–6th century A.D.*; hewn out of the rock, with surface modelled in stucco; H. 53 m.; in situ.*

Bāmiyān is famous for the two colossal images of the Buddha hewn out of the conglomerate in the mountain-side. The technique used to portray the folds of the cloak is worth noting: they were modelled in stucco over ropes fastened to the image by means of wooden pegs. Here the propensity to the colossal is revealed to the full; the Bāmiyān statues did not fail to excite the admiration of the Chinese traveller Hsüan-tsang, who described the larger of the two as follows: 'To the north-east of the royal city there is a mountain, on the declivity of which is placed a stone image of Buddha, erect, in height 140 or 150 feet. Its golden hues sparkle on every side, and its precious ornaments dazzle the eyes by their brightness.' (Beal, *op. cit.*, 1, pp. 50–51).

148. Bejewelled Buddha

From niche D, Fondukistān, Afghanistan; 7th century A.D.*; painted unbaked clay; Musée Guimet, Paris.*

In one of the niches around the stupa court in the monastery of Fondukistān was found a complex sculptural decoration, in the centre of which was a Bodhisattva image. On the side-walls of the niche were two damaged Buddha figures seated on lotus flowers; that on the right was a 'classical'-type Buddha with a large halo bordered by spurts of fire encompassing the whole torso; that on the left was the bejewelled Buddha, the best specimen of this interesting iconographical type from Afghanistan. Other examples of bejewelled Buddhas in Afghanistan are known from Haḍḍa, Bāmiyān and Tapa Sardār. The suggested date takes into account both the style of the image, which seems to derive from Mathurā designs of the Gupta period, and the style of the paintings in the recess, which are reminiscent of the Ajantā cave paintings.

149. Bodhisattva Maitreya

From Fondukistān, Afghanistan; 7th century A.D.*; paint on dry clay plaster; Kabul Museum.*

The main room of the Fondukistān monastery excavated by the French Archaeological Delegation in Afghanistan in 1937 is in the form of a square and was probably barrel-vaulted. In the centre is a stupa and on each side of the room there are three niches. In one of these (which the excavators indicated by the letter E) was the extremely important group representing a royal couple, now housed in one of the rooms in the Kabul Museum. The outer columns of the niche are decorated with paintings depicting the Buddha (on the left) and the Bodhisattva figure shown here, which was probably intended to represent Maitreya, the Buddha of the future. A blue lotus flower (*utpala*) is held in the right hand, and dangling from the left hand is the small flask characteristic of this Bodhisattva. In this figure, even more than in the images of the Buddha, we see how profound was the iconographic renewal of which Fondukistān affords an exceptionally valuable example—a renewal due also but not solely to the influence of Indian painting in the Gupta tradition.

150. Buddha head

From Shrine 17, Tapa Sardār, Ghazni, Afghanistan; 8th century A.D.

The inner walls of Shrine 17 of the Tapa Sardār were decorated with meditating Buddha images set in niches and arranged in tiers on each side of the colossal central image. This latter is seated in the 'European' fashion, and is probably the Future Buddha, Maitreya. The head shown here belongs to one of the many Buddhas in the decorative group, where details are necessarily of less importance than the general effect. Stylistically, there is an obvious affinity between all the late works produced at Tapa Sardār and those produced at Fondukistān, although the latter site is of a more refined character.

151. Another early painting of the Buddha

Wall painting; from Shrine 3, Mirān; 3rd century A.D.*; H. approximately 45 cm.; National Museum of India, New Delhi.*

This is a detail from a fragment showing the Buddha followed by six disciples. The position of the right hand has been interpreted as the attitude of the teacher. In fact, it is more likely to be a gesture of reassurance, the *abhaya-mudrā*. Gandhāran art, in fact, represents a stage in which iconographical details had not become immutable and there were many variations. That this Mirān style of painting derives from Gandhāran painting, of which nothing remains in Gandhāra itself, has been well argued by Bussagli (see his work *Painting of Central Asia* [Geneva, 1963], pp. 19–29).

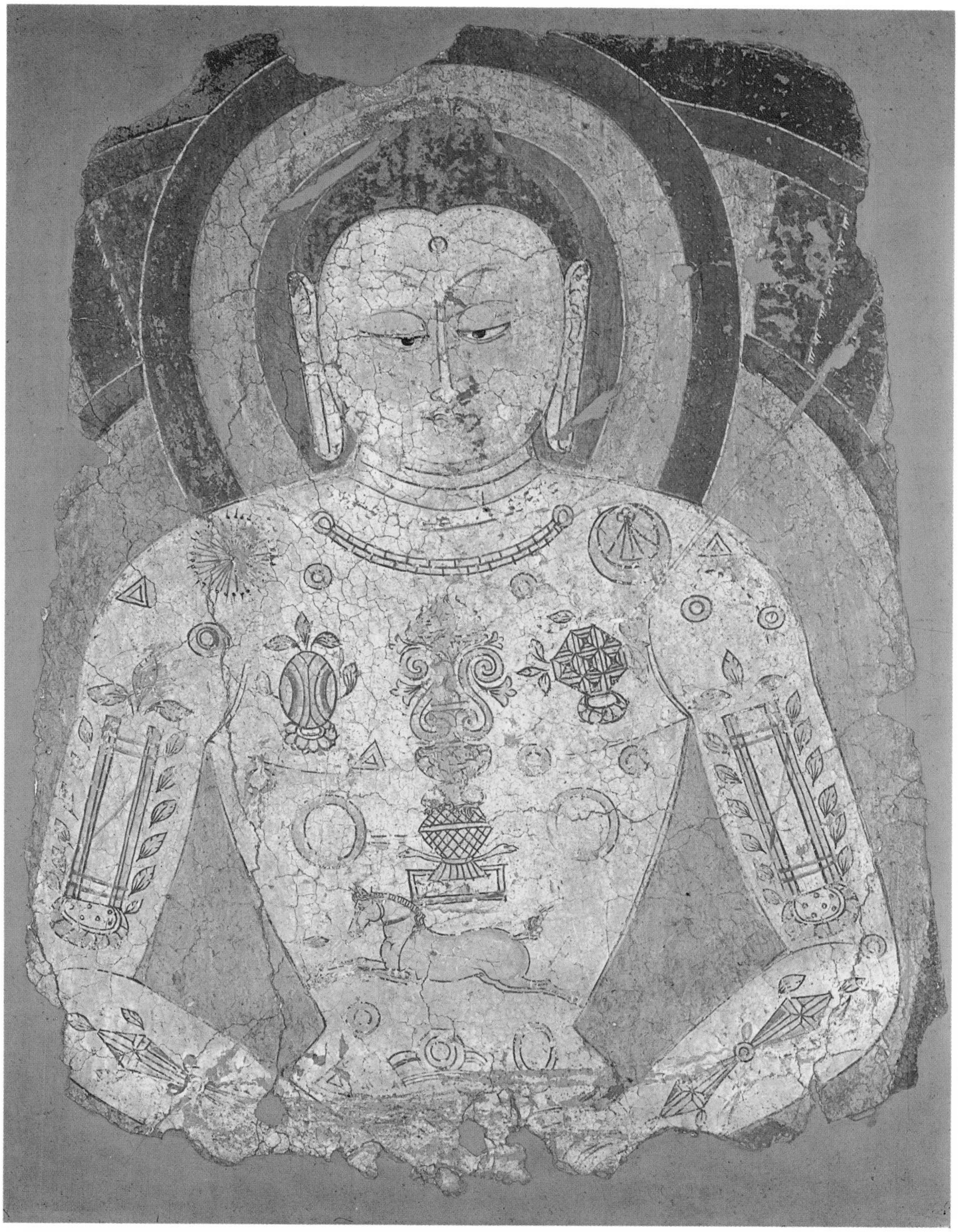

152. Buddha in meditation (cosmic Vairocana)

Wall painting; probably from Balawaste, Keriya; 6th century A.D.*; H. approximately 80 cm.; National Museum of India, New Delhi.*

This is one of the finest examples of the cosmic Vairocana, with many different signs or symbols on the body, an image frequently found in the Khotan region where the Mahāyāna prevailed. As Eiichi Matsumoto has shown, this iconography was based on the *Avataṃsaka-sūtra*, the dissemination of which took place largely in the Khotan region. The concept 'all in one and one in all' or 'all is one and one is all' was illustrated in images such as this. Each of the 'symbols' is to be understood as one of the forms that the Buddha can assume. To quote J. Williams, 'A typical passage [of the *Avataṃsaka-sūtra*] describing this cosmological inter-relationship runs thus: "The transformations of the Buddha exist sometimes in the form of Mt. Sumeru, of rivers, of whirlwinds, of whirlpools, of circle-nets, of earth altars, of forests, of towers, of mountain peaks, of all square things, of wombs, of lotuses, of gold, of the bodies of all sentient beings, of clouds, of the thirty-two major and eighty minor signs, of a radiant halo, of pearl nets, of gate panels, and of all sorts of ornamentation." And elsewhere, similar highly repetitive passages describing the universal seas include lion thrones, octagonal jewels, wish-granting jewels, circles, forms neither square nor circular, rivers, wheels, trees, crescents, half-necklaces (and other pieces of jewellery), *vajras*, tortoise-shell shapes, and triangles.'

153. Buddha in meditation

Wall painting; from Shrine 1, Bezelik; 8th–9th century A.D.*; National Museum of India, New Delhi.*

This wall painting comes from a rock-cut shrine in Bezelik, the most important of the Buddhist sites in the Turfān group. The decorative group to which it belonged consisted of a series of similar Buddha images, each one in a shrine with an unbaked brick foundation and a wooden roof topped by a stupa-shaped ornament with a parasol and pennants. In the photo reproduced here one can see the lower part of a shrine with the image of the Buddha and the upper part of the shrine belonging to the image below. The repetition of the Buddha image is a typical motif of Buddhist art of this period, and not only in Central Asia. It was also from the tenth century onwards a common feature of temple wall decoration in Ladakh and western Tibet, probably following similar styles of painting in Buddhist temples in pre-Moslem Kashmir.

which was due to the fact that there was no official state religion, frequently led to forms of syncretism that, moreover, were not unknown in Afghanistan itself (cf. the Durgā image at Tapa Sardār).

Yet in Soviet Central Asia it is not easy to distinguish trends towards iconographical renewal with respect to the representation of the Buddha. The small figures (isolated or in small groups of worshippers) depicted on the gilded bronze plaques of Ak-Beshim[42] amid intricate plant patterns show the Buddha clad in a monastic robe, in the posture of meditation; there are typological traces of Gandhāran and Indian influence here, although the style in general is not derivative. Similarly, the clay sculpture of Kuva (Ferghāna)[43] is memorable for the riotous imaginativeness of its demoniacal figures (rather than for the great head of the Buddha Maitreya), which, although not an innovation (there are many examples among the Haḍḍa stuccoes), became more and more common in Central Asia as a setting for images of the Buddha. So this demoniacal element becomes a common motif throughout Central Asia, as far as Sinkiang and Khotan, on the southern caravan route, and Tumshuq and Turfān on the northern route; it contrasts strongly with the image of the Buddha, who was now portrayed as a noble but detached being, clothed in simple but rich monastic garments, ready to turn benevolently towards the worshipper or disciple portrayed at his side, yet distant because of his halo of divine light and his lotus throne.

It would be pointless to list the plastic and pictorial works of art, many of them justly famous, that various archaeological missions—British, French, Japanese, Russian and German—have removed, usually with thoughtless frivolity, from structures buried in the sands of Sinkiang to enrich collections such as those of the British Museum, the Musée Guimet in Paris, the Hermitage in Leningrad and the Berlin and New Delhi museums.[44]

We shall rather turn our attention to two groups of representations among these. The first group is amply documented, particularly at Khotan (a city on the southern caravan route); the second is less reliably documented with well-known illustrative material, but it is mentioned in the texts and, like the first, it is of particular conceptual importance.[45] The first group consists of representations of the cosmic Vairocana whose body is marked with symbols such as the stupa, the *vajra*, the running horse, the scroll book, the triangle, etc., which represent the various forms that the Buddha may at times assume (Pl. 152); there is an affinity here, on the conceptual level, with the representations of innumerable Buddhas radiating out from one central figure. This is not a new form; it can be traced back to such Gandhāran representations as those of the 'Great Miracle of Śrāvastī'. Thus, on the one hand, we have the Buddha containing in himself all possible forms of his manifestations, and, on the other, the Buddha multiplying himself as he radiates out towards all

[42]Brief accounts of the excavations at Ak-Beshim in Belenitsky, *op. cit.*, pp. 141–43, figs. 66–67; L. I. Albaum and B. Brentjes, *Wächter des Goldes* (Berlin, 1972), p. 174, figs. 168–69.
[43]Also for Kuva, see Albaum and Brentjes, *op. cit.*, pp. 173–74, figs. 161–67.
[44]An excellent summary of studies of the painting of Central Asia (especially that of the Tarim Basin), particularly as regards the history of styles, is the previously cited work by Bussagli. There is a full bibliography in the work by M. Paul David, M. Hallade, and L. Hambis, *Toumchouq*, Text, *Mission Paul Pelliot*, 2 (Paris, 1964).
[45]For both groups, see J. Williams, in *East and West*, 23 (1973), particularly pp. 117–29.

the points of the cosmos, always both changing and changeless, to reabsorb himself finally in one central unity.

The second group of representations is to some extent different in nature from the cosmic Vairocana; it consists of reproductions of the so-called Famous Images, among them the celebrated one believed to have been executed during the life of the Buddha by King Udāyana of Kauśāmbī. Hsüan-tsang, the pilgrim, wrote of it: 'Here [i.e., in Khotan] there is a figure of the Buddha in a standing position, made of sandalwood. The figure is about twenty feet high. It works many miracles and reflects constantly a bright light. Those who have any disease, according to the part affected, cover the corresponding place on the statue with gold-leaf, and forthwith they are healed. People who address prayers to it with a sincere heart mostly obtain their wishes. This is what the natives say: This image in old days when Buddha was alive was made by Udāyana, king of Kauśāmbī. When Buddha left the world, it mounted of its own accord into the air and came to the north of this kingdom, to the town of Ho-lo-lo-kia' (Beal, *op. cit.*, 2, p. 322). Because of the unworthiness of the inhabitants, the miraculous image transferred itself from that city to the site (Pimā) where Hsüan-tsang saw it.

Thus we see represented in these two groups of images the two basic tendencies, speculative and devotional, that characterize Buddhism; they have perhaps always been present, but their success has alternated. The art of Chinese Turkestan between the fifth and ninth centuries gave ample scope to both of them.

5. CHINA: GROWTH AND MATURITY

It is certain that Buddhism first reached China during the *pax imperia* of the second century A.D., when the power of China, the Kuṣāṇa state and Rome made the highroads across Asia safer and busier than ever before. Missionaries arrived with increasing frequency from the mid-second century onwards. Initial distrust of a creed coming from outer darkness was gradually relaxed (though some basic reasons for hostility never became extinct). The process was facilitated by the degeneration, from the 170's onwards, of everything that had once made the Chinese proud and confident. As decline darkened into savage wars, the old religions showed themselves pitifully irrelevant. The early victories of Buddhism in China, like those of Christianity in the West, were multiplied by local despair. When an uneasy peace was won in the third century, conversions continued. Around 300, in the two metropolitan centres of Ch'ang-an and Lo-yang, it is said that there were 180 monastery temples and some 3,700 monks.

The barbarian explosion that destroyed the whole northern half of the empire between 310 and 316 divided China and its Buddhism for 270 years. The south held out behind formidable natural barriers. Though greatly reduced at the end, it managed to keep its capital region, modern Nanking, and many of its important secular and religious centres intact. For most of the period its culture was brilliant, alive with creative enthusiasm. Most of the famous missionaries from the west made their homes there and carried out the bulk of the early translations of sacred books from Sanskrit. In the south Buddhism found a rich field for conversions, or for stimulating opposition, among the well-educated gentry, who enjoyed sharpening their wits in arguing the new philosophy. At the same time the emotional appeal of Mahāyāna began to draw groups of devotees into special cults, most often the belief in the Pure Land of Amitābha, or in the golden age to come under Maitreya.

The southern emperors were usually at least superficial adherents, and in the sixth century were notably devout. A few of them painted icons; most dedicated temples and commissioned images, sometimes twice human scale or in great numbers. The most honoured material was bronze, normally gilded. Other materials were clay, lacquer and wood, except in the far west, where an abundance of good stone was available. The famous painters, particularly Ku K'ai-chih and Chang Seng-yu, turned to Buddhist themes, executed on a grand scale on temple walls.

There are indications, however, that great numbers of the South Chinese still clung to the more primitive beliefs that had been loosely organized in late Han under the name of Taoism, and particularly to the cult of the goddess of long life, Hsi Wang Mu.

We know that the north passed through a 'Dark Age' of about a century after 316, when the tribes that had settled there struggled viciously against each other for lands and Chinese slaves. In time one group, the T'o-pa, emerged as victors on an imperial scale. Their dynasty, the Wei, enjoyed a century of grandeur, but even at its height much was owed to the talents (and the overwhelming numbers) of its captive Chinese. In the end the latter's numerical and cultural superiority virtually obliterated T'o-pa control. In the 580's the whole empire was reassembled under a Chinese régime of renewed magnificence, the Sui.

The Buddhist missionaries who penetrated the north in the chaotic first century found rulers utterly unlike the educated gentry of the south. In these cases conspicuous successes were won through displays of magic, particularly by tricks useful in war. When the Wei showed clear signs of primacy, the officially named superintendant of Northern Buddhism buttressed his position by calling the T'o-pa ruler 'a present-day Buddha, to whom it is entirely proper for monks to pay reverence'. Though accepted as an instrument of state, Northern Buddhism was nearly annihilated when the greatest conqueror, T'ai Wu Ti, was persuaded in 444 that its growth threatened his own rule. For five years a ferocious proscription was enforced. In the end it failed, and since there were still survivors to begin rebuilding, a quick and thorough restoration was permitted.

In a few years the leader, T'an-yao, was able to persuade the new ruler to make a grandiose act of penitence by excavating in a cliffside near the capital, now called Yün-kang, five colossal cave shrines, each to contain a giant rock-cut image, presumably on behalf of the preceding five emperors. The next emperor (reigning 466–71) continued the work in altered form by opening twin cave chapels, presumably dedicated to his deceased parents. This latter precedent was followed at intervals throughout the next century near later capital sites, sometimes with a third chapel room added alongside for the living ruler.

At Yün-kang these great early caves, Nos. 16–20 and 7–8, used Buddha types that were manifestly western in origin. This monopoly was spectacularly broken in the 480's by the substitution of a more congenial form. The decision was probably a personal one, made by the North Chinese lady who then was all-powerful as regent for the boy emperor, her step-grandson. Under her protection, Chinese traits began to appear openly at the court level, and talented Chinese gained a new importance. It is possible that the new Buddha model was imported from the south, a bronze colossus that had been working miracles in a border city taken by the Wei in 467. The new style was introduced in a new pair of caves alongside 7 and 8, but was totally different. Cave No. 6, the most elaborate and original of all, was probably intended by the dowager empress for her own benefit. Cave No. 5, a modernized version of the original imperial five, centres like them on one gigantic Buddha. He cannot have stood for anyone in the T'o-pa line; I believe that he stood—by a supremely arrogant act of filial piety—for the dowager's Chinese father (who had been executed by the Wei as a traitor).

The earliest Buddhists in China were content to worship a single seated Buddha on a lion throne, certainly intended as Śākyamuni (cf. Pl. 157). By the fifth century it was customary to add a standing Bodhisattva on either side (Pl. 154). At the one imperial cave at Lung-men, c. 510, two small standing monks appear between the major figures, one the wrinkled Kāśyapa, the other the chubby Ānanda, summing up the group of human disciples. Toward the end of the Wei, as times again grew dark, two athletes dressed as gods were placed as bastions at the outer corners (cf. Pl. 162). By the 560's the group might again be enlarged by adding two odd figures, dressed like monks but with conical hair, the Pratyekabuddhas, who have achieved Enlightenment, but only for themselves.

Late in the same period a more obvious change with broader implications is seen in two long lintels from Caves Nos. 1 and 2 at the Northern Ch'i cave site of South Hsiang-t'ang Shan: a palace garden setting, where the lotus pond and the seated poses indicate the Pure Land of the West, presided over by Amitābha (Pl. 165). An earlier special group is a pair of Buddhas sitting side by side, an allusion to the central miracle of the *Lotus Sutra*, when Śākyamuni summons from the remote past a second Buddha identical to him, Prabhūtaratna (Pls. 161, 164). Often this scene, which took place on earth, is surmounted by a Bodhisattva figure sitting with crossed ankles: Maitreya, the Buddha of the future, biding his time in the Tuṣita heaven.

A useful feature of early Buddhist art in China is the frequency of inscriptions. By good fortune the site richest in early sculptures, Lung-men, has an exceptionally high proportion of inscriptions, most of them dated and many full of details. The cult preferences revealed in the early votive inscriptions show dedications as follows:

A.D. 495–575: Śākyamuni, 50; Amitāyus (Wu-liang-shou), 9; Bhaiṣajyaguru, 1; Prabhūtaratna, 3; Dīpaṅkara, 2; Maitreya, 36; the Seven Buddhas, 3; the 53 Buddhas, 1; the 1000 Buddhas, 1; unnamed dedications, 116. (Avalokiteśvara has 23.)

Sui and T'ang, out of a total of 601: Śākyamuni, 11; Locana, 3; Amitāyus, 3; Amitābha (O-mi-t'o), 122; Bhaiṣajyaguru, 2; Maitreya, 13; the Seven Buddhas, 2; the 16 Buddhas, 1; the 25 Buddhas, 2; the 35 Buddhas, 1; the 53 Buddhas, 1; the 1000 Buddhas, 4; unnamed dedications, 312. (Avalokiteśvara has 43.)

The most natural prayer for a Chinese is phrased at its simplest on a small gilded bronze Buddha made in 437 under the Nanking Sung dynasty (Pl. 155):

> . . . The disciple Han Ch'ien has reverently had this Buddha image made, praying that his deceased parents, his wife, his son, and his brothers may encounter the Buddhas and ever abide with the Three Jewels.

At the other extreme, an inscription of 498 in the Ku-yang cave at Lung-men gives the prayer of a high-born priest for his deceased father:

> . . . May he in spirit fly above the three [realms] . . . . May those of an earlier generation, the monks who taught me, my father and mother and their household soar like the *fêng* phoenix to the place of Enlightenment, or mount like the *luan* bird to the Tuṣita heaven. If they should re-awaken in some lower state among men, let it be among [the grandees of the land]. May the hosts of creatures in all conditions of life benefit in like manner from this prayer.

When the secular state loomed closest to the Church, it was natural to begin with prayers for the ruler, his consort, his heir, occasionally even the bureaucracy. Most of these pious wishes conclude with a longed-for destination, either the Western Pure Land of Amitāyus/Amitābha, or the world itself in that golden age when Maitreya descends to become Buddha.

Mahāyāna scriptures like the *Lotus Sutra* teach that the act of making a holy image is a work of the highest merit. In some branches of Buddhism and Hinduism, the conclusion is drawn that an image need not survive beyond the period required for its ceremonial recognition. In China, Buddhist images were made to survive, and in principle to be continually worshipped. Given the numbers involved, their actual functions are unclear. A small figure or group, made by a single householder, would presumably enter a family chapel, and be worshipped there perhaps for many generations (cf. Pls. 155, 157, 161, 163). In the southern records a number of colossal images of gilded bronze are mentioned as having been specifically made for famous named temples. On the other hand, what happened to 'the myriad stone images' said to have been commissioned by the last Northern Wei emperor, Chuang Ti (reigning 528–30)? If they, or the even larger bronze sets cited elsewhere, were actually executed, were they distributed to favoured individuals and to semi-official temples throughout the realm? There must have been a limit to what the latter could receive without disrupting their existing installations. The figures on altars in the main or subsidiary halls of early temples were presumably single, or set out in small groups according to rules, as in the surviving early buildings in Japan.

Evidence suggests that metropolitan temples did acquire great numbers of images beyond those they could properly install and care for. The eye-witness text that describes the Wei capital in its last years of magnificence, the *Lo-yang ch'ieh-lan chi*, tells of the annual Buddha's birthday festivities, when all the temples round about paraded their treasures, accompanied by guards, musicians and entertainers. The rendezvous was the imperially erected Ching-ming-ssu; the statues brought there would amount to over a thousand. Most must have been made of readily portable materials, lacquer, clay, wood, or hollow

154. Buddha flanked by Bodhisattvas

Painting on the wall of Cave No. 169, Ping-ling-ssu, Kansu Province, China; dated corresponding to A.D. *420.*

One of many votive groups, sculptural or painted, that are irregularly disposed in a very large natural cavern; one is inscribed with a date corresponding to A.D. 420 under the barbarian Western Ch'in régime. The figures here are outlined in black, lightly coloured, with conspicuous white highlights on flesh. The Buddha wears a Gandhāran-style robe, sinicized to suggest long sleeves, and sits in the pose of meditation on a lotus seat raised on a clumsily drawn pedestal; above is an umbrella-like canopy. The body aureole, inherited from Central Asian practice, seems to have been filled with Chinese-style flames. The haloed flanking figures, though garbed like monks, are called Bodhisattvas in their otherwise illegible cartouches.

155. Seated Buddha

Inscribed with a date corresponding to A.D. *437 under the South Chinese Sung dynasty; gilt bronze; H. 29.3 cm.; private collection, Japan.*

Now the robe has become rigidly symmetrical; the throne is a high moulded pedestal, its upper plinth based on the symbolic silhouette of the cosmic peak Sumeru and its bottom a cusped Chinese-style dais. The jutting flames of the aureole follow a Chinese tradition going back to late Chou. The inscription includes a prayer that the disciple-donor's 'deceased parents, his wife, his son, and his brothers may encounter the Buddhas and ever abide with the Three Jewels'.

156. Standing Buddha

Dated corresponding to A.D. *477 (Northern Wei dynasty); gilt bronze; H. 140.3 cm.; Metropolitan Museum of Art, New York.*

This is the 'King Udāyana' type of figure, ultimately Gandhāran but perfected in its formal symmetry in Central Asia. The two hands are balanced, one pointing upwards and the other downwards in expressive gestures; this is a culminating touch of formality apparently invented in China. Chinese preferences are seen in the piquant face and linearized, spiralling hair. The once pegged-on aureole has been lost; perhaps it originally bore an inscription, the gist of which was rudely copied around the base with a date corresponding to A.D. 477 and the name Maitreya. Irregularities in wording suggest it may be spurious; the iconographic type is still Śākyamuni's. The lotus base shows another Chinese characteristic—double staminodia bosses on each petal.

157. Seated Buddha

From Hopei Province, China; dated corresponding to A.D. *477 (Northern Wei dynasty); gilt bronze; H. 40.3 cm.; private collection, Japan.*

The drapery follows the Gandhāran 'open' mode, with the outer robe worn like a sling to partially cover and support the right arm; a western preference is still obeyed in using the left hand merely to hold the robe ends. Other characteristics are those perfected in China; firstly, the great flaming outer aureole, surrounding an inner area of stillness with seven tiny meditating Buddhas. There are two small lions in the round at the front corners of the 'Sumeru throne' and a cusped dais, with a godling kneeling or standing on the front and side leg panels. At the back of the dais, an inscription, after recording the date and place of origin (modern Hopei Province), names the figure as Śākyamuni and adds prayers for the donor's household: peaceful lives and rebirth where they may hear the Buddhas preaching. The aureole reverse is crowded with groups in low relief: the twin Buddhas of the *Lotus Sutra* at the top, scenes from Śākyamuni's birth-cycle at the bottom, and a preaching Buddha assemblage between.

158. Buddhist stele

Unearthed at Kao-p'ing-hsien, Shansi Province, China; first half of sixth century A.D. *(Northern Wei dynasty); H. 182 cm.; sandstone.*

The great number of miniature Buddha niches carved on the front make this a Thousand Buddha stele, of the sort that became current in the sixth-century phase of Northern Wei. This stele has no inscription but also may be considered a work of the sixth-century phase of Northern Wei. It is said to have been unearthed at Kao-p'ing-hsien in Shansi Province, and so may be attributed to the Shansi school of sculpture. In such details as the shapes given the two attendants and the deities that fly across the top, the special quality of Shansi sculpture may be recognized.

159. Colossal seated Buddha

From Cave No. 3, Yün-kang, north Shansi Province, China; 5th century A.D. and later; cut from the rock.

This is the central Buddha figure in a cave begun under the Northern Wei and completed later, perhaps in the eleventh century. It is the best preserved of all the colossal images and can be photographed the most effectively. The figure's way of sitting with pendent legs is Western. Its right hand makes the conventional "fear not" gesture, *abhaya-mudrā*. On each side of the Buddha figure stands a Bodhisattva, wearing a pseudo-Indian costume with a jewelled crown.

160. Seated Buddha identified as Amitāyus (Wu-liang-shou)

Recently unearthed in Szechwan Province, China; dated corresponding to A.D. *483 (Southern Ch'i dynasty); stone; Ch'eng-tu Provincial Museum.*

This is the earliest Buddha image so far found re-designed in a fully Chinese manner: the outer robe is worn opened down the front, kimono-fashion; a conspicuous sash is knotted with dangling ends; and the highly elaborate pleated robe overhangs in three tiers covering the legs and throne. The hand-gesture (*mudrā*) is interesting: the left hand is turned down to balance the upturned right, with a new distinction between open and closed fingers like a Christian gesture of blessing. The rear of the pier has an unfinished standing figure with the same characteristics. A conspicuous lack of any aureole or hair details is perhaps because both were originally painted.

161. Pair of enthroned Buddhas

Dated corresponding to A.D. *518; gilt bronze; H. 27 cm.; Musée Guimet, Paris.*

The two epitomize the spectacular central miracle of the *Lotus Sutra*, the meeting and conversation between Śākyamuni as Buddha of the present age and a Buddha recalled from the remote past, Prabhūtaratna. Unusual are the return to the informal Indian *rāja*'s way of sitting and the contrast between plain hair surfaces on one Buddha and tiny Gupta-style curls on the other. The work displays a climax of nervous exaggeration; the quality originated in South China and was common in both north and south by A.D. 518. On the throne are two tense adoring monks, two lions, and a central lotus-shaped incense-burner, supported by an earth deity.

162. Stele with standing Buddha and attendants

Unearthed from the ruined temple site of Wan-fo-ssu, Ch'eng-tu, Szechwan Province, China (from which a very similar piece was found, dated corresponding to A.D. *522); Liang dynasty; red sandstone; W. 31 cm.; Szechwan Provincial Museum.*

Both the Buddha and Bodhisattva types had by this time become standard in both South and North China. The Wan-fo-ssu stele, presumably following Liang court standards, is exceptionally rich, both in the number of figures and in technical variety, the relief ranging from partially free-standing lions and donors to the almost flat quartet of deities across the back. Athlete guardians at the bottom corners round out the iconographic scheme. The preserved half of the aureole shows, instead of flames or tiny figures in rows, picturesque narrative scenes, probably drawn from the cycle of the Buddha's Entry in Nirvana. This innovation seems to bear witness to the rapidly growing prestige of Buddhist painters in the south.

163. Standing Buddha Maitreya

Dated corresponding to A.D. *536 (Eastern Wei régime); gilt bronze; H. 61 cm.; University Museum, University of Pennsylvania, Philadelphia.*

This figure is a fully developed version of the completely sinicized Buddha type, with the flattened body concealed by folds that flare widely as they descend. We note a short vertical accent in the dangling sash ties, balanced up and down hand-gestures, and a tall thin neck, head and *uṣṇīṣa*. The pointed aureole has a border of darting flames, and around the lotus of the head halo is a flat lotus scroll. The inscription identifies the figure and adds a prayer for peace, one most appropriate in an age of catastrophic civil wars.

165. Frieze with Buddha assemblage

From a lintel position at the front of Cave No. 2 of the southern half of Mt. Hsiang-t'ang, on the Honan-Hopei border, China; Northern Ch'i work for an imperial patron, probably c. A.D. *570; stone; H. 157.5 cm.; Freer Gallery of Art, Washington, D.C.*

The composition shows the Pure Land Paradise of the Buddha Amitābha, identifiable by the stone bordered lotus pool in which the new arrivals are being reborn from lotus buds. At either side of the pool are the chief Bodhisattva agents, Avalokiteśvara and Mahāsthāmaprāpta. Lesser Bodhisattvas sit or stand at the rear and small Buddha groups swoop down from above as visitors from their own realms. An unprecedented weighty opulence is evident in canopy and foliage and in sturdy figures that almost seem nude. Only the flanking garden pavilions are in purely Chinese style; the rest must depend on some lost Indian prototype.

◁ 164. Broken stele

Dated corresponding to A.D. *554, the final year of the Western Wei régime; stone; H. (of remaining part) 215 cm.; Museum of Fine Arts, Boston.*

This is the most richly varied (and compositionally unified) example of a type of multi-tiered stele developed in China. The main group shows a seated Buddha flanked by named leading disciples Kāśyapa and Ānanda, flanked in the outer panels by unnamed Bodhisattvas and thunderbolt-bearing guardians. Above, twin Buddhas under a canopy represent the *Lotus Sutra* miracle (cf. Pl. 161). The lower half of the stele gives an unusual emphasis to the lions, incense-burner, donors with horses, and an inscription square. The style is the last phases of Wei, with obtrusive parallel folds falling in heavy swages or flat, petal-like sheaths; the swiftness and tension of the dying style survive only in incidental details. The long inscription opens with a typical theological cliché, names as chief beneficiary the emperor, and asks that all may be reborn to attend the Three Assemblies of Maitreya. Over two hundred donors are spoken of, and beyond the grandees on the front, the rear is filled with one hundred and twenty-two of the rest, standing in identical rows.

166. Standing Buddha Amitābha

Dated corresponding to A.D. *557 (Northern Ch'i regime); stone; H. 268 cm.; Royal Ontario Museum, Toronto.*

This is a complete antithesis to the Wei standard, except in the lingering flatness below the waist and the discreet curlicues at the bottom of the robe and under-garment. The widely spaced robe folds fall in symmetrical catenaries derived from India and thought in China to imitate an original carved for Emperor Aśoka. Notable are the roundness of the head with a very low, domical *uṣṇīṣa* and the small curls. A long base inscription lists donors' names.

167. Standing Buddha lacking head and hands

Stone; Freer Gallery of Art, Washington, D.C.

The robe is covered, front and rear, with crowded, small-scale, low relief cosmological representations. The shoulders and chest show the Tuṣita heaven, with Maitreya as a Bodhisattva enthroned in the central pavilion. Down the rib axis runs the hourglass-shaped mountain Sumeru, encircled by a pair of giant *nāga* kings and flanked by two titanic standing *asuras*. The middle of the body focusses first on a miniature city; then on a confrontation between two figures in architectural enclosures, with an enigmatic horse between, perhaps to symbolize the animal passions. Just below, the centre is occupied by deities and monks worshipping a stupa of Gupta period type, flanked by the many-armed Hindu gods, Śiva on his bull and Kārttikeya on his peacock. At knee level, demi-gods emblematic of the primal phenomena of the earth—wind, fire, mountains, etc.—are seated between trees. At the bottom is a judgement scene in hell.

168. The interior of Cave No. 11 at Lung-men, Honan Province, China

Dated corresponding to A.D. *673; W. 379 cm.*

A priest's donor inscription identified the central throne figure as a Maitreya (shown by anticipation as a Buddha), and adds a prayer on behalf of the imperial family. The image is seated in the 'European' posture (*bhadrāsana*), as borrowed from late Gandhāra and Gupta practice, and the high-backed throne is also Indian. The figures have the amplitude and solidity of the mature T'ang style but they are not yet exaggerated; the Buddha's face expresses gentleness and intelligence, with a touch of child-like sweetness.

169. Wall painting of the Pure Land Paradise of Amitābha

Side-wall of Cave No. 321 (in Pelliot's system, 139A), Tun-huang, Kansu Province, China; datable to c. A.D. 775.

This is the most happily proportioned and brilliantly detailed version of the palace-garden formula common at Tun-huang from the mid-eighth through to the eleventh century. The architecture, the perspective formula, and the costumes of the small figures in the border scenes are high T'ang. The arbitrary sizes of the deities and their attendants, and the dark brown skin colour come directly from India. The central Amitābha's body has the tense slenderness of the Pāla style; in the flanking Bodhisattvas and Buddhas something of the languorous plumpness of the Chinese eighth century has been added. The scenes in the side strip on the viewer's right tell the tragic story of King Bimbisāra, Queen Vaidehī and their murderous son Ajātaśatru. On the opposite side are the sixteen degrees of visualization prescribed to Vaidehī as a means of reaching true knowledge of Amitābha and his Pure Land in her mortal body.

170. Triptych 'pillow shrine'

Brought back to Japan in A.D. *806 as a present from his Chinese masters in esoteric lore, by the Shingon founder Kūkai (i.e., Kōbō Daishi); sandalwood; H. 23 cm.; Kongōbu-ji, Kōya-san (Mt. Kōya), Wakayama Prefecture.*

It is a doubly puzzling piece, since it is obviously not 'Indian' as Kūkai's list of gifts notes, and is in no discernible way tantric. Instead it looks like an imitation of some lost sculpture of Northern Ch'i type, in both style and iconography; there are many points of resemblance with the Hsiang-t'ang Shan cave sculptures.

171. Block-printed frontispiece to a printed handscroll edition of the *Vajracchedikā-sūtra*

Found by Sir Aurel Stein at Tun-huang, Kansu Province, China; dated corresponding to A.D. *868; H. 23 cm.; British Museum, London.*

Śākyamuni, wearing a robe with the complex fold and hem treatment of late T'ang, carries on a dialogue with his kneeling disciple, the aged Subhūti, on the left. Note a symbolic lion, two thunderbolt-wielding guardians, the nine other 'great disciples', a king with his ministers and two Bodhisattvas inserted at the rear (testifying to the relatively early date of the sutra). It is energetically drawn, with a typical late T'ang mixture of realism and formality.

bronze. Very likely it was the aftermath of such displays that was lamented by the devout crown prince of the Liang dynasty in the south, when he described the unseemly crowding into cabinets and chests of the images that had made so fine a show the day before.

Except for such texts, almost everything that we know about Buddhist image-making in the early centuries is provided by extant sculptures in stone, most less than life-size but including a few free-standing giants. Recent finds under a ruined temple at Chü-yang in Hopei Province have revealed over 2,200 fragments carved in the local white marble, dating from late Northern Wei to mid-T'ang. Many may have been broken from a single original; but even so, the total accumulated by the end of Northern Ch'i, the period when enthusiasm for Buddhism was at its height in the north-east, must have been so large that they could be stored only in special halls or temple courtyards and worshipped *en masse* (like the outdated ancestor tablets of a millennium earlier).

A good many of the largest remaining sculptures are stelae of the dragon-topped form; and these, though they include niches with figure groups, have spacious shafts that permit lengthy inscriptions. Often these texts record not merely the act of carving the stone itself, but the erection of a temple building, or even a first founding. Such stones were important as almost indestructible historical documents, and so were probably given prominent places in the temple courtyard or hall, where they could be read as history and their calligraphy admired. The fact that they also included small figures of the types worshipped elsewhere was probably accepted as routine, these being given only perfunctory reverence. The majority of the large, stone, stele-like pieces that remain with legible inscriptions may speak of scores or hundreds of donors, or represent them in miniature with names attached (Pl. 164). There will be a place-name, but usually no mention of a temple. Perhaps most of these sculptures, too large and costly, and involving too many local families to be merely taken for storage, were set up in cloister corridors. Under the most primitive conditions they may have had only wooden shelters, and so have functioned as wayside reminders.

The Sui coup d'état in 580 terminated one of the three most disastrous periods for Buddhism, the proscription ordered from 574 on under the Northern Chou. The new emperor made his government a positive agent in restoring religion. As a donor of holy images he is said to have had 1,508,940 restored, and 106,580 made anew in various sizes, in gold, silver, sandalwood, lacquer, ivory and stone. Thereafter Buddhism took its place among the major institutions of the Chinese empire, never seriously threatened until its third crisis in the 840's. Its temples around the capital vied in splendour with the imperial palaces, and must indeed have been artistically richer, since most of the great painters of the time did monumental murals on their walls.

Worship of the Buddha may be said to have undergone three conspicuous changes during the Sui and T'ang periods. In the Six Dynasties, deities had multiplied, and cults had grown and competed, without any control from above. These cross-currents and conflicts, which seemed to mirror political fragmentation, must have seemed intolerable to those who looked towards unity as the ultimate ideal. The concept of a single, supreme Buddha as the sum of all lesser aspects of divinity begins to enter the records of image-making with marked frequency in the second half of the sixth century. The almost universally used name for this being is Locana (in Mandarin, Lu-che-na; in Japanese, Roshana). The choice was an old-fashioned one, since the Buddha so-called had been the central feature of the *Sutra of Brahmā's Net*, translated at the end of the fourth century. There he is revealed by Śākyamuni—the eternal preacher, but now in a celestial setting—as enthroned on an immense lotus of a thousand petals, each containing its own cosmos made up of a hundred million worlds like our own, each of them with the standard Mount Sumeru at its centre and its own Buddha Śākyamuni. Such a theme was far beyond the capacities of even the Sui and T'ang artists, who seem to have merely made still taller colossi, in lacquer or on cliffsides. The imperial Lu-che-na of 679 at Lung-men is merely a huge seated Buddha, on a throne too damaged to aid any attempts at further identification and with the conventional attendants. The most ambitious of remaining examples in Eastern Asia is the bronze Roshana of 747 at Tōdai-ji in Nara, seated on a twenty-petal lotus, each engraved with a central seated Buddha group, and with horizontal striations below to stand for separate worlds. The prayers addressed to Locana preserved in votive inscriptions merely continue the formulae worked out for Śākyamuni.

The imagery of the *Sutra of Brahmā's Net* reappears in still more stupendous forms in the much longer *Avataṃsaka-sūtra*. That, too, had an early translation, but was represented in art chiefly on the basis of a second one, made in the late 690's. The new work may have been first tried out in a wall painting done for the Lo-yang temple, Ching-ai-ssu, which the usurper Empress Wu built on behalf of her parents. The title recorded is *Hua-yen pien*, i.e., *Avataṃsaka* scenes. The cosmic Buddha is now Vairocana (P'i-lu-che-na, or Birushana), an obvious enrichment of the earlier name, but the means used to elucidate his sutra are entirely different. There is no giant central Buddha; instead, as seen in a number of late wall paintings at Tun-huang, the composition is a display of nine preaching groups enclosing a centrally placed Mount Sumeru rising from the cosmic sea. Each group is filled with celestial listeners surrounding a preaching Buddha, but their scale is so small that they seem like brilliantly coloured blossoms. Each of the nine Buddhas is Śākyamuni, shown as he moves from one place of assembly to another on earth or in the heavens. Vairocana is suggested throughout, but not represented; Buddhist art here returns to the doctrine that the highest level of truth, the *dharmakāya*, is utterly beyond normal perception.

'*Vairocana*' in Sanskrit means 'resplendent' (see p. 135); T'ang stressed the quality of universal radiance, presumably testifying to the passage of Buddhism on its mission to the Far East, through Iranian light-worshipping lands. The name appears later in the group of scriptures of the Esoteric sect, the Vajrayāna, brought to China from India by sea in the early eighth century. In their translations the sublime name is rendered with audacious simplicity as 'Great Sun Tathāgata' (Ta Jih Ju-lai; Japanese, Dainichi Nyorai).

The Vajrayāna was highly influential for a brief period in China, particularly after the disasters of the mid-eighth century when its repertory of magical defenses promised a desperately needed barrier. It seems to have been in favour at the T'ang capital in the early years of the ninth century, when the two Japanese student-priests Saichō and Kūkai came to penetrate its mysteries. Whereas the new sects that they founded, Tendai and Shingon, won a dominant position that they maintained for many centuries in Japan, the school in China seems never to have gained more than a few strategic strongholds, and for that reason suffered most grievously in the great proscription of 842–46.

Thus almost all evidence for Vajrayāna art in China has been preserved in Japan, in much the same way that most of the evidence for Vajrayāna art in India has been preserved in Tibet. The iconographic traditions certainly passed through China to Japan, just as they passed from India to Tibet, but because of the destruction that the Buddhist tradition suffered both in India and in China, the later recipients have remained the main beneficiaries certainly so far as Vajrayāna art is concerned. In T'ang times Dainichi (Vairocana) was normally represented not as a single Buddha figure, but as the centre of a Five Buddha mandala, exactly as in the earliest known Indo-Tibetan tradition. These mandalas are often extremely complex, for they include besides the Five Buddhas also the four chief goddesses surrounded by attendant Boddisattvas, minor goddesses, guardians of the four quarters, etc. It is interesting to note that at some stage the Sino-Japanese tradition seems to have replaced certain of the goddesses by Bodhisattvas. The main geometrical designs are known as the *Garbhadhātu* (the Sphere of the Embryo of Buddhahood) and the *Vajradhātu* (the Elemental Sphere), in Japanese the Taizōkai and the Kongōkai. Several early examples of these have been preserved in Japan (see Pls. 202, 202–a,202–b). Also preserved is a Chinese handscroll of iconographic drawings, called the *Gobu-shinkan* (Fivefold Contemplation), given in A.D. 855 to the Japanese student monk Enchin (Fig. E, p. 418). T'ang Buddhists as a whole worshipped a variety of novel or recently popularized deities, most of them manifestations of Avalokiteśvara, culminating in the Thousand-handed, Thousand-eyed, Greatly Compassionate, Greatly Merciful One. What was typical of temple layouts, at least in the north-west, may be assumed from the standard followed from the eighth century on at the busy Caves of the Thousand Buddhas site near Tun-huang in far western Kansu. There the typical high T'ang cave is a large open room, expanded by a wide recess at the rear that holds the clay images aligned on either side of an enthroned Buddha. These are usually traditional; the Buddha seems to be either Śākyamuni, with legs crossed, or Maitreya, with legs down.

The entire wall surface of the room on the worshipper's left is occupied by a monumental presentation of the Pure Land of the West (Pl. 169). The figures, headed by an oversized Amitābha, sit in a palace garden setting, with a frame of monumental buildings behind and a formal pool in front. To left and right of the pool two unidentifiable minor enthroned Buddhas address small groups. The ends and sometimes the bottom of the paradise scene are usually framed by accessory illustrations. One border will be a vertical series of panels telling the tragic story of the pious royal pair Bimbisāra and Vaidehī, and their cruel son, the parricide Ajātaśatru. The opposite frame will show Vaidehī performing the series of sixteen meditations that led her from the horrors of her life to a full absorption in the beauties of Amitābha and his Pure Land. The typical bottom sequence differentiates the nine degrees of welcome to Paradise granted the believer's soul at the moment of death.

The matching composition on the observer's right will be the Eastern Paradise of the Buddha of Medicine, Bhaiṣajyaguru. Since the latter's special scripture admits that his realm is just like that of the West, the artists at Tun-huang were content to make only minor modifications. The host around this Buddha should feature his twelve demon-like guardians, who lead the assault on the demons of disease. Natural subjects for use as side frames are his Twelve Vows of saviourhood, and the nine forms of violent death from which he can perform rescues.

At Tun-huang two alternative side-wall compositions, with the same large scale but no necessary orientation, celebrated Śākyamuni's preaching the *Lotus Sutra* and the golden age to come under Maitreya. Since the *Lotus Sutra* was preached on the Vulture Peak, with no architectural background, a great palace in miniature, spread out under the top frame, refers to the Tathāgata's promise that the earth itself will be revealed as an eternal paradise. Maitreya's assembly will be very much like Amitābha's, with a similar palace garden setting, distinguished chiefly by the fact that small scenes set outside the main group, in an irregular landscape, illustrate the prelude to the prophecy of Maitreya's final descent.

The summary descriptions of Buddhist wall paintings at the T'ang capitals, Ch'ang-an and Lo-yang, included in the mid-ninth century painting history *Li-tai ming hua chi*, make it clear that from the artists' standpoint the most challenging works were individual figures, not of Buddhas, but chiefly of lesser deities or of monks. Five Western Paradise scenes are cited, two by the great *Wu Tao-tzu*, but none show the rival Pure Land of Bhaiṣajyaguru.

6. KOREA

The Three Kingdoms

It was during the second half of the Three Kingdoms period, fourth to sixth centuries, that Buddhism supplied the motivation for the art of sculpture in Korea. Buddhism was introduced into Koguryŏ and Paekje in the late fourth century, but it was not until the first half of the sixth century that it became the official state religion in Silla. During this period, foreign monks and craftsmen were responsible for the erection and decoration of Buddhist temples. An example of an image that may be taken as a product of this period is a seated figure made of gilt bronze, discovered accidently at Tuksŏm near Seoul in April, 1960. This very small piece deserves special mention because its place of discovery is authenticated, though the story of its acquisition is not known in detail. Its discovery is significant in that it suggests that sculptural relics in Korea may possibly date back earlier than the fifth century. This seated image of Buddha is only 5 centimetres high, but judging from its style and especially its socle, it is assumed to be an early gilt bronze Buddha of the type produced in the north-western part of China around A.D. 400, and it also has characteristics typical of early Korean sculpture.

The Koguryŏ Kingdom (37 B.C.–A.D. 668). The Koguryŏ relics, which usually consist of small images, are divided into three categories: those of metal, those of stone, and those of clay. In a discussion of metal Buddhist images, we must first mention the well-known triad excavated at Koksan-gun, Hwanghae Province. This consists of a statuette of Amitābha

172. Standing Buddha, dated 7th year of Yonka

Discovered in 1963 at Ŭirŏng, South Kyŏngsang Province, Korea; 6th century A.D. *(*A.D. *539 or 599); gilt bronze; H. 16.2 cm.; National Museum of Korea, Seoul.*

The image stands on a round lotus pedestal and is backed by an oblong halo with an incised pattern. The body is covered with a thick robe and the two hands make regular symbolic gestures. The face shows a slight smile. On the back of halo an inscription of 47 characters in 4 lines gives the date, name of country and the monks concerned. It is noteworthy that this Buddha of the Koguryŏ kingdom was found in the territory of Old Silla.

173. Bodhisattva in reflective pose

Three Kingdoms period, early 7th century A.D.*; gilt bronze; H. 93.5 cm.; National Museum of Korea, Seoul.*

This Bodhisattva image is famous for its size and excellence. He is seated in a reflective pose which is a modification of the 'sportive' gesture (*lalitāsana*). See also Pl. 186 for a possible identification as Maitreya, and for the pose compare Pl. 222. The right elbow rests on the right knee and the fingers of the right hand barely touch the cheek. The right leg is crossed over the left knee and the left leg rests on a nearly flat lotus pedestal. The crown is three-cusped but very flat. The softly rounded modelling is suggestive of reserve and quiet vitality. At Kōryū-ji temple in Kyoto, is a wooden image very close in style and feeling despite the different medium.

174. Buddha triad

From Sŏsan, South Ch'ungch'ŏng Province, Korea; Paekje dynasty, early 7th century A.D.*; rock-cut relief; H. of central Buddha 280 cm.; H. of seated Bodhisattva 160 cm.; H. of standing Bodhisattva 170 cm.; in situ.*

This, newly discovered triad is located in a deep valley near Sŏsan in the south-western part of Korea. A huge eastward-facing rock preserves this triad in its lower section. The Buddha has a petalled halo behind the head and a lotus support under the feet. The tall body is covered with a very thick robe and the two hands show regular symbolic gestures. The Bodhisattva on the right sits in a 'playful' posture (*lalitāsana*) and a smile plays on his rounded face. The Bodhisattva on the left holds a round jewel with two hands and his face also has a slight smile. This triad is a masterpiece of Korean stone sculpture.

175. Standing Maitreya

From Samyangdong, Seoul, Korea; Old Silla period, 6th century A.D.*; gilt bronze; H. 20.7 cm.; National Museum of Korea, Seoul.*

The image was discovered in Seoul in 1967 and is probably from the site of an old temple. It stands on a round pedestal carved in the lotus pattern. The crown is triangular with a small inset Buddha image. The rectangular face has rather swollen eyes and a solemn appearance. The left hand holds a water-pot and the drapery hangs on a two-tiered U-shaped style. This figure represents one of the most important discoveries of very old bronze images in Korea.

176. The Buddha of a triad

From Samhwa, Namsan, Kyŏngju, Korea; Old Silla period, early 7th century A.D. *(c.* A.D. *644); stone; H. 160 cm.; Kyŏngju National Museum.*

This triad was originally located on the peak of Samhwa ('Three Flowers') on Namsan, south of Kyŏngju, and was probably enshrined in a stone cave that was artificially constructed. According to the style and to literary evidence, the main Buddha appears to be Maitreya. The figure is seated on a lotus-patterned base with the feet resting on separate platforms. The drapery is marked with curving lines that are one of the characteristic features of this figure. Because of the childish expression of the face, this triad is generally called 'the infant Buddha'.

177. Seated Buddha

Discovered in the three-storeyed stone pagoda of Hwangbok-sa, Kyŏngju, Korea; United Silla period, c. A.D. *700; gold; H. 12.2 cm.; National Museum of Korea, Seoul.*

The image sits enthroned on a raised lotus seat. Deep folds of drapery conceal his crossed legs and the front of the seat. The halo has a border of scrolls and flames done in low relief openwork with a punched and incised pattern behind the body. The right hand makes the gesture of blessing and for this reason we identify the image as Amoghasiddhi, but it might equally well be intended as Śākyamuni.

with a Bodhisattva on either side. The halos are carved and the inscription on the piece is believed to correspond to the year 571. The style of the images themselves also supports this claim and is reminiscent of sculptures of the Northern Wei, while its detailed technique reflects the influence of the late Six Dynasties.

A superb example of a single figure of the Buddha made of gilt bronze was discovered at Ŭiryŏng, South Kyŏngsang Province, in 1963. It is 16.2 centimetres in height (Pl. 172), stands on a lotus socle and is adorned with a boat-shaped halo. The four-line inscription of forty-seven characters on the back of the halo gives the date, the name of the region and the persons involved. The date reading "the seventh year of Yonka" is understood to correspond to sometime in the sixth century. The gentle smile on the oval face and the thick fall of drapery over the shoulders are all expressive of the style developed by the Northern Wei. It is also interesting to note that a work produced in Koguryŏ, which was located in the northern part of the peninsula, was discovered in the southernmost region of the country.

The Paekje Kingdom (37 B.C.–A.D. *661).* From the time of its foundation Paekje was under constant attack, and several efforts were made to establish the capital further south. However, the reign of King Sŏng (523–53), who had his court at Puyŏ, seems to be especially noteworthy for the importation of Buddhist civilization, resulting from the contacts with the Northern and Southern dynasties of China, and especially with the Liang of the Southern Dynasty. The Paekje arts prospered in the course of a period of 120 years during the reign of King Sŏng, and of the two kings who succeeded him, Wi-dok (554–97) and Mu (600–40).

Triads in gilt bronze occur frequently and may have been produced in the period from the end of the sixth to the beginning of the seventh century. Although these works display a simple technique derived from Chinese models of the Northern Wei, they also show a certain softness and warmth, which may be the contribution of Paekje. Apart from these inscribed images, small figures of Buddhas and Bodhisattvas have also been discovered. Two standing Bodhisattvas that show the influence of the Chinese style of the Sui period were unearthed at Kyuam, Puyŏ, at the beginning of this century. Another gilt statuette of a standing Bodhisattva, excavated at Kunsu-ri, Puyŏ, in 1937, is a typical example of the Paekje images and is thought to have been produced in the second half of the sixth century.

Among all the gilt bronze images of the Three Kingdoms period that deserve notice is the Bodhisattva image seated in the *lalitāsana* posture, now owned by the National Museum of Korea (Pl. 173). Produced towards the end of the Three Kingdoms period in the seventh century, it is the finest work of its kind ever made in Korea.

Carvings in stone were made at Sŏsan, South Ch'ungch'ŏng Province, and around Iksan, North Chŏlla Province. At the former location, two fine examples of a triad of Buddha figures carved on a huge rock were discovered in 1957. Such new finds allow us to conjecture that Buddhist stone sculpture may have originated in Paekje in the sixth century, since these two examples are believed to date from the early seventh century (Pl. 174).

Sculptural technique in Puyŏ was outstanding, and certainly superior to that of the other two kingdoms in the Three Kingdoms period. Its influence reached not only neighbouring Silla but also Japan.

The Old Silla Kingdom (57 B.C–A.D. 668). Official recognition of Buddhism came later in Old Silla than elsewhere in the three kingdoms. There is no trace of any sculptural activity before the sixth century and thus the acquisition of technique and individual style in Silla seems to have been surpassed by that in the other two kingdoms. No gilt bronze triads, like those found at Paekje, have been discovered in Silla. Only the gilt bronze standing statue of a Bodhisattva, found at Samyangdong, Seoul, in 1967, is assumed to be a product of Old Silla because of the definite location of its discovery (Pl. 175).

Almost no stone statues predating the sixth century are known. However, the ten figures of Buddhas and Bodhisattvas at Sinsŏn-sa on Mt. Dansok, So-myon, Wŏlsŏng-gun, North Kyŏngsang Province, discovered in 1969 and believed to have been produced around A.D. 600, are remarkable. The well-known figures of the two Deva Kings, carved in relief on the sides of the stone pagoda at Punhwang-sa, the stone Maitreya on Mt. Songhwa, and the Maitreya triad from Samhwaryong (Pl. 176) on Mt. Nam, Kyŏngju, are all thought to date from the first half of the seventh century.

The United Silla Period

The Early Days. Sculpture in the early days of United Silla had an advantage over that of Old Silla, since it could make use of the advanced techniques and accumulated experience of Paekje and Koguryŏ. A period of peace and stability after a long war provided a suitable background for the blossoming of Buddhist culture around Kyŏngju, the capital of the new kingdom. In the early United Silla period, sculpture may be regarded as representing a kind of provisional phase, continuing the style of the previous period but also at the same time providing a starting point for the discovery of a style of its own. During this period, a new foreign style was introduced from T'ang China, which resulted in a mixture of the old and the new. However, no large gilt bronze statue is extant, and only a few statuettes of Buddhas and Bodhisattvas are known. The seated Buddha (Pl. 177) and the standing figure of Maitreya, both made of gold alloy and found in the three-storeyed stone pagoda at the site of Hwangbok-sa, Kyŏngju, may be regarded as products of this period. With regard to stone images, huge Buddha statues carved in relief on rock in the conventional style were prevalent, and the method of carving gradually evolved into that of sculpture in the round. One specific feature that attracts notice in these early works of sculptured rock is that these Buddha images are enshrined in stone cave shrines or niches.

The above-mentioned statues belong to the early days of United Silla and display features typical of the style of the Three Kingdoms period. In the case of the triad of images (Pl. 178) at Kunwi, it is noticeable that the style of the detailed areas, the technique of carving a fall of drapery on the square pedestal of the central Buddha figure, and the face and the ornaments of the standing Bodhisattvas beside him reveal a great affinity with those of the stone or metal statues belonging to the Puyŏ period of Paekje.

Other important works ascribed to this period are seven stone statues that were discover-

178. Buddha triad

From Kunwi cave, North Kyŏngsang Province, Korea; United Silla period, c. A.D. *700; granite; H. of main Buddha 288 cm.; in situ.*

At the lower part of a huge cliff, located near a stream, is the Kunwi cave, in which is seated an enthroned Amitābha with two standing Bodhisattvas. The Buddha has smooth hair and a thin robe that falls covering the rectangular base on which he sits. The Bodhisattvas have a three-sided crowns, two-tiered U-shape robes and one holds a water-pot. This cave was discovered in 1958 and was found to have been carved about A.D. 700, prior to the famous stone cave on Mt. T'oham in Kyŏngju.

179. Stele erected by the Chun family of Piam-sa

From South Ch'ungch'ŏng Province, Korea; United Silla period, dated A.D. *673; soapstone; H. 43 cm.; National Museum of Korea, Seoul.*

This stone stele is the most representative one so far discovered in Korea, even if it lacks both the base and the upper part. It was discovered in 1958 in a small temple in South Ch'ungch'ŏng Province. In the foreground is a seated Buddha triad with guardians that are carved with halos and lotus pedestals. On both sides and the back are carved seated *apsaras* with musical instruments and other seated images. The inscription incised on the front gives simply the appellation of Buddha and the donors with dates corresponding to A.D. 673. This stele was carved by a noble family that was living in the Paekje kingdom just after its destruction.

180. Budda Vairocana

From Kyŏngju, Korea; United Silla period, c. second half of 8th century A.D.*; gilt bronze; H. 177 cm.; Pulguk-sa, Kyŏngju.*

This Buddha is one of the three colossal bronze Buddhas of the United Silla period that survived in the Kyŏngju area in Korea. Lacking the lotus base and halo, this Buddha is now enthroned in the Paradise Hall of Pulguk-sa with a gilt bronze Amitābha of the same size and age. The flat face and the hand-gesture (*bodhyagrī-mudrā*, see p. 369) suggest the latter half of the eighth century. This bronze Buddha served as the model for stone-carvings of this style, which prevailed from the ninth century to the end of the Silla kingdom.

181. Standing Maitreya

From Kamsan-sa, Kyŏngju, Korea; United Silla period, A.D. *720; H. 183 cm.; National Museum of Korea, Seoul.*

This standing image has an octagonal lotus base and an oblong halo, which has carved inscriptions on the back. According to the inscriptions, this image of the Bodhisattva Maitreya was carved in 720 and dedicated by the official Kim Chi-song to his deceased parents. It has jewelled robes, an ornamented crown, ear-rings and a necklace The drapery is well carved according to the style of the period. This image was enthroned in Kamsan-sa together with an Amitābha Buddha carved in the same year.

182. Seated Buddha

From Sŏkkur-am cave, Kyŏngju, Korea; United Silla period, A.D. *750; H. 326 cm.; in situ.*

In the centre of this stone cave, which is located near the summit of Mt. T'oham, Kyŏngju, this huge granite Buddha is enthroned on a lotus base. It has a serene face and majestic body with the hands in the 'earth-witness' posture, typical of the Silla period. Facing the south-eastern direction with the Eastern Sea in view, this image has remained in his elaborate niche for more than 1200 years. It was constructed because of the anxious desire for peace on the part of the Silla kingdom and dates to A.D. 750.

183. Bodhisattva Samantabhadra

From Sŏkkur-am cave, Kyŏngju, Korea; United Silla period; H. 218 cm.; in situ.

Two Bodhisattvas stand on either side of the entrance to Sŏkkur-am cave. Among these images, one in the northern wall is especially noteworthy for his slender body and delicate carving. Facing the inside of the cave, this Bodhisattva stands on a round lotus pedestal, but gives the suggestion of motion.

ed in Yŏn'gi-gun, South Ch'ungch'ŏng Province, in 1959. The most notable are the Buddha triad, bearing an inscription informing us that it was erected in A.D. 667 at the Piam-sa temple by someone named Chun (Pl. 179), and the monument-like stone statue of the Buddha triad at the Sŏkwang-am, Chochiwŏn. Such works not only reflect the influence of Paekje sculpture but also preserve traces of the old association with the Chinese style of the Six Dynasties period. It is even more significant that these sculptures were completed by the surviving Paekje craftsmen immediately after the fall of the Paekje kingdom.

No large clay images of the early United Silla have survived, but plaster images of the Four Deva Kings, unearthed at the Sachonwang-sa site, are representative of this period. These images have a strong appeal because of their refined technique and graceful style. A similar group of the Four Deva Kings, even more valuable as an artistic piece, was discovered in the western three-storeyed stone pagoda at the site of Kamun-sa, near Kyŏngju.

The Middle United Period. From the beginning of the eighth century, Silla sculpture began to display special characteristics of its own. Not only did the number of sculpture works increase but the area of activity also widened. Especially noticeable during this period is the prevalence of small gilt bronze statues, indicating that Buddhism had gained popular support. The great scarcity of large images may be due to their destruction in a later age. A statue of Bhaiṣajyaguru, Buddha of Medicine, at Paekyul-sa, and statues of Amitābha and Vairocana (Pl. 180) at Pulguk-sa may date back to about 800.

Among the stone statues of this period whose dates are ascertained are the two standing statues of Amitābha and Maitreya that have survived at the site of Kamsan-sa (Pl. 181). However, the best of eighth-century Silla sculpture may be the statues enshrined in the rock chapel of Sŏkkur-am on the crest of T'ohamsan; of these the seated Buddha, the central figure in the cave, is exquisite in its harmony (Pl. 182). Among the numerous images carved on the surrounding walls, the four Bodhisattvas to the right and left of the entrance are certainly masterpieces (Pl. 183). The Eleven-headed Kuan-yin standing behind the seated Śākyamuni is tall, slender and elegantly robed. The ten disciples, carved on the walls to the left and right of the central figure, are shown engaged in ascetic practices or spiritual discipline.

The Final Years. Towards the end of the eighth century, Silla sculpture became conventionalized. This period lasted until 918, when Silla's fate was sealed. Characteristic of these years is the prevalence of iron statues and especially the appearance of the iron statue of Buddha with datable inscriptions. An example of this is the seated figure of Vairocana (cast in the second year of King Hunan of Silla, that is, in 858)at Porin-sa, in Changhung, South Chŏlla Province.

Of the gilt bronze statues of the period, only a few smaller pieces have survived. Many stone works were produced, but the statues of this period display a rather stiff formality, although their pedestals are often finely worked. Many such examples are preserved in provincial temples.

7. JAPAN

The Introduction of Buddhism and Buddhist Art

It was as late as the sixth century that Buddha's teachings and his image finally arrived in Japan. The oldest official history of Japan, compiled in A.D. 720 reports that 'a gilt bronze image of Buddha Śākyamuni, some banners and baldachins, and volumes of the canon and commentaries' were sent as gifts to the royal court of Japan by the king of Paekje, a southern Korean kingdom very friendly to Japan, at a date that is thought to have been 538. It seems certain, however, that even earlier, in the beginning of the sixth century, Buddhism was already professed by some people in Japan.

Despite the opposition of a conservative faction adhering to the worship of traditional Japanese gods, the Buddhist cause, aided by Prince Shōtoku, an ardent believer who held the rank of regent during the reign of his aunt, the Empress Suiko, made rapid headway throughout the country. Although there is much uncertainty today about what Japanese Buddhism in its earliest stage consisted of and how it was understood by the people, its artistic remains show us that it was a Chinese-type Mahāyāna Buddhism that revered Śākyamuni, Bhaiṣajyaguru, Amitābha and other Buddhas and such Bodhisattvas as Avalokiteśvara and Maitreya.

The advent of the faith naturally led to the introduction of Buddhist art-forms already highly developed in China and Korea. The relics of the Buddha and the holy images required shrines and pagodas to accommodate them; dormitories were needed to house the monks, as were ritual implements and other decorations and utensils. The Japanese invited from the Korean Peninsula the craftsmen needed for making them; they also invited monks and nuns to perform the rites and preach the doctrine. At first Buddhist images were worshipped at private homes, but later monasteries were built. The statistics of 624 show that there were already as many as 46 monasteries in existence, with 816 monks and 569 nuns, making a total of 1,385. Its spread to this extent in less than a hundred years following the introduction of Buddhism must be regarded as truly remarkable.

Not all of the monasteries had complete sets of buildings; yet excavations at their sites show that the larger ones as a rule had a pagoda, the equivalent of the Indian stupa, erected over a container enshrining the relics of Buddha. There were also a *kondō* (golden hall) to house images of the Buddhas as the objects of worship, an assembly hall in which the monks congregated and engaged in discussions, and monks' living-quarters (*vihāra*). All main buildings except the living-quarters were surrounded by cloisters with gates; all were arranged in an orderly formation. Several variations have been found in the arrangement of the buildings on the premises of such *garan* (*saṅghārāma*), or monasteries, but the component buildings themselves are the same in all. The concept of these structures originated in India, but they were given distinct forms in China and reached Japan through Korea.

Certainly, the arrival of Buddhism and Buddhist art was one of the most important, epoch-making events in the entire history of Japanese culture. It enriched the spiritual life of the people, and at the same time prompted them to adopt the highly advanced culture that had developed together with Buddhism on the Asian continent.

184. Shaka Sanzon (Śākyamuni triad)

By Tori; Asuka period, dated A.D. *623; gilt bronze; H. of central image 87.5 cm.; H. of two attendants 92.3 cm. (proper left), 93.9 cm. (proper right); H. of halo in the form of a lotus petal 60.3 cm. (concave); the principal image, Kondō, Hōryū-ji, Nara Prefecture.*

This triad is counted first among the representative images produced in the Asuka period. It bears an inscription to the effect that the master sculptor Tori was commissioned to make it as a memorial to Prince Shōtoku in 623, which makes it one of the very few ancient works whose artist and precise date are both known. The Śākyamuni in the middle is distinguished by the peculiarly Chinese-style robe over both his shoulders and the mannered rendering of the decorative moiré pattern on the skirt of the robe draped over the pedestal. This, together with his slim face and the gestures of his hands, makes him a close counterpart of the late Northern Wei style represented by the principal image in the Pin-yang Cave at Lung-men (505–23). The attendant Bodhisattvas at his sides, identical in appearance, are also derived from prototypes in Chinese Buddhist sculpture of the first half of the sixth century and in early Korean images of the Three Kingdoms period. It is true that in this Śākyamuni triad each statue assumes a pose that is rigid, awkward and frontal, lacking in movement; still, they express both sternness in form and inner strength in spirit, making them quite effective as objects of worship. Even in early Japanese Buddhist sculpture, a unique national style with its own, distinctly Japanese physiognomy was emerging under the influence of the forms imported from China through Korea.

The Development of Early Styles

Concerning the first Buddha image sent from Paekje, we know only that it was a gilt bronze Śākyamuni 'majestic in appearance', but we may picture it roughly similar to the sixth-century bronze Buddhas discovered in Korea or to the earliest Buddhist statues surviving in Japan, the Śākyamuni triad in the Kondō of Hōryū-ji (Pl. 184). There are unexpected variations in sculptural forms, which means that the Japanese must have adopted various Chinese art styles, i.e., not only the style of the late Northern Wei, but of other dynasties as well, such as Northern Ch'i and Sui, mostly brought by immigrants from China or Korea.

Buddhist sculpture of this early period survives in considerable quantities because most are made of gilt bronze. There are also some wooden and clay figures, but almost none in stone, the medium that was popular on the continent. There is little variation in subject-matter and form among the Buddhist images: the first Buddhas depicted were Śākyamuni and Bhaiṣajyaguru, and later they were joined by Amitābha and Maitreya. More widely worshipped were two Bodhisattvas, Avalokiteśvara, the merciful saviour, and Maitreya, the Future Buddha. There are also unidentified Bodhisattvas such as the attendants in the Śākyamuni triads. It may be added here that most of the Buddhist sculptural remains of this period, together with a few minor art objects and paintings, have been preserved at Hōryū-ji, near Nara, which also contains the oldest wooden religious edifices in the world.

As for paintings from this early period, there are those on the doors and the pedestal of the Beetle Wing Miniature Shrine (Tamamushi Zushi) at Hōryū-ji. The shrine itself, despite a few alterations, is equally as important as an example of the Asuka architectural style; on the doors are images of *dvārapālas* and Bodhisattvas; and on the pedestal, scenes of worship and two illustrations of *jātaka* stories. It is interesting to find *jātaka* scenes made in Japan as in other countries in the early stage of Buddhism, but the two illustrations depicted there are remarkable in that they are both based on stories told in Mahāyāna sutras. These paintings are done in pigments mixed with oil over a black lacquer base and skilfully depict human figures and mountain forms in a unique style derived from one established in Northern Wei China, as was the case with the Asuka sculpture. The Embroidered Curtain of the so-called Land of Heavenly Longevity (Tenjukoku Shūchō), fragments of which survive at Chūgū-ji, is said to have been made on the design drawn by an immigrant painter from Korea in the year of Prince Shōtoku's death (622). Depicting a paradise in which the prince had supposedly been reborn, it is the oldest surviving piece of Japanese pictorial art, quite archaic in its expression.

The Classical Style: The Early Nara Period

The mid-seventh century and thereafter seems to have been a transitional period in which styles of diverse origins were mixed, some derived from the earlier Japanese period, others from the late Southern and Northern dynasties in China. Here we must remember that the Korean Peninsula of the time was undergoing violent political changes, such as the successive downfall of Paekje and Koguryŏ and the emergence of a unified Korea under

185. Kannon (Avalokiteśvara), known as 'Kuze Kannon' (Avalokiteśvara the Saviour)

Asuka period, first half of 7th century A.D.*; wood, painted; H. 179.9 cm.; with crown of metal openwork, 29 cm.; H. of halo 111.2 cm.; Yumedono (Dream Hall), Hōryū-ji, Nara Prefecture.*

Though made of wood, it is very well preserved for it was long hidden from view. Except for the two hands holding a jewel (*maṇi*) in front of the chest, an iconographic motif, the image closely adheres to the same tradition as the attendant Bodhisattvas in the triad featured in Pl. 184; the ends of the scarves are likewise rendered like fins turned sideways; also his facial expression, though unique, is similar to that of the Śākyamuni. Still the facial features and his tall proportions attest an artistic level advanced beyond that found in the triad. Moreover, the tall crown consisting of elaborate metal openwork and the jewel-shaped halo covered with flowing patterns were made by a more sophisticated artist who was probably living at a later time than that of the Śākyamuni triad. Another figure of approximately the same date is the famous slender wooden statue of the 'Kudara Kannon' (literally, Paekje Avalokitéśvara), deposited in the treasure house of Hōryū-ji. He stands tall with a long, flowing scarf, his peculiar body with exaggerated suppleness and his small lovely face that suggests an exotic femininity. These attractive features set him apart from other Northern Wei-style Buddhist statues typical of the Asuka period, and some scholars are inclined to interpret them as indications of his stylistic origins in the southern dynasties of China.

186. Bodhisattva in a reflective pose (Bosatsu Shi-i)

Asuka period, dated in the sexagenary cyclic year, possibly A.D. *606 or 666; gilt bronze; H. 41.8 cm.; originally at Hōryū-ji, now in Tokyo National Museum.*

This is one of the most beautiful examples of the collection of small gilt bronze images originally kept at Hōryū-ji. Its overly large head has the face slightly turned downwards and the expression is sharp and stern. Its composition is rather elegant as a whole, with sloping shoulders, slender limbs and a trunk that is boldly formed. The sexagenary cyclic year mentioned in its inscription has been the subject of a controversy, and is interpreted as either 606 (being more possible) or 666. The appealing pose of a Bodhisattva who sits on a pedestal with one foot hanging down and who gently touches his cheek with one hand, deep in thought, originated in Gandhāra; in China it first appeared as early as the fifth century and was quite popular in the Northern Ch'i dynasty in the latter half of the sixth century; it was also common in Korea in the late Three Kingdoms period. It is interesting to note that such figures were actively produced in Japan only in the earliest times. Most remains in this category belong to the seventh century, in number about twenty, of both bronze and wood. These include two famous wooden images—the crowned figure in Kōryū-ji, Kyoto, and the one with a double topknot in Chūgū-ji, near Hōryū-ji. From the inscription found on one of them, they are generally identified as Maitreya.

Silla. At the same time, Japan, preoccupied with the hostile relationship with Silla, had little opportunity to absorb the latest developments in the arts from the Asian mainland. In the fourth quarter of the seventh century, Silla's rule had become stabilized and intercourse with Japan was resumed. It may be no accident that about this time there appeared a new type of Buddhist image, with a well-proportioned physical beauty and an expression of solidity and wealth. It was the advent in Japan of a new style to be called that of the early Nara, or Hakuhō, period. In fact, it had originated in the early T'ang period and was transmitted to Silla, which was increasingly affected by T'ang culture, and by the middle of the late Nara period (c. 710–94), also given the name 'the Tempyō period', the high T'ang style had become the dominant force in Japanese Buddhist art.

In 670, early in this period, Hōryū-ji was burned and its buildings reconstructed. A group of clay figurines in the Five-storeyed Pagoda there, completed by 711, already show characteristics that are found in the high T'ang works and these give evidence of the process of rapid sinification. It was also roughly in the fourth quarter of the seventh century that the great government-built monasteries of Yakushi-ji and Daian-ji, and the private Yamada-dera and Taima-dera were constructed, and some of their original Buddhist images, mostly in bronze, are still extant. Those illustrated in Plates 187–90 are among the outstanding sculptural remains of this period.

The famous wall paintings in the Kondō of Hōryū-ji are thought to have been done in the same early Nara period. Their date is a matter of conjecture, but is generally thought to be about 700, and most were destroyed by fire in 1949; what is left retains little of their original beauty. We must remember, however, that these paintings have survived over 1,200 years and were done on the walls not of a rock cave, but of a wooden building standing on the surface of the ground. They depict four preaching Buddhas on the four major walls, usually interpreted as illustrations of the paradises of Bhaiṣajyaguru, Śākyamuni, Amitābha and Maitreya, the Buddhas most widely worshipped at the time. The eight minor walls are filled with Avalokiteśvara and other Bodhisattvas, among whom, interestingly enough, are the oldest Japanese representations of the Eleven-headed Avalokiteśvara and Samantabhadra riding the elephant. The artist defined the forms with a powerful, unmodulated line; the colours are bright, with a slight modelling of high-lights and shadows to enhance the sense of mass, a relatively advanced drawing technique suggestive of the early T'ang style influenced by Central Asian techniques. Of those paintings, only the scenes of flying *deva*s drawn on the triforia of the sanctuary, repeated twenty times in identical form, escaped the fire and preserve the original colours and lines.

The Classical Style: The Tempyō Period and the Maturity of Japanese Buddhist Sculpture

The eighty years or so in which the capital was located in Nara formed one of the most dramatic eras in the history of Japanese art. Called the Tempyō, or late Nara, period (710–94), it was characterized by vigorous, large-scale construction of palace and monastery buildings in the new capital and by the achievement of a classical style of Buddhist sculpture that reflected the mature sophistication of high T'ang art. The Buddhist pantheon

187. Buddha head

Early Nara (Hakuhō) period, A.D. *685; gilt bronze; H. 106.8 cm.; Kōfuku-ji, Nara.*

This head of the Buddha Bhaiṣajyaguru, originally the principal image in the Assembly Hall of Yamada-dera (Jōdo-ji) at Asuka, enshrined in 685, is the earliest datable example of the new style of the Hakuhō period. Later in the middle ages the statue was moved to Kōfuku-ji, where it was destroyed in a fire, leaving only the damaged head. The head, however, reveals the influence of the early T'ang style, in the simple, clear-cut and balanced formation of its face brimming with lively dynamism.

188. Miroku Butsu (the Future Buddha, Maitreya)

Early Nara period, last quarter of 7th century A.D.*; clay, lacquered gold leaf; H. 220 cm.; the principal image, Kondō, Taima-dera, Nara Prefecture.*

This seated figure of the Buddha Maitreya, the principal image in the Kondō of Taima-dera, has a tall, stately body that is at once full of virile massiveness yet mild and warm, owing to the feeling of its material—clay. This image, the oldest clay Buddhist figure in Japan, occupies a very important position in the history of Japanese sculpture, as do the statues of the Four Lokapālas in the same Kondō (except for the Vaiśravaṇa, which is a later addition)—the oldest dry-lacquer figures. This may be from about the same time as the Buddha head of Pl. 187.

189. Shō Kannon (Ārya Avalokiteśvara)

Early Nara period, end of 7th century A.D.*; gilt bronze; H. 188.9 cm.; H. of pedestal, 47.5 cm.; Tōin-dō, Yakushi-ji, Nara.*

This Avalokiteśvara, one of the largest and best-preserved of the gilt bronze images from this period, is especially remarkable in the idealized T'ang-style proportions and the sense of dynamic power. Somewhat rigid in its frontal posture, it conveys a sense of brimming power, with its slender body well proportioned and solidly modelled, and its face firmly set and majestic. This image has no characteristic other than the hands in the *vitarka-mudrā*, the gesture of explanation, the left raised and the right pendant, to identify it as an Avalokiteśvara. Unlike other works of the time representing the same Bodhisattva it lacks both a crown and an emanation Buddha on its top-knot. Yakushi-ji was built in the fourth quarter of the seventh century, and it is said that in 697 a Yakushi (Bhaiṣajyaguru) Buddha was enshrined there with a prayer for the reigning empress's recovery from an illness.

190. Amida Sanzon (Amitābha triad)

Early Nara period, beginning of 8th century A.D.*; gilt bronze; H. of central image 34 cm., H. of lotus pedestal, 13.2 cm.; installed in the so-called Lady Tachibana's Miniature Shrine, with metal screen; Daihōzōden Repository, Hōryū-ji, Nara Prefecture.*

The Buddha Amitābha sits on a lotus flower rising from a pond, flanked symmetrically by Avalokiteśvara, with an emanation Buddha on his crown, and Mahāsthāmaprāpta, with a water jug on his crown, a very finely balanced triad. The nimbus of the Buddha has a refined vine pattern in exquisite metal openwork on the rear screen, done in remarkable low relief. A group of worshippers is shown seated on the lotus flowers of the paradise in which they were reborn amid the harmonious curves of long undulating lotus stalks and flowing scarves. Though not too easily datable, most scholars, in consideration of the original shrine that houses it, agree to assign it to a time somewhere at the beginning of the eighth century. Other distinguished contemporary works are the Śākyamuni of Jindai-ji, west of Tokyo, the so-called Dream-conjuring Avalokiteśvara (Yumeta-gae Kannon) of Hōryūji, and the Avalokiteśvara of Kakurin-ji, Hyōgo. Prefecture. All with youthful faces, they are very graceful, uncomplicated, and charming, and the folds of their robes are skilfully rendered.

worshipped at this time included those deities worshipped earlier: Śākyamuni, Bhaiṣajyaguru, Amitābha, Maitreya and Avalokiteśvara. It was expanded, however, by the arrival of the Buddha Vairocana as described in the *Avataṃsaka* literature and by tantric aspects of Avalokiteśvara, shown in the forms of the Unfailing Noose (*Amoghapāśa*), Eleven-headed (*Ekādaśamukha*) and the Thousand-armed (*Sahasrabhuja*). There also appeared, in connection with the idea of the protection of the state by the religion, the Four Lokapālas and other guardian and fertility deities in the *kondō*. Thus the principal image, which used to be alone or in a triad, was now accompanied by many attendant figures, such as the Twelve Divine Officers of Bhaiṣajyaguru and the Ten Disciples of Śākyamuni, thus adding much more sculptural variety.

Holy images were produced in great quantities to meet such demands. Their style, while nourished by that of the high T'ang period, retained a certain independence. This style combined a sense of literalness or worldly realism with lofty spiritual conceptions expressed through idealized forms. At the same time, there was great experimentation with sculptural techniques, some of them newly introduced from the mainland. The old techniques of bronze casting were applied on an unprecedented scale to make the Great Buddha of Tōdai-ji. Newly introduced techniques of modelling in clay and hollow dry lacquer produced a new freedom of expression and endowed sacred images with an emotional range and a feeling for the material hitherto unknown. The oldest examples of the new media are the Maitreya in clay (Pl. 188) and the Four Lokapālas in dry lacquer, both in the Kondō of Taima-dera. In the techniques most widely used in the Tempyō period, a clay image was either plain, painted with colour, or finished with an overlay of lacquer and gold leaf. In the hollow dry-lacquer technique, the sculptor first made a rough form with clay, strengthened by a wooden core and frames, then pasted over it several layers of cloth soaked in lacquer, and added the finishing touches in lacquer. He next hollowed it out by removing the clay inside. The resulting image was quite light in weight and not unlike a kind of *papier-mâché*. In the latter half of the Tempyō period, however, this technique was replaced by the use of wood-core dry lacquer, in which the surface details were modelled in lacquer applied heavily over a rough-hewn wooden form. This technique became more common as it was less troublesome than the hollow type, but the change resulted in works that were less accomplished.

Among the many surviving Buddhist images from the Nara period, the first to be mentioned is the Bhaiṣajyaguru triad, the principal images of the Kondō of Yakushi-ji (Pl. 191). The most prominent undertaking in the Nara period was the construction of Tōdai-ji and its principal image, the Great Buddha (*Daibutsu*). Originally, Tōdai-ji was built as the provincial monastery for Yamato but was later given control over all other provincial monasteries. The first stage of its construction was the casting of the bronze statue of the Great Buddha. This difficult project, which took more than thirteen years before the image alone was completed, is so well documented that we have detailed knowledge about the process of the founding, the quantity of materials required, the original height of the image (16.21 metres tall), the organization of the Tōdai-ji Construction Agency (*Zō Tōdai-ji Shi*), and the kinds and number of the workers. In 752 the bronze casting of the image itself was finished and a grand consecration ceremony was held, but the gilding of some parts as well as the production of lotus petals and a great nimbus had to be continued, along with the construction of both the Kondō to house the image and the other buildings of the monastery. Finally in 789, the great undertaking that had lavishly consumed the wealth of the nation was officially declared complete. The colossal image was that of Buddha Vairocana (Resplendent One), who is described in the *Avataṃsaka* texts. Its equally colossal forerunners are found in China, in Cave No. 18 of Yün-kang dating from the late fifth century and at the Feng-hsien-ssu cave of Lung-men, dated 675. This Buddha is believed to rank above all other Buddhas and Bodhisattvas (see p. 135). Like the sun, shining brightly, pervading all things and encompassing the whole universe, it must have been chosen as the most appropriate deity in a religious enterprise commissioned by the emperor and supported by the government. Unfortunately, the original statue was severely damaged and even later restorations were destroyed in the fires caused by civil wars. The present image, except for a few of the original lotus petals forming a part of the pedestal, was made as late as 1692, somewhat reduced in size (14.73 metres tall) and with changed proportions.

At the time of the founding of the Great Buddha, the making of other images was also under way at Tōdai-ji. The monastery's Sangatsu-dō, also called the Hokke-dō, houses fourteen large images with typical features of the classical style, made in hollow dry lacquer and clay. The lovely gilt bronze figure of the infant Śākyamuni standing in a basin and the Four Lokapālas (in clay) of the Kaidan-in, skilfully harmonizing realism with idealism, must also be noted.

Kōfuku-ji prospered as a family monastery of the Fujiwara clan, but suffered frequent damage from fires, losing many buildings and holy images; yet the monastery still has such masterpieces as groups of hollow dry-lacquer images of the Eight Kinds of Supernatural Creatures (*Hachibu Shū*) and the Ten Disciples of Śākyamuni, which along with the images in the Sangatsu-dō of Tōdai-ji are representative works of the early half of the Tempyō period. Also dating from this time are the Twelve Divine Officers of Bhaiṣajyaguru in clay at Shin Yakushi-ji (Pl. 193), a monastery said to have been built in the mid-eighth century. Surely made earlier, in the early part of the Tempyō period, are the group figures in clay on the lowest storey of the Five-storeyed Pagoda of Hōryū-ji, which constitute three-dimensional illustrations of Buddhist narrative stories (*hensō*); they represent the Nirvana of Buddha Śākyamuni to the north, his cremation and the distribution of his ashes to the west, the scene of a disputation between Vimalakīrti and Mañjuśrī based on the text of the *Vimalakīrtinirdeśa-sūtra* on the east, and the view of the paradise of the Future Buddha, Maitreya. These small clay figurines already demonstrate the distinct influences of sophisticated high T'ang sculpture.

The late Tempyō period, or the latter half of the eighth century, is represented by images at Tōshōdai-ji and Saidai-ji. The former, founded in 759 by Ganjin (Chien-chen), a Chinese monk, still preserves several original buildings including the Kondō and the Kōdō (Assembly Hall) and many original sculptures, including the large hollow dry-lacquer statue of Vairocana (Pl. 194). The seated statue of Ganjin at the Kaisan-dō is another hollow dry-lacquer masterpiece whose original colouring is well preserved; it is valued as one of the

191. Yakushi Sanzon (Bhaiṣajyaguru triad)

Late Nara (Tempyō) period, early 8th century A.D.; *gilt bronze; H. of central image (Buddha) 254.7 cm.; H. of attendant on proper left (Nikkō Bosatsu, or Sūryaprabha) 317.3 cm.; H. of attendant on proper right (Gakkō Bosatsu, or Candraprabha) 315.3 cm.; the principal image, Kondō, Yakushi-ji, Nara.*

The Buddha achieves the highest level of artistic perfection, with its majestic plump face and with its feeling of firm flesh; the massive body exudes a sense of power. The two attendant Bodhisattvas flanking him, Sūryaprabha and Candraprabha, stand over three metres tall, each raising one hand lightly and letting the other fall. Their pose is a moderate form of the Indian *tribhaṅga*, with an artistic expression of tenderness and sternness suitable to a Bodhisattva. Concerning the date of their origin there are two contradicting theories: one maintains that they must be the original images completed in 697 as stated in the official history; and the other, based on their mature and sophisticated style, insists that they were made anew after the removal of the monastery from Asuka, probably during the Yōrō-Jinki era (718–26). The large square pedestal of the Buddha is remarkable for the grape-vine and small floral patterns decorating it and the four Chinese animal symbols of the four cardinal points. Also found on it are reliefs of several groups of naked demons with fangs and curly hair which are all depicted with an exotic sense of archaism.

192. Fukūkensaku Kannon (Amoghapāśa Avalokiteśvara)

Late Nara (Tempyō) period, mid-8th century A.D.*; hollow dry lacquer, lacquered gold leaf; H. 362 cm.; Hokke-dō (Sangatsu-dō), Tōdai-ji, Nara.*

This majestically tall dry-lacquer statue, standing upright with eight arms and a stern face, is the principal figure of fourteen large images in the Sangatsu-dō hall. On his head is a silver crown set with many jewels, and on his back a copper nimbus of unconventional design represents rays shooting out in all directions. The two clay Bodhisattvas, generally known as Sūryaprabha and Candraprabha, standing at his sides with folded hands, probably did not belong in this temple originally. They are, however, typical examples of Tempyō sculpture, with their clean and beautiful forms. In the same hall are also eight large hollow dry-lacquer guardians and two clay goddesses; and in the rear chamber of this building is a clay figure of Vajrapāṇi clad in armour, which is known for its realistic representation of strength.

193. Mekira, one of the Twelve Divine Officers of the Buddha Bhaiṣajyaguru

Late Nara (Tempyō) period, mid-8th century A.D.*; clay, painted; overall H. 166.7 cm.; Hondō, Shin Yakushi-ji, Nara.*

The Shin (New) Yakushi-ji was first built around 745 at the behest of Empress Kōmyō, lost its main buildings in a fire of 780, and was rebuilt around 793. Its principal image, the wooden Bhaiṣajyaguru belongs to the time of the reconstruction, and is important as the earliest example of the Jōgan style. Except for one that is a later addition, the clay figures of the Twelve Divine Officers, now placed in a circle surrounding the principal image, are earlier in time than the principal image, and most probably belong to the initial Shin Yakushi-ji. They are represented as armed guardian deities clad in armour, whose bristling hair and wrathful eyes are realistically executed in a powerful formative representation. According to the *Bhaiṣajyaguru-sūtra*, the Divine Officers, as strong military men, were thought to protect devotees day and night, and usually accompanied Bhaiṣajyaguru.

194. Roshana Butsu (Buddha Vairocana)

Late Nara (Tempyō) period; hollow dry lacquer, lacquered gold leaf; H. 304.5 cm.; the principal image, Kondō, Tōshōdai-ji, Nara.

The Tōshōdai-ji, founded by the T'ang Chinese monk Chien-chen (Ganjin), appears to have had the majestic Main Hall (Kondō) only since sometime between 770 and 780, after the founder's death. This gigantic image, the Buddha Vairocana described in the *Avataṃsaka* literature, massive and majestic in appearance, uses the orthodox hollow dry-lacquer technique of the high Tempyō period. His nimbus is adorned with a thousand Buddhas, also original, symbolic of his role as the source of all other deities. Representing the same Buddha as the Tōdai-ji image, this Vairocana (though not cast in bronze as that was) helps us to imagine what the original Great Buddha, of which there now remains only a later reconstruction, was like. Also in the same Main Hall are colossal Thousand-Armed Avalokiteśvara and Buddha Baiṣajyaguru figures that date from a little later.

two realistic portrait sculptures of ancient times, along with the figure in hollow dry lacquer of Gyōshin Sōzu at the Yume-dono of Hōryū-ji. Most of the other sculptures at Tōshōdai-ji, however, including the large Bhaiṣajyaguru and Sahasrabhuja Avalokiteśvara in the Kondō, are done in wood-core dry lacquer or carved wood, indicating a transitional stage in the coming of wood sculpture. Moreover, those images are characterized by a ponderous and rigid form, a trait that is commonly called the Tōshōdai-ji style. Saidai-ji, founded in 765, was a great *saṅghārāma* (monastery) completed at the end of this period and possessing, as records tell, a rich variety of holy images and pictures. Most of them were lost in fires, and the fortunes of the monastery declined, leaving only a few works including lacquered and gilt wooden images of the four cosmic Buddhas. According to the tradition of the monastery, they are to be identified as the four directional Buddhas—Akṣobhya, Ratnasambhava, Amitābha and Amoghasiddhi—and were originally enshrined in the lowest storey of a pagoda there.

As for pictorial art, we can quote only the scene of the Buddha's preaching on Mt. Gṛdhrakūṭa, based on the text of the *Saddharmapuṇḍarīka*, and the Great Goddess (Śrī Mahādevī) preserved at the Hachiman Shrine of Yakushi-ji. The former, originally kept at the Hokke-dō (Sangatsu-dō) of Tōdai-ji but now in the possession of the Boston Museum of Fine Arts, depicts the Buddha—with attendant Bodhisattvas and others against a background of mountains and valleys—on a sheet of hemp cloth, and it is remarkably rich in the elements of T'ang painting. The figures include a plump T'ang-style lady clad in gorgeously ornamented robes also painted on a sheet of hemp cloth. It closely resembles pictures of beautiful court women preserved at the Shōsō-in, attesting to the strong influence of T'ang pictorial art. Embroidered or woven images and illustrations of stories seem to have been produced at that time, but the only surviving specimen is the fragmentary woven illustration at Taima-dera of the paradise of Amitābha, which was probably imported.

Esoteric Buddhism and Its Art

A new phase in Japanese cultural history began with the removal of the capital from Nara to Kyoto in 794. The first century of the new period is known as the early Heian, or Jōgan, period. In this period the long-standing cultural intercourse with T'ang China entered its last stage, the most remarkable incident of which was the introduction of new types of Buddhism, especially genuine Esoterism, and the rise of new art-forms accompanying it. In the field of sculpture, still dominated by Buddhist images, this was an age of woodcarving for all sects, old and new. Sculptural style was from the beginning marked by a sense of massiveness and power appropriate to Esoteric Buddhism; yet, generally speaking, the stylistic basis of Jōgan sculpture was the result of an amalgamation of well-established T'ang Chinese elements with the ones introduced by the new form of Buddhism. This Jōgan style, however, went through a gradual transformation, and became more distinctly Japanese in expression. In the pictorial arts, continuous importation and copying of Buddhist paintings kept them under even heavier influence of the T'ang Chinese than was the case with sculpture. Yet many of these works contain nuances of expression that are unique to Japan. In T'ang China, however, the so-called Hui-ch'ang persecution of 845 dealt a severe blow to the Buddhist religion and its art from which they never quite recovered; and Japan decided to discontinue the long practice of sending embassies to China in 894. Now freer from continental influence, Japanese Buddhist art was able to follow a more independent course of development in the following period.

The new-type Buddhism of the Jōgan period was represented by two new sects, Shingon and Tendai, introduced by two learned Japanese monks who studied in China in the early ninth century. The new sects quickly replaced the old and dispirited Nara schools of Buddhism as leaders of the religious world of Japan and remained vital for a long time. The Shingon sect, introduced by Kūkai, transplanted in its entirety Esoteric Buddhism as it had been systematized in China. The Tendai sect, introduced by Saichō, was originally a school of Exoteric Buddhism based on the *Saddharmapuṇḍarīka*, but thanks to the efforts of Ennin and Enchin who went to China later, it incorporated so many teachings of Esoteric Buddhism that it began to compete with the Shingon sect. The two Esoteric sects, the Tōmitsu (literally, the Esoterism of Tō-ji, i.e., the Shingon sect) and the Taimitsu (the Tendai sect), were quite active all through the Jōgan period, and became a major force in Japanese art by commissioning numerous carved and painted images of Esoteric divinities.

This Esoteric or Tantric Buddhism introduced from China into Japan requires special explanation. It was a Chinese variant of the Mantrayāna, and the process of its formation can be more clearly traced through abundant Chinese versions of Indian sutras, rather than in surviving native Indian documents. In its earliest form, it consisted mainly of simple magic rituals like the chanting of mantras (*mantra*) or dharanis (*dhāraṇī*) to drive away evil and illness and to bring happiness and peace. Later, elaborate religious symbolism became one of its hallmarks, with complicated mystic rites performed before images of divinities. When one of the merciful Bodhisattvas was invoked, he was given many faces or arms (Eleven-headed Avalokiteśvara or Thousand-armed Avalokiteśvara, for example). The functions of power, subjugation or destruction of evil were symbolized in the exaggerated forms of wrathful deities (those belonging to the classes of Vajrasattva and Vidyārāja, etc.). Great Hindu gods were borrowed outright and converted into guardian deities, taking advantage of their magical powers. This kind of unsystematized Esoterism (Zōmitsu, 'ungenuine' Esoterism) that concentrated on magical rites is known to have spread widely in China in the late seventh century and onwards. It was this 'ungenuine' Esoterism that entered Japan in the eighth century and resulted in the many-headed and many-armed images of Avalokiteśvara discussed earlier.

In contrast to this, genuine Esoterism was based on two mutually independent texts, the *Mahāvairocana-sūtra* and the *Sarvatathāgatatattvasaṃgraha*, supposedly originating from the Buddha Vairocana in his *dharmakāya* (Absolute Body). Early in the eighth century, soon after their composition in India, the two texts were brought to China and translated into Chinese. They underwent further doctrinal unification and centred on the adoration of Vairocana resulting in a religion of high intellectual and spiritual content. This kind of Esoteric Buddhism was hindered by the Hui-ch'ang persecution (845) from further growth in China, but in Japan, where it had been introduced in the early ninth century, it prospered and created a lively atmosphere.

Genuine Esoterism holds that the Buddha Vairocana in his *dharmakāya* is the supreme and absolute deity pervading all time as well as all space, and that all other Buddhas, Bodhisattvas and gods are only his manifestations or emanations in different times and on different occasions. In accordance with this doctrine, the Esoteric practiser who performs religious rites to a particular deity, forms a *mudrā* with his hands, chants a mantra, concentrates on the deity in his mind and strives to achieve spiritual union with him. Through this process he becomes one with Vairocana, immerses himself at once in the absolute state while still in his normal body, and at the same time he is able to produce religious wonders and miracles. This mystic and magical practice is called *shuhō* (*sādhana*) in Esoteric Buddhism. Originally, each *sādhana* required a mandala (*maṇḍala*), a platform built with soil on which carved or painted images of the principal deity and related gods and guardians were arranged, but the platform was replaced later by a pictorial mandala painted in colour. The arts were indispensable to Esoteric Buddhist rituals and the new religious movement required countless new paintings and statues in the Jōgan period. In the performance of *sādhana*, these images were interpreted not just as worshipped divinities, but as manifestations of the Buddha Vairocana himself. Thus each detail of the *sādhana*, of the appearance of the deities and their position was minutely followed to ensure the secrecy and so the detailed knowledge of their practice was as a rule transmitted only orally from the master to his disciples. From this derives the notion of the secret and exclusive knowledge of the priesthood that is fundamental to the Esoteric sects.

The Jōgan Period and Wood Sculpture

Although the Jōgan period saw extensive propagation of the new types of Buddhism as discussed above, the art-works surviving from this period, especially numerous sculptures, belong not only to Esoteric temples but also to Exoteric (non-Esoteric) or more traditional Mahāyānist sanctuaries. It was in this period, too, that Shintō shrines began the production of images of its gods in imitation of Buddhist iconography.

In Jōgan sculpture, the use of bronze and hollow dry lacquer for statuary in previous times was almost completely replaced by wood. Not only was good wood readily available, but this phenomenon must be related to the fact that both bronze and dry lacquer were scarce and expensive, requiring a high level of skill and much time for production. There is a historical logic to this development as well, since hollow dry lacquer was supplanted by wood-core dry lacquer in the late Tempyō period, and then, in the Jōgan period, the latter was further simplified to carved wood. At the very beginning of this period many works were created by methods of wood-core dry lacquer, but soon after there was a rapid inclination towards wood sculpture. Many wooden images were left unpainted, emphasizing the beauty of the wood itself, while the rest were totally painted or lacquered and then covered with an outer layer of gold leaf. Some statues were life-size or even larger; seated figures were about two metres high, based on a module called '*jōroku*' (or 'sixteen feet', that is, double life-size). A single block of wood was used to carve the main portion of a statue. The mode of 'single-block carving' is one of the outstanding features of Jōgan sculpture, though usually the main block was supplemented by an additional piece to form such parts as the arms or the knees of a seated figure. Also part of the inside of the torso was commonly hollowed out in order to lighten the weight or prevent cracking.

Many Buddhist images of the Jōgan period have survived to this day, even though they are made of wood, a material prone to decay. Encompassing both Exoteric and Esoteric deities, the most numerous among them are Buddha Bhaiṣajyaguru, who had already been worshipped in previous times and many kinds of Avalokiteśvara, including the Esoteric Eleven-headed and Thousand-armed, but Śākyamuni, Amitābha, Maitreya, Kṣitigarbha and the Four Lokapālas are also frequent. Among the Esoteric deities that were newly introduced were Vairocana, the Five Buddhas, Acala and other Vidyārājas, Cintāmaṇicakra Avalokiteśvara, and the Five Ākāśagarbhas. Thus, Esoteric Buddhism greatly enriched both the number of the deities and the variety of their iconographic expressions.

In comparison with Tempyō sculpture, which was marked by harmony and sophistication under high T'ang influence, the early Jōgan images are subdued, rough and rigid. They achieved a sense of virility and august power, thereby forming a prototype for the new style to develop thereafter. Two Bhaiṣajyaguru Buddhas, the standing one of Jingo-ji, Kyoto (Pl. 195), and the seated one of Shin Yakushi-ji, Nara, are the earliest examples of the Jōgan style. Needless to say, there are also Jōgan images that preserve both the style of previous times and techniques of wood-core dry lacquer or clay. Either Exoteric or Esoteric, they are endowed with balanced, rich forms and a subdued expression related to their materials: the seated Bhaiṣajyaguru (wood-core dry lacquer) of Jingo-ji, Kyoto, and the Cintāmaṇicakra Avalokiteśvara (clay, with later repairs) of Oka-dera, Nara Prefecture, from early in the period, as well as the colossal seated Amitābha in the assembly hall of Kōryū-ji, Kyoto.

The earliest of the genuine Esoteric images of the Jōgan period are in the assembly hall of Tō-ji (Kyōōgokoku-ji) in Kyoto, built in the last years of Kūkai's life, probably according to his own plans. Containing statues of the Five Buddhas, the Five Bodhisattvas, the Five Vidyārājas, Brahmā, Indra and the Four Lokapālas, twenty-one in all, they were completed after Kūkai's death in 839. One can deduce that these divinities symbolized the Esoteric view of universe underlying the *Vajradhātu-maṇḍala* (see p. 225), the very basis of Shingon doctrine, and at the same time formed a mandala based on the *Jen Wang Ching* (*Ninnō-kyō*, or *Sutra of the Benevolent King*) to ensure peace for the state. This group of statues thus formed a unique mandala combining two symbolic systems. Of the extant images, all the Five Buddhas and the central of the Five Bodhisattvas are later restorations, and the original works have been repaired to a considerable degree. The four original Bodhisattvas are done in wood-core dry lacquer, showing traits of the traditional Tempyō style in their balanced, calm, yet majestic expression, while the three-headed, four-armed Brahmā who sits on four addorsed geese (*haṃsa*) and Indra riding an elephant follow the Indian iconographical style imported along with Esoteric Buddhism; they are totally different from the earlier Chinese-style representations of Indra and Brahmā. Of the Five Vidyārājas of the same hall, see Pl. 196 where one of them, the Trailokyavijaya, is illustrated. Other outstanding Esoteric works are the Five Ākāśagarbhas of Jingo-ji, the Acala in the Miei-dō of Tō-ji, and the Cintāmaṇicakra Avalokiteśvara of Kanshin-ji, Osaka Prefecture (Pl. 197).

195. Yakushi Nyorai (Buddha Bhaiṣajyaguru)

Early Heian (Jōgan) period, end of 8th century A.D.; wood; overall H. 170 cm.; the principal image, Kondō, Jingo-ji, Kyoto.

This standing figure represents the new style of early Jōgan sculpture together with a seated Buddha at Shin Yakushi-ji, Nara. Both are Bhaiṣajyaguru, dating back close to the end of the Tempyō period or the very end of the eighth century, and exuding a sense of massiveness, power and gravity. The statue illustrated impresses us with its virile countenance, full of spirituality, and its somewhat rigid and weighty torso. The seated Shin Yakushi-ji figure is striking for its large body nearly two metres tall and the long, unusually large eyes. Next comes the Bhaiṣajyaguru of Gangō-ji, Nara, of which the draped robe is arranged in a manner typical of the early Jōgan period. The distinctive arrangement of the folds of the robe had already appeared in the Tōshōdai-ji statues of the late Tempyō period, and it continued as a distinct feature of Jōgan sculpture; it was to be perfected as a unique trait called the 'rolling wave' (*hompa shiki*) in the middle Jōgan period.

196. Gōzanze Myō-ō (Trailokyavijaya Vidyārāja)

Early Heian (Jōgan) period, A.D. 839; wood, painted; H. 174 cm.; Kōdō, Kyōōgokoku-ji (Tō-ji), Kyoto.

The Five Vidyārājas, Esoteric deities who symbolize the wrathful energies of the Five Buddhas, are characteristically powerful and dynamic, with an emphatic expression of violent anger. Except for the central figure of Acala, they are given many heads with grotesque features and many arms, suggesting ceaseless motion. This Trailokyavijaya has three heads, each with three eyes, and eight arms, and he assumes the pose of trampling under his feet Maheśvara (Śiva) and Umā (Pārvatī), supreme deities of the Hindu religion, who were often opposed to the Buddhas. The other three Vidyārājas are Kuṇḍalin, Yamāntaka and Vajrayakṣa.

197. Nyoirin Kannon (Cintāmaṇicakra Avalokiteśvara)

Early Heian (Jōgan) period, mid-9th century A.D.*; wood, painted; H. 108 cm.; Kanshin-ji, Osaka Prefecture.*

One of the most excellent images of the fully fledged Esoteric divinities newly introduced in the Jōgan period, this figure attracts by its unique pose and charmingly sensual face and torso. Cintāmaṇicakra Avalokiteśvara is a Bodhisattva whose great capacity for salvation is symbolized in a wish-fulfilling jewel (*cintāmaṇi*) and a wheel (*cakra*); iconographically he is said to have two to twelve arms, but in most cases is represented seated and with six arms. The earliest example of this Bodhisattva is the one painted in the Takao Mandara (Pl. 201), of which this is an almost exact carved copy. Traditionally hidden from public view, it is very well preserved and affords an idea of the beauty of the initial colouring.

198. Jūichimen Kannon (Ekādaśamukha Avalokiteśvara)

Early Heian (Jōgan) period, mid-9th century A.D.*; wood; H. 194 cm.; Kōgen-ji (Togan-ji), Shiga Prefecture.*

The figure stands in a beautiful pose, with hips slightly turned, and is obviously in the main current of T'ang sculpture. The way the eleven heads are arranged is unprecedented, two large heads having been added to both sides of the main face. This style comes from T'ang Chinese influence and marks the different view of the Jōgan from that of the Tempyō period.

199. Shaka Nyorai (Buddha Śākyamuni)

Early Heian (Jōgan) period, late 9th century A.D.*; wood, painted; H. 238 cm.; the principal image, Kondō, Murō-ji, Nara Prefecture.*

Preserved in good condition, this well-proportioned statue of the late Jōgan period has a formal beauty, rich in its sense of power and mass. Moreover, in this image the lines of the 'rolling wave' folds of the robe are delicately arranged in a decorative fashion, and the fold lines that flow from the stomach down to beneath the knees are more formalized than on the Bhaiṣajyaguru of Jingo-ji (Pl. 195).

200. Yakushi Nyorai (Buddha Bhaiṣajyaguru)

Early Heian (Jōgan) period, end of 9th century A.D*; wood, lacquered gold leaf; H. 137 cm.; Shōjō-ji, Fukushima Prefecture.*

This seated Bhaiṣajyaguru, long a hidden image, was recently brought under scientific study and proved to be a masterpiece from the late Jōgan period (end of ninth century). The beautiful, yet virile face and body were carved by a sophisticated hand, which neatly arranged the broad folds of the robe in the 'rolling wave' style.

There are also works in a different stylistic vein that must have come from T'ang Chinese influence in the Jōgan period: e.g., a Bodhisattva of Hōbodai-in, Kyoto, and the Eleven-headed Avalokiteśvara of Kōgen-ji, Shiga Prefecture (Pl. 198). And as those of the later style, several statues including the standing Śākyamuni (Pl. 199) of Murō-ji, Nara Prefecture, should be noted.

The Introduction of Esoteric Buddhist Painting

In comparison with sculpture, it is regrettable that only a few examples of Jōgan painting have survived, since they were mostly done on silk or paper, materials hard to preserve. Almost all of the surviving works depict fully-fledged Esoteric Buddhist subjects of the kind that was newly introduced in this period. As mentioned earlier, an Esoteric Buddhist *sādhana* inevitably required an image of its proper divinity, either carved or painted. In China, where silk was readily obtainable, coloured paintings of deities and mandalas came into use, and this trend was transmitted to Japan as part of Esoteric Buddhist doctrines. Also in this school of Buddhism, where the texts of the sutras and the manuals of ritual practices were extremely difficult to interpret and the secret nature of religious rites was jealously protected, a course of instruction in secret practices between a master and his successor was customarily accompanied by pictorial illustrations, including simple un-coloured drawings. The art of painting was thus given special importance by Esoteric Buddhist monks and the popularity of the school greatly stimulated the pictorial arts.

The first Esoteric paintings of this period were T'ang Chinese works brought back to Japan by monks who had studied in that country. The Chinese portraits of the five Shingon patriarchs brought back by Kūkai are still preserved at Tō-ji, and two more patriarchs, Nāgārjuna and Nāgabodhi, were added to them in 821 by Japanese artists in imitation of the Chinese style; these, too, are preserved at Tō-ji. The Mandala of the Two Principles (*Ryōkai Mandara*), also brought back by Kūkai, was copied several times and one of the copies is still extant as the Takao Mandara (Japanese spelling of *maṇḍala*) at Jingo-ji (Pl. 201). The Mandala of the Two Principles consists of two parts, the *Garbhadhātu-maṇḍala* (*Mahākaruṇāgarbhodbhava-maṇḍala*), based upon the text of the *Mahāvairocana-sūtra* and the *Vajradhātu-maṇḍala*, based upon the text of the *Sarvatathāgatatattvasaṃgraha*, each representing a different system of organizing all the Esoteric divinities under the central figure of the Buddha Mahāvairocana in his *dharmakāya*. Both parts symbolize the fundamental doctrines and the cosmology preached by genuine Esoterism and play an extremely important role in Esoteric rituals. The Chinese interpreted the Two Principles as mutually complementary, giving rise to the Mandala of the Two Principles, in which the *Garbhadhātu* was to be hung on the eastern, and the *Vajradhātu* on the western wall of a ceremonial hall, or *kanjō-dō* ('initiation hall'). Not a single example of this kind of mandala survives in China, however, while in Japan many are preserved, including this Takao Mandara and ones made in subsequent times.

Stylistically, the Takao Mandara is followed by the Twelve Devas of Saidai-ji, Nara, in which each of the serene and stately gods rides his particular animal or bird. Its meticulously drawn lines and peculiar shading and gradation of colours all show strong T'ang influence. Most probably based upon a coloured original imported from China, this Saidai-ji group seems to belong to a time not later than the mid-ninth century. There must have been a vast number of T'ang coloured paintings and uncoloured drawings of Buddhist themes that were brought back by monks and others, but most have perished, with two important exceptions: the uncoloured drawings of the *Gobu-shinkan* kept at Onjō-ji and the *Susiddhikara-mudrās* at Tō-ji.

The Yellow Acala, normally kept as a secret image hidden from the public at Onjō-ji, Ōtsu, is said to have been painted by a Japanese artist at the order of Enchin (814–91), founder of the monastery, who one night had had a vision of the *vidyārāja*. It is an unusual form of Acala, resembling no other similar work. Standing with exaggerated muscles and a powerful but grotesque countenance, it does not correspond to descriptions in sutras and ritual manuals, nor does it seem to be based upon an imported T'ang original. Yet it is an outstanding masterpiece, excelling in its skilfully drawn lines and dynamic expression. The medium-sized Mandala of the Two Principles at Tō-ji (Pl. 202), remarkably well preserved, is also ascribed to the end of the ninth century.

201. Nyoirin Kannon (Cintāmaṇicakra) ▷

Detail of the Garbhadhātu Mandala, one of a pair of the Mandala of the Two Principles (Takao Mandara); early Heian (Jōgan) period, between A.D. *829 and 833; two hanging scrolls painted with gold and silver lines on reddish-blue silk (damask); size: Garbhadhātu, 446.4 × 406.3 cm., Vajradhātu, 411 × 366.5 cm.; Jingo-ji, Kyoto.*

The mandala shown is not coloured, but drawn with gold and silver lines on a reddish-purple dyed ground (damask). Despite peeling and other damage, its fluid but steady lines define with precision the many divinities in a rich, well-ordered and elegant expression. Though it is a copy of an original painting imported from China, it reveals mature artistic skill in its reflection of the original T'ang style.

202. Detail of Taizōkai, Ryōkai Mandara (Mandala of the Two Principles) (See also Pls. 202–a, 202–b)

Two hanging scrolls; early Heian (Jōgan) period, end of 9th century A.D.*; painted on silk; size: Garbhadhātu (Taizōkai), 183.6 × 164.2 cm.; Vajradhātu (Kongōkai), 183.5 × 163 cm.; Tō-ji, Kyoto.*

This is the earliest remaining example of these mandalas painted in colour. The Taizōkai consists of a single mandala with a crowned figure of Dainichi (Vairocana) at the centre and the other four Buddhas (see p. 135) for the four main directions and Bodhisattvas for the four intermediate directions (cf. Pl. 344). The central lotus flower, on the petals of which they are enthroned, is surrounded by a great concourse of Bodhisattvas, gods, goddesses and guardian divinities. The Kongōkai is an arrangement of the set of nine mandalas of Dainichi (Vairocana). The top central one contains a single manifestation of Dainichi. The top right one contains Dainichi in his Five Buddha manifestation with the four main goddesses in the intermediate directions. The top left repeats the Five Buddha manifestation with *vajra* symbols in the intermediate directions. The three mandalas of the central row and that of the bottom left reproduce the Five Buddha pattern in a more complex manner, whereby each of the Five Buddhas manifests himself as fivefold. The remaining two mandalas below consist entirely of *vajra* symbols, thus suggesting the transcendence of all personalized forms.

202–a Taizōkai, Ryōkai Mandara

202–b Kongōkai, Ryōkai Mandara

V. LATER VARIATIONS AND DEVELOPMENTS

1. INDIA: THE LAST STAGES

Historical Background

From the eighth century onwards the history of northern India is conditioned by one great overwhelming event—its gradual conquest, beginning in the far north-west, by Islam. Steadily from west to east the same pattern of events was repeated—first a series of devastating and murderous raids upon people, who, whether Hindu, Buddhist or Jain, were all regarded as equally idolatrous, then the eventual settlement of the area under Moslem rule, followed by the same kind of raids in the areas then further east, then settlement, and then further raids—until the whole of North and Central India was at last under Moslem rule. The process lasted five centuries and more, for it was usually strongly resisted by the surviving Hindu dynasties. Thus it was not until the early eleventh century that Kanauj, once the capital of the great Harṣa in the upper Ganges Valley and now the capital of a Rājput dynasty, the Pratihāra, fell to Mahmud of Ghazni. Under constant threat of Moslem raids, Hindu rule was re-established and it was not until the end of the twelfth century that Kanauj was finally absorbed within the sultanate of Delhi. Meanwhile in the lower Ganges Valley, roughly from Gayā eastwards, the Pāla dynasty remained in control. The first known king of this dynasty is Gopāla (in power about 765–70), who founded the famous Buddhist monastery of Odantapurī, intending it as a great centre of learning like Nālandā (already founded in the fifth century under the Guptas), which continued to enjoy the protection of the Pāla kings in whose domains it happily lay. The Pālas were avowedly Buddhist and thus it was within their territories, comprising most of modern Bihār, West Bengal, and present-day Bangladesh, that Buddhism continued to prosper during the eighth to twelfth centuries, even though it had already been utterly destroyed in ancient Gandhāra (modern Pakistan) and led a precarious existence in the upper Ganges-Jumna region, where a Hindu dynasty under constant pressure from Moslem invaders was fighting for its very existence. Subsidiary to the protecting Pālas, who survived until the twelfth century, were the kings of the Candra dynasty (c. 900–1050) in South-East Bengal, and the Bhauma-Karas (eighth to tenth centuries) and the Somavaṁśis (tenth to thirteenth centuries) in Orissa. With the Pālas one must mention the Senas, who set themselves up as independent rulers of the area between Orissa and the Ganges delta during the twelfth century. It is common to speak of the art of this whole period as Pāla-Sena.

The Pālas were certainly the chief protectors of Buddhism, and since their domains covered a considerable part of eastern India, it is a mistake to assert, as is all too often in histories of Buddhism in India, that the influence of this religion practically came to an end in the eighth century A.D. To the north the Pāla domains remained open to Nepal and Tibet, and it was precisely during this period that the whole of the Indian Buddhist tradition, religious practices of all kinds, a vast literature, and styles of art and architecture and painting were imported from India to Tibet. The enormous heritage that the Tibetans received bears witness to the highly prosperous state of Buddhism in eastern India from the eighth to the twelfth centuries. Particularly famous were the great monastic universities of Bodhgayā and Nālandā, now under Pāla protection, as well as the actual Pāla foundations of Somapur, Odantapurī and later Vikramaśīla. These places were still the centre of a vast Asian Buddhist missionary effort, of which it is hard to imagine the scope when nowadays all but nothing remains. Students and teachers flocked to them from all over the Buddhist world, from Tibet in the north to Sumatra in the far south-east. Typical of the great scholar-abbots of those times is the famous Indian Buddhist missionary, Dīpaṅkara Śrījñāna, popularly known as Atīśa in Tibet; he arrived in Tibet in 1042 after many invitations, and remained working and teaching there until his death in 1054. However, before going to Tibet he had not only studied and taught in the three Pāla universities of Bodhgayā, Odantapurī and Vikramaśīla but had also been on a missionary journey to Sumatra.

Literary records about this last great period of Buddhism in India are not so abundant in South-East Asia as in Tibet, while in India itself they are non-existent. Here we have to rely upon the archaeologist's spade, which has unearthed an enormous number of Buddha images of all kinds relating to the Pāla-Sena period. Apart from the major establishments, there were numerous smaller ones, of which the original Buddhist names will never now be known. One may note that despite the great fame of Vikramaśīla, well attested in mainly Tibetan literary sources, its actual site remains unidentified, such was the destruction that it suffered. We may also mention other great Buddhist establishments recently discovered on hilltops, Lalitgiri and Ratnagiri, some sixty kilometres from Cuttack (Orissa). Their ruins cover a large area, and famous as they must once have been, it is impossible to identify the original names with certainty, such has been the break in Buddhist tradition in the land of its origin.

Until their final disappearance at the end of the twelfth century the Hindu-Buddhist dynasties of eastern India maintained cultural links with the various Hindu and Buddhist kingdoms of South-East Asia. But having consolidated their hold on northern India, the Moslems gradually likewise assumed control of overseas trade with the result that Islam came to supplant Hindu-Buddhist religious and cultural influences overseas. In the south, Sri Lanka remained a Buddhist land, and its strong Theravādin traditions continued to provide missionary incentives, finally ousting from the South-East Asian mainland (Burma, Thailand, Cambodia and Laos) the Mahāyāna influences that had previously reached there from eastern India. The South-East Asian islands (modern Malaysia and Indonesia) became predominantly Moslem, but spectacular Buddhist monuments remain to this day, especially in Java.

From the eighth century onwards the advance of Islam had already cut off China from its overland route through Central Asia to Gandhāra and North-West India, and thereafter Chinese, Korean and Japanese Buddhism go their own way, modifying to suit themselves those Indian Buddhist traditions that they had already received. Thus during the later period under consideration in this present chapter there is no longer any direct contact between Indian and Far Eastern Buddhism.

Between the eighth and twelfth centuries the Tibetans were active in transferring to their own country all they could find of Indian Buddhism, mainly from eastern India by way of Nepal. Soon after they in turn converted the Mongolians to the new religion, and still later the Manchus, who as emperors of China up to 1911 remained Tibetan Buddhists in religion. This, however, had little, if any, influence on Chinese Buddhism itself, which had long since gone into decline.

Thus from 1200 the Buddhist world survives as three rather distinctive areas, namely, the Theravādin lands of Sri Lanka and South-East Asia, the Tibetan-Mongolian area maintaining a frontier connection with Nepal to the south, and, lastly, Far Eastern Buddhism.

East India

For the reason given above comparatively few Buddhist remains from the later period have been found in the upper Ganges and Jumna region. However, since some images of Buddhas and Bodhisattvas have been found, we may be sure that some small Buddhist centres still continued to exist. One such centre may have been responsible for the Buddha image on a high throne pedestal that was found originally at Farrukhabad and is now in the State Museum, Lucknow. This image is shown in the earth-touching gesture (*bhūmi-sparśa-mudrā* and is flanked by two Bodhisattvas, Padmapāṇi Avalokitésvara and Vajrapāṇi. It may be identified as Akṣobhya, that is to say, as the Buddha Imperturbable before the attacks of Māra, and thus is an aspect of Śākyamuni that was very popular in eastern India (Pl. 203).

However, when we move further eastwards into the land once subject to the Pālas, we come upon the ruins of numerous monastic establishments, which have yielded to the spade of the archaeologist hundreds of Buddhist images of all kinds such as were typical of the latter stage of Mahāyāna religious practice. Buddha images remain the most popular, either alone or flanked by attendant Bodhisattvas, but we note the existence of separate Bodhisattva images, as well as of protecting divinities, male and female, and also Buddhas and Bodhisattvas coupled with a feminine partner, known usually as *prajñā* (Transcendent Knowledge) in Buddhist tantric works, not as *śakti*.

Small-size octo-alloy (*aṣṭadhātu*) cast-metal images of Buddhas and Bodhisattvas seem to have been very much in demand, since they were easily portable and could be used as pilgrim mementos or votive offerings. To meet this demand, foundries and workshops seem to have sprung up at places like Nālandā and Kurkihar in Bihār, and perhaps also at Nāgapaṭṭiṇam in Tamil Nadu, Jhewari in Chittagong and in one or two other places in what is now Bangladesh. Hoards of such cast-metal icons have been recovered, for instance,

203. Buddha in the 'earth-witness' posture

From Farrukhabad, Uttar Pradesh, India; 9th century A.D.*; sandstone; State Museum, Lucknow.*

This is Śākyamuni as Akṣobhya (the Buddha Imperturbable), who makes the gesture of 'touching the earth' (*bhūmisparśa-mudrā*). This is by far the most common Buddha manifestation in eastern India and hence also in Nepal. This scene relates specifically to the scene of the Enlightenment at Bodhgayā, and it has been noted that Akṣobhya is the Buddha of the eastern quarter (see p. 135). The main image is flanked by Padmapāṇi (Avalokiteśvara) and Vajrapāṇi, and the throne is supported by both lions and elephants, suggesting that while Akṣobhya is the Buddha of the east, he is also the Supreme Buddha.

204. Seated Buddha

From Gayā, Bihār, India, where it remains in the local sculpture shed; 10th century A.D.*; black stone.*

There appears to be an inscription on the base of this image, but regrettably it has proved impossible to obtain a copy of it (Editor's note).

205. Colossal seated Buddha

From Jagadispur, near Patna, Bihār, India; 11th century A.D.*; sandstone; in situ.*

The Buddha is making the gesture of calling the earth to witness *(bhūmisparśa-mudrā)*, encompassed by the army of Māra and surrounded by figures representing other great events in his life.

from Kurkihar, Nālandā, Nāgapaṭṭiṇam and Jhewari. In artistic and iconographic form these icons of a given centre are so similar as to suggest that they were turned out in hundreds, more or less mechanically from moulds. The Jhewari icons are sometimes distinguishable from one another by their facial and physiognomical form as well as by their shape and style, but the Nālandā and Kurkihar cast-metal icons are all but interchangeable in art and iconographic form. Elegant and sophisticated, refined and even graceful at times, the cast-metal icons of the Master and the Bodhisattvas tend to be monotonous in style and iconography.[1]

The stone images are more varied and interesting, especially those of Orissa. Of the important monastic establishments of this period, which were the abodes of the icons of the Buddhas and Bodhisattvas, the more well-known are those of Nālandā, Kurkihar and Bodhgayā in Bihār, Jagaddal (in Varendri), Vikrampur and Pattikera (present Mainamati) in Bangladesh, and Lalitgiri, Udayagiri, Ratnagiri, Baudh, Balasore, Chauduar and Khiching in Orissa. Mostly it is from the ruins of these monastic establishments that the better-known figures have reached us. But similar icons, not a few of which are very large in size and artistically remarkable, have come also from places where no important monastic establishment is yet known to have existed. Quite a few of them are still *in situ*. It is not unlikely that such icons belonged to the once existing shrines of smaller establishments, but they are nevertheless significant and deserve notice.

Gayā in Bihār has been for a long time an important Brahmanical centre, but nonetheless it has yielded a number of Buddha figures, one of which is reproduced here (Pl. 204). The presence of these images, all datable to the tenth to twelfth centuries, presumably indicates that there were Buddhist establishments in Gayā at a time when the Pālas were patrons to the great monastic establishment at Bodhgayā, ten kilometres from Gayā itself.

At Jagadispur, a village near the modern city of Patna, there is *in situ* a large stele in relief representing the seated Buddha making the gesture of calling the earth to witness (*bhūmisparśa-mudrā*) (Pl. 205). He is encompassed by the army of Māra and surrounded by subsidiary images representing other great events in his career. The precise and clear carving of these relatively small figures in agitated movement, together with the surrounding reliefs representing the other important incidents of his life, throw the huge main icon of the central Buddha into high relief. Also significant are the facial expressions and the plastic treatment. The face is oval with a pointed chin, pointed and closed lips and a pair of sharply chiselled closed eyes in harmony with the lips and the chin. The treatment of the plastic surface is soft but disciplined and smooth, yet not of a metallic smoothness. The monastic robe is treated integrally with the modelling of the plastic surface, but, following the idiom of fifth- to sixth-century Mathurā, the folds are shown in regular conventional lines mechanically arranged, becoming rather coquettish and decorative below the folded

[1]For a detailed and profusely illustrated study of the cast-metal icons of East India, see N. Ray, *Eastern Indian Bronzes* (New Delhi, Lalit Kala Academi), forthcoming. For the art and iconography of the stone sculptures and bronzes of Bihār, Bengal and Orissa, see S. Kramrisch, 'Pāla and Sena sculptures', *Rupam* (Calcutta, 1928); R. D. Banerji, 'Eastern Indian school of medieval sculpture', *Archeological Survey of India* (Delhi, 1933), and *History of Orissa*, vol. 2 (Calcutta, 1932); N. K. Bhattasali, *Iconography of the Buddhist and Brahmanical Sculptures in the Dacca Museum* (Dacca, 1929); and especially Charles Fabri, *History of the Art of Orissa* (Calcutta, 1974).

legs on the lotus seat. The total impression is one of elegance and sophistication, both in terms of aesthetic feeling and of ideological understanding and interpretation. From palaeographical indications, this icon should be assigned to about the eleventh century.

By far the largest number of Buddha icons of these four centuries, made in stone, stucco or terracotta or fabricated in cast-metal and recovered from the ruins of Nālandā and Kurkihar or from any other site of Bihār, West Bengal and Bangladesh, would by and large conform to the art-form and style of the icons, which have been described and analyzed above in some detail. The type of the crowned Buddha seems to have become very popular in the tenth and eleventh centuries, more in its cast-metal version than in stone, if one can judge from the relative numbers that have come down to us, and Kurkihar seems to have turned them out in hundreds (Pl. 206).

Fairly high-relief stelae, large and small, carved out of dark grey or black sandstone quarried from the Rajmahal hills that divide South Bihār from Bengal, and presenting the Buddha seated or standing, flanked by two Bodhisattvas, one on each side, with or without the principal episodes of the Master's life along the two sides and the top, have been found in good numbers from all over Bihār and Bengal (Pl. 207). Orissa, too, has yielded such reliefs but in smaller numbers. In Bihār and Bengal these relief stelae can be dated, palaeographically and stylistically, from about the eighth to about the first half of the twelfth century, that is, to the so-called Pāla period. The arrangement of these Buddha stelae is stereotyped, the same form being repeated from stele to stele, though the physiognomy and plastic treatment change with time. Aesthetically these icons are not therefore of much significance and do not reveal any new interpretation of the Buddha-Bodhisattva idea. However, the iconographic form was certainly very popular in East India, whence it was exported to South-East Asia on the one side, and to the Himalayan lands of Nepal and Tibet on the other.

Certain iconographic forms seem to have become fixed during this period and to have repeated themselves from figure to figure. As one reviews the countless number of icons of Bihār and Bengal, one cannot help noticing at once that with very few exceptions the Buddha is shown seated in *bhūmisparśa-mudrā*, and this is true of the contemporary Buddha images of Orissa as well. This means that in East India over these four centuries the great event of the Enlightenment is primary (see p. 135). In those reliefs where other incidents of his life are represented, the central and by far the larger part of the relief would be occupied by the Buddha sitting in *bhūmisparśa-mudrā* and seven other incidents would be arranged around him, with the *parinirvāṇa* scene placed invariably at the top and the birth scene at either the right or left bottom (Pls. 206, 208).

A ninth-century stele from West Bengal presents the Buddha in bold round relief, seated on a lotus flower base (*ambuja-pīṭha*) holding the pot of honey offered him by a monkey, which is shown at the bottom left below the Buddha figure (Pl. 209). The palaeography of the Buddhist formula inscribed around the figure would support the date that it has been assigned. This figure can perhaps be usefully compared with the huge seated Buddha figure *in situ* at Nālandā (Pl. 210). The latter, which is in *bhūmisparśa-mudrā*, is in the round—not altogether an unusual phenomenon in Indian art. From the point of

206. Buddha in the 'earth-witness' posture

From eastern India, exact provenance unknown; 11th century A.D.*; basalt; H. 28 cm.; British Museum, London.*

This is a crowned image of Akṣobhya, conceived of as the Supreme Buddha, for he is surrounded by subsidiary manifestations though in what appears to be a rather haphazard manner. Midway on either side he is shown in his preaching manifestation. Above to the right he makes the *abhaya-mudrā* (gesture of fearlessness), while above to the left as well as at the bottom right, he makes the *varada-mudrā*. At the top, his Final Nirvana is represented, while at the bottom left his birth scene is suggested.

207. Śākyamuni as Akṣobhya

From Nālandā, Bihār, India; 11th century A.D.; sandstone; Nālandā Museum.

Here Śākyamuni as Akṣobhya is surrounded by subsidiary images representing other aspects of his great actions (compare Pls. 206, 208).

208. Buddha in the 'earth-witness' posture

From Nālandā, Bihār, India; 10th-11th century A.D.; sandstone; Nālandā Museum.

Here, Śākyamuni as Akṣobhya Buddha is surrounded by subsidiary images representing particular Buddha gestures, such as those of meditation, generosity, fearlessness, and 'historical' incidents, such as the Nativity, First Sermon and Final Nirvana.

209. Śākyamuni with a pot of honey

From West Bengal, India; 9th century A.D.*; sandstone; Asutosh Museum of Indian Art, Calcutta.*

The pot of honey was offered to Śākyamuni at Vaiśālī and this event came to be included as one of the Eight Great Events of his life, associated with eight main places of pilgrimage (see p. 45). The legend is certainly an old one, for the scene is already depicted on the northern gateway of the great Sāñcī stupa. Hsüan-tsang visited the site and for his description, see Beal (reference on p. 185), 2, p. 68. A. Foucher discusses this particular 'miracle' in *La vie du Bouddha, op. cit.*, pp. 289–93.

210. Buddha in the 'earth-witness' posture

From Nālandā, Bihār, India; c. 10th century A.D.*; black stone; in situ.*

See p. 277.

view of facial and physiognomical form the two figures are similar; the plastic treatment of the rounded volumes is also more or less similar. But the monastic robe in the former covers both shoulders and the conventionally rendered folds are heavier; in the latter it covers the left shoulder alone and the folds are rendered lightly and more gracefully.

In the next century the face becomes slightly longish and the chin somewhat pointed; the body and the limbs shed much of their weight. At the same time, the monastic robe is treated integrally with the plastic treatment of the body, which is softer and more sensitive. The result is an elegant, delicate and sophisticated figure tending to be pretty and modish.

To this stage of aesthetic perception belongs the majority of the Buddha icons cast in metal of Nālandā and Kurkihar (Pl. 211). At Nālandā we have a human form that is light, tall and slim, with long legs (Pl. 212). At Kurkihar the legs are longer still, with a trunk that is shorter and more robust, with broader shoulders and a more expanding chest than at Nālandā. The plastic treatment conforms, however, to the same idiom, but at Nālandā the conventional monastic mantle is treated more lightly and sensitively than at Kurkihar, where the folds are given a volume and are arranged in a much more mechanical manner. The Kurkihar standing icon shows in its right hand the *varada-mudrā*, while the Nālandā ones show the *abhaya-mudrā*. Belonging more or less to the same aesthetic perception but perhaps to a somewhat earlier date is a Kurkihar icon of the Buddha seated in *bhūmisparśa-mudrā* on the lotus pedestal of an elaborately decorated throne (Pl. 213). Here the facial type is less elongated and the plastic treatment is somewhat severe. The treatment of the robe in heavy folds adds to the rather ponderous impression given by this whole piece. In European terms one might describe it as baroque.

Notice must be taken here of a number of Buddhist palm-leaf manuscript paintings originating from Bihār and Bengal and belonging to the eleventh, twelfth and thirteenth centuries. The earliest chronologically and the best examples aesthetically are preserved in the Cambridge University Library and in the Library of the Asiatic Society, Calcutta. Quite a few of these miniatures represent Buddhas and Bodhisattvas in familiar postures and stances, either independently or in compositions presenting Buddhist legends. In form and style these paintings are somewhat thinned and flattened versions in miniature sizes of what remained of the fully rounded and modelled volumes of Ajantā and Bagh cave-paintings. Eastern India exported this form and tradition of Buddhist painting to South-East Asia, to Nepal and Tibet.

During these four centuries or so, Orissa seems to have rendered a better account in regard to the understanding of the connotation of the term 'Buddha', and to its interpretation in terms of an image, in other words, in terms of art.[2]

The ruins of the Buddhist monastic establishment at Lalitgiri have yielded a number of refined and graceful Bodhisattva images belonging to the seventh and eighth centuries, a few of which are housed in the Indian Museum, Calcutta. These Bodhisattva images, for instance, the one of Avalokiteśvara Padmāpaṇi, deserve more than casual notice (Pl. 215). Tall, supple and slender, the figure stands in a slight *tribhaṅga* pose, holding the slender

[2]Concerning Orissa and Ratnagiri in particular, see Debala Mitra, *Buddhist Monuments* (Calcutta, 1971), pp. 223–33.

211. Standing Buddha making the hand-gesture of generosity (*varada-mudrā*)

From Kurkihar, Bihār, India; 11th century A.D.*; cast octo-alloy metal; Patna Museum.*

The Buddha is attended by Brahmā and Indra. Cf. Pl. 234.

212. Standing Buddha

From Nālandā, Bihār, India; 11th century A.D.*; cast octo-alloy; Nālandā Museum.*

The Buddha is making the gesture of blessing (*abhaya-mudrā*) with his right hand and holds his robe with the gesture of generosity (*varada-mudrā*) in his left hand.

213. Buddha Akṣobhya

From Kurkihar, Bihār, India; 11th century A.D.*; cast octo-alloy; Patna Museum.*

Akṣobhya is identifiable by the 'earth-witness' posture and by the lion supports of the throne, which is unusually ornate. It follows the pattern of those shown in Pls. 204, 206.

214. Crowned Buddha, presumably again Akṣobhya

10th–11th century A.D.*; sandstone; Nālandā, Bihār, India.*

The small inset images above represent the Buddhas of past. present and future, that is, the timelessness of Buddhahood.

215. Bodhisattva Avalokiteśvara Padmapāṇi

From the site of the mediaeval monastery at Lalitgiri, Orissa, India; sandstone; Indian Museum, Calcutta.

See p. 281.

and supple stalks of the lotus flower, the curves of which follow the soft, melting lines of the physiognomical form. The plastic treatment of the rounded forms of the body and the limbs, too, are soft and somewhat melting, and the face articulates an expression that is full of compassion. Here is indeed a clear echo of the tradition of Sārnāth, an echo that is still heart-warming.

Lalitgiri Bodhisattvas are more or less well known to all students of Indian art and iconography, but the Buddha figures of this once important monastic establishment are less known, though there is reason to believe, from their large size and imposing presence, that these were images that were installed as icons at the main shrines of these monastic establishments. This is true of the majority of the large-size Buddha images of other monasteries of Orissa, for instance, at Udayagiri and Ratnagiri, at Baudh and Balasore. Indeed, it seems that apart from the character of the facial and physiognomical form and its sensitive plastic treatment, the huge size and heroic proportions of the figures were but additional means by which the craftsmen sought to convey the greatness of the *mahāpuruṣa-cakravartin* that the Buddha was. It may be noted in parentheses that quite a few of these large images were made not out of one single block of stone but of more than one, and hence in sections. Practically all the Buddha images of Orissa belong to a period ranging from about the eighth to about the twelfth century; those from Lalitgiri are perhaps the earliest, and the one that is reproduced in this album may even belong to about the end of the seventh century. All the other sculptures reproduced, including the Lalitgiri colossus, are *in situ*, in the midst of the ruins, except a smaller rectangular relief that is now housed in the Cuttack Museum.

Of the large images, that of Lalitgiri is the best preserved, but it is most unfortunate that a modern beautifier has made an attempt to improve it, and so has dot-marked the neckline, lips, the nose-tip and line, the eyes, the forehead line, including the hanging ear-lobes, and the first line of the 'snail-shell' curls with indelible white paint. But it was not the motive of beautification alone that disfigured this remarkable image; the person responsible also wanted to turn the image into one of Śiva, and therefore put the Śaivite mark on the forehead. Such is the sad situation of these long-abandoned monastic sites. This dignified image is seated in the *bhūmisparśa-mudrā* and characterized by broad shoulders and an expanding chest, the latter gradually and gracefully attenuating towards the waist. The arms and legs are long and roundly modelled. The figure has indeed the fresh fullness of mature youth, an impression that is also heightened by a soft and graceful plastic treatment that does not hide the feel and character of the stone itself.

This is indeed the general common feature of all the large Buddha images of Lalitgiri and Udayagiri belonging to the eighth and ninth centuries. Even the smaller but high relief slabs retain this character. They are all pure, straightforward articulations of the Buddha idea in terms of simple but heroic dignity, of inwardness of being and of tender mellowness of feeling that is not in any way fastidious. Even the colossal head of the great Buddha figure at Ratnagiri, which should be dated earlier than the tenth century, would deserve this characterization, despite its mutilation. But much more mutilated is the colossus from Balasore, which is perhaps still later. Because of its mutilation no mean-

216. Buddha seated in the 'earth-witness' posture

From the site of the mediaeval monastery at Ratnagiri, Cuttack, Orissa, India; 11th century A.D.; sandstone; now in site shelter, Ratnagiri.

217. Buddha Vairocana

From the site of the mediaeval monastery at Ratnagiri, Cuttack, Orissa, India; 11th century A.D.; sandstone; now in site shelter, Ratnagiri.

This image of a preaching Buddha may be identified in Mahāyāna tradition as Vairocana (see p. 135). He is seated on a lion-supported throne, marked by the Wheel of the Law. This is flanked by two deer, referring to the Deer Park near Vārānasi. The tree motif commemorates the moment of the Enlightenment at Bodhgayā.

ingful comment can be made, but from its size and from some of the portions that are still somewhat intact, namely, the right arm, the left hand and the shoulders, one can perceive that it was at one time a very dignified image, tall and robust but at the same time mellow and sensitive.

Towards the end of the tenth and in the eleventh century, the Buddha images of Ratnagiri and other places in the Cuttack district at any rate are informed by a certain amount of conscious grace, elegance and sophistication (Pl. 216). Smaller in size, they still retain their heroic physiognomical form, but in certain instances the waist tends to be narrower than in others. The plastic treatment becomes generally somewhat tight and hard and the surface smooth. Conventional decorations abound. The face, with sharp nose, lips and half-closed eyes, all cut sharply and with refinement, wears a light smile (Pl. 217).

South India

Although mainly known as a result of the important discoveries of bronze images (some 350 items) at Nāgapaṭṭiṇam since 1856, the later developments of Buddhist art in the south bear witness to its quite surprising vitality in most of the ancient cultural centres. Often benefitting from the solicitude of the Cōla kings and from the tolerance of the Hoysala, maintaining also close links with Sri Lanka and South-East Asia, especially Burma (cf. the inscriptions of Kalyāṇi, the end of the fifteenth century), Buddhism maintained itself successfully in the south under the rulers of Vijayanagar and even under the Nayaks of Tanjore, at least until the beginning of the seventeenth century. While Theravādin Buddhism, being the best attested, seems to have maintained itself the longest, the activity of the Mahāyāna should not be overlooked, and if we accept the testimony of the surviving images, it seems to have ceased not very much sooner than the Theravāda.

From the artistic standpoint, until about the fourteenth and fifteenth centuries the orientation remains much the same as during the previous period (see Chapter 3: 5), merely affirming perhaps the principal tendencies that we have already noticed. Buddha images show the two-fold influence of the primitive tradition on the one hand, and of the art of Nālandā on the other. Bodhisattva images follow the evolution of Cōla art, then that of the Vijayanagar, while respecting generally the same iconographic principals as those of the north (Bihār, Nepal, etc.) The later Buddha images, often of stone and of which the greater number have been placed in Brahmanical temples, show stylized exaggerations in which the influence of Sri Lanka is certainly not absent.

As for the previous period, and doubtless for much the same reasons, no sanctuary or monument has been preserved. Even the great *caitya* of several storeys at Nāgapaṭṭiṇam (nicknamed *Puduveli-gopuram*, 'The Chinese Pagoda') was demolished in 1867 by the Jesuits.[3] Nevertheless, as we shall see later on, a few votive stupas that possess a certain iconographic interest preserve perhaps some memory of architectural forms.

Apart from the consideration of actual postures, seated or standing, which should not be expected in any case to provide critical evidence, the Buddha images of Nāgapaṭṭiṇam

[3]A description and drawing of this interesting building will be found in *The Indian Quarterly*, 7 (1878), pp. 224–27. See also Mitra, *op. cit.*, pp. 193–97.

218. Buddha Akṣobhya

In the compound of the Karikala Aman, Kāñchīpuram, Tamil Nadu, India; stone; H. 75 cm.

Note the flame-like *uṣṇīṣa*, so typical of the Buddha image in Sri Lanka.

219. Meditating Buddha, possibly intended as Amitābha

From Kāñchīpuram, Tamil Nadu, India; 12th century A.D.*; stone.*

The cult of Amitābha, which has had so large a following in Far Eastern Buddhism has left few traces in India. This image may have been intended as a meditating Śākyamuni, but in the Mahāyāna period the *dhyāna-mudrā* became typical of Amitābha. See p. 135fn.

can be separated into three main groups. The first of these reflects the persistence of the early traditions of the Āndhra region. The second remains faithful to the tendencies made manifest during the second period from the sixth to seventh centuries onwards. The third is characterized by the passing adoption of the iconography of Nālandā. No matter to which group the images belong, all adhere to the same aesthetic principles: simplification of the general lines; large and regularly shaped oval heads, eyes almond-shaped and wide open; a low forehead; the hair arranged in curls, which tend to be flattened; the *uṣṇīṣa* rather reduced and sometimes conical in shape, but always surmounted by an ornament in the form of a flame that recalls at once the *siraspota* of the Buddha images of Sri Lanka. The attitudes and the gestures, which vary but little, bear witness to the influence, whether direct or indirect of Nālandā (Pls. 218, 219).

In the first group, which is probably the oldest (approximately tenth to eleventh centuries), the arrangement of the robe and the gestures belong to those of the school of Amarāvatī (pp. 78–79). The stylization of the faces, the disappearance of pleats and the adoption of a scarf thrown over the left shoulder are the only signs of change. Very often the manner of the gesture is modified, and as we shall note in the case of the second group, it tends to associate the *abhaya-mudrā* of the right hand with the *vitarka-mudrā* of the left hand.

In the second group (approximately tenth to fourteenth centuries) the arrangement of the robe accords generally with the reversed mode that appeared in post-Gupta art: thus the rear end of the robe instead of being thrown across the back is brought in front; crossing the left side of the chest, it passes over the left upper arm before falling free. The first and second groups have inspired a large number of later images, such as the extremely beautiful Buddha in *samādhi*, accompanied by two *nāga* kings (Pl. 220). This comes from Nāgapaṭṭiṇam and is probably of the thirteenth century or so. Another example is the great standing Buddha making the gestures of fearlessness (*abhaya*) and generosity (*varada*), which was found at Tanjore and is kept in the Madras Museum (Pl. 221). This probably belongs to the end of the sixteenth century. It is noticeable that the images of the directional Buddhas (Jina), identifiable on votive stupas, are sometimes seated in the attitude known as *vīrāsana* (cross-legged), which is characteristic of South India, and that the same monuments also show Buddhas seated in the 'European' fashion and teaching with the *vitarka-mudrā* (gesture of explanation). These are rare survivals of attitudes and gestures that won the favour of the schools of South-East Asia, in particular that of Dvāravatī.

The third group, which may be attributed to the period of the thirteenth to sixteenth centuries largely on the basis of palaeographic indications, recalls the iconography of Nālandā, although it is not always possible to decide if we are dealing with the survival of styles established before the destruction of Nālandā at the end of the twelfth century, or if it is a matter of later influences transmitted through Burma as intermediary. Whatever the case, the images of the third group, while preserving the aesthetic norms of South India and keeping the ornament of the *uṣṇīṣa* in the form of a flame, also adopt the gestures, attitudes and arrangement of the robe according to the Pāla-Sena tradition. Typical of the gestures adopted are those of fearlessness (*abhaya*) associated with generosity (*varada*) and the 'earth-witness' (*bhūmisparśa*). The most common attitude adopted is that of the

220. Meditating Buddha enthroned

From Nāgapaṭṭiṇam, Tamil Nadu, India; c. 13th century A.D.*; bronze; overall H. 74.5 cm; Government Museum, Madras.*

This haloed Buddha seated in the meditation posture on a large lotus throne is one of the most beautiful examples of South Indian mediaeval Buddhist art. The simplicity of the figure of the Tathāgata shaded by a parasol is emphasized by the magnificence of the surrounding ornamentation that acknowledges his pre-eminence: the back of the throne flanked by rearing lions, the large ornamental plaque decorated with luxuriant flowering foliage, the bejewelled *nāga* kings bearing fly-whisks. The attire and ornaments of these *nāga* kings indicate a work of the Cōla period. The composition is reminiscent of the Gal Vihāra cave (Pl. 226).

221. Buddha beneath an arch decorated with a sea-monster

From Tanjore (Thanjavur), Tamil Nadu, India; c. 15th–16th century A.D.*; bronze; overall H. 105.5 cm.; Government Museum, Madras.*

This hieratic Buddha shown in a frontal representation with a highly stylized anatomy is making a dual gesture combining blessing (*abhaya*) and generosity (*varada*), a feature that seems to have been taken from Pāla-Sena iconography whose influence is much in evidence at Nāgapaṭṭiṇam. However, the facial features, hair and flame-like ornament shooting from the *uṣṇīṣa*, which is here very prominent, continue the South Indian tradition. The figure stands on a lotus support beneath an openwork arch that is supported at either end by a sea-monster (*makara*) and that is surmounted by a grotesque mask (*kīrtimukha*). These are traditional themes and the degree of their stylization reflects their lateness.

222. Bodhisattva Avalokiteśvara seated on a lotus throne in a 'sportive' posture (*lalitāsana*)

From East India, exact provenance unknown; 12th century A.D.*; bronze; H. 26.2 cm.; British Museum, London.*

This late Pāla-style image relates directly with Nepalese workmanship of the same period.

223. The Final Nirvana and the cult of the stupa

From East India, exact provenance unknown; 10th century A.D.*; basalt; H. 54.4 cm.; British Museum, London.*

224. Standing Buddha

From East India, exact provenance unknown; 10th–11th century A.D.*; bronze; H. 19.2 cm.; British Museum, London.*

The Buddha is making the gesture of blessing or fearlessness (*abhaya-mudrā*), and is wearing a crown and ornaments, surmounted by a garlanded umbrella, topped by the symbols of sun and moon, which represent 'wisdom' (*prajñā*) and 'means' (*upāya*)—the two co-efficients of Enlightenment (see p. 416).

225. Votive stupa
225-a. The same stupa with the dome removed

From Nāgapaṭṭiṇam, Tamil Nadu, India; c. 13th century A.D.*; overall H. 22 cm.; Government Museum, Madras.*

This votive stupa, inscribed with the name of a female donor, has been dated palaeographically to the end of the Cōla period, although similar works were apparently being produced at Nāgapaṭṭiṇam from the end of the ninth century. It will be noted that the combination of a stupa and a building containing cella appears to reproduce architectural features that were probably evolved in the Magadha area (Kolvi, Binnayaga), traces of which are also to be found in South-East Asia (Thailand, Indonesia). The image of Avalokiteśvara on the wall opposite the door is proof that the work is Mahāyāna. The Buddha concealed within the moveable body of the stupa is shown making the earth-witness gesture and should be identified with the Buddha of the east, Akṣobhya.

cross-legged meditation posture (*vajrāsana*). Standing images with the robe covering both shoulders very often preserve the large concentric folds with the lateral edges regularly and symmetrically turned back in the manner that is so well attested in the art of Bihār (Nālandā, Kurkihar).

The images of Bodhisattvas, mainly of Avalokiteśvara (Pl. 222) and of Maitreya with two or four arms, are seated in the elegant posture known as *lalitāsana* or in the meditation posture (*vajrāsana*) following the tradition of the north, or again they may be standing, broad-hipped, in the attitude so much favoured by Dravidian sculptors. They generally hold their symbolic devices between the raised index and middle fingers, once again in the Dravidian manner, and they wear ornaments and head-dresses very similar to those of Brahmanical divinities, which thus helps to date them. The head-dress of Maitreya is generally decorated with the small inset stupa that characterizes him, but only exceptionally does Avalokiteśvara wear a small inset image of Amitābha Buddha, so typical in the north.

The votive stupas of Nāgapaṭṭiṇam (Madras Museum) that we mentioned above are interesting for several reasons (Pls. 225, 225-a). Dating from the Cōla period (tenth to thirteenth centuries) and of Mahāyānist inspiration, they reveal to us what Buddhist architecture would have been during that period and bear witness to an unusual conception of the role and meaning of the stupa. While those that seem to be the most ancient preserve the usual shape, others represent styles that are far more evolved. Some that possess a high square base ornamented with niches containing images remind us of the stupas of Nālandā and Bodhgayā. Others suggest actual shrines crowned with a stupa like those of Kolvi and Binnayaga (Rājasthān, approximately sixth century) or the small sanctuaries of Caṇḍi Sewu (Java, ninth century). From the iconographic point of view, the small monuments of Nāgapaṭṭiṇam (average height: 20–25 centimetres) are especially interesting. A door decorated with three figures in high relief opens into their base. Amongst these figures one recognizes the Buddha preaching the First Sermon, marked by the Wheel of the Law and two deer, and seated either in the 'European' or in the 'Indian' fashion, or again another Buddha figure, teaching, making the 'earth-witness' gesture, or seated in *samādhi*. Such figures are probably to be identified according to Mahāyāna tradition as the various cosmic Buddhas (see p. 135). Other than such Buddha figures one may find a Bodhisattva, identifiable as Avalokiteśvara, and seated in the posture known as *lalitāsana*. The stupa that crowns the sanctuary is bulbous and ornamented with four flowers in full bloom. It is moveable and shelters another Buddha image always in the 'earth-witness' posture, which may therefore be identified with Akṣobhya, the Buddha of the eastern quarter. One should notice that in the case of such compositions, the figure in the sanctuary facing west is that of Avalokiteśvara. The inscriptions sometimes found are unhappily too short and vague for us to be able to deduce the sects to which such stupas might be attributed.

Finally, despite its unequal aesthetic value, the late Buddhist art of the south presents an undeniable interest, revealing the extraordinary durability of the school and its traditionalism. It also furnishes us in retrospect with precious information on the evolution and the various changes that we could not otherwise imagine for the whole period from the fifth to the ninth centuries, such are the gaps in other information available to us.

2. SRI LANKA AND SOUTH-EAST ASIA (10TH–19TH CENTURIES)

Schools of Buddhist Art

An iconographic tradition, if not doctrinal unity, seems to have been established in Sri Lanka after the ninth century despite political difficulties, and it ensured the genuine continuity of art; but this was not so in South-East Asia. The radical changes that occurred at different times in the various kingdoms sometimes led to the total transformation or the actual disappearance, maybe followed by the re-appearance, of the Buddhist workshops that had grown up during the first period.

Generally speaking, it can be said that after the remarkable artistic flowering of Buddhism in the eighth and ninth centuries inspired mainly by the rapid spread of Mahāyāna doctrines, there was a general decline in almost all regions, sometimes a total eclipse. Pervading most of the schools of South-East Asia for varying periods, this decadence often affected the importance of the schools more than the quality of their art. Its causes appear to have been manifold: the progress and strengthening of Brahmanic religions in close conjunction with the exercise of political power in most of the kingdoms, a deterioration in the political climate, ethnic movements and the appearance of new rulers in place of the old. As a result of such a period, so unfavourable to the sustained influence of the *saṅgha*, the 'Community', Buddhist art emerged much changed. It was, however, during the long period stretching roughly from the tenth to the fourteenth centuries that the major Buddhist schools of South-East Asia that have survived to the present time achieved their true originality. This originality was such that genuine local iconographic traditions grew up and became so firmly established that no further external influence has succeeded in modifying them until virtually the present day.

It appears that it was towards the end of the twelfth and the beginning of the thirteenth century that influences from India left their last visible, though somewhat short-lived, marks on the art of the Indo-Chinese Peninsula. The exodus and dispersal of Indian monks following the destruction of Buddhist universities when the troops of Muhammad-ibn Bakhtyar conquered Magadha led to the complete renewal of a large part of the iconographic repertoire. But the lessons thus learned were more easily forgotten than assimilated by schools that were already firmly attached to their own traditions, and the introduction of Sri Lanka Buddhism at much the same time, though of such decisive importance for the religious history of South-East Asia, seems to have had just as little effect so far as the production of images was concerned, except for the Sukhothai school (see p. 314). The influence exerted by the Indian monks on doctrine and on the organization of the communities was not strong enough to interfere with stylistic traditions, often centuries old and generally based on the cult of a particular image. In fact, the aura of fame surrounding certain images by virtue of the events (e.g., Victory over Māra) or places (the site of the Enlightenment) they evoked and, above all, the protection they afforded sites and individuals conferred on them the value of archetypes, which was in itself an invitation to mass copying. The notion of a 'copy' should not be taken literally in the sense of a purely formal imitation entailing simply the execution of facsimiles, but rather as the production of a work that participates in the benevolent power of the 'model'. Thus traditionalism, however necessary, is not to be associated with stagnation. Throughout the whole of Buddhist South-East Asia, art has always remained very much alive. Everywhere aesthetic concepts changed over the centuries, accentuating differences between schools. To the initial idea of the grandeur and ideal beauty of the Buddha was added the search for features indicative of the signs (*lakṣaṇa*) that at his last birth identified the great being who would renounce the world and become a Buddha. The supramundane beauty thus conceived transcends human reality and lends itself most successfully to the boldest of stylized treatments. After a long evolution it may sometimes appear to an eye trained in Western classicism to show signs of a certain dryness. The fact is that the later ideal is primarily inspired by the desire—manifested more artistically in some cases than in others, but always with the same faith—to magnify the image by attempting to express what is felt to be inexpressible.

The choice of attitudes and gestures, designed to represent each of the great moments in the career of the Buddha, reveals similar preoccupations. Breaking the Mahāyāna tradition, according to which each Jina had his own *mudrā*, or gesture, whereby he could be identified at a glance, the images inspired by the Theravāda attempt to illustrate primarily the life and miracles of the historical Buddha. As interest ceased to concentrate on the Eight Great Events (Pl. 232), a wider choice of notable events was portrayed by means of a whole repertoire of appropriate gestures and attitudes, codified to a greater or lesser degree and in some few cases indicated by the depiction of protagonists. Without necessarily having recourse to painted compositions or narrative bas-reliefs, Buddhist art from the end of the medieval period onwards provided the devotee with a widely varied choice of edifying images. No doubt closely associated with the veneration of particular images, which was often bound up with considerations of a national character, the renewed favour apparently enjoyed by the cult of relics gave fresh impetus to art. In Sri Lanka, wall paintings recounted in epic style the history of some relic, while in the Indo-Chinese Peninsula numerous 'copies' were produced of the venerated Buddha footprint (*buddhapāda*), thus returning to the early traditions of Buddhist art.

Sri Lanka

From the ninth century to 1803, the date of the annexation of the kingdom of Kandy by Britain, three historical periods can be distinguished that had influence on Sinhalese religious art.

The End of the Anurādhapura Period and the Cōla Occupation. From the ninth to the eleventh centuries the history of Sri Lanka was dominated by a recrudescence of the activity of the Pāṇḍyas from India, and, more important, from the tenth century onwards, of the Cōlas, who destroyed Anurādhapura in 993. Appropriating to themselves 'all the treasures of Laṅka', they dominated the island more or less effectively until 1070. Apart from the devastation and pillaging, this Hindu domination does not seem to have made much difference to the position of Buddhism, which remained more or less the same as in previ-

226. General view of the Gal Vihāra

Group of rock carvings at Polonnaruwa, Sri Lanka; 12th century A.D.*; average H. 7–8 m.*

This group, executed in a manner that is sober and impressive, was part of the Uttārāma Monastery built by Parākramabāhu I (1153–86) and comprises four colossal images, one carved within an excavated rock and the other three originally protected by separate constructions. Two of the statues are seated in the *samādhi* position; the third, standing with hands folded on the breast, shows the Buddha in the second week following the attainment of the Supreme and Perfect Enlightenment (see Pl. 228) and not, as is often suggested, his disciple Ānanda; the last image, 14.12 metres long, is a Buddha in the *parinirvāṇa* posture, the most remarkable Buddha in Sinhalese sculpture.

ous centuries, and a prey to the same rivalries. The arrival in the ninth century of an Indian member of the Vajraparvata sect who settled at Abhayagiri to teach the Vajrayāna doctrine does not seem to have produced any noticeable iconographic changes, nor does the artistic tradition seem to have been modified in any way.

While it is not possible to give exact dates, it seems that most of the colossal rock-carvings, in a style similar to that of Avukana (Pl. 95), may be ascribed to this period: the standing Buddha at Sasseruwa, the Buddha seated in the *samādhi* and the reclining Buddha at Tantirimalai seem, like the reclining Buddha at Attaragollewa, to prefigure the Gal Vihāra images (Pl. 226). Even more typical of the trend, though more mediocre as art, is the large Mahāyāna group at Buduruvegala, showing two triads of Bodhisattvas on either side of a 15-metre-tall Buddha in high relief. All these images have very stylized garments, and the sculptors seem to have been more concerned to suggest supernatural power than to portray living beauty. Wall paintings, however—judging solely from fragments discovered in the reliquary chamber at Mahiyaṅgana-thūpa (in particular, the Victory over Māra, 11th century?)—are executed with restraint and dignity, and reveal a deeply sensitive art.

Polonnaruwa Period. A royal residence for the first time in the seventh century and the seat of Cōla power in the eleventh century, Polonnaruwa became the capital of Vijayabāhu I and his successors after the recovery of national independence. Considerably enlarged and enriched at the time of Parākramabāhu I (1153–86), it was finally abandoned in 1293 in favour of a site less threatened by invasion. Entirely dominated by the achievements of Parākramabāhu I, the Polonnaruwa period was outstanding from both the political and the religious point of view. Parākramabāhu I equipped the island with a remarkable irrigation system devised as much for religious and political as for economic ends (he wished to be a 'universal monarch'); and he was also the sovereign who put an end to the protracted rivalry and decadence of the Sinhalese Buddhist communities and united the dissident sects within the purified and regenerated Mahāvihāra, probably around 1165. Though a very important reform, accompanied by the creation of numerous wealthy religious foundations, this did not result in major changes as regards iconography. While a number of the statues at the Polonnaruwa site obviously predate his reign and appear to have been brought there from ruined foundations—a practice of which there are many examples elsewhere (Thailand, Pl. 104)—the most representative style seems to be that of the Gal Vihāra group (Pl. 226), at least three of whose images are ascribed by the *Cūḷavaṃsa* to the reign of Parākramabāhu I. The trend in art seems to continue towards a representation of the Buddha with somewhat impassive majesty, the forehead already narrow and rather sloping, characteristics that tend to become more marked in later iconography. The treatment of the drapery is also different, the folds being finer and more regular, and emphasized by a double line. The great monuments of Polonnaruwa maintain the tradition of the colossal statues (Laṅkātilaka Vihāra, Tivaṅka Piḷimage, etc.). In stuccoed brick, the figures are of a suppleness unknown in the earlier period, sometimes even standing in a relaxed position. It should also be stressed that the four *samādhi* images of the Vaṭadāge at Polonnaruwa form a unique group, characterized less by the fact that there are no folds in the garments than by the kind of smooth, totally unadorned head-dress that apparently covers the skull. Wall painting is still of high quality (fragments from rock shelters at Dimbulāgala and in the vicinity are unfortunately very much worn away, but are masterly in their draughtsmanship, e.g., the Buddha sitting on the Seat of the Enlightenment); above all are the lively, well-balanced drawings, of great distinction and executed in sober colours—red ochres, yellows and greens—of the huge complex at Tivaṅka Piḷimage (Pl. 227).

The Period of Decline. At the time of the subsequent Tamil incursions in the thirteenth century, Buddhist communities were persecuted, and towards 1280 the tooth relic was actually carried off, though it was returned shortly afterwards. Polonnaruwa was abandoned in favour of Kuruṇegala, which was less exposed, and later for Gampola, Rayigama and finally Kōṭṭe, where the Portuguese landed in 1505. Throughout this troubled period there was still much artistic activity, chiefly at Gampola. The most ancient works still resemble Polonnaruwa art, but the more recent ones often show a marked falling-off from the classical standard. Nearly all the images are seated in the *samādhi* attitude; stone images appear to be rare, particularly since it is now difficult to make out the exact nature of some large statues (Gadalādeniya, Laṅkātilaka at Gampola, Pl. 228), covered as they are in stucco and paint. In bronze statues, many of which are gilded, a greater attempt is made to portray hieratic grandeur, lines and volumes being severe. The robes, with their folds represented as completely stylized parallel waves, suggest materials pleated before being used (Pl. 229). The hair, dressed in small pointed curls, is surmounted by a very large flame (*siraspota*) in the form of a lyre.

After 1505 the determination of the victorious Portuguese to force Catholicism upon the island took the form of brutal persecution and large-scale destruction. While somewhat less serious during the time of the Dutch, who were in sole possession of the island from 1658 onwards, the situation of Buddhism remained very serious, and it fell to the kingdom of Kandy, which remained independent until annexed by the British in 1803, to maintain both the religion and its art. The decadence of the *saṅgha* led the sovereigns to send several missions to Burma and Thailand in order to restore the rules of the Community, but the situation of art was not as critical as it is often said to have been. Through persecution, religion acquired a national character that, while not always leading to quality in works of art, encouraged their production in large numbers and protected them from the influence and contamination of European art. Statuary seems to have been protected to a certain extent by its fidelity to iconographic treatises like the *Śāriputra*, which laid down the canon of images (Fig. A). Usually made of metal, they are only in exceptional cases of wood, ivory or crystal (the crystal Buddha in the Temple of the Tooth, Kandy). Bas-reliefs seem to be kept for divinities, who, as protectors of the island, are increasingly shown associated with the image of the Buddha (Pl. 229). The large reclining Buddha at Dambulla (length, 14.75 metres), which may belong to the seventeenth century, is unique in its workmanship, and stands out from an otherwise unremarkable series of works. Painting developed extraordinarily during the Kandy period. Essentially didactic in character, it expresses an ideal that is very different from that of the former school. Its images are large-

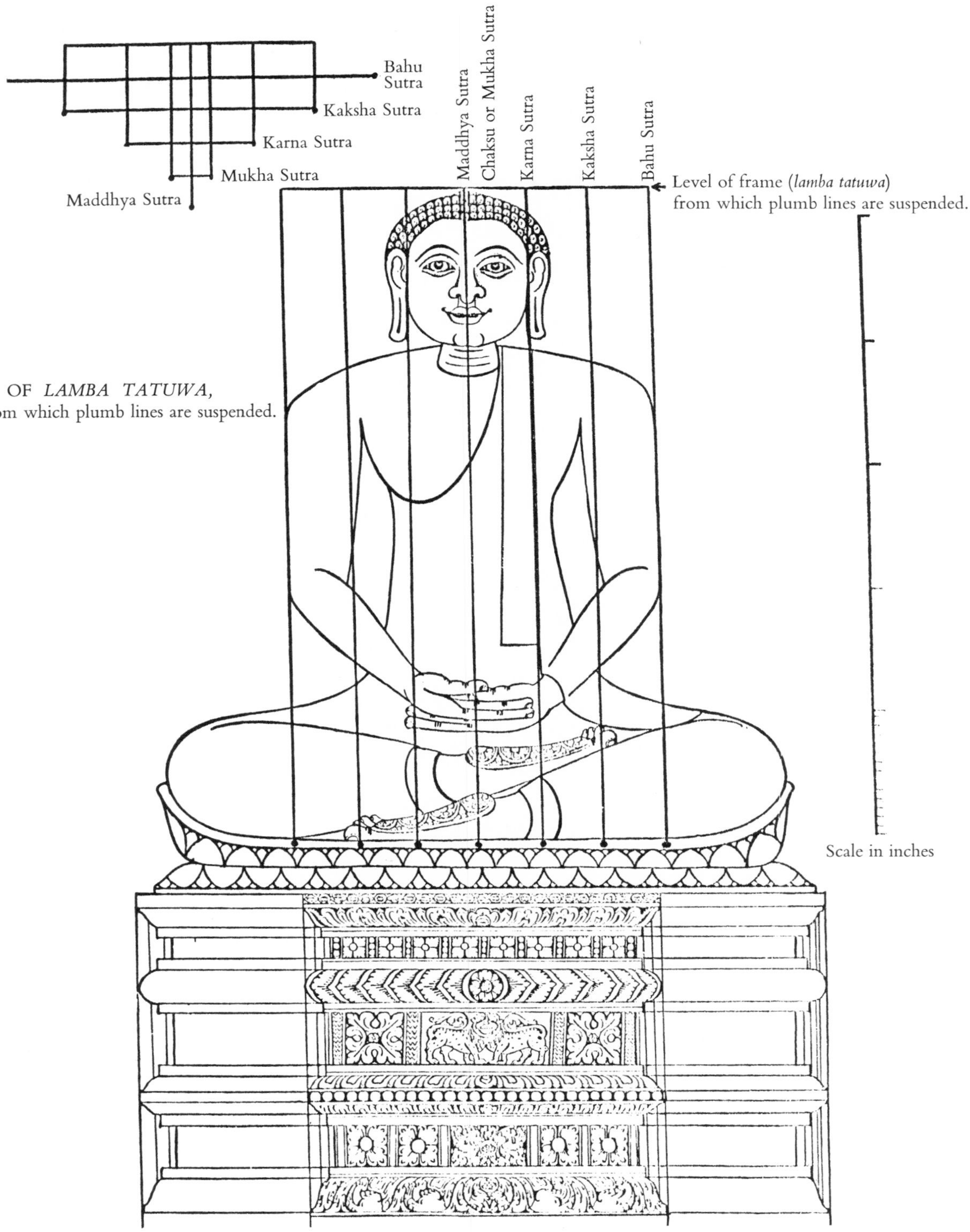

Fig. A. Sketch of a seated image, after D. S. Muhandiram (A. K. Coomaraswamy, *Medieval Sinhalese Art* [New York, 1956]).

scale, of conventional draughtsmanship, and in bright colours. Highly decorative, frequently forming a continuous narrative, they spread over walls and ceilings, even those of earlier buildings. Scenes dealing with the most celebrated *jātaka*s, the last life of the Buddha, or the establishment of Buddhism in Sri Lanka frequently receive epic treatment. Among the most remarkable eighteenth-century groups, mention should be made of those at Degaldoruwa, Telvatte, Mulgiragala and, above all, the great rock temple at Dambulla.

227. The Descent from the Heaven of the Thirty-three Gods

Wall painting at the Tivaṅka Piḷimage, Polonnaruwa, Sri Lanka; 12th–13th century A.D.*; in situ.*

Most of the wall paintings at the Tivaṅka Pilimage illustrate *jātaka*s, but some are of scenes from the last existence of the Buddha. This one, the Descent from the Heaven of the Thirty-three Gods, where the Buddha had gone to preach the doctrine to his mother who had been reborn among the gods (Pl. 107), is one of the finest illustrations of the miracle that is described in detail in the texts. There is a good copy of the painting, which has suffered from the elements, in the National Museum, Colombo.

229. Standing Buddha

From the region of Kandy, Sri Lanka; 17th–18th century A.D.*; brass; H. 16 cm.; National Museum, Colombo.*

The refinement of style and highly decorative interpretation of this small group are indicative of the modern trend in Sri Lanka Buddhist art. Here the tendencies shown at Gampola (Pl. 228) are confirmed. The highly hieratic, stylized treatment confers on the image an undeniable grandeur, emphasized by the *makara* triumphal arch and the presence of four divinities brandishing swords.

228. Colossal Buddha in the meditation posture

The most important image of the Laṅkātilaka Vihāra, Gampola, Sri Lanka; second half of 14th century A.D.*; bronze; in situ.*

This shows the rapid progress of the stylized treatment of the image of the Buddha in Sri Lanka. Instead of naturalism, the aim is to convey an impression of magnificence, emphasized by the very decorative character of the paintings in the chevet; and the systematic treatment of the folds of the *uttarāsaṅga* contributes to the effect. The paintings decorating the pillars on either side of the apse illustrate the seven weeks that followed the Enlightenment.

230. Standing Buddha

From the East Gandhakuṭī, Shwezigon Pagoda, Pagan, Burma; end of 11th century A.D.*; bronze; H. approximately 4 m.; in situ.*

Each of the four sanctuaries (*gandhakuṭī*), situated at the four cardinal points of the main stupa, enshrines a colossal image of the Buddha, the right hand making the *abhaya-mudrā* gesture and the left hand holding the border of the robe. Attention has rightly been drawn to the affinity between these images, held to represent four successive Buddhas (this being the Konāgamana Buddha), and the great statue from Sulṭāngañj in Birmingham Museum (Pl. 62). Though this is an indication of the prevailing inspiration in the art of Pagan, Burmese art nevertheless aims at a hieratic effect, especially in the very stylized robe treatment.

231. The Cutting of the Hair

From Nanda Temple, Pagan, Burma; end of 11th–12th century A.D.*; stone high relief, gilt; H. approximately 110 cm.; in situ.*

This relief, which is part of a large group, illustrates the same scene as the Borobudur composition (Pl. 113), but in a very different manner that was generally adopted throughout the peninsula. The scene is reduced to essentials: the seated Bodhisattva cuts his hair, swept up into a very elaborate twisted strand, while a god (not visible here) carries his gold tiara to the Heaven of the Thirty-three Gods. It should be noted that the very supple, indeed graceful, attitude of the Bodhisattva is in marked contrast with the hieratic style of the standing Buddhas of the Shwezigon Pagoda (Pl. 230).

232. The Eight Great Events of a Buddha's career

From Upali Thein, near Pagan, Burma; 11th–12th century A.D.*; high relief, steatite; H. 12.7 cm.; Pagan Museum.*

This slab, like some others of the same type, illustrates with astonishing technical virtuosity the classical series of the Eight Great Events (see p. 45). The style derives directly from the Pāla tradition (cf. Pl. 205). The central figure (Akṣobhya) represents the Victory over Māra, whose routed army is scattered among the foliage. Seated on a lotus throne, the Buddha is flanked by two Bodhisattvas and adored by two *nāga* kings; the treasures of the *cakravartin* monarch decorate the base.

233. The birth of Śākyamuni

Wall painting from Nandamaññya Temple, Minnanthu (East Pagan), Burma; 13th century A.D.*; in situ.*

This interpretation of the traditional theme of the tree in the park of Lumbinī bending towards Queen Māyā, who grasps a branch, with her left hand round the shoulder of her sister Mahāprajāpatī Gautamī, is an obviously deliberate attempt at a stylized decorative treatment, and the attending gods are relegated to the lower part of the composition. It will be noted that the future Buddha is shown twice, at the right of his mother and also at her feet.

234. The Descent from the Heaven of the Thirty-three Gods

From Pagan, Burma; 11th–12th century A.D.*; high relief, wood; H. 70 cm.; Pagan Museum.*

This wood-carving, one of the rare examples preserved from this period, shows the same qualities as the relief at the Nanda Temple (Pl. 231). The episode concludes the miracle illustrated at the Tivaṅka Piḷimage, Sri Lanka (Pl. 227). Standing on a lotus, the Buddha has just descended at Sāṅkāśya from the Heaven of the Thirty-three Gods. Accompanied by Śakra (Indra), who is bearing the begging-bowl, and Brahmā, who is holding the parasol and is recognizable by his many faces, the Buddha is welcomed at the foot of the triple ladder by his disciple Śāriputra, who is kneeling with his hands clasped together. The difference in height emphasizes the pre-eminence of the Buddha over all mankind.

Burma

In what is necessarily a very brief description, it is difficult to relate the history of Buddhist art in Burma to a political and religious history of which the chief feature is its complexity, since the diversity of ethnic groups promoted both political rivalry as well as the particularism of the schools. We shall therefore merely indicate, in their temporal and spatial context, a few outstanding characteristics of images without attempting a more general survey.

In the Mon country (Rāmaññadesa), Thaton retained its importance notwithstanding the foundation of Pegu around 825, which later supplanted it. At Pegu stands the Shwemawdaw Pagoda, one of the most venerated stupas in Burma. Rebuilt and enlarged several times, it is traditionally held to have been founded by Tapussa and Bhallika to house the two hair relics they had received from Śākyamuni himself. It was also at Pegu that the colossal Shwethalyaung was constructed in 994; it is a stone image of the reclining Buddha, 55 metres long and almost 16 metres high, restored in the fifteenth and at the beginning of the twentieth century. Theravādin Buddhism spread from Rāmaññadesa to Pagan in the eleventh century, introducing the Pāla-Sena technique and iconography that had been flourishing at Thaton for several centuries.

The Pagan Images. The fortifications of Pagan, the most impressive religious city in South-East Asia, are reputed to have been constructed in 849. It subsequently succeeded Tagaung, a city considered the cradle of Burmese civilization, but whose statuary stylistically differs little from that of Pagan, which does not really begin its history until the reign of Aniruddha (Anawrahta, 1044–77). In the field of religion, the conversion of the king to the Theravāda by a Mon monk was followed by the conversion of the followers of the Mahāyāna and of the worshippers of local spirits. The conquest of the kingdom of Thaton in 1057 brought to Pagan not only the canonical texts but also architects and image-makers who introduced Thaton art to the capital, where it prospered until the city was taken by the Mongols in 1287.

The iconographic importance of the Pāla-Sena tradition (the frequency with which images are seated in the *vajrāsana* attitude and shown making the *bhūmisparśa-mudrā* or *dharmacakra-mudrā* gestures, the stylized treatment of the robes, etc.) is probably due as much to the influence of the Thaton school as to the importance of Bodhgayā (the holy place of Buddhism) for King Aniruddha, who had his seals decorated with a representation of the Mahābodhi Temple there. The site was, moreover, so renowned that a copy of the Mahābodhi Temple was erected in the capital in the first half of the thirteenth century. Nevertheless, while the image of the Buddha, with or without jewels, certainly took its inspiration from the art of Bengal and Bihār, the Pagan school rapidly began to diversify attitudes and gestures in such a way that most of the miracles in the last life of the Buddha could be conveyed with the utmost economy, depicting only the personages who were needed to identity the scene (Pls. 231, 232). The trend began with the construction of the Nanda (or Ānanda) Temple by Kyanzittha in 1091. A new type of image gradually appeared, in stone, stuccoed brick, bronze, and more rarely, wood (Pl. 234); a heavy torso, a short neck and a

Fig. B (a). Sketch of a late seated image, Burma.

Fig. B (b). Sketch of a late bejewelled image, Burma.

slightly inclined head were characteristic of the Burmese Buddha. Wall paintings in abundance (previous Buddhas, *jātakas*, the life of Śākyamuni, the Buddhist cosmogony) were initially reminiscent of the tradition of western India and, later, of the schools of Bengal and Nepal.

Burma after the Fall of Pagan. The temporary downfall of the kingdom of Burma in 1287 led to the fragmentation of power, but did not involve any great changes in the fields of religion or art. The Mon kingdom of Haṅsavattī (Pegu), reconstituted in 1369, maintained the earlier tradition. The growing importance of Sinhalese Buddhism, especially in the reign of Dhammaceti (1472–92), may have fostered imports and even copies of certain images from Sri Lanka and the Nāgapaṭṭiṇam school, but the major achievements of the reign remains the construction of the Shwegugyi, another copy of the Mahābodhi Temple, together with seven edifices grouped beside it, commemorating the seven weeks that followed the Enlightenment.

The Burmese Renaissance. It was from Taungu, where the Burmese state had withdrawn in 1347, that the second unification of Burma was effected. In the second half of the sixteenth century, the work of Bayinnaung was particularly important: the reconstruction of Pegu (1566) and, above all, the construction of a copy of the Mahācetiya of Sri Lanka to house a replica of the tooth relic (Mahazedi Pagoda, 1576). The four colossal images of the Buddha in the Kyaikpun Pagoda, seated with their backs against a huge pillar and shown calling the earth to witness, are of approximately the same date. Although in the Pagan tradition (the Thandawgya image), the stylized treatment of their robes seems already to foreshadow later images (Figs. B-a, B-b). We cannot go into the question of the complex stylistic development of images from the end of the sixteenth century onwards, but it will be noted that a genuine 'Burmese canon' gradually evolved from models that appeared at the end of the Pagan period. At the same time, Chinese influence is seen in a number of images, while the importance attached to ornaments leads in some cases to surprising developments of themes that have been inherited from Pāla-Sena art. Painting, represented chiefly by illustrated manuscripts, moves towards a more specifically Burmese style. Although revealing a certain affinity with contemporary painting in Thailand, this highly decorative stylized manner takes its place in the trend of which the forerunners were the thirteenth-century paintings of the Nandamaññya Temple (Pl. 233).

Thailand

Towards the end of the ninth and the beginning of the tenth century, Buddhist art seems to have experienced a period of decadence throughout the whole of what was later to be Thailand. The influence of the kingdom of Śrīvijaya and the spread of the Mahāyāna, which it had encouraged, now declined, and the Theravādin communities that had certainly been weakened did not regain their earlier vitality. There seem to be few foundations that can be ascribed to this period, and statuary (stucco work associated with restoration, bronze images) is often sadly mediocre. Not until the eleventh century were there any signs, and then chiefly in the eastern region, of a genuine renaissance—very much Khmer in its inspiration—consequent on the Khmer expansion towards the Maenam Basin. This trend characterized the 'Lopburi school', which achieved its full flowering roughly from the twelfth to the end of the first quarter of the thirteenth century; and it persisted in some regions long after Cambodia had ceased to exert its authority there. During the same period, in the north of the country, the Mon kingdom of Haripuñjaya (now Lamphun) seems to have preserved something of the Dvāravatī stylistic heritage, possibly already affected by Pāla-Sena and Khmer influences, the former from the Rāmaññadesa, the latter a result of the Cambodian expansion. In the second half of the thirteenth century, the growth of the first independent Thai kingdoms led to the appearance of new schools. These reached their maximum number in the fourteenth century, and then decreased; following more or less closely on the unification of the kingdom, Buddhist art in Thailand did not achieve unity until modern times. We must therefore analyze, at least briefly, each of the quite different styles that at times existed side by side and at other times succeeded each other for a period of nearly six centuries.

We may pass rapidly over the Haripuñjaya school, known chiefly for works such as that shown in Plate 235, the date of which generally appears to be about the time of the absorption of the kingdom by the recently constituted kingdom of Lan Na in 1292, but we must spend a little more time on the 'Lopburi school'. This was never, except perhaps in the reign of the great king of Angkor, Jayavarman VII (1181–c. 1218), either a genuinely Khmer or a merely provincial school. As a centre of Mahāyāna culture for many centuries, the region of Pimai undoubtedly played a part in the elaboration of Khmer Mahāyāna iconography; and while a whole category of images reveals the existence of contacts with workshops in the Pāla-Sena tradition, it is also obvious that the Lopburi school did much to maintain a number of Khmer-like trends and influenced the artistic development of the kingdom of Ayutthaya.

The Sukhothai Style. This is, if not actually the oldest of the genuine Thai styles, at least the one whose dates we know with most certainty. It is doubtful whether it had been evolved when the kingdom gained independence towards the middle of the thirteenth century, but it certainly had by the reign of Ram Kamheng (1277–c. 1299) and its originality was obvious by the beginning of the fourteenth century. It has sometimes been suggested that Sukhothai art was a reaction against the tendencies of the former Khmer rulers. This is certainly not the case. The beauty conceived by Sukhothai artists is supernatural, designed to evoke the characteristic 'signs' of the *mahāpuruṣa* ('Great Man') by which, according to the texts, one can recognize every being destined to become a Buddha. There may also be some reminiscences of Sinhalese art, but in essence the style is peculiar to Sukhothai (Fig. C-a): seated Buddha images, calling the earth to witness, are shown making a gesture that is virtually unknown in Sri Lanka; and while the walking Buddha seems to be foreshadowed at Polonnaruwa (Pl. 226), his depiction in high relief (for example, at Wat Trapang Thong Lang, Sukhothai) and, above all, in the round (Pl. 237) is one of the major inventions of Sukhothai art and probably that which best expresses its ideal. The school, which was extremely active, excelled in all forms of art: monumental images and compositions in stuccoed brick, bronze statues of excellent workmanship, paintings of which only too few examples survive. Judging from inscriptions, it was also responsible for the renewed favour enjoyed by *buddhapāda* (Pl. 330). Lastly, the style only declined gradually as a result of the linking up of the kingdom with that of Ayutthaya in 1438, though it exerted a decisive influence on Ayutthaya art.

The Chieng Sen Style. Chieng Sen is the name traditionally used to designate the art of the former northern kingdom of Lan Na (with its capital, Chieng Mai), which was set up in 1292. The images that appear to be the oldest and are of high plastic quality (Pl. 239) reflect an ideal that is entirely different from that of Sukhothai, and they are governed by entirely different iconographic principles. The Pāla-Sena influence appears to predominate (in particular, the frequency of the seated cross-legged *vajrāsana* attitude: Fig. C-b). This influence appears to diminish fairly rapidly as the quality of the images declines. In the second half of the fourteenth century, the fame enjoyed by the monks of Sukhothai led to the development of contacts, thus greatly promoting the influence of the Sukhothai style at Chieng Mai. This resulted to a certain extent in a renaissance of the Chieng Sen style, but above all in the transforming of its iconography by that of Sukhothai, producing a mixture of styles that combined the characteristics of the two schools in varying proportions. From the middle of the fifteenth century, which was marked by great artistic activity, almost up to the present time, this composite character persisted in works in the Chieng Sen style, which, moreover, varied considerably in quality. The choice of attitudes is more varied in Lan Na statuary than in the contemporary Sukhothai and Ayutthaya styles, which are faintly reminiscent of the trends of the Pagan school. This style has not left behind it so many monumental images as the Sukhothai style, and seems to have achieved excellence mainly in the art of bronze-working.

235. General view of Wat Kukut

From Lamphun, Thailand; Haripuñjaya school, 12th–13th century A.D.*; brick, laterite, terracotta, stucco; H. of the large* caitya *approximately 23 m.*

Built and remodelled by the last sovereigns of the Mon kingdom of Haripuñjaya (now Lamphun), which was absorbed at the end of the thirteenth century into the Thai kingdom of Lan Na (capital: Chieng Mai), these monuments were considered until recently as representing an architectural tradition inherited from Dvāravatī. This is not in fact the case; the multiplicity of images of the Buddha, all similar, is beyond all doubt a generalization of a Pāla principle. The originality of the Haripuñjaya school seems to lie in the choice of a standing attitude for all the images; the style appears to combine reminiscences of Dvāravatī art with certain influences of the Khmerizing Lopburi school.

236. Buddha Akṣobhya

From Sukhothai, Thailand; Sukhothai style, 14th century A.D.*; bronze; H. 92 cm.; private collection, Bangkok.*

The Sukhothai style is certainly the one that carried farthest the attempts to express the supramundane characteristics of the anatomy of the Buddha; it succeeded in elaborating an entirely original canon of beauty. The face seems reminiscent of Sri Lanka art of the period, but the attitude is in no way influenced by Sri Lanka, where the 'earth-witness' gesture is almost unknown.

237. Walking Buddha

From Sukhothai, Thailand; Sukhothai style, 14th century A.D.*; bronze; H. 220 cm.; Wat Benchamabopit, Bangkok.*

Even more than the preceding statue, this walking Buddha shows the style at its best. The stupendously huge image suggests great spirituality. The walking attitude, which is very rare in statues of the Buddha, may be regarded as a Sukhothai invention; and it is entirely consonant with the texts, which define walking as one of the four attitudes of the Buddha, evoking either the Descent from the Heaven of the Thirty-three Gods, the great miracle of Śrāvastī (see Pl. 107), or his ambulation in the third week following the Enlightenment.

238. Buddha marking the imprint of his foot

From Chieng Mai, Thailand; late Chieng Sen style, A.D. *1482; bronze; H. 47 cm.; National Museum, Bangkok.*

Somewhat mediocre as to line, this image, which has its date inscribed, shows the influence of the Sukhothai aesthetic, and gives us a new version—to our knowledge, unique—of the walking theme. The miracle takes place at Sāṅkāśya (see Pl. 234) at the time when the Buddha, having descended from the Heaven of the Thirty-three Gods, marks the imprint of his foot on the very spot where all the past Buddhas (here indicated by three footprints) set their foot after having gone to teach the doctrine to their mothers. The footprint of the historical Buddha is the smallest; we learn from the *Buddhavaṃsa* that the height and the duration of life of each being diminishes from one *kalpa* to another.

239. Buddha head

From Chieng Sen, Thailand; Chieng Sen style, 13th–14th century A.D.*; bronze; H. 38 cm.; National Museum, Bangkok.*

This head, of a thoroughly classical beauty, is evidence of an ideal that is very different from the one prevailing about the same time at Sukhothai. While Pāla influence is often very noticeable in the Chieng Sen style, here we have an entirely original tradition. Moreover, works of this quality are very rare, and those found in Chieng Sen are exceptional. The origin of this one is certain because of a special technical feature, the dove-tailed mortise joint, which is found only in works produced in Chieng Sen workshops.

240. Buddha head

From Suphanburi, Thailand; U Thong style, end of 13th–first half of 14th century A.D.*; bronze; H. 25 cm.; National Museum, U Thong.*

Combining reminiscences of the Dvāravatī school with a certain ideal of serene grandeur inherited from the Khmerizing Lopburi style, and apparently also showing an affinity with the Haripuñjaya school (in particular, in the treatment of the hair), this work is nevertheless entirely original, and probably one of the finest examples of the U Thong style in its early or 'A' period.

241. The great miracle at Śrāvastī

Wall painting from Wat Ko Kaew Suttharam, Phetburi, Thailand; Ayutthaya style, A.D. *1734; H. approximately 100 cm.; in situ.*

A series of stupas and temple roofs are decorated with events from the Buddha's life and cosmological patterns. The main scene here illustrates one of the Eight Great Events, namely, the miracle at Śrāvastī, when the Buddha flew into the air and emitted flames and streams of water from his body in order to convert heretics. Compare Pl. 107.

242. Bejewelled standing Buddha

From Ayutthaya, Thailand; Ayutthaya school, 18th century A.D.*; gilt bronze; H. 78 cm.; National Museum, Bangkok.*

Known as 'Song Krüang' ('decked with royal jewels'), these images are in the line of a long tradition and have retained great importance in Theravāda Buddhism. In the Ayutthaya style, the Buddha is generally portrayed standing, making the gesture of fearlessness (*abhaya*) with his right hand or with both hands. The robe is usually treated in a highly stylized manner, and the jewels are represented with a wealth of luxurious detail. Contrary to the conservative tendency of Buddhist art, the jewels follow the evolution of the crown jewels from reign to reign.

243. Defeat of the army of Māra

Wall painting from Wat Tusitaram, Thonburi, Thailand; continuation of the Ayuttaya style or beginning of the Bangkok style, end of 18th or beginning of 19th century A.D.*; in situ.*

Seated in the *samādhi* attitude, the Bodhisattva impassively watches the vain attacks of the army of Māra, represented with much picturesque detail. Rising up at the call of the Bodhisattva, the earth-goddess wrings from her hair the water that has accumulated on the occasion of the countless gifts made by the Buddha-to-be during his previous lives. Such is the flood that it submerges and disperses the army of Māra. This version, examples of which are to be found in images as early as the twelfth century, is peculiar to the peninsula, and appears to be taken from the *Paṭhamasambodhi*, the 'Life of the Buddha' in Pāli, well known in Thailand, Cambodia and Laos.

(a)

(b)

(c)

Fig. C (a). Sketch of a seated image in the Sukhothai style, Thailand.
Fig. C (b). Sketch of a seated image in the Chieng Sen style, Thailand.
Fig. C (c). Sketch of a seated image in the Chieng Sen style, Thailand (mixed styles).

The Ayutthaya Style. Characteristic of the kingdom founded in 1350 and overthrown in 1767, when the capital was taken by the Burmese, Ayutthaya art nevertheless survived, almost to the present time, in the styles of Thonburi (1767–81) and Bangkok (1782 to the present), which are directly descended from it.

The images executed in the region at the time of the rise of the kingdom belonged to the U Thong school (recalling the name of the prince who founded Ayutthaya), which combines Khmer-like traditions similar to those of the Lopburi school with traces of Dvāravatī art in works that sometimes achieve great serenity (Pl. 240). This early style A (Fig. C-d) was first modified by the adoption of iconographic features, such as the flame surmounting the cranial protuberance, which are reminiscent of the Sinhalese tradition (style B: Fig. C-e). At the beginning of the fifteenth century the influence of Sukhothai became predominant and radically modified the aesthetic of images, though without imparting its

(d)

(c)

(f)

Fig. C (d). Sketch of a seated image, the U Thong school, Thailand (style A).
Fig. C (e). Sketch of a seated image, the U Thong school, Thailand (style B).
Fig. C (f). Sketch of a seated image, the U Thong school, Thailand (style C).

spirituality to them and even sometimes giving them a certain insipid affectation (style C: Fig. C-f). It was the style C that engendered the Ayutthaya style proper, characterized by a search for technical perfection and a somewhat severe classicism that readily veers towards conventionalism, rather than by a genuine ideal of supramundane beauty. The Buddha is frequently portrayed standing, in a hieratic attitude, making the *abhaya* (absence of fear) gesture with one or both hands. Bejewelled images are numerous, increasingly heavily laden with jewelled ornaments as the centuries pass (Pl. 242). The style is nevertheless much concerned with diverse attitudes and gestures in order to represent all the incidents in the career of the Buddha as faithfully as possible; it is in the wall paintings and black and gold lacquers of the seventeenth and eighteenth centuries that its qualities appear to best effect. The wealth of inspiration, inventiveness, power of observation and distinguished draughtsmanship of the Ayutthaya style link it with the grand tradition of narrative imagery.

Cambodia

Pre-Angkorian art had not resulted in the elaboration of a single unique style for the image of the Buddha, and no such style appeared until the end of the tenth century. Deeply influenced by contemporary Hindu art, it followed its stylistic evolution very closely—frequently even showing the hair plaited rather than curling, and even introducing the convention of the completely nude torso (Pl. 245)—until the time when the short-lived triumph of the Mahāyāna at the end of the twelfth century brought the Buddhist aesthetic to the fore.

Angkorian Art. The newly created kingdom of Angkor (ninth–tenth centuries) had paid little attention to Buddhism; and in the second half of the tenth century a dignitary assumed the task of regenerating the fast-declining religion and restoring sanctuaries. An inscription at Wat Sithor states that 'having brought back from a foreign country a host of books. . .', he 'spread their study far and wide'. Unfortunately the foreign country cannot be identified from the text, but it does at least indicate the Mahāyāna and Vijñānavādin trends that prevailed for more than two centuries. While remaining profoundly Khmer, the images seem to suggest the influence of Mahāyāna schools originating in the south of India (Pl. 246). From then onwards the image of the Buddha sheltered by the *nāga* Mucilinda (Pls. 244, 245), which was unknown in pre-Angkorian art, acquired an importance that it retained until at least the thirteenth century, Cambodia long according it the supremacy that many other schools accorded to the Buddha Akṣobhya calling the earth to witness his victory over Māra. Up to about the middle of the twelfth century the art of minority Buddhism is represented solely by this type of image and a few scenes incorporated in a small number of decorative lintels. Yet apparently about the same time we have richer and more varied scenes (lintels, tympana of pediments, Pl. 251) inspired by the Theravāda, for example, at Prah Palilay, Angkor Thom.

The Bayon Style. This style (end of the twelfth–beginning of the thirteenth century) marks the triumph of the Mahāyāna, which was adopted as the royal religion, and that of Buddhist iconography and a new aesthetic (Pls. 247, 248). We shall not dwell on the magnitude of the architectural achievements of the time or the wealth of the Mahāyāna pantheon portrayed, but merely emphasize that apart from a highly original conception of the beauty of the Buddha due to its deep humanity, the style seems to owe much to Pimai art. It was probably from Pimai that the Bayon style took the tradition, inherited from Dvāravatī, of standing Buddhas, with or without jewels, shown with both hands making the 'explanation' or 'absence of fear' gesture, a tradition that was long preserved (Pl. 250). Bas-reliefs (Pl. 251), only too often defaced during a brief and exceptional period of Śaivite reaction, preserve—mainly in the region of Angkor—a mere fraction of the scenes that illustrated the life of the Buddha, sometimes intermingled with ornamental foliage (Pl. 252).

Post-Angkorian Art. As throughout the peninsula except for Vietnam and Malaya, post-

244. Buddha sheltered by the *nāga* Mucilinda

Monolithic caitya *from Kbal Sre Yay Yin, Phnom Srok, Cambodia; Angkorian art, last quarter of 10th century* A.D.*; sandstone; overall H. 230 cm.; Musée Guimet, Paris.*

The composition of this *caitya* seems to derive from various votive stupas in the Pāla tradition: Mahāyāna in inspiration, its high base is decorated with standing figures of Vajrapāṇi, Prajñāpāramitā (Goddess of Wisdom) and Avalokiteśvara, and the Buddha, seated in the *samādhi* attitude on two coils of the body of the *nāga* king, whose sevenfold hood opens out to a great height in front of an ornamented chevet that balances the compositions on each of the other sides. We have here one of the most ancient Khmer representations of a theme that was to acquire extraordinary favour in Angkorian art. Compare the Amitābha image from Nepal (Pl. 92).

245. Bejewelled Buddha sheltered by the *nāga* Mucilinda

From the region of Sisophon, Cambodia; Angkorian art, first half of 12th century A.D.*; sandstone; H. 87 cm.; National Museum, Phnom Penh.*

Indicative of the Khmer conception of this miracle, this image, with the acme of stylization, emphasizes the sovereign majesty and equanimity of the Buddha. While retaining some features of the serpent, the *nāga* has become a kind of throne for the Buddha, who is much more the universal monarch than the peerless religious teacher. The head-dress, with its conical crown, is that of divinities decked out like the kings of Angkor; the hair is plaited, not curled; and the torso appears to be completely naked, as if the convention of the transparent garment had been carried to the extreme. Nevertheless, the *samādhi* attitude and the closed eyelids clearly suggest the imperturbable meditation of the Buddha.

246. Standing four-armed Avalokiteśvara

From Tuol Chi Tep, Cambodia; Angkorian art, third quarter of 10th century A.D.*; sandstone; H. 115 cm.; Musée Guimet, Paris.*

This statue, unfortunately mutilated, is a typical example of the Banteay Srei style whose characteristics—aesthetics, dress, coiffure—are all illustrated here. It is one of the most representative works of the Buddhist renaissance that is indicated in the literature of the second half of the tenth century in Angkorian Cambodia. The stylistic influence of contemporary Hindu imagery, which was very strong during that period, is amply demonstrated in this statue.

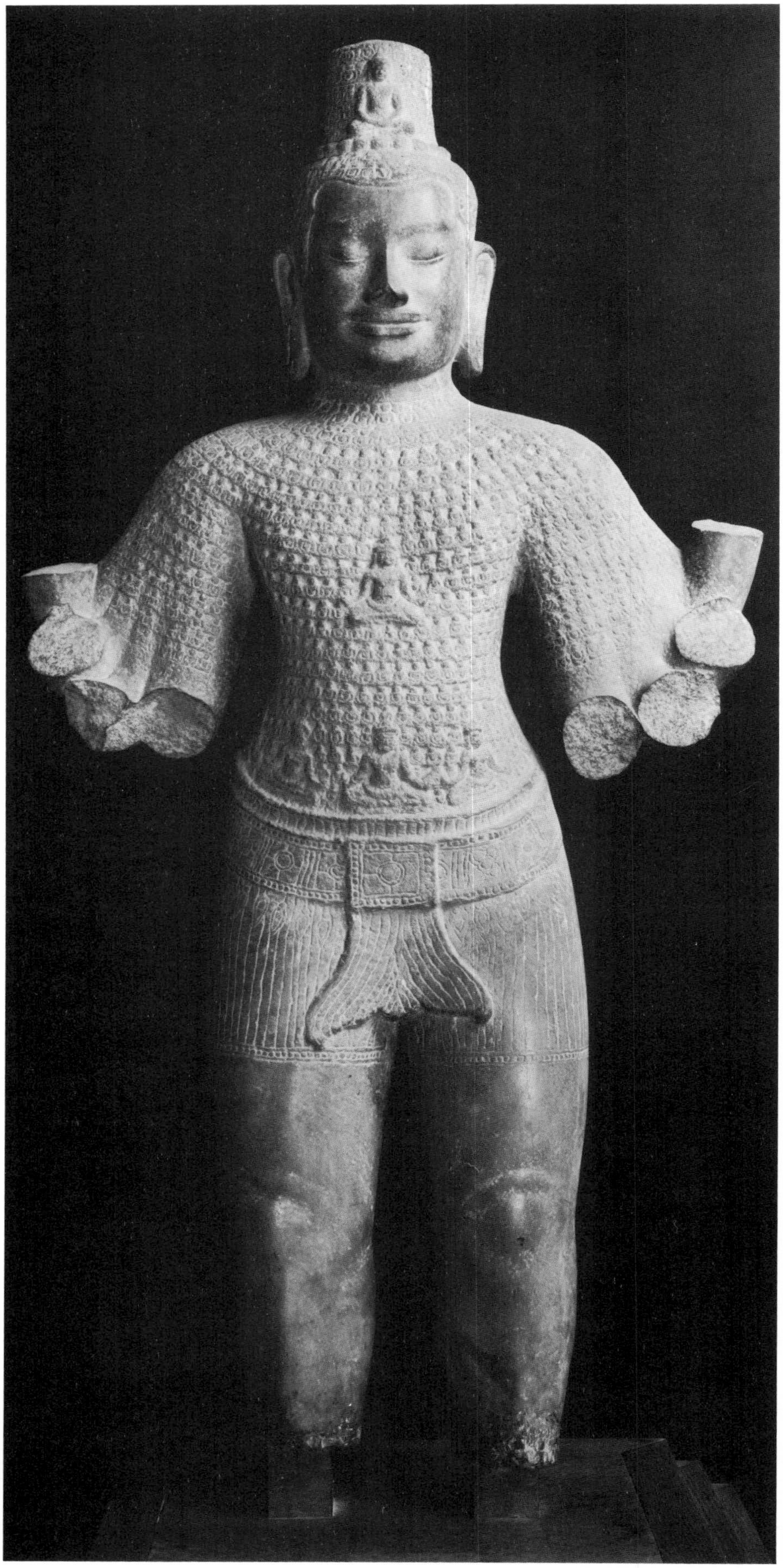

247. 'Radiant' eight-armed Avalokiteśvara

From Prah Thkol, Cambodia; Angkorian art, end of 12th–beginning of 13th century A.D.*; sandstone; H. 130 cm.; Musée Guimet, Paris.*

This image is characteristic of the Mahāyāna art of the reign of Jayavarman VII (1181–c.1218) and of the style of the Bayon. Its iconography is as interesting as its plastic form, which marks a break in its naturalism and humanity with previous Angkorian traditions. The body and the head radiate a multitude of small Buddhas seated in the *samādhi* position, together with some larger images of divinities; thus this type of image has been called 'radiant'. It would seem to illustrate a passage from the *Kāraṇḍa-vyūha-sūtra*, a text known to have existed in Cambodia as early as the second half of the tenth century, which emphasizes that each of the pores of the Bodhisattva's skin, being a true macrocosm, contains the whole universe.

248. Standing four-armed Avalokiteśvara

From the Gate of Death, Angkor Thom, Cambodia; Angkorian art, end of 12th–beginning of 13th century A.D.*; sandstone; H. 212 cm.; National Museum, Phnom Penh.*

The forearms of this monumental statue were assembled by means of sandstone supports. Of the same period and style as the preceding example, it provides even more decisive evidence of the desire for naturalism that emerged during the reign of Jayavarman VII. It represents another aspect of Avalokiteśvara, one of the most popular divinities in Cambodia and Champa, having as attributes a rosary, a book, a water vase and a lotus (here missing). Unlike the figure from Champa, this statue is clothed only in a tiny loin-cloth that in the absence of jewellery would seem to indicate an ascetic aspect of the Bodhisattva. It is, however, more likely that the figure had moveable clothes and jewels, which are referred to in inscriptions of that reign.

249. Buddha head

From Tep Pranam, Angkor Thom, Cambodia (Angkorian art); end of 12th–beginning of 13th century A.D.*; sandstone; H. 41 cm.; National Museum, Phnom Penh.*

Found among the objects deposited at the foundation of a colossal sixteenth-century statue, this head belongs to what is known as the Bayon style (reign of Jayavarman VII), and it shows tendencies very different from those prevailing half a century earlier (Pl. 245). An impassive ideal of superhuman beauty is replaced by a highly sensitive search for human truth. The Buddha, like the Mahāyāna or Brahmanical divinities of the time, ceases to be supernatural. Overflowing with compassion, he reverts to the human state and appears in the form of a Khmer.

250. Bejewelled standing Buddha

Exact provenance unknown; Angkorian art or Lopburi school, end of 12th–first half of 13th century A.D.*; bronze; H. 50 cm.; private collection, Bangkok.*

The images of the Buddha standing and making the gesture of explanation with both hands continue a type of which there are many examples in Dvāravatī art (Pl. 106). The ornaments are even richer than in the twelfth century (Pl. 245) and are becoming excessive; the girdle and the central section of the robe are ornamented, presaging the trend that has continued up to the present day (Pl. 242).

251. Seated Buddha surrounded by devotees

Fragment of a pediment from Prah Palilay, Angkor Thom, Cambodia; Angkorian art, 12th century A.D.*; sandstone; H. 133 cm.; National Museum, Phnom Penh.*

It is difficult to say what scene is illustrated on this very incomplete pediment. However, it may be that it depicts the praise offered to the Buddha after his victory over Māra (cf. *Lalitavistara*: 23), since he is seated under the bodhi tree in the attitude of calling the earth to witness (an attitude exceptional in Angkorian art) and surrounded by devotees, among whom can be recognized a *nāga* king (with a diadem decorated with five serpents' heads), a sovereign (with a triple crown), celestial beings of whom only the bust is shown, and, probably, *devas* in the lower part of the pediment.

252. The assault by the army of Māra

Pediment from D terrace, Angkor Thom, Cambodia; Angkorian art, 13th century A.D.*; sandstone; L. 194 cm.; National Museum, Phnom Penh.*

Set out symmetrically at levels one above the other, the scene represented on this pediment is a clash between two armies rather than an assault directed against the Bodhisattva. In fact, this opposition is possibly not fortuitous, and may illustrate one version of the assault comparable to that contained in the *Lalitavistara*, where a band led by the 'demon' Sārtavūha stands to the right of the Bodhisattva, recognizing his power, which is 'rooted in intelligence', and opposes the army of the Evil One (Māra) standing on his left. It should be noted that the Bodhisattva does not call the earth to witness, but makes the gesture of fearlessness and that the gods, who are supposed to have fled at the army's approach, here remain close to the Blessed One.

253. Bejewelled standing Buddha

From Angkor Wat, Cambodia; post-Angkorian art, c. 17th century A.D.*; wood; H. 98 cm.; National Museum, Phnom Penh.*

As in Burma, Thailand (Pl. 242) and Laos, bejewelled images of the Buddha are much favoured in Cambodia, where they have a long tradition behind them (Pl. 245). During the post-Angkorian period, various schools of sculpture can be distinguished, characterized by a certain fidelity to the Angkorian models. Some common features should be noted: for instance, the vast majority of these images are carved in wood. While the gestures and attitudes are those prevailing in Thailand today, the aesthetic is quite different, as are the ornaments.

254. Buddha Akṣobhya

From Wat Wixun, Luang Prabang, Laos; c. 14th century A.D.*; bronze; overall H. 32.5 cm.; collection of H.M. the King of Laos, Luang Prabang.*

Directly related to the art of Lan Na, this beautiful image, unfortunately corroded, of the Buddha calling the earth to witness shows the characteristics of the Chieng Sen style, although the hair is shown in tiny curls and the facial features are slightly different. It was probably taken to Luang Prabang before 1514, the date of the founding of That Mak Mo, where it was discovered among the 140 miscellaneous items forming the sacred treasure. Its smooth headgear of gold is adorned with cabochons of precious stones. Several of the images at That Mak Mo have the same coiffure, examples of which are also seen at Lan Na in finely wrought gold (Wat Chedi Luang, Chieng Mai).

255. Standing Buddha in *abhaya-mudrā*

Exact provenance unknown; c. 17th century A.D.*; bronze; overall H. 185 cm.; Wat Phra Keo Collection, Vientiane.*

This figure, which is shown with both hands making the gesture of fearlessness, illustrates a pose often found in Thai art. It is nevertheless distinguished by the extremely stylized treatment of face and ears, the size of the ornament surmounting the *uṣṇīṣa*, certain details of the robe and the form of the pedestal. The fairly naturalistic treatment of the hands, the fingers of which are still of unequal length, makes one inclined to attribute this statue to the seventeenth rather than the eighteenth century, in view of the increasingly marked tendency to make the fingers of Buddha images of equal length.

Angkorian art is Theravādin in inspiration. Despite the political role of the kingdom of Ayutthaya, which exerted no appreciable influence on art until the end of the sixteenth century, Cambodia almost always preserved its essential originality. Generally, this was expressed in the numerous wooden statues that tended to replace stone images during this period. An abundance of painting, whether mural or in manuscripts, reflects the vitality of the tradition, but is represented only by late works.

Laos

The anointing of Fa Ngum in 1353 confirmed the foundation of the kingdom of Lan Chang (now Laos), which enjoyed spiritual and material aid from the court at Angkor. Receiving Khmer monks and artists, the kingdom should in theory have developed a type of art very close to that of Cambodia, whose artistic influence had moreover already been demonstrated much earlier in the regions to the south. The Pra Bang, the protective image at Luang Prabang, is a standing statue in the tradition of the Bayon style or the Lopburi school, but if the date ascribed to the colossal bronze statue (in ruins) at Wat Manoram (1372) is correct, it must be admitted that the influence of the Sukhothai style had become predominant even before the end of the reign of Fa Ngum. Nevertheless, the influence of the Lan Na school lasted longer than any other in Laos, and this can be explained simply by historical contacts. While most works are marked by the late 'mixed' iconography of the Chieng Sen style, there are also some at Luang Prabang (the Royal Collection) that may rank among the best in this particular style (Pl. 254). Burmese influence, notwithstanding several periods of tutelage, seems to appear solely in architecture, and then only sporadically. The influence of Ayutthaya and, later, Bangkok is noticeable in images whose dominant features are their hieratic attitude and extremely stylized treatment (Pl. 255). Despite these persistent trends, the marked feeling for decoration and the sensibility of Laotian artists occasionally achieved works of an undeniable originality.

Champa

With the transitory triumph of Mahāyāna Buddhism, the end of the ninth century saw the flowering of the most original and most unusual style of the art of Champa. In the tenth century the importance of Buddhism decreased, and art returned to a more classical ideal. A single image, a standing bronze statue at Dai-huu that has quite unexpected characteristics, may possibly be ascribed to this period. Depicted in an attitude recalling the Dvāravatī tradition, its clothing seems to combine late Gandhāran reminiscences with features apparently borrowed from Nālandā art. While, judging from inscriptions, the Mahāyāna regained genuine importance during the eleventh century, the few images of the Buddha known to us, which are defaced, tell us little about the evolution of an art that, at Thu-thien, seems to have followed a tradition somewhat reminiscent of Sri Lanka. From the end of the twelfth century to 1220, the Khmer occupation of Champa led simply to a transplantation of works in the Khmer Bayon style (Buddha in royal attire on the *nāga*, found at the Silver Towers). In the thirteenth century, when independence was regained, inscriptions still recall a much more tantric aspect of the Mahāyāna than in Cambodia,

256. Buddha head

From Rawapulu, Surabaja, Java; Majapahit art, c. 14th century A.D.*; stone; H. 33 cm.; Djakarta Museum.*

Unlike the divinities in the syncretistic Vajrayāna pantheon, few images of the Buddha can be ascribed to the last period of Buddhist activity in Indonesia. This head differs appreciably from the earlier tradition (Pl. 119). While its somewhat impassive dignity is reminiscent of the famous Prajñāpāramitā in the Leiden Museum, it seems related by its iconography to some of the works of the peninsula (development of the *uṣṇīṣa* and the bud-like treatment of the *siraspota*). On the other hand, the elongated halo without any ornamentation is probably an Indonesian feature because the tendency there was to treat images in high relief against a vertical surface rather than genuinely in the round.

suggesting some relationship with the Buddhism practised at that time in Java. No image can be related to the few texts where in 1265 there occurs what is probably the last mention of the Buddha. Yet a statue, of which unfortunately little is known as yet, may perhaps confirm that Buddhism still existed in Champa towards the end of the fourteenth or beginning of the fifteenth century. After 1471, the date of the capture of the capital, Vijaya, by Vietnam, the Buddhist school of Champa finally disappeared. After its conquest of the greater part of Champa, Vietnam remained faithful to the iconography of the Chinese tradition, which had been propagated there together with the doctrine from the third to the sixth centuries.

Indonesia

It appears that before the end of the first quarter of the ninth century the power of the Buddhist Śailendras declined in Java. Barely a quarter of a century later they took refuge in Sumatra (Śrīvijaya), while the Śaivite princes from Mataram regained power in Central Java. The Mahāyāna was ousted and the great foundations were henceforth Hindu (Lara Janggrang). In 929, with the final transfer of the capital to the east of Java, began what is known as the eastern Javanese period. We have scarcely any archaeological traces of this period. On the other hand, a treatise on the Vajrayāna composed in the first half of the tenth century, the *Sang Lyang Kamahāyānikan*, has fortunately come down to us, and is the best source for a study of Buddhist architecture and iconography in Java. It is probably to the tenth century that we should ascribe the remarkable group of some ninety bronze statuettes discovered near Ngandjuk (now in Djakarta Museum); it constituted a *Vajradhātu-maṇḍala*, in which four Jinas and a complete Buddha pantheon are grouped around the Supreme Buddha, shown with four faces and crowned.

Eastern Java (13th–15th Centuries): The Kingdoms of Singhasari and Majapahit. While the number of works of art, frequently Buddhist in inspiration, again increases, there are very few images of the Buddha (Pl. 256). The Buddhism practised at the end of the thirteenth century by King Kṛtanagara (1268–92), the Kālacakra, was essentially tantric. From a monist viewpoint based on a syncretism between Buddhism and Śaivism, the king is the incarnation of a Śiva-Buddha entity. Images such as the Singhasari Cakra-cakra (in Leiden Museum) or the colossal Bhairava (in Djakarta Museum) from Sungai Langsat, Sumatra, clearly reveal the unusual features of iconography during this period. Though Buddhist literary activity continued until the fourteenth century, statuary chiefly depicts deified kings; and images such as that a Amoghāpaśa, at Caṇḍi Jago (c. 1280), reproduced in numerous copies, show only minute Jinas among the companions of the magnified Bodhisattva.

The situation is no different in Sumatra, where the Śailendras had withdrawn in the ninth century, and the central part of the island passed under Javanese domination in 1347. The large complexes of monuments at Muara Takus and Padang Lawas (c. thirteenth–fourteenth century), original in their conception, have yielded no more images of the Buddha than have the monuments in Java, where in any case all Buddhist activity seems to have ceased long before the final disappearance of the Majapahit kingdom in 1528.

3. KASHMIR AND NEPAL; TIBET AND MONGOLIA

These four countries need to be considered together, since it was mainly through Kashmir and Nepal that Buddhist religion and art reached Tibet, and it was subsequently by the efforts of Tibetan missionary lamas that the whole tradition was later spread to Mongolia. Again, it is mainly from Tibetan historical accounts that we learn something of the renowned Buddhist teachers and craftsmen from Kashmir and Nepal who were active in Tibet from at least the eighth century onwards, and maybe even a century earlier, when the Tibetans are recorded as first making contact with their Buddhist neighbours.

Kashmir

The reign of Lalitāditya-Muktāpīḍa (c. 725–56) to which we have referred in the last chapter as the period of Kashmir's greatest power and prosperity, when religious treasures of all kinds including images for Buddhist as well as Hindu cults were seized from abroad and when craftsmen were freely imported from distant lands, resulted in the creation of an extraordinarily rich heritage. However, even while it was being built up, it was already being pillaged by invading Tibetans, who were then at the height of their power in Central Asia. They later became fervent converts exclusively to the Buddhist, not to the Hindu, traditions that they found in Kashmir, and in the troubled centuries that followed upon the break-up of Lalitāditya's short-lived empire, Kashmiri scholars and craftsmen found a ready welcome as well-paid scholars and craftsmen in Tibet. In Kashmir itself, centuries of internal strife and foreign invasion resulted in the total dissipation and destruction of what must have been an extraordinary civilization.[4] In 1337 the country was finally taken over by the Moslems, and forcible conversion soon put an end to whatever survived of Buddhist and Hindu religion. Buddhist and Hindu tradition survived, interestingly enough, in Moslem architecture, but that does not concern us here. As to the Buddha image, the result was deliberate and almost total destruction. Thus in a land and a period of which much might be written in a book such as this, there is very little indeed to describe.

All that remains, in fact, apart from the ruins and broken pieces described in the last chapter, are the very few stone images, mainly preserved in the Srinagar Museum, and a number of interesting bronze images, unearthed at various times and now in the possession of various museums and private collectors. A very useful article by Douglas Barrett resumes the little that may be known of these items, and thus here we need only refer to their special features.[5] They are so few that no general observations may be safely made about the style of the Buddha image in Kashmir from the eighth to the fourteenth century except for the most general of all observations, namely, that Kashmir clearly belonged to the Indian sphere of cultural influence, including such traces of Gandhāran motifs as had already been absorbed into Indian iconic traditions.

Two traditions existed side by side in the portrayal of the religious robes. These might

[4]See H. Goetz, 'The medieval sculpture of Kashmir', *Marg* 8, 2 (Bombay, March 1955), p. 65 ff., reprinted in *Studies in the History and Art of Kashmir and the Indian Himalaya* (Wiesbaden, 1969), pp. 68–76.

[5]D. Barrett, 'Bronzes from North-West India and Western Pakistan', *Lalit Kalā*, no. 11 (April 1962), pp. 35–44.

either cling closely to the body in the manner typical of the Mathurā images and of most Gupta images, thus clearly a Ganges-Jumna tradition, or they might be arranged in heavy folds, often covering both shoulders in the manner typical of the earlier Buddha images of Gandhāra (Pl. 41). Similarly, the lion-supported throne represents a clear Indian tradition so far as Kashmir is concerned, whatever its earlier origin may have been, while the throne of lotus flowers, despite its later popularity in India, is more likely to have been of Gandhāran provenance. Even so, combined with the lion motif on the throne there is sometimes a small Atlas figure, clearly of Greco-Roman origin but later taken over by the Tibetans from Kashmir as a possible Buddha 'vehicle'. Added to the lion, the elephant, the horse, the peacock and the *garuḍa*, it provided a sixth item, useful when a sixth Supreme Buddha, who comprehends the Supreme Pentad, was conceived. The fact that the use of such symbols is not yet stereotyped on these surviving Kashmiri images, suggests a certain freedom of style, readily associated with the disturbed social conditions of Kashmir.

A well-preserved image, probably of the central Buddha Vairocana, the Resplendent One, now reposes in the Los Angeles County Museum of Art (Pl. 257). The robe is neither very full in the Gandhāran manner, nor does it cling to the body; it is reproduced, if without special elegance, certainly with realism, and the right shoulder is left bare in the traditional Indian manner. As hand-gestures became stereotyped for the various members of the Supreme Buddha Pentad, the preaching gesture became typical of Vairocana, and since the traditions surrounding this particular Buddha manifestation were already well established in Central Asian Buddhism, we need have little hesitation in so naming this Buddha image from Kashmir. A similar image, but with close-fitting robe, exists in the British Museum collection (Pl. 258), and many examples, certainly of Kashmiri inspiration, if not of actual workmanship, are found in western Tibet from the tenth century onwards. Another interesting type is that with the gift-giving (*varada*) gesture, namely, with the right hand, palm open outwards, resting by the right knee of the cross-legged figure. This is but an iconographic variation of the typical earth-touching (*bhūmisparśa*) gesture, where the fingers of the right hand touch the ground and the palm is always turned inwards. A fine example of such a gift-giving Buddha now belongs to the British Museum (Pl. 259). It is further distinguished by an unusual five-pointed flame-like protuberance on the head, a rather special development of the *uṣṇīṣa*, of which the South Indian form has been noted (see p. 127). This again suggests creative initiative on the part of Kashmiri craftsmen. It may be compared with the more solid conventional image, representing the same type of Buddha, which now belongs to the Los Angeles County Museum of Art (Pl. 260). The gesture of gift-giving came to be associated with Ratnasambhava (Jewel-Born), Buddha of the south, but this manifestation, devised to complete the Pentad, became seldom if ever the centre of liturgical cycles like Vairocana, Amitābha, Akṣobhya and Amoghasiddhi. In these Kashmiri images the gesture is probably to be interpreted as simply a typical Buddha gesture without any special differentiation. Judging from the available images, the gesture seems to have been a popular one in the north-west. It is also typical of some Bodhisattva images preserved in the British Museum (Pl. 261).[6]

[6] *Ibid.*, figs. 13 and 14.

257. Buddha Vairocana

From Kashmir; 8th century A.D.*; bronze with silver inlay; H. 40.6 cm.; Los Angeles County Museum of Art.*

The preaching gesture (*dharmacakra-pravartana-mudrā*) allows us to identify this image as Vairocana (see p. 135), who by the eighth century was well established in the north-west of the Indian subcontinent and thence throughout Central Asia and in China as the supreme Buddha manifestation. The style is already quite distinctive. Although the robe is arranged rather as on Gupta images of the period, it hangs with a fullness that recalls the heavier Gandhāran type of garment. The earlier 'snail-shell' curls on the head have become simply neat little blobs on the images, and this will very soon be produced in western Tibet. The throne is elaborate, with pillars, lions, winged dragons and a central 'Atlas' figure.

258. Buddha Vairocana

From Kashmir; 8th century A.D.*; bronze; H. 19.8 cm.; British Museum, London.*

259. Seated Buddha

From Kashmir; 9th century A.D.; bronze; H. 23.1 cm.; British Museum, London.

This unusual image has rather extravagant hand-gestures, a five-pronged flame springing from the *uṣṇīṣa*, and a very elaborate throne with the Wheel of the Doctrine and two small deer at its foot. Images such as this suggest an extraordinary freedom of creation in Kashmiri imagery.

260. Seated Buddha

From Kashmir; 8th–9th century A.D.; yellow alloy of bronze with silver inlay; H. 10 cm.; Los Angeles County Museum of Art.

Perhaps rather solid and clumsy in appearance, this image serves to illustrate the seeming variety of styles current in Kashmir. One may note an unconventional combination of gestures: that of generosity (*varada*) with the right hand, and that of explanation (*vitarka*) with the left. The robe is of the heavy Gandhāran type. The throne consists of a double lotus flower. Possibly intended as Śākyamuni, this image may have had a specific local name, which we now cannot surmise.

261. Bodhisattva Avalokiteśvara

From Kashmir; 10th–11th century A.D.*; bronze; H. 23.7 cm.; British Museum, London.*

This is a six-armed manifestation of Avalokiteśvara, identifiable by the small image of Amitābha set into his head-dress, as well as by the large lotus flower that he holds and the antelope skin draped over his shoulders. Other hands hold a rosary and a bell, while the lower right hand makes the gesture of generosity (*varada*). The throne seems a curious arrangement consisting of a lotus flower set upon a bench-like structure with four deer as a decorative motif. The deer are usually associated with the Wheel of the Doctrine (see Pls. 217, 259), but here the craftsman has exercised the freedom that seems typical of these works from Kashmir. The arrangement of the hair and of the lower garment suggest the princely style of the period.

262. Śākyamuni flanked by two Bodhisattvas

Probably from Kashmir; c. 7th–8th century A.D.*; wood; Tsaparang, Tibet.*

This remarkably well-preserved image of Śākyamuni, flanked by the Bodhisattvas Avalokiteśvara and Vajrapāṇi, was noted by Professor Giuseppe Tucci at Tsaparang (western Tibet). It is probably of Kashmiri provenance and could be seventh to eighth century. The Gupta inscription below the images is the regular formula: 'The Tathāgata has told the cause of the elements', etc. (see p. 174). (Reproduced from G. Tucci, *Indo-Tibetica* [Rome, 1932–41], vol. 3, part 2, pl. 30; text reference, pp. 89–90.)

After the fourteenth century not only the Buddhist tradition itself, but also the actual memory of it was lost in Kashmir, and thus we have to rely upon Tibetan literary sources for the little that is known of the earlier centuries. Certainly many scholars and craftsmen from Kashmir continued to work in Tibet. We might mention Jñānaśrībhadra, a prolific writer and translator of the eleventh century, and certainly Śākyaśrībhadra (1127–1225), known popularly in Tibet as the Great Kashmir Scholar. He travelled all around Tibet from 1204 to 1213, visiting all the holy places and personally founding four new monasteries, all of which required internal decoration and frescoes, as well as images to place in the shrines. Such was the fame of this great Kashmiri that nearly all the leading religious men of Tibet of the time, whatever their particular school or sect, claimed the honour of having been his pupil. Although the life of such a man, told from the Tibetan point of view, tells us little directly about Buddhism in Kashmir, we have sure indications of the high scholarly and artistic standards that must still have obtained in Kashmiri monasteries (Pl. 262). Much of their artistic workmanship survives in Ladakh and in the other ancient monasteries of western Tibet, which we will be considering below.

Nepal

Although Buddhist traditions, in close association with Hindu ones it is true, have survived in Nepal more or less up to present times, we still depend to a large extent upon Tibetan interest in Nepal and upon Nepalese craftsmanship as practised in Tibet itself to appreciate the full range of Nepalese endeavour. From the eighth century until the thirteenth, Nepal served as a half-way house between the lower Ganges Valley and central Tibet. After the Gupta traditions mentioned in the previous chapter, the Pāla and Sena traditions of north-eastern India penetrated Nepal, and then crossed the Himalayas, where the Buddhist were avidly collecting all they could of Indian Buddhist civilization. When Islam finally put an end to the Indian Buddhist establishments, Nepal still continued to provide Tibet with works of art and with the services of her craftsmen, for the potential Buddhist market, extending from the thirteenth century into Mongolia and Mongol-ruled China, far exceeded the limitations of the small Kathmandu Valley, which was still the only Nepal of those days. The inhabitants refer to themselves as Newār, merely a phonetic variant of Nepāl from a linguistic point of view, but since the conquest of the valley by the Gorkhas in 1768–69, the name Newār has come to distinguish them from all the other different ethnic groups that go to make up the people of modern Nepal. It is with the Newārs, the original inhabitants, and with them only that the Tibetans have continued to maintain cultural and social relations. The Nepalese community in Lhasa was a Newār community, and it is with Newārs and not with other Nepalese that Tibetans not uncommonly intermarry. Thus the Buddhist tradition of Nepal, great as has been its influence, has been the creation of what is now an ethnic minority in a very much larger country.

Apart from the early images in Gupta style to which reference has been made in the previous chapter, we may note one or two later stone images of impressive grace and elegance. As the Buddha image itself tended to be stereotyped, one must look for the best examples amongst Bodhisattvas and even goddesses, where the tradition allows rather

263. Bodhisattva Avalokiteśvara with two attendant goddesses

In a wayside shrine near the Yampi-bāhā, Pātan, Nepal; stone.

There is no satisfactory way of dating this image but it might well derive from the twelfth century or thereabouts. The legs are short and the arms appear elongated by comparison. Note the very beautiful mandorla, which with its elaborate patterns has progressed considerably from those seen on Pls. 64 and 215.

264. Śākyamuni on a lotus throne, supported by gods

From Nepal; c. 10th century A.D.*; schist; H. 29.2 cm.; British Museum, London.*

Śākyamuni is here flanked by two famous disciples, Śāriputra and Maudgalyāyana.

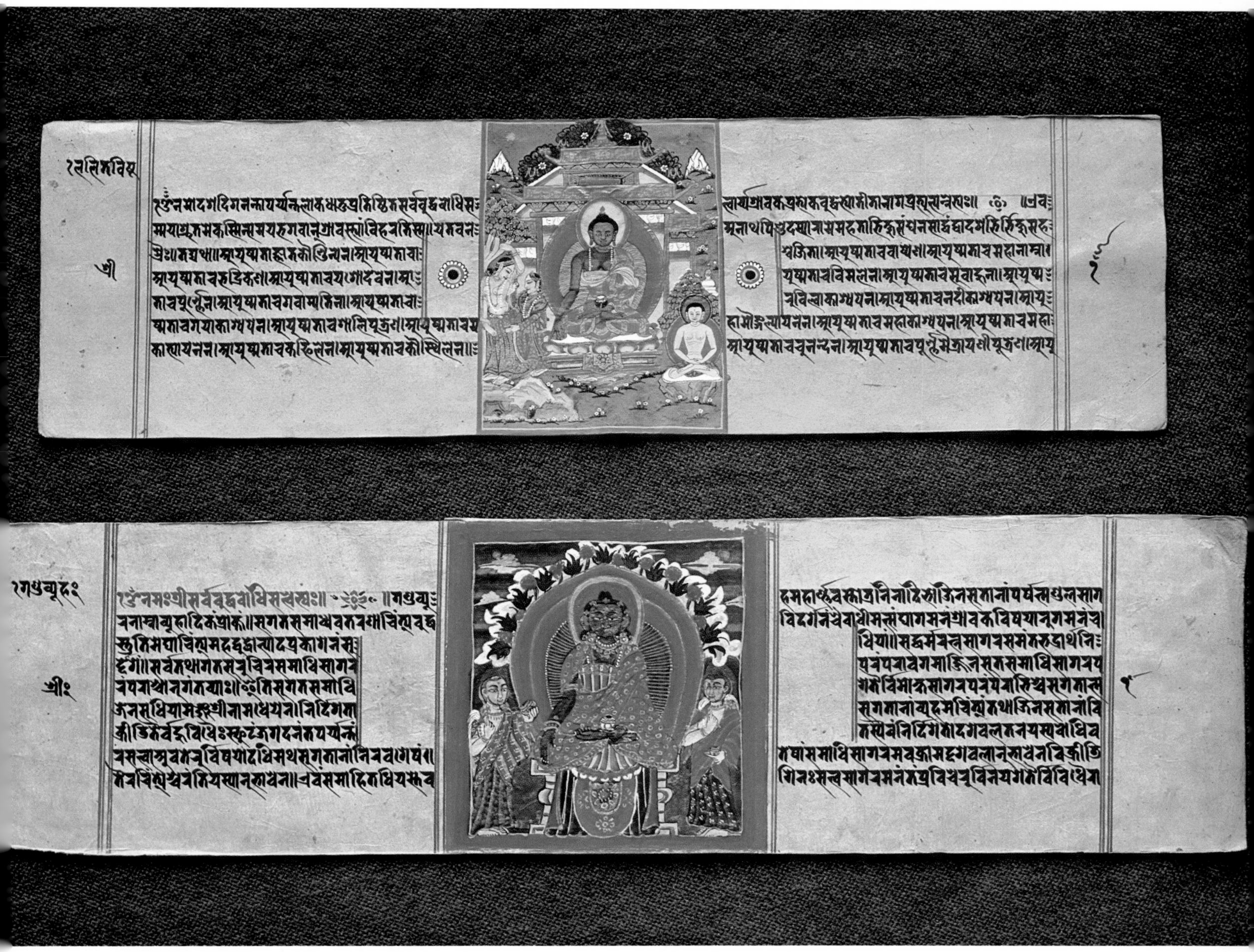

265. Manuscript illustrations

Manuscripts; c. 19th century A.D.*; National Art Gallery, Bhadgaon, Nepal.*

These illuminations are from pages of different manuscripts, the *Lalitavistara* and the *Gaṇḍavyūha*; both were popular works, continually copied by scribes as late as the nineteenth century, the probable date of these mansucripts. They are both of Śākyamuni with a begging bowl, but the gesture of touching the earth (*bhūmisparśa-mudrā*) and the blue colouring imply local identification as Akṣobhya. Note the birth scene and that of meditation under the bodhi tree arranged as subsidiary scenes in the upper miniature. An effort has been made to produce Indian styles of dress for the Bodhisattva's mother. The lower painting is interesting for it illustrates very well the way in which such Buddha images are dressed and adorned with jewelled ornaments in the shrines of Nepalese monasteries (*bāhā*) to this day. The two worshippers are males, dressed in traditional Newār costume.

266. Buddha Ratnasambhava

Painted scroll; probably 13th–14th century A.D.*; Los Angeles County Museum of Art.*

This early scroll (Sanskrit: *paṭa*; Tibetan: *thang-ka*) could be either Newār or Tibetan in origin, but in any case Indian inspiration is clear (see p. 343). It represents the Buddha of the southern quarter, Ratnasambhava (Jewel-Born) with attendant Bodhisattvas. Originally reproduced by Professor Giuseppe Tucci in his *Tibetan Painted Scrolls* (Pl. E), it passed into the Heeramaneck Collection and is at present in the Los Angeles County Museum of Art.

more freedom of representation. Although goddesses in general lie outside the scene of this book, we may fairly include an image in deep relief of his birth scene, where his divinized mother, Māyā, stands grasping the branch of a tree in a manner not unlike that of the *yakṣinī*, or tree-nymphs, who adorned the railings and archways of the early Buddhist stupas of central India. The theme is an ancient Indian one, but long since adapted in Buddhist mythology as representing the manner of the birth of a potential Buddha (namely, from the side of his mother while she stands upright supporting herself against a tree), it now finally reaches Nepal in a carefully balanced but slightly florid form, suggesting the inspiration of Pāla craftsmen (Pl. 131). Among several Bodhisattva images of this period we may note a small wayside shrine containing a standing Avalokiteśvara with two attendant deities at his feet (Pl. 263). The graceful stance of the main figure and the delicate tracery of the background which frames the image represent the best of Pāla tradition in Nepalese form.

Stone-carving was clearly an imported craft, and with the disappearance of the Buddhist tradition in India, the Newārs concentrated upon wood-carving, metal-work and painting, which seem to have been much more to the local taste. Pāla and Sena bronze images certainly provided the models, just as styles of wood-carving and painting were strongly affected by Indian influences, but these were the crafts that the Newārs took up and developed at home and in Tibet throughout succeeding centuries, as though they themselves were the prime instigators. Apart from manuscript illustrations, of which surviving examples date from about the tenth century, very little Newār Buddhist painting has survived that has not been absorbed into the very much larger and more active Tibetan tradition of religious painting (Pl. 265). We may mention an early painted scroll (Sanskrit: *paṭa*; Tibetan: *thang-ka*), that is usually associated with Nepal (Pl. 266).[7] It serves, however, to illustrate the sameness of styles prevalent amongst Buddhist artists in northern India from the tenth century onwards, which passed into Tibet both via Kashmir and Nepal.[8] With the Gorkha take-over of the valley in 1768–69 and the consequent loss of patronage of leading Newārs, Newār painters, relying on a Tibetan market, produced works in the related Tibetan style, itself once of Newār origin, and all distinction between Newār and Tibetan styles was finally lost. In such cases they can be recognized as Newār only by an inscription if present.

In metal-casting and wood-carving the Newārs have remained complete masters of their craft, and the greater freedom they are permitted by tradition, the greater is the scope for the exercise of their skill. The many temples and stupas that still adorn the valley are enriched with inset images of all kinds, directional Buddhas, attendant Bodhisattvas and goddesses, and such is the richness and variety that we here can only draw attention to a few examples (Pls. 92, 93, 267). Larger images occupy the main shrines, and as these are still sacred places and the object of daily worship, inquisitive access to them is unwelcome. Happily accessible to all who approach with respect is a magnificent copper gilt image of

[7]See *The Arts of India and Nepal: The Nasli and Alice Heeramaneck Collection* (Museum of Fine Arts, Boston, Massachusetts, 1966), pl. 122. One may note also their pl. 121, another early *thang-ka* of similar style. See also below our Pl. 280 (from Ladakh) on p. 355.

[8]See D. L. Snellgrove and T. Skorupski, *The Cultural Heritage of Ladakh* (Warminster, England, 1977), pp. 16–17.

267. Bodhisattva Mañjuśrī surrounded by attendant divinities
From the Cā-bāhī, Kathmandu, Nepal (see Pl. 327); 17th century A.D.*; stone; in situ.*

Avalokiteśvara that is kept in an upper shrine room of the Kwābhū-bāhā (Hiraṇyavarṇa-mahāvihāra) in Pātan. The impression given of meditative detachment, combined with elegance and delicacy, is quite overwhelming (Pl. 268). In the British Museum is a standing image of Vajrapāṇi, who is often paired with Avalokiteśvara and who is here conceived in much the same style. They are presumably of more or less the same period, fourteenth to fifteenth centuries, and represent Newār craftsmanship when, with the disappearance of Indian models, it had come entirely into its own (Pl. 269). As observed above, actual Buddha images tend to be conventional and perhaps sometimes too solid or even too ornate in appearance. Contrasting examples of a heavy robed figure and one whose robe is so light as to be transparent, revealing an over-solid body beneath, may be seen in E. and R. L. Waldschmidt, *Nepal*, Plates 37 and 38. A cult of the former Buddha Dīpaṅkara persists in Nepal, and of him there are many beautiful effigies, some complete statues but others put together for the occasion using masks and hands fitted on a frame and then dressed (Pl. 275).

Good wooden carvings are far more rare simply because of their greater fragility (Pls. 272, 273). Formerly the decorative piece (*toraṇa*) set over doorway entrances was often of wood, but these have been replaced increasingly with duplicates in metal. The central figure on these is often Akṣobhya, the most popular of members of the Great Buddha Pentad in Nepal, or it may be a comprehensive ten-armed Buddha figure, known locally as Nāmasaṅgīti, literally, 'The Recitation of the (Buddha-)Names', thus comprising in one image all the Five Buddhas (Pl. 274).

268. Bodhisattva Avalokiteśvara, reposing in an upper shrine room of the Kwābhū-bāhā, Pātan, Nepal.
C. 14th century A.D.*; bronze; H. 91.4 cm.*

269. Bodhisattva Vajrapāṇi
From Nepal; c. 15th century A.D.*; gilt copper; H. 44.5 cm.; British Museum, London.*

270. The Future Buddha, Maitreya

From Nepal; c. 10th century A.D.*; gilt copper; H. 26.6 cm.; British Museum, London.*

Seaten in the 'European' posture (*bhadrāsana*), Maitreya makes the hand-gesture of explanation (*vitarka-mudrā*). Already in the Gandhāran period (see Pl. 139), Maitreya, who is properly a Bodhisattva, appears by anticipation, as it were, as a Buddha. This is a very beautiful image indeed, and one may note especially the transparent delicacy of the robe.

271. A Bodhisattva, perhaps Samantabhadra

From Nepal; 15th–16th century A.D.*; gilt copper; H. 38.1 cm.; British Museum, London.*

The ear of corn suggests an identification as the Bodhisattva Samantabhadra as this is listed in some texts as his implement. He stands in a *tribhaṅga* posture, making elegant hand-gestures, which appear to be a combination of that of explanation (*vitarka-*) and that of generosity (*varada-mudrā*).

272. Part of a *toraṇa*

Wood-carving; from Nepal; perhaps 16th century A.D.*; Nepal Museum, Kathmandu.*

This is part of a *toraṇa* (a decorative piece over a doorway), illustrating Śākyamuni subjected to the rowdy assault of Māra, the Evil One, and his host. Probably it was once over the doorway of a Nepalese monastery courtyard.

273. Stele of Dīpaṅkara

Wood-carving; from Nepal; end of 17th century A.D.*; National Art Gallery, Bhadgaon.*

On this stele, the Buddha Dīpaṅkara, who is very popular in Nepal, is shown with two divine attendants. It is dated by its inscription to the end of the seventeenth century (c. 1680).

274. The all-comprising Buddha manifestation Nāmasaṅgīti (Recitation of the [Buddha-]names)

Toraṇa *of beaten metal in a Nepalese monastery.*

Above the Buddha figure is Garuḍa, the mythical Indian bird with a human face who consumes snakes, and on either side are *makara*, an Indian mythical form of crocodile. These are often shown as a kind of decorative design around the Buddha image in Nepalese and Tibetan tradition.

275. Effigies of Dīpaṅkara

These effigies of the Buddha Dīpaṅkara are set up for the occasion and consist of masks and hands in metal fixed to a frame and then elaborately dressed. The workmanship is modern, but the special cult of this Buddha in Nepal is certainly a well-established tradition.

276. Standing Buddha

Inset in the wall of one of the buildings that surround the Great Stupa of Svayambhu (see Pl. 328), Nepal; c. 11th–12th century A.D.*; stone.*

This image follows the tradition of earlier images illustrated above (Pls. 126, 127), but is probably several centuries later, maybe eleventh to twelfth century.

Tibet and Mongolia

The first Buddha images were brought to Lhasa from Nepal in the first half of the seventh century, according to traditional accounts. The most holy image in Tibet is reputably one such image, known as Jo-wo, the 'Lord', which represents Śākyamuni as a young prince. Until recently it reposed in the main temple in Lhasa, the Jo-khang, or 'House of the Lord'. It was so swathed in garments and jewellery that no one could ever investigate it closely. Over the centuries Lhasa itself, with the Dalai Lama's fort-like palace, the Potala, and the many nearby monasteries, has become one vast treasure-house of books, paintings and images, which scarcely anyone has ever had the opportunity of examining in detail. Older images, replaced by newer ones, find their way to store-rooms and inner chapels. It is known that Sa-skya Monastery, founded in 1073 in western Tibet, some 300 kilometres from Lhasa, possessed a collection of Indian bronzes, mainly from the Pāla period, and even a small-scale model of the great Buddhist monastery at Bodhgayā as it used to be before its dereliction in the thirteenth century.[9] The only part of ancient Tibet that has been investigated systematically is the far western region, the districts of Gu-ge and Pu-rang, which were in close contact with North-West India from the tenth century onwards, when strong local dynasties were ruling there. When the centre of power removed later to central Tibet, these far western areas remained much as they were, since few people bothered to repaint the walls and replace old images with new ones. Many of the temples there were surveyed in the 1930's by Professor Giuseppe Tucci, and his *Indo-Tibetica*, vol. 3, contains numerous illustrations of Kashmiri styles of wood-carving, painting and Buddha images from that early period.

Ladakh—once a flourishing independent western Tibetan kingdom but since 1834 annexed to the state of Jammu and Kashmir—also preserves traces of late Indian, specifically Kashmiri, Buddhism amongst its more prevalent Tibetan heritage. One may note the many wayside rock-carvings in relief, illustrating Buddhas and Bodhisattvas, especially Avalokiteśvara and Maitreya (Pls. 277, 278). Some even survive in the western reaches of Ladakh, which have gradually become entirely Moslem over the last five centuries, while those closer to Leh are treated with respect and reverence. Most of these rock-carvings would seem to date from the seventh century onwards. Also many bronze images, clearly of Kashmiri origin (thirteenth century and earlier), may be seen in the monasteries of Ladakh. These are similar to those already illustrated (Pls. 257–61) and belong to the period when Kashmir was still a Buddhist land.

Of several early monastic foundations in Ladakh the only one to survive in its original state is the monastery of Alchi, near Saspol, some sixty-five kilometres west of Leh. Here the temples are adorned with wall paintings, taking us back to the twelfth and thirteenth centuries, when early Tibetan art was so clearly dependent on Indian models. The foremost Buddha image of this time is Vairocana, centre of the Five Buddha mandala (Pls. 279, 280).

[9]Sa-kya Monastery was visited by the Indian scholar Rahula Sañkrityāyana in 1936. See his article 'Second search of Sanskrit palm-leaf manuscripts in Tibet', *Journal of the Bihar and Orissa Research Society*, vol. 23 (1937), pp. 1–57; see especially Pāla images illustrated opposite p. 9, and the model of the Mahābodhi (complex of temples and stupas at Bodhgayā) opposite pp. 16 and 17.

Even earlier, from the seventh century onwards, Tibet was in close contact with the Central Asian city-states of the Takla Makan (modern Chinese Turkestan), and especially with Khotan, and Buddhist influences carried by Khotanese monks and craftsmen certainly reached Lhasa. These early influences were, however, submerged in the flood of Buddhist culture that arrived subsequently from India, mainly via Kashmir and Nepal, during the eleventh and twelfth centuries. From then on, Newār craftsmanship, as noted above, began to amalgamate with Tibetan craftsmanship with the result that a single indistinguishable style was created. This happened all the more easily as communities of Newār craftsmen settled in Lhasa, where there was always great demand for their productions.

In the thirteenth century, the abbots of Sa-kya Monastery became the first accredited representatives of Tibet at the court of the new Mongol (Yüan) dynasty in China, and for their task of converting these barbarian overlords to the Tibetan religion, they took with them not only scholars but also craftsmen, some of whom came originally from Nepal. Even after the fall of the Mongol dynasty in 1368, the Tibetans continued their missionary activities amongst the various Mongol tribes, but it was not until the Manchus, also foreigners to China proper and also converts to Tibetan Buddhism, drove the former Ming dynasty from the Chinese throne in 1644 that it becomes possible to speak with certainty of a reciprocal Chinese influence on Tibetan art. However, this influence affected rather the details of religious painting, such as cloud-motifs, waterfalls, the representation of houses and temples, and sometimes the general arrangement of the main figures; it has scarcely affected the form of the Buddha image, which has remained faithful to the canons of Indian Buddhist art as received mainly through Kashmir and Nepal.

The Tibetans imported Indian Buddhism during the very last period of its organized existence in the land of its origin. Since so much has disappeared in India, Buddhist iconography in Tibet, with its exuberant tantric pantheon of Buddhas in tranquil and fierce aspects and coupled male and female manifestations, tends to be treated in histories of Buddhist art as a special Tibetan aberration. In fact this whole art was clearly received from India, and the Tibetans added very little indeed to it—a few local saints, a few local divinities supposedly converted to Buddhism, their own hierachies of religious superiors (lamas), and that is about all. The Buddha forms are mainly of Indian inspiration and Tibetan 'Buddhology' simply reproduces the last stage of Indian developments. Supreme Buddhahood is represented by the Pentad already described above, sometimes conceived as a sixth all-comprehending manifestation. The names of this supreme Buddha vary. In Nepalese tradition he is often represented as the 'Recitation of the Buddha-Names' (Nāmasaṅgīti), as mentioned above (p. 344), or as the Primary Buddha (Ādibuddha), or he may be known as the Resplendent One (Vairocana), central Buddha of the Five Buddha mandala (Pl. 344). In Central Asian and later Tibetan tradition the Buddha of the west, whether known as Boundless Light (Amitābha) or Boundless Life (Amitāyus) (Pl. 282), seems to have become increasingly popular and he appears on many wall paintings and painted scrolls. In such supreme manifestations as these, the conception of Buddhahood receives its most cogent and positive form, far removed perhaps from the inert and negative expression of absolute being, as first symbolized by the stupa. Yet this apparently positive conception of

277. Bodhisattva Maitreya

Rock-carving on the roadside at Mulbek, in the western (Kargil) district of Ladakh; H. approximately 350 cm.; c. 8th century A.D.

From iconographic features, this image may be dated approximately to the eighth century. Older rock-carvings, such as this one, are carved 'in the round'. Compare the following plate.

Buddhahood is still interpreted philosophically in terms of the non-committal assertions of the 'Perfection of Wisdom' teachings. Thus it is taught that the supreme representation of Buddhahood still remains 'void' (*śūnya*) in his true nature (*svabhāva*).

In the expression of Buddhahood we may note a gradual change from the quasi-historical approach, as represented by the special cult of Śākyamuni Buddha, to a mystical and fully

278. The Five Buddhas

Rock-carving on the roadside below the old citadel of Shey, 12 km. east of Leh, Ladakh; H. (of central Vairocana) 250 cm.

The Buddhas can be distinguished by the hand-gestures and by the creatures beneath their feet. The date of such rock-carvings remains quite uncertain. This one might be dated at a guess to the eleventh/twelfth century.

279. Buddha Vairocana

At Lamayuru Monastery, Ladakh; 11th century A.D.; stucco; in situ.

This painted image of the central Buddha Vairocana, surrounded by the four other Buddhas of the set of five (see p. 135), not shown here, has survived in an old, scarcely used temple, known as Senge-sgang, within the complex of buildings which go to make up Lamayuru. The foundation of this particular temple must go back to an early period, typical of the foundations attributed to the great Tibetan translator and founder of monasteries, Rin-chen bZang-po (958–1055).

280. Buddha Vairocana

Wall painting from one of the smaller temples, known as Lha-khang So-ma at Alchi Monastery, near Saspol, Ladakh; 12th–13th century A.D.; in situ.

This monastery certainly goes back to the period associated with Rin-chen bZang-po (see above), who worked largely on tantras and commentaries associated with Vairocana in his various manifestations. Compare the following plate and also the mandala illustrated on Pl. 344. Many of the same tantric texts and traditions also reached Japan via Central Asia and China. Compare Pl. 202. This particular temple was founded rather later than the main Alchi ones.

281. The 'Omniscient One' (Sarvavid), a form of Vairocana

Wall painting on the upper storey of the 'Three-tier' (gSum-brtsegs) Temple at Alchi, near Saspol, Ladakh; 11th–12th century A.D.*; in situ.*

This temple belongs to the earliest foundations of the monastery (cf. Pl. 280), but an inscription informs us that it was repaired and apparently to some extent repainted in the sixteenth century (cf. Pl. 344). The central figure of Sarvavid is flanked by a pair of Bodhisattvas, whose close Indian associations are unmistakable. For the general composition of the piece one may also compare the two flanking Bodhisattvas in Pl. 66. The sequence of transmission was Gandhāra, then Kashmir, then western Tibet.

282. Buddha Amitāyus (Boundless Life)

Tibetan painted scroll (thang-ka)*; probably 17th–18th century* A.D.*; Victoria and Albert Museum, London.*

283. Śākyamuni

Tibetan painted scroll (thang-ka)*; dated by inscription to the 24th year of the Manchu emperor K'ang-hsi, who reigned from* A.D. *1662; Victoria and Albert Museum.*

Śākyamuni is represented in the usual 'earth-witness' posture, surrounded by scenes from his life. The small surrounding scenes start from the left-hand side of the painting, but so much detail is introduced that it has proved impossible to follow a completely consecutive order and at the same time maintain an overall balance in the design, which the artist clearly sought to achieve. Thus, on the left we see Śākyamuni receiving *kuśa* grass from the grass-cutter Svastika. Below him and to the right of this little scene are the figures of sickness, old age, death and the religious life, the vision of which determined him upon his religious quest. To the top of the painting he is seated on the *kuśa* grass under the bodhi tree at the moment of achieving Enlightenment. On both sides, top left and right corners, groups of gods pay him homage at this historic moment. To the right of the picture he is seen preaching to the gods, and just below (near the left knee of the main central figure) four gods bring him bowls of offerings. The small stupa nearby symbolizes his full and perfect Enlightenment. In the bottom central scene he appears preaching to the five ascetics, his first converts in the world of men. Nearby two *asuras* (demonic beings) offer him the throne that his divine status merits, while layfolk in various circumstances make him offerings. On the left again, just below the figures of sickness, old age and death mentioned above, he is shown in a transcendent heavenly state illuminating the world with the divine ray that emanates from the top-knot (*uṣṇīṣa*) on his head.

284. Śākyamuni

Tibetan painted scroll; Victoria and Albert Museum, London.

This is the seventeenth of a set of thirty-one *thang-ka*s that illustrate the 108 stories from the Buddha's previous lives, as narrated in the eleventh-century work, the *Avadānakalpalatā* ('The Paradise Tree of Heroic Acts'), by the eleventh-century Kashmiri poet Kṣemendra and his son Somendra. The paintings have been produced according to block-print (xylograph) designs, printed in sNar-thang, probably in the eighteenth century. This type of painting is included since it represents much earlier traditions; because of their fragility, older examples are difficult, if not impossible, to come by. This particular one illustrates stories Nos. 53, 54, 55. Throughout the set the central figure of Śākyamuni appears with five alternately recurring hand-gestures, those of the 'earth-witness', 'Turning the Wheel of the Doctrine' (as here), that of 'giving' (*dāna*) that of 'contemplation' (*samādhi*), and that of 'elucidation' (*vitarka*). For a description of the complete set, see G. Tucci, *Tibetan Painted Scrolls* (Rome, 1949), pls. 100–30, pp. 437–534.

285. Śākyamuni in the typical 'earth-witness' posture, seated on a double-lotus throne.

From Tibet; perhaps 14th century A.D.*; copper, gilded and painted; H. 41.9 cm., W. 36.7 cm.; Victoria and Albert Museum, London.*

This is one of the finest pieces in the Victoria and Albert Museum Tibetan collection.

divinized one, where all ideas of a particular historical Buddha manifestation are transcended completely. The first approach is typical of the earliest known Buddhism, of the Śrāvakayāna (Hīnayāna) generally and of the Theravāda in particular as it survives to this day. The second is typical of the Mahāyāna, which produces a gradual elaboration of envisaged Buddha manifestations. Yet these two types of approach are never quite mutually exclusive. From early times onwards the stupa cult represented a mystical and even a divinized approach to the Buddha ideal, and this was later formalized diagrammatically in the conception of Buddhahood as a fivefold cosmic force. At the same time, Śākyamuni as a quasi-historical manifestation of Buddhahood was never forgotten. This is attested not only by the persistent popularity of pilgrimages to the holy places in India but also by the continuing demand for paintings illustrating the scenes of his last life and the events of his previous lives (Pls. 283, 284).

An important work translated from Sanskrit into Tibetan with the help of Kashmiri scholars was the *Uttara-tantra-śāstra*, the 'Treatise of Supreme Tantra', attributed to the Bodhisattva Maitreya and promulgated by his disciple, the famous scholar Asaṅga, in the fourth century. It was translated into Tibetan in Srinagar towards the end of the eleventh century. This work assumes that Buddhahood is an ideal transcendental state, to which all living beings and men in particular may properly aspire in so far as the Buddha-nature is already present in them in embryonic form. The Buddha Śākyamuni, while certainly an historical figure from our worldly point of view, is none the less in essence a divine manifestation, whose life on earth assumes the stereotyped form of the Great Events of a Buddha.

> Just as Brahmā, without moving from the state befitting Brahmā,
> Manifests effortlessly his apparition everywhere in the divine worlds,
> Just so the Sage, without moving from the Absolute Body (*dharmakāya*),
> Reveals his manifestations without effort to those who are worthy in all spheres of existence.
> He descends from the Tuṣita heaven. He enters his mother's womb.
> He is born. He lives in his father's palace.
> He indulges in the easy life of the harem,
> (Abandoning the world,) he lives in solitude,
> He overcomes the Evil One. He attains to Supreme Enlightenment.
> He shows the way leading to the land of peace.
> The Sage, though performing such acts,
> Does not come within the vision of those who are unworthy.[10]

Such a text as this provides the necessary nuance that one must give to the interpretation of images and paintings of the historical Buddha Śākyamuni, which still remain very common in the art of later Mahāyāna Buddhism.

[10]Translated by the Editor from the *Ratnagotravibhāga Mahāyānottaratantraśāstra*, as edited by E. H. Johnstone (Patna, 1950), p. 107, vv. 53–54, 57. Tibetan version in the *Taishō Tripiṭika*, vol. 108, p. 30, folios 70b–71a. The whole work has been translated by J. Takasaki, *A Study on the Ratnagotravibhāga* (*Uttaratantra*) (Rome, 1966). For the passage quoted see his pp. 368–69.

4. CENTRAL ASIA

Although in no way losing its original characteristics, Buddhist painting in Central Asia after the ninth century A.D. may be said to be Chinese painting, although there were still traces of elements from many different sources. To be more precise, whatever was new in Sino-Indian painting in this last period was part of the development of Chinese art.

First and foremost, it must be remembered that Central Asia was no longer culturally united, as it had been in the past, despite numerous local variations. The firm economic basis that had been provided by long-distance trading had been broken up as a result of political and military developments that led to the division of Central Asia between Turks, Mongols, Arabs, Tibetans and Chinese, and Buddhism disappeared from vast areas. In the first half of the seventh century, Kashgar, Khotan, Kuchā and Qarashahr passed from the Chinese to the Tibetans, then back to the Chinese in the ninth century and from them to the Turks; in 652 the Arabs occupied Tokharestan and the city of Balkh in ancient Bactria, which became an active centre of Islamic culture.

Thus the gradual Islamization of Central Asia began (the same fate befell Afghanistan); the new religion, not merely a new creed but also and most significantly a new form of social organization, became a great attraction to ordinary people; henceforth it was to be the Islamic world that came into contact with China in the sphere of Central Asian culture, whilst India gradually withdrew.

'In the tenth century', writes Mario Bussagli in a useful summary, 'the civilizing mission of the Sino-Indian region had practically ceased. The variety of languages had vanished, commerce flagged, all capacity for original artistic creation was exhausted, and the process of Islamization was not yet complete. There remained in fact considerable numbers of Buddhists and Nestorians, who also, after the expansion of Mongol power, exerted a marked influence on the relations between Christianity and the followers of Genghiz Khan.'[11]

Bussagli has undoubtedly laid his finger on one of the root causes of the drying up of artistic activity, both Buddhist and non-Buddhist, in the Sino-Indian region: the decline of commerce. It did not, however, cease completely; for some decades longer a great deal of merchandise came into India via Kashgar. This commercial decline was itself a consequence of the partition of the lands of Central Asia amongst different rulers and peoples of differing cultures, all at war with each other.

Yet, from the standpoint of cultural vigour and artistic creativity, the fate that befell the western territories (Ferghana, Sogdiana, etc.) of Central Asia was different from that of Sino-India. In the former we see a considerable capacity to adapt elements inherited from the local culture to the demands of Islamic iconography; in the latter, an unconditional surrender to Chinese artistic culture.

This may well have been due to the very different weight of Chinese artistic and icono-

[11] M. Bussagli, in M. Bussagli, L. Petech, and M. Muccioli, 'Asia Centrale e Giappone', *Nuova storia universale dei popoli e delle civilità*, 20 (Turin, 1970), p. 138. Another good summary of the history of Central Asia is M. Bussagli, *Culture e civilità dell' Asia Centrale*. (Turin, 1970).

graphical tradition by comparison with that of Islam, which was then almost non-existent. But perhaps it is worth recalling a point that has often been made by both Soviet and Western scholars, notably by Bussagli, and that seems more and more demonstrably true: the art of western Turkestan influenced not only Afghan art but also that of the Sino-Indian region to such an extent that what used to be considered Iranian influences in the painting of the caravan centres of Sino-India should be understood as 'Oriental-Iranian', that is to say, originating in Soviet Central Asia.[12] These caravan centres had lost their former creative impulses as a result of their enforced separation from the western territories of Central Asia, which had come under Islamic domination.

It should not be thought, of course, that the Arab conquest meant that Buddhism suddenly died out: Litvinskij[13] has rightly maintained that the opposite is in fact the case. But it is also true, as the same scholar writes, that while in the tenth century Buddhism 'had won many supporters among the Turks, Sogdians, Sakas, Tokharians and Chinese in Eastern Turkistan' so that 'one may speak not only of the revival but even of the flourishing of Buddhism at that time', in western Turkestan on the other hand it was really a question of survival and of a later and 'short-lived revival'.

The cultural decline of the centres in Sino-India where Buddhism continued to hold its ground can be exemplified by what occurred at Tun-huang, where, quoting from a particularly apt passage by Basil Gray: 'Up to the Tibetan conquest it appears that the hollowing of the caves, and their decoration with Buddhist paintings were financed out of the donations of visiting pilgrims. But from the mid-ninth century onwards dedications of new work and of repairs show mainly local support, above all from the two dominant families at Tun-huang, the Chang and the Ts'ao.'[14] Painting on cloth seemed to take on greater importance; Tun-huang itself has yielded many examples of such painting.[15]

This is not the place, however, to discuss the stylistic stiffness of these late works at Tun-huang; we are more concerned with the image of the Buddha. Yet even on this subject there is little or nothing that we can add to what has been said in the previous chapter: traditional designs became fossilized through repetition; the lack of change in iconography was paralleled by an absence of fresh theories (Pls. 286–89).

Nevertheless, the oldest Central Asian painting retained its renown; it was openly copied in China in the eleventh century at the court of the Sung emperors. The celebrated painting in the Boston Museum of Fine Arts is probably an example of this. It portrays the Buddha Śākyamuni under the flowering mango tree; Ch'ên Yung-chih is said to have copied it from a work by the Khotan painter Yü-ch'ih I-sêng (7th century); this work, however, is entirely in the manner of Chinese iconography, and there would be no point in comparing it—unless by contrast—with the artistic output of Central Asian Buddhism.

12 M. Bussagli, *Painting of Central Asia* (Geneva, 1963), pp. 35–36; B. A. Litvinskij, 'Outline History of Buddhism in Central Asia', International Conference on the History, Archaeology and Culture of Central Asia in the Kushan Period, Dushanbe, 1968 (Moscow, 1968), p. 63.

13 *Ibid.*, pp. 66–68.

14 B. Gray, *Buddhist Cave Paintings at Tun-huang* (London, 1959), p. 21.

15 The examples collected by Paul Pelliot's expedition have now been systematically and very accurately described: see K. Riboud and G. Vial, *Tissus de Touen-houang conservés au Musée Guimet et à la Bibliothèque Nationale; Mission Paul Pelliot*, 13 (Paris, 1970).

286. Śākyamuni standing on the Vulture Peak

Silk embroidery from Tun-huang, Kansu Province; 10th century A.D.*; British Museum, London.*

The Enlightened One is represented between two Bodhisattvas and two Arhats and standing on the Gṛdhrakūṭa ('Vulture Peak'), one of the five hills around Rājagṛha. The Gṛdhrakūṭa was the favourite resort of the Buddha Śākyamuni and the scene of many of his sermons. One of the most important texts of Mahāyāna Buddhism, the *Saddharmapuṇḍarīka*, for instance, opens by depicting an assembly of disciples on the Vulture Peak; and it is in the *Saddharmapuṇḍarīka* that the Tathāgata represents himself to be *dharmarāja*, the judge rewarding the pious after their death by showing himself to them.

287. Preaching Buddha

This painting is a variant of one of the most common iconographies in Central Asian Buddhism: the Buddha in *dharmacakramudrā* (the gesture of preaching) under a canopy and a sacred tree, between Bodhisattvas and monks. Also in this painting the representation is Indian in its origin, presumably Gandhāran. Indeed, some schist stelae from the Peshawar and Mardān area may quite possibly be the source for this iconography.

288. Bodhisattva Vajrapāṇi

Painting on silk from Tun-huang; 10th century A.D.*; British Museum, London.*

This and the following plate of an anonymous Bodhisattva are reproduced side by side in order to show their contrast in style. Although both are derived from Indian prototypes (this Vajrapāṇi has often been described as 'Nepalese' following Sir Aurel Stein in his *Serindia*, 2, p. 862), it is useful to compare the transformation that our unnamed Bodhisattva has undergone through direct Chinese influence.

289. An unidentified Bodhisattva

Painting on silk from Tun-huang; 10th century A.D.*; British Museum, London.*

5. CHINA: THE POST-T'ANG PERIODS

After the persecution of the 840's had ended, efforts were made to restore the losses. However, it was not long before the civil wars at the end of T'ang brought renewed destruction. During most of the tenth century the treasures of the past were guarded and the arts of the time were still employed for religious purposes in remote southern provinces.

When the Sung régime had restored imperial unity (960), the first decades were spent in the traditional task of rebuilding on the old patterns. The Buddhism favoured in the first Sung century was still traditional (see Pls. 290, 292), with strong conservative influences emanating from old headquarters, especially T'ien-t'ai Shan in the south-east and Wu-t'ai Shan in the north-west, the pilgrimage centres that the Japanese students of Tendai and Shingon, the two Esoteric sects, had visited in the ninth century. By good fortune we possess a mid-eleventh century Japanese pilgrimage diary that outdoes Ennin's in its bountiful detail, the *San Tendai Godaisan-ki* set down in 1072–73 by the Tendai priest Jōjin. Jōjin, scion of a Fujiwara family and generously backed, was fortunate in being allowed to visit all that he had hoped to see, at a time of dynastic strength and general prosperity. His rhapsodies on the beauties of the various temples he entered are almost monotonously ecstatic. Though he must have been familiar with the ultimate Fujiwara achievement of his own time, the Regent Michinaga's great Hōjō-ji in Kyoto, he found in China between Hang-chou and Wu-t'ai Shan so much gold, silver, and jewels, such hosts of sacred images, so much cunning artistry, belvederes and pagodas of such breathtaking height that his final comment could only be 'indescribable . . . unimaginable'.

In the main Buddha halls he entered, Jōjin usually found three throned Buddhas with long-familiar names, golden or gilded at twice life-size. Śākyamuni usually occupied the centre, flanked by Maitreya and Amitābha; once the Buddha of Medicine (Bhaiṣajyaguru) took the place of Maitreya. Occasionally Maitreya took the central place. He saw two-storeyed buildings used to distinguish degrees of importance, the most traditional case being one with the Buddha of Medicine on the ground floor and a twice life-sized Locana above, throned on a lotus whose petals—once again—contained one thousand images of Śākyamuni. He found lesser halls dedicated to single deities, to Buddhas, Bodhisattvas, or great human saints of the past. What must have been to him the greatest surprise was to find Arhat (*lo-han*; Japanese: *rakan*) figures everywhere, carved or painted, in their then canonical sets of sixteen and five hundred, sometimes accompanying a main image, elsewhere worshipped in Lo-han chapels of their own. At the Sung capital, in the imperial temple Hsiang-kuo-ssu, the climax was reached. In the top storey of the main pavilion was a Śākyamuni surrounded by five hundred Arhats, all life-sized and gilded. In a connecting tower to the west was a chapel enshrining Mañjuśrī on his lion, supplemented by Samantabhadra on his elephant to the east—these being constant attendants of Śākyamuni since high T'ang.

Accounts of the wall paintings at Hsiang-kuo-ssu tell that it contained Pure Land compositions, one for Maitreya's golden age and another, apparently, for Amitābha. Other subjects, however, seem to have been chosen for their spectacular or even merely entertaining qualities. Thus we find not merely the ancient epic of the Victory over Māra, but a new Buddha, Tejaprabha, in an astrological role as custodian of the eleven great heavenly bodies (Pl. 291). There is even the frankly comic story of Śākyamuni's kidnapping the baby son of the ogress Hārītī, a kind of parody of the Māra theme. Two more compositions with a similar mixture of magic and comedy involved the Buddha's disciple Śāriputra, and a southern high priest of the Six Dynasties, Chih-kung. A fresco series with scenes from the legendary career of the Emperor Aśoka probably featured a battle that was both exciting and fantastic. A 57-foot-long handscroll (Pl. 293) displays seriatim a Buddhist pantheon painted in the late 1170's for the king of the Yunnanese state of Ta-li, independent but under strong Sung influence. The principal artist, one Chang Sheng-wen, was probably a specialist brought down for the purpose from the adjacent Sung province of Shu (i.e., Szechwan). Chinese elements predominate in both style and iconography, with the degree of conservatism that seems to have been peculiar to Shu. Near the start is a Victory over Māra scene, probably so placed in order to associate that supreme victory with the power claimed by the Ta-li king. There is a very large Śākyamuni assembly, followed by another equal in size and richness centring on the Buddha of Medicine (Pl. 293); both are full of traditional details, rendered in the slightly over-ripe fashion of the time. Bhaiṣajyaguru is further represented by small narrative panels illustrating his Twelve Vows to help mankind; and finally by a remarkable standing Buddha figure against a scroll background, which looks like a copy of a non-Chinese icon. Maitreya, dressed as a Buddha, is shown by three throned figures in a row, to match the Three Meetings he will hold in the age to come. Vairocana is probably shown three times. Once he takes the pose of Śākyamuni calling the earth to witness, but is called the 'Great Sun (i.e., Dainichi), Universally Shining Buddha', in the label alongside. Next comes a seated figure with an illegible title, probably identified by the miniature representations of the cosmos that appear on his robe (see Pl. 167). The third time he is shown with the name Pi-lu-che-na Fo (Vairocana), crowned and making the hand-gesture (*mudrā*) that symbolizes the unity of 'wisdom' and 'means', the female and male co-efficients of Enlightenment, according to the Vajrayāna. There is also a unique composition that shows a small Buddha at the centre of a multi-petalled lotus, who may be Amitāyus—otherwise absent—in a special form (Pl. 294).

The scroll is also full of minor deities, particularly manifestations of the Bodhisattva Kuan-yin, especially popular as a tutelary divinity in Yunnan. A good part of its length is given over to series of saints, the Sixteen Arhats and Nine Patriarchs, with seven more at the end who were probably local holy men (one a king).

The first groups to be designated as Arhats in early Buddhist literature were the personal followers of Śākyamuni (see above, p. 85), five hundred of whom are supposed to have attended the first council after his Entry into Nirvana. The teaching that Sixteen Great Arhats, individually named, had been preserved by the Buddha's will from death to protect the *dharma* was rendered into Chinese by the seventh century. They became important cult figures by the end of the ninth. In one sense they were an extraordinary intrusion: only two bore names associated with the historic disciples, and all were characterized as solitary ascetics like those of pre-Buddhist tradition in India—or, to the

290. Seated Buddha

Plausibly attributed to the Liao dynasty in the north, 10th–11th century A.D.; gilt bronze; H. 26 cm.; Nelson Gallery of Art, Kansas City.

T'ang tradition is followed, but all the details of the robe, the lotus seat and the simulated cabinet-work of the throne have been altered to produce manneristic novelties. A bare spot in the hair at the base of the *uṣṇīṣa*, already visible in Pl. 171, is now orthodox. If the *mudrā* made by the hands is to be interpreted in the usual fashion, the figure represents the Buddha Amitābha as he is revealed to the worthiest of his worshippers.

291. Celestial procession

Japanese hand-drawn copy, misleadingly entitled a North Star Mandala, of a lost Chinese original, presumably Sung and about a century earlier; dated corresponding to A.D. *1148; H. 112.5 cm.; Tokyo Fine Arts University.*

The picture purports to illustrate the meeting between a T'ang emperor and a star goddess in A.D. 839. Its chief emphasis is given to a celestial procession showing the astrological Buddha Tejaprabha surrounded by personifications of the heavenly bodies he was believed to control: the five planets, the sun and moon, the two Indian eclipse demons Rāhu and Keṭu, and tiny crowds standing for the signs of the zodiac and the stations of the moon; all but the demons are in voluminous Sung-style robes.

292. Seated Buddha

Ascribed to Liao and Northern Sung dynasty; gilt bronze; H. 24.1 cm.; collection of Mr. and Mrs. Ivan B. Hart.

The *bodhyagrī-mudrā*, symbolizing the union of 'wisdom' and 'means' (see p. 416), identifies the figure as the tantric Vairocana. The T'ang tradition is still active, but re-proportioned to emphasize the *uṣṇīṣa* with its bald spot, dwarfing the body and making the face over-delicate; the drapery folds are arbitrarily formalized.

293. Detail from a very long handscroll showing a great variety of Buddhist deities

Painted at the court of the Ta-li kingdom (modern Yunnan Province); dated corresponding to A.D. *1178; H. 30.4 cm.; National Palace Museum, Taipei.*

The named artist, Chang Sheng-wen, was probably a visiting specialist from Southern Sung China. The detail shows part of the assemblage surrounding a throned Buddha identified by a cartouche as Bhaiṣajyaguru. His way of sitting with legs down, the draping of his robe, the 'Sumeru' throne and its high cusped back, all derive from T'ang models but are more lavishly enriched. The same increase in opulence has affected the coiffures and costumes of the Bodhisattvas (no longer even remotely Indian) and the armour of the guardians. There is a new emphasis on realistic facial characterization; the drawing is fine-scaled but still energetic.

294. Seated Buddha surrounded by a kind of lotus-shaped aureole

Detail from the Ta-li scroll, dated corresponding to A.D. *1178; see Pl. 293.*

His flesh golden, his robes red, the lotus white, the Buddha wears a kind of pectoral ornament resembling somewhat the Chinese character *shou*, 'long life', other variations of which are repeated on the lotus petals. His robed body is drawn with gnarled lines and a tortuous silhouette suggesting an old tree; perhaps this peculiarity, plus the *shou*-like cryptogram, identify him by peculiarly Chinese means as Amitāyus, the Buddha of long life (not elsewhere represented in the scroll's pantheon). The whole composition seems to be a vision granted to the dark-skinned, nearly naked holy man kneeling at the lower left.

295. Seated Buddha Śākyamuni

Ascribable to the Southern Sung dynasty, 13th century A.D. *(?); painted in ink and colours on silk; H. approximately 145 cm.; Tōfuku-ji, Kyoto.*

The scroll is supplemented by two narrow hanging scrolls showing the Bodhisattvas Mañjuśrī and Samantabhadra, seated on recumbent 'vehicles,' the lion and elephant respectively. Executed in the free, dynamic brushwork usually found on Ch'an (i.e., Zen) figure paintings, and with the beasts typically late parodies, the triad is also half-traditional in costumes and in in the Buddha's gesture, apparently a tantric *mudrā* made doubly secret by being muffled in the robe.

296. Śākyamuni emerging from the mountains

Signed by the Southern Sung master Liang K'ai (late 12th–early 13th century A.D.*); painted in ink and restricted colours on silk; H. 148 cm.; private collection, Japan.*

This subject is closer to the heart of Ch'an teaching than Pl. 295, since it emphasizes anew the humanity of the historic Buddha (note the unorthodox beard), his stoical endurance of suffering, and even his foreignness. The subject was a fairly popular one in Sung times, and is here dramatized by Liang K'ai's composition and draftsmanship.

Chinese, like their own Taoist recluses. In another sense the Sixteen, being men, earthbound in their movements and wonder-working, must have seemed a welcome relief from the mind-shattering powers, numbers, dimensions, and distances of late Mahāyāna.

With the Sixteen came the Five Hundred, transported en masse to a new home on the South Chinese coast on Mt. T'ien-t'ai. As the titular leader of both groups, the Buddha Śākyamuni returned to a central role, in belief and in art.

In 1082 the Sung emperor established two new Ch'an precincts under eminent priors at the imperial temple Hsiang-kuo-ssu. Thereafter the sect consolidated and extended its position at court and among the gentry, until at Hang-chou a century later, in the heyday of Southern Sung, its monasteries enjoyed a virtual monopoly. Behind this success there lay the inevitable payment. Had Ch'an leadership remained in the hands of men like those of the early centuries, such lonely heroes could never have created an order capable of survival and growth, versatile enough to compete with its entrenched rivals, able not merely to catch the fancy of a handful of restless intellectuals, but to demonstrate its value to the state.

A monastery in the hills around Hang-chou was in many ways strikingly different from those at Ch'ang-an four centuries before, when Saichō and Kūkai were probing new mysteries. The veil of magic had lifted; most of the phantasmagoria of deities—holders of squares or circles in the mandalas, visitors from outermost space, hell demons—had been blown away. In the main hall the high altar was relatively small and bare. Śākyamuni was the dominant figure. On the altar, however, he was shown with nothing like the human vulnerability pictured by some Ch'an painters (Pl. 296). He was enthroned, wearing brocaded robes very much like those of the throned abbots whose portraits were also part of the new iconography. Since the Ch'an in ageing had turned again to books, especially to the *Avataṃsaka*, he might also be shown with an elaborate crown, like Vairocana's, and with the two Bodhisattvas whom that sutra had given him as main attendants, Mañjuśrī and Samantabhadra with their steeds (Pl. 295). A different trio returned to what had been most familiar by showing three nearly identical Buddhas spanning past, present and future: the historic Buddha with Amitābha and Maitreya. Descending to a more human level, the two on the sides would be the old Mahākāśyapa and the young Ānanda. A set of Arhats, either the Sixteen or the Five Hundred, would usually fill the upper storey of the main gatehouse. Among the few other beings preserved for sentimental reasons would be a special form of Avalokiteśvara, shown sitting on a rock above water; and a novel guardian, Veda (Chinese: Wei-to), whose odd name seems to derive from a mistranscription of a character in the name Skanda, the Hindu god of war.

What the Japanese found this time (and reanimated by their zeal) was in fact a well-ordered part of the Sung Establishment, running somewhat sluggishly, but comfortably well fed. Its main halls were erected, like any other public building, with the small-scale, feminine tidiness of the Southern Sung building code. Its icons were often overloaded with ornamentation; the once-energetic lion and elephant steeds lay prostrate or else curled in sleep.

By the end of Sung the Arhat type had eased into grotesque old men, or conventional

297. Śākyamuni in a pose suggesting deep thought

Probably Yüan dynasty; gilt bronze; H. 44.2 cm.; Cleveland Museum of Art.

This is a novel conception of the meditating Śākyamuni, both emphasizing his humanity and, by its curious medley of elaborate details and almost architectonic stiffness, suggesting a new conception of religious art, totally different from that of Pl. 296.

298. Seated Buddha

Attributed to the Yüan dynasty; ch'ing-pai *porcelain; H. 26.7 cm.; Royal Ontario Museum, Toronto.*

This piece is an incongruous combination of sweetness and sensuous shimmer with an extravagant *mudrā* borrowed from the gesture repertory of gods of wrath; the whole is a piece of *bijouterie* rather than an icon.

Chinese monks. The 'Water-moon Kuan-yin' seemed an oddly dressed Sung gentleman enjoying a nature walk. The mailed guardian Wei-to, instead of brandishing a weapon or stamping in fury, stood meekly, hands folded in prayer, his weapon merely a horizontal club supported at the elbows. When the Mongols broke in as conquerors (reaching the far south in 1278) they superimposed their own preferred form of Buddhism, namely, the Tibetan version (see above p. 352). Chinese craftsmen of great skill were available to give the new subjects a wealth of precise details, with a medley of realism and decorative boldness. At least one novel interpretation of Śākyamuni seems to have been widely accepted, a bearded, hermit-like, kneeling figure, rigid and harsh in expression (Pl. 297). What the Chinese could do on their own to domesticate the tantric Buddha theme is shown in the porcelain image of Plate 298, all pretty curves and slick surfaces.

In its final centuries Chinese Buddhism finally lost the support of most of the scholar class. Its sects blended with each other, and with a flood of Taoist superstitions. Religious art became progressively more and more decadent.

6. KOREA

The Koryŏ Period (A.D. 918–1392)

In the wake of United Silla, the Koryŏ dynasty established Buddhism as a state religion. An important undertaking of Wangkon, founder of the Koryŏ, was the erection of ten Buddhist temples in his new capital at Kaesŏng. Thereafter each successive king of this dynasty showed special enthusiasm for his favourite temples and thus Koryŏ became a distinctive Buddhist kingdom. This revival of Buddhism led naturally to a flourishing of Buddhist art, with many opportunities for the restoration of earlier traditions. Despite contemporary fashion, which pursued extreme delicacy and elegance, we note a new spirit of majesty and power now beginning to pervade Buddhist art. Although contemporary sculpture was not concerned exclusively with religious practice, there is no doubt that the principal motive of sculptural activity at this time was provided by Buddhism.

Koryŏ sculpture inherited the tradition of the previous era and so started with a firm foundation. But the stability of the kingdom and the increasing demand for Buddhist images provided the necessary opportunities for the encouragement of new enterprises in Koryŏ sculpture. Chinese influence is noticeable, especially that of the early Sung and Liao and the late Yüan dynasties. Changes in Koryŏ sculpture were, however, not so much due to alien influences as to the effects of domestic achievements. Thus in contrast with the works of the Three Kingdoms period, which are idealistic, Koryŏ products appear rather realistic. While the sculptures of Silla radiate an inner strength and are bright and cheerful in impression, their Koryŏ counterparts are warm-hearted as well as graceful and elegant. This characteristic of Koryŏ sculpture may be regarded as a reflection of Koryŏ Buddhism. To account for such a phenomenon, it may be possible to point to the gradual prevalence of the Son (Zen) sects of Buddhism. Ever since the end of Silla, this had brought about a decline of interest in Buddhist statues, while the dissemination of wood-block prints of the *Tripiṭaka* and other Buddhist scriptures may have led to a certain desultoriness in technical

299. Iron Buddha

From Kwangju, near Seoul, Korea; Koryŏ period, first half of 10th century A.D.*; H. 288 cm.; National Museum of Korea, Seoul.*

This is the largest iron Buddha surviving from the temple site at Kwangju, near Seoul. From the beginning of the ninth century, iron Buddhas were popular throughout the United Silla kingdom, and a few examples are preserved in temples. It has now been moved the National Museum of Korea in Seoul. The face is slightly thin and the 'earth-witness' hand-gesture is typical of the Silla period. Both base and halo are missing. According to stylistic indications and investigations at the temple site, the date is estimated to be about the earlier half of the tenth century, which corresponds to the early Koryŏ period.

300. Seated Bodhisattva

From Hansong-sa, Kangwŏn Province, Korea; Koryŏ period, 10th–11th century A.D.*; marble; H. 92 cm.; National Museum of Korea, Seoul.*

This image is one of the rare examples of marble sculpture in Korea. Originally it survived at the site of a temple near the seashore at Kangnung, in Kangwŏn Province. The crown, probably made of metal, was missing. The face is mild and its body has decorative jewels and drapery. This image on a lotus pedestal is one of the very fine carvings of the early Koryŏ period dating from around the eleventh century.

innovation. Now, in the Koryŏ period, a fusion of renewed Buddhist faith and popular art styles resulted in a certain secularization of Buddhist art. This tendency gradually increased and finally resulted in the production of works of no artistic value.

Buddhist sculpture in the Koryŏ dynasty may be divided roughly into two parts. The former covers the period from the founding of the dynasty (918) to the beginning of the thirteenth century. With the stability of national power, sculptural activity was first based on traditional techniques and patterns inherited from the Silla period. Moreover, in the same period, according to literary evidence, Buddhist images as well as actual craftsmen arrived from Sung and Liao China.

The second period dates from the middle of the thirteenth century to the end of the fourteenth century, during which Koryŏ was under the close control of the newly established Mongol (Yüan) dynasty in China and it is not surprising that sculpture stagnated in this period. Gradually, however, the enthusiasm of the Yüan dynasty for Tibetan Buddhism began to have its effect even in Korea, with the result that Yüan influence on Koryŏ Buddhist art in the second period was far greater than in the first.

The chief materials used in the creation of Koryŏ sculpture were not so very different from those employed in the Silla period, namely, metal, stone, clay and wood, and statues were also of Buddhas, Bodhisattvas, generals of divine power, Arhats, and so forth. Apart from the statues enshrined inside the temples and monasteries, there also came into fashion colossal sculptured images cut out of gigantic walls of rock located at scenic spots, especially steep mountains or deep valleys. This came to be a speciality of Koryŏ sculpture and most surviving examples of huge stone statues that we see today by Buddhist temples and monasteries in the mountains across the country are conjectured to be products of the Koryŏ period. This is especially true of the area that was beyond the territorial boundary of Old Silla.

7. JAPAN

The Japanese Buddhist community continued to prosper in the tenth, eleventh and twelfth centuries when its counterparts in India and China had begun to decline. It was in this rather late period that a thoroughly Japanese style of Buddhist statues and paintings was produced and painting itself achieved a golden age. The dominant types of Buddhism at this time were the Pure Land doctrines, which had begun to spread rapidly in the latter half of the tenth century, and Esoterism. Both of these attained remarkable prosperity in the plastic arts, for they enjoyed the devotion and protection of the aristocracy in a society in which the aristocracy was all-powerful. In the late twelfth century, however, as the political power of the military clans took a firm hold on Japan, Buddhist statues and paintings began to show increasing signs of regression in style and technique, despite temporary outbursts of creativity in both the old and new types of Buddhism. Buddhist art continued to deteriorate unchecked throughout the warrior régimes of the fourteenth century, and suffered a serious blow in the nation-wide civil wars of the fifteenth and sixteenth centuries. Yet it is noteworthy that at the same time Zen Buddhism, with its strongly spiritual intent, adopted as its own art-form a monochrome, Chinese-style ink painting, thus opening up a new field of expression in Japanese art.

The Emergence of a Japanese Style

The Heian period, during which Kyoto was the political centre of the empire, is usually divided into two parts by art historians: the first half is the Jōgan period already discussed; the second half, covering about two hundred and fifty to three hundred years, is called the Fujiwara period. The latter began in the late tenth century as the Fujiwara clan monopolized power and social status by intermarrying with the imperial family. Fujiwara supremacy continued through the latter half of the eleventh century, but in an atmosphere of heightened tension, as emperors who had retired from the ceremonial restrictions of the throne attempted to regain control of the government. The Fujiwara were finally replaced by the powerful Taira clan, who none the less maintained the cultural traditions of the Heian capital. But with the fall of the Taira towards the end of the twelfth century, the age came to a close.

During the Fujiwara period, the archetypes of Japanese conceptions of beauty were formed, featuring sophisticated harmony and decorative elegance. Culture was dominated by the aristocrats who had grown rich from the incomes of their vast estates, and by the clergy of the great monasteries who reflected the taste of their patrons. Buddhist art was a major aspect of this culture, for the construction of monasteries and images was zealously promoted by the aristocracy. One cannot fail to notice, moreover, the phenomenon of indigenization in all aspects of Japanese culture that took place after the official interchanges with the Asian continent were discontinued towards the end of the preceding period. Buddhist statues and paintings of this period absorbed less and less Chinese influence and became more and more Japanese in spirit, culminating in the graceful and well-proportioned style of the eleventh century, one that is called *wa-yō*, or the 'Japanese style'—elegant, sumptuous, then delicate, and even at the end decadent.

Religious activities of this period were almost totally dominated by the Tendai and Shingon sects. However, doctrinally they propagated two greatly different types of Buddhism—Esoterism and the Pure Land creed—among the imperial courtiers, the aristocracy and the masses at large. Esoterism, consisting of the Tōmitsu, i.e., the Shingon sect, and the Taimitsu, which made up a part of the Tendai sect's teachings, largely concerned itself with the so-called *shuhō* (*sādhana*), magical rituals intended to achieve material welfare in this world. Highly effective in attracting people with its emphasis on mysticism, Esoterism was at the same time apt to encourage superstitions and evil beliefs. The Pure Land doctrines had been present in Japan since the Nara period, but in the Jōgan period and thereafter they were fostered mainly by the Tendai sect and spread rapidly. The attractive belief in Amitābha's *raigō*, his coming to welcome the soul of the deceased, and the latter's rebirth in paradise won many adherents from the latter half of the tenth century onwards. Interestingly enough, as far as extant works of this period are concerned, images of Amitābha and other Pure Land subjects are found mostly in sculpture, while among Buddhist paintings Esoteric themes are far more numerous. Also the *Saddharmapuṇḍarīka*, which is central

301. Central Buddha of Yakushi Sanzon (Bhaiṣajyaguru triad)

Late Heian (Fujiwara) period, A.D. 907–13; wood, lacquered gold leaf; H. 177 cm.; Yakushi-dō, Kami-daigo, Daigo-ji, Kyoto.

302. Amida Nyorai (the Buddha Amitābha)

By Jōchō; late Heian (Fujiwara) period, A.D. *1053; wood, lacquered gold leaf; H. 279 cm.; H. of pedestal 179 cm.; H. of halo 330 cm.; the principal image, Hōō-dō (Phoenix Hall), Byōdō-in, Uji, near Kyoto.*

The Hōō-dō (Phoenix Hall) was constructed after the fashion of the palace buildings depicted in paintings of the Pure Land, and the principal image enshrined in it was therefore the Buddha Amitābha, lord of Sukhāvatī. The statue sits with grave composure on a lotus base (*padmāsana*) with the hands joined in a *dhyāna-mudrā* attitude peculiar to Amitābha. Its harmonious proportions are reflected in the soft, generous physical presence and the composed, compassionate expression of the face. Jōchō created, with a most highly polished technique, an archetype of Japanese beauty in keeping with the ideals of the nobility of the time. This style of Buddhist sculpture, unique to Japan, was the result of a century of direct development from Jōgan forms; in this statue the *wa-yō* (Japanese style) found its most perfect expression. It was not without reason, therefore, that Amitābha statues in the so-called Jōchō style appeared successively thereafter, such as those of Manju-ji, Hokkai-ji, and Hōkongō-in, all in Kyoto, from the late eleventh to the twelfth century.

303. Ichiji-kinrin (Ekākṣara-uṣṇīṣacakra)

Late Heian (Fujiwara) period, late 12th century A.D.*; wood, painted; H. 76 cm.; Chūson-ji, Hiraizumi, Iwate Prefecture.*

This statue, with its narrow eyes and small mouth, realistically and skilfully captures the personality of a youth, and differs from those in the Konjiki-dō hall in its rich realism and colouring reminiscent of live flesh. It is unusual in that it is made according to the *yosegi-zukuri* technique but resembles high relief; it consists only of a frontal part and is joined at the back to the nimbus. Ekākṣara-uṣṇīṣacakra (Ichiji-kinrin, or, more fully, Ichiji-kinrin-butchō) is one of the group of personifications of the *uṣṇīṣa* (*butchō*), one of the thirty-two aspects (*lakṣaṇa*) of a Buddha; as the highest deity, whose *mantra* (*shingon*) is the syllable '*Bhrūṃ*' and whose symbol is a wheel (*cakra, kinrin*), he is compared with the *cakravartin* (universal monarch). He is represented almost in the same way as Mahāvairocana of the *Vajradhātu* and he makes the gesture of Enlightenment (*bodhyagrī-mudrā*). An Ekākṣara-uṣṇīṣacakra mandala is formed with this deity at its centre, surrounded by the seven jewels of the *cakravartin*.

to the Tendai doctrine, emphasizes the copying and illustration of that text. The production of beautifully ornamented and illustrated sutras thus became a major characteristic of the Fujiwara period, along with the belief in the coming of Maitreya, the Future Buddha. In order to preserve holy texts and religious implements until his coming, deposits of such things were buried in so-called sutra mounds throughout Japan.

Spurred by such beliefs, powerful nobles and local gentry of the eleventh and twelfth centuries rivalled each other with the construction of monasteries and statues, causing Buddhist art to prosper greatly. According to documents, the number of monasteries built in this period seems limitless, but the larger ones were built in and around Kyoto by the imperial house and the court nobles. It is interesting to note that most of the great establishments had on their premises many halls enshrining Buddhas, Bodhisattvas and other deities who were thought to be especially effective, regardless of whether they were Esoteric or Exoteric. This may have been caused by the polytheistic tendency of Japanese Buddhism, but such lavish projects reveal how assiduously the people of that time, and particularly the ruling class, constructed monasteries and images simply in the expectation of great religious efficacy, without adhering to any particular sect or belief. Backed by political power and material wealth, they competed among themselves in the grandeur and sumptuousness of the monastic buildings and the number and size of holy images enshrined there. It was only natural that such projects should embody the finest creations of aristocratic culture, and it is not too much to say that Fujiwara arts blossomed around the monastery building. Unfortunately, most of these structures have been lost, mainly in fires, leaving very few that still preserve traces of their original splendour. Among them, the Five-storeyed Pagoda of Daigo-ji, Kyoto, built in 951, is the earliest Esoteric building still retaining a Mandala of the Two Principles in wall paintings (Pl. 304) intact on the inside of the first storey. The Hōō-dō (Phoenix Hall) of Byōdō-in, built at Uji near Kyoto in 1053, was an especially sumptuous temple of Amitābha, and, together with the gilded wooden votive statue and internal decorations, it represents the highest achievement of Fujiwara Buddhist culture. It should be pointed out also that Amitābha temples were built in provincial areas (e.g., those of Ganjō-ji, Fukushima Prefecture, and Fuki-dera, Kyushu), many of them taking on distinctive new stylistic traits in both sculpture and architecture. The Konjiki-dō (Golden Hall) of Chūson-ji, Iwate Prefecture, built in 1124, is a rare example of provincial Buddhist architecture, sculpture and decorative arts, on which the local magnates in the remote Tōhoku area lavished their wealth.

The Fujiwara Period and the Perfection of Sculpture in Wood

As a result of the highly increased demand for Buddhist images, production rose to unprecedented quantities, and the many skilled *busshi* (specialized sculptors of Buddhist images of the Fujiwara period) perfected a revolutionary technique of wood sculpture made by joining together many pieces of carved wood.

Fujiwara wood sculpture started as a continuation of the Jōgan technique of carving solid tree trunks, which were hollowed out from the rear or bottom to allow uniform drying and shrinking of the wood without cracking and to lighten the weight of the statue. Then, to facilitate the hollowing process, a new technique was invented of cutting the head and torso of a statue vertically from front to back, hollowing out the centre, and then rejoining the two pieces. This further developed into the technique of *yosegi-zukuri*, of carving several wood parts separately and assembling them afterwards. In this technique, there were restrictions regarding the assembly of the parts; for example, the frontal parts of the head and torso had to be carved from either a single piece of wood or from *tomogi*, paired pieces made by cutting a single piece down its median line, while the back part was made in the same way. This new technique, which greatly facilitated the hollowing process, was not only far more advantageous to the sculptor than solid block carving but also made possible the production of very large statues and the division of carving labour. In this way the sculpture workshops were able to fulfil continuous demands for statuary. This technique appears to have been invented in the last years of the tenth century and spread widely in the first half of the eleventh; it may not be coincidental that the dates roughly correspond to the time when the many halls of Hōjō-ji were being commissioned by Fujiwara no Michinaga. Legends ascribe the invention of the *yosegi-zukuri* technique to the master Jōchō (died 1057), who was active in the sculpture projects for Hōjō-ji; actually, he should be regarded as the one who perfected, rather than invented, this technique. After his time, the *yosegi-zukuri* spread and eventually became the main technique of Japanese Buddhist sculpture.

This period produced not only Jōchō but also many other *busshi* who were busily engaged in supplying holy images to the monasteries. Contemporary and later documents record their names and genealogies, and reflect an increasingly high social status given to their activity. From the time of Jōchō and his disciple Chōzei (1010–91), high monastic ranks were awarded to those in charge of making holy images, a phenomenon related to the practice that men who carved the sacred likenesses of the Buddhist pantheon were usually ordained and received into the ranks of the clergy. Each leading *busshi* had his own workshop with many apprentices, an arrangement that enabled him to produce large statues in a short time. Diaries of court nobles and other contemporary sources give detailed accounts of how actively the *busshi* produced images for the great monasteries under patronage of the imperial house and the aristocracy, but regrettably, very few of the works of this era survive today. However, one masterpiece remains, Jōchō's statue of Amitābha (Pl. 302) for the Byōdō-in, the Fujiwara family temple at Uji.

The stylistic development of Fujiwara sculpture did not follow a course of consistent improvement through the period's three-hundred-year duration. Based upon a stylistic analysis of extant works, the period may be divided into three parts: a peak in the early and mid-eleventh century in which the so-called Japanese-style sculpture was perfected; the tenth century in which are found efforts leading towards that peak; and the twelfth century during which the Fujiwara style was on the decline. Generally, the tenth-century Buddhist images continued the Jōgan style and technique with many mannerisms. At the same time, however, there is found in them an increasing tendency to depart from the previous T'ang Chinese style and to seek a more harmonious and lyrical expression in accordance with the national taste, the so-called Japanese style (*wa-yō*). This tendency grew stronger in the latter half of the tenth century. It was also in those last years that sculptors began to experiment sporadically with *yosegi-zukuri* while still continuing the solid block carving technique. An exceptional piece of sculpture, one that was to have enormous influence in later generations, was the Śākyamuni made in 985 and brought from China by the monk Chōnen. Said to be a copy of an ancient Indian statue, it became an object of devout worship throughout Japan. It is in the Seiryō-ji, Saga, Kyoto.

In the following century, Buddhist sculpture achieved the remarkably high level of development made possible by the golden age of Fujiwara aristocratic culture, and is best represented by the Amitābha of the Amida-dō (or Hōō-dō) of Byōdō-in (Pl. 302). It is only through historical documents that we learn about the immediate prototypes of the Amitābha statue and the Byōdō-in, namely the works at Hōjō-ji in the early and the middle parts of the century. There Jōchō and his father, Kōjō, made holy images for the many monastic halls. But of all the products of this group of sculptors, only the Amitābha of Byōdō-in survives. However, a considerable number of sculptures from other workshops remain, and from them we notice that the *yosegi-zukuri* technique was becoming common.

For about a hundred years after 1086, Japan was governed by an irregular political system in which a measure of real power was in the hands of retired emperors, or *insei*. The *insei* period was culturally a continuation of Fujiwara aristocratic culture, but in many ways this culture was already past its zenith. In sculpture in particular, the mannerisms of *wa-yō* reached an advanced stage, tending to degenerate into mild, even weak forms lacking in expressive power. Emperors and ex-emperors in this period built numerous monasteries concentrated in the Shirakawa district of Kyoto (the Hosshō-ji, for example), or in the Toba district (the Shōkōmyō-in, for example). They and other wealthy patrons seeking greater religious merits, through the sheer quantity of their donations, often had identical holy images produced in large numbers, such as the thousand statues of the Thousand-armed Avalokiteśvara of Rengeō-in (popularly known as the Sanjūsangen-dō). Pure Land Buddhism was more popular than ever, and there are many Amitābha images surviving from this period throughout many parts of Japan, both those in the Jōchō style and those that are not. There also appeared for the first time groups of statues representing Amitābha's *raigō*, his coming to receive the reborn in paradise.

Other important works in the late Fujiwara style are: the sophisticated Samantabhadra Riding his Elephant, now in the possession of the Ōkura Shūkokan Museum; the Amitābha triad of Chōgaku-ji, Nara Prefecture, made in 1151 with the earliest known instance of crystal eyes inset from within the head, a technique that was to become common in the following period; the colossal Hayagrīva Avalokiteśvara of Kanzeon-ji, Kyushu, an Esoteric image; and the Yamāntaka Vidyārāja Riding a Water Buffalo in the Maki no Oodō, Kyushu, another Esoteric image. There are no provincial Fujiwara sculptures, however, that rival the holy images of Chūson-ji, a cultural heritage of the city of Hiraizumi, Iwate Prefecture, a small version of Kyoto built in remote north-eastern Japan. In the famous Konjiki-dō of that monastery are the coffins of the three successive lords of the Hiraizumi Fujiwara clan placed beneath the altar. Over each coffin is a set of statues, each set containing an Amitābha triad, six Kṣitigarbhas, and guardian figures, made from 1124 to 1187. Those statues, elegant but expressively somewhat weak, were made in the style then current in the Japanese capital (Pl. 303).

The Golden Age of Japanese Buddhist Painting

Japanese Buddhist painting entered its golden age in the Fujiwara period. The T'ang Chinese elements dominant in the past were supplanted by a Japanese style of artistic expression, the *wa-yō*, similar to that which developed in sculpture against the same background of aristocratic culture. There are far more extant paintings from this period than from the Jōgan; yet only a few of them survive from the tenth century or the eleventh, which marked the high point aesthetically of Japanese Buddhist painting; most are from the twelfth century in which the art-form was on the decline and in a transitional state to a newer style. An overwhelmingly large number of surviving Fujiwara-period works were made for Esoteric rituals that required pictorial representation of the central divinities. Exoteric paintings also survive in considerable quantity, but in contrast to the large numbers of Amidist sculptures remaining from this period, only a few of them depict Pure Land themes. Let us now outline the stylistic development of Buddhist painting in the Fujiwara period.

There are only two survivals from the tenth century; the Go Dairiki (Five Great Powers) Bodhisattvas of Mt. Kōya (Wakayama Prefecture), and the wall paintings in the Five-storeyed Pagoda of Daigo-ji (Pl. 304). The former is a set of five hanging scrolls, each showing a Bodhisattva in a wrathful aspect who is said to protect the nation in the older version of the *Jen Wang Ching* (*Ninnō-kyō*). Two of the scrolls are missing, but the remaining three, and the central one in particular, retain the solemnity and power characteristic of the Jōgan painting style, and are thus believed to date from the early part of the century.

Then, in the eleventh century we have three masterpieces: the Amida Shōjū Raigō in the Phoenix Hall, Byōdō-in; the Ao Fudō (Blue Acala) of Shōren-in, Kyoto; and the *parinirvāṇa* scene of Mt. Kōya, Wakayama Prefecture. They mark the perfection of the so-called classical Buddhist style in Japanese pictorial art (Pls. 305–307).

In the twelfth century, or the *insei* period, the production of Buddhist painting continued without interruption, but the art began to lose substance and expressive power; the general trend of the day was in the direction of elegance, delicacy and decorativeness corresponding to the aristocratic aestheticism of that time. While the Fujiwara style was declining, new trends began to emerge in the middle part of the period as a more emphatic, calligraphic drawing technique and a distinctly new colour sense—probably an influence from Sung China—which anticipated the style of the coming Kamakura period.

Yet the early and middle parts of the twelfth century produced some works which, in the tradition of the finest Buddhist painting of the previous century, achieved a new kind of beauty. The first to be mentioned among them are the Five Vidyārājas and the Twelve Devas produced in 1127, both originally at Tō-ji but the latter recently purchased by the Japanese government (Pl. 308). From about the same time in the *insei* period are produced the Red Śākyamuni of Jingo-ji and the Mahāmāyūrī in the Tokyo National Museum, both maintaining a pleasant harmony between rich *kiri-kane* (gold leaf cut into decorative patterns and applied to paintings and sculpture) patterns and sumptuous colours. This type of traditional Buddhist painting, however, grew in delicacy, and the tendency became even more pronounced in the latter half of the century.

Another new school of Buddhist painting was also gaining currency, one that emphasized lines and had a more restrained colour sense. The oldest remaining example of this school is the Zennyo Ryūō (Nāga-rāja) by Jōchi, dating from 1145. Then came the famous Coming of Amitābha in Welcome (*raigō*) at Mt. Kōya (Pl. 309).

Buddhist Art in Decline: Buddhist Doctrine and Art in The Kamakura Period

The latter half of the twelfth century was the time of the turbulent downfall of the ancient political system and the birth of the warrior régime. Under the rule of a military overlord, or shōgun, the new political order of the Japanese middle ages became feudal in nature. Kamakura replaced Kyoto as the centre of government authority, and the Kamakura period, which opened in 1185, lasted for the next century and a half. From the viewpoint of the history of Japanese Buddhism, major efforts were made to spread the faith among the populace at large, both by the new schools of Buddhism and by a revival of the older ones. Yet Buddhist art did not necessarily prosper. One of the outstanding aspects of Kamakura-period arts was the marked development of realism in Buddhist sculpture in the early part of the period. In the late part, Zen Buddhist arts began their rise in importance, and throughout the entire period, Pure Land imagery was produced in great quantities. As a whole, the decline of traditional Buddhist sculpture and painting from the extraordinary achievements of the eleventh century becomes increasingly apparent over the span of the Kamakura period.

In the Buddhism of this period, the Esoteric sects declined as new religious movements began rapidly spreading among the populace in an atmosphere of great political and social instability. The new movements simplified the beliefs in the paradise of Amitābha and the *Saddharmapuṇḍarīka* that had been current primarily among the aristocracy in the previous period. Towards the end of the twelfth and into the thirteenth century, several new sects appeared—the Jōdo-shū, Jōdo Shin-shū, and Jishū—that focussed their devotions on Amitābha, and the Nichiren-shū that made the *Saddharmapuṇḍarīka* the centre of its creed. Two Zen sects also appeared at the same time, and in response to the spread of the new schools, the older sects with headquarters in Nara began a restoration movement of their own. This heightened spirit of revival was stimulated by the rebuilding of Tōdai-ji and Kōfuku-ji, the two most representative monasteries of Nara, which had been almost completely destroyed by fire during civil disturbances in 1180.

The great burgeoning of the plastic arts in the early Kamakura period started with this reconstruction of buildings and holy images at Tōdai-ji and Kōfuku-ji. Among sculptors, Unkei, Kaikei and their successors produced a vast number of excellent wood-carvings, thereby establishing a fame and reputation that has not been forgotten. Their products are usually accompanied by inscriptions or records concerning their production, often giving the names of the carvers and the dates (Pl. 311). The most outstanding works include the

Maitreya Buddha of the Hokuen-dō, Kōfuku-ji, the imaginary portraits of the Indian sages Asaṅga and Vasubandhu of the same monastery, the two colossal guardians, done jointly by Unkei and Kaikei, of Tōdai-ji (Pl. 312), and the Thousand-armed Avalokiteśvara, by Tankei, of Rengeō-in, Kyoto. They are all characterized by extreme realism and a sense of physical dynamism, and particularly in the statues of wrathful or protective deities, emphasis is on a powerful likeness to living forms. In the images of distinguished monks, it is on the representation of individualized countenances. The technique of inlaid crystal eyes, which became widespread in the Kamakura period, strongly reinforced these realistic tendencies. However, it is universally recognized that realism as an aesthetic principle is not well suited to convey a sense of spirituality. Even an idealized, well-proportioned statue of a Buddha or Bodhisattva loses its sense of divinity if the face is realistically similar to that of an ordinary mortal human being. The realism of Kamakura sculpture is generally thought to have been influenced by Sung Chinese art, since contacts with the mainland had been growing since the last part of the previous period. There are several clear instances of Sung Chinese influence both in sculptural styles and in the kinds of the divinities chosen as subjects, but it is not as pronounced as in architecture and painting.

The greatest number of carved Buddhist images from this period has been preserved in the Nara, Kyoto and Kamakura regions. The most distinguished pieces are dated prior to the mid-thirteenth century; after that, as time passed, the deterioration of both sculptural forms and techniques became more and more pronounced. From the late Kamakura into the Muromachi period, with the exception of the portrait statues, Buddhist sculpture declined steadily, notwithstanding the spread of popular Buddhism.

Buddhist painting did not undergo the remarkable activity seen in sculpture. The chief development was the amalgamation of the new style, with its strong line quality, with the old, which continued Fujiwara traditions. The latter half of the thirteenth century, however, saw an increasing decline in both style and technique. Pictorial works from that time exist today in large numbers; they were produced in connection with the lively religious movements of the period—Esoteric, Exoteric and Pure Land alike; many new subjects and new types of compositions appeared, giving more diversity in content to the art, but in quality they usually compare unfavourably with earlier paintings.

Esoteric painting was still very much alive in this period, producing mandalas and holy images required in the practice of *sādhana*; occasionally it invented such novel forms as the Twelve Devas standing upright and the Running Acala. In Exoteric painting, the religious revival movement caused production of works depicting the scenes from Śākyamuni's life and his Nirvana. Archaistic pieces were done in the manner of Tempyō painting. At the same time there were also painted many scenes illustrating the textual content of the *Saddharmapuṇḍarīka* (*Hokke-kyō hensō*), the pilgrimage of Sudhanakumāra, based on the text of the *Gaṇḍavyūha*, images of Mañjuśrī Crossing the Sea, and Samantabhadra with the Ten *Rakṣasī*. Also noteworthy in Kamakura Buddhist painting are works made for the Pure Land sects. These include paintings of Amitābha's paradise and of his coming, scenes of Maitreya's paradise and of his coming, and pictures with such novel themes as the

304. Tenkuraion Nyorai (Divyadundubhimeghanirghoṣa)

Detail of the Garbhadhātu Mandala; late Heian (Fujiwara) period, A.D. 951; painted on wooden boards, north face; total size 242.8 × 67 cm.; first storey of the Five-storeyed Pagoda, Daigo-ji, Kyoto.

The Daigo-ji wall paintings, inside the first storey of a pagoda completed in 951, are unique in that they depict in colour major divinities from the Mandala of the Two Principles, on a white clay undercoating over wooden boards and pillars. Though peeled and damaged in places, the divinities are well proportioned and skilfully composed, showing a transition from the severity and dignity of the T'ang style as seen in the Takao Mandara, towards a milder, more brightly coloured idiom—the earliest remaining example of the trend to the *wa-yō* in painting.

305. Amida Shōju Raigō (Amitabha with a host of Bodhisattvas coming from paradise to guide the soul of a deceased devotee)

Detail of the scene of the Gebon-jōshō (the 7th of 9 classes of the Amitābha's Raigō); late Heian (Fujiwara) period, A.D. *1053; painted on a wooden door panel; total size 383.7 × 149.8 cm.; Hōō-dō (Phoenix Hall), Byōdō-in, Uji, near Kyoto.*

The Amida-dō, or the so-called Hōō-dō (Phoenix Hall), of the Byōdō-in is as precious a monument of the painting of the golden age of the Fujiwara aristocracy as it is of architecture, sculpture, and decorative craftsmanship. Unfortunately, however, the paintings are in a poor state of preservation and many areas are a complete loss due to discolouration and damage. These scenes of the coming of Amitābha painted on the inside of four wooden doors are the most noteworthy among them. They are visionary scenes in which the Buddha Amitābha, accompanied by a crowd of divinities, descends in a stately way from his paradise and then returns there guiding the soul of a dead person to rebirth under his protection. Landscapes of the four seasons in the lower part of the compositions depict settings not unlike the mountains and rivers in the Kyoto area. Based on the doctrine that there are nine ways of the Buddha's coming to welcome the faithful of nine different levels of virtue and devotion, there were originally nine such scenes painted on the interior walls and doors of the building, the oldest remaining examples of *raigō* scenes. The Buddha and Bodhisattva figures are all outlined with supple, fine lines; their faces are full and lively; the atmosphere has a lyrical harmony of a kind that appears only in Japanese Buddhist painting; the landscapes, too, are very much those of the local environment. But, regrettably, the pictures have so deteriorated that now we cannot savour their original beauty to the full.

306. Ao Fudō (Blue Acala Vidyārāja)

Hanging scroll; late Heian (Fujiwara) period, mid-11th century A.D.*; painted on silk; size 203.3 × 148.4 cm.; Shōren-in, Kyoto.*

Known as the Blue Acala because of the conspicuous dark blue colour of his body, he assumes a fierce appearance, eyes full of wrath and hair bristling, surrounded by brightly coloured flames, indicating his violent but imperturbable character. However, his countenance lacks the exaggerated sense of anger found in continental works, and his bodily attitude is also restrained and in balance with the two attendant boys standing one on either side. Highly sophisticated in both drawing and colouring, it represents the classical beauty of Fujiwara taste in an Esoteric Buddhist subject.

307. The Final Nirvana

Hanging scroll; late Heian (Fujiwara) period, dated A.D. *1086; painted on silk; size 266.2 × 270.9 cm.; Kongōbu-ji, Kōya-san (Mt. Kōya), Wakayama Prefecture.*

This scene is not only a rare work of the eleventh century whose date, 1086, is precisely recorded, but because of its expressive powers it occupies the highest rank among the extant Buddhist paintings of Japan. It is an unusual scene of Śākyamuni's Final Nirvana, in that the Buddha on his deathbed is attended not only by a crowd of weeping and wailing disciples and lay believers but also by several Mahāyāna Bodhisattvas who, standing at his head, gaze on him and meditate the meaning of the Buddha's Nirvana. It illustrates graphically the Mahāyāna conception, as taught in the Mahāyāna *Mahāparinirvāṇa-sūtra* that the Nirvana of a Buddha is not extinction but eternal life. This oldest example of a Japanese painting of the Nirvana was to be followed by many later ones of similar Mahāyānist intent. Outstanding features of this picture are the complex composition that skilfully combines the Buddha lying with eyes closed at the centre and the surrounding crowd of Bodhisattvas, disciples and believers. With its disciplined lines and luminous tones of colour, it is a truly refined expression of religious emotion. Also treating the Buddha's Nirvana, the Śākyamuni's Resurrection, or Emergence from the Golden Coffin, at the Matsunaga Art Museum depicts a highly dramatic scene in which he briefly comes back to life to preach the *dharma*.

308. Taishakuten (Indra), one of the Twelve Devas

Hanging scroll, originally in Kyōōgokoku-ji (Tō-ji), Kyoto; late Heian (Fujiwara) period, A.D. *1127; painted on silk; size 144.2 × 126.6 cm.; Agency for Cultural Affairs, Tokyo.*

In these paintings of Twelve Devas or tantric guardian deities, the artists used bright colours, painted with a most refined technique, and, on the costumes and elsewhere, applied varied patterns both in colour and in *kiri-kane* (thin strips of gold and silver leaf pasted to the surface), which greatly enhanced the decorative effect and is a reflection of the aestheticism typical of the period.

309. Amida Shōju Raigō (Amitabha with a host of Bodhisattvas coming from paradise to guide the soul of a deceased devotee)

The central one of three hanging scrolls; late Heian (Fujiwara) period, late 12th century A.D.*; painted on silk; size 210.8 × 210.6 cm.; Yūshihachiman-kō, Kōya-san (Mt. Kōya), Wakayama Prefecture.*

This plate depicts the Buddha, seated frontally, descending from his paradise upon a cloud and accompanied by numerous Bodhisattvas and musicians. Completely filling the width of the three silk panels, its grand composition conveys a sense of dynamic movement, making it the very best of the Amida's *raigō* patterns. The Bodhisattvas are full of movement, with bright colours and strong red lines, anticipating future stylistic developments.

310. Yama-goe Amida (Amitābha Appearing over the Mountains)

Hanging scroll; Kamakura period, early 13th century A.D.*; painted on silk; size 138 × 118 cm.; Zenrin-ji, Kyoto.*

The Coming in Welcome (*raigō*) of Amitābha was painted in several different compositions. In most cases, the Buddha is depicted as riding a cloud and descending to earth, followed by the joyous crowd of music-playing, singing and dancing Bodhisattvas (see Pls. 305, 309). In the Amitābha Appearing over the Mountains, however, the sense of his Coming in Welcome is conveyed by having the upper half of his body tower over a mountain range. The present example neatly expresses the idea by simply placing on this side of the mountains, where they have already arrived, the two attendant Bodhisattvas and the standard-bearing boys who lead the procession. It is also possible to interpret this Amitābha as the mental state induced by solar meditation (*nissō-kan*), in which one is supposed to visualize the Western Paradise while staring at the setting sun and contemplating deeply. Thus this picture could be interpreted as showing Amitābha preaching in his Pure Land, as the *dharmacakra-mudrā* suggests.

311. Miroku Butsu (the Future Buddha, Maitreya)

By Unkei; Kamakura period, A.D. *1208–12; wood, lacquered gold leaf; H. 142 cm.; H. of pedestal 110 cm.; Hokuen-dō, Kōfuku-ji, Nara.*

312. Niō (one of a pair of *dvārapāla*, or guardians)

By Unkei and Kaikei, jointly; Kamakura period, A.D. *1203; wood, painted; H. of A (with open mouth; not shown) 836.3 cm.; H. of Hūṃ (with mouth closed) 842.3 cm.; Nandai-mon, Tōdai-ji, Nara.*

This is one of the two figures, the *dvārapāla*, or divine gatekeepers, who stand on either side of the Nandai-mon, main gate to the Tōdai-ji, built in 1199. Muscular and exaggeratedly wrathful in appearance, they overwhelm us by their sheer size and the impression of power they convey. Unlike the usual *yosegi-zukuri* type statues, they were carved out of several large logs joined together lengthwise, and are said to have been completed in just seventy days by twenty sculptors under the direction of Unkei and Kaikei. Their gloriously powerful forms as giant wrestlers represent an archetype of the new realistic style that characterized the Kamakura period.

313. The Monk Tan-hsia Burning a Wooden Image of the Buddha

Fragment of a handscroll, now mounted as a hanging scroll; by Yin-t'o-lo (Yüan-dynasty painter, mid-14th century A.D.*); ink on paper; size 35 × 36.7 cm.; collection of K. Ishibashi, Tokyo.*

White Path to Paradise between Two Rivers of Wordly Vice and the Six Worlds of Reincarnation. It was also in this period that Shintō shrines required paintings similar to Buddhist narrative scenes and mandalas, such as the Kasuga Mandara, the Kumano Mandara, the Sannō Mandara.[16] These are called *suijaku* paintings, and show the relationship between Buddhist and Shintō deities.

Kamakura Buddhist painting developed in an interaction between the technical tradition of the previous period and new tendencies mainly influenced by Sung Chinese painting. The latter influence had been apparent already in the mid-twelfth century, and in the period currently under discussion produced the remarkable Twelve Devas on folding screens by Takuma Shōga, of Tō-ji, dated to 1191. Such a distinguished achievement aside, however, many Kamakura Buddhist paintings are characterized by stiff lines and unrefined colours not found in earlier works, unusually exaggerated movement in wrathful deities, faces often inelegant though realistic and well drawn—traits often ascribed to influences from Sung China, where traditional Mahāyāna votive painting had begun to decline. The general tendency of this period may be summarized as follows: having achieved a high level of aristocratic elegance, grace, and decorativeness in the Fujiwara period, Buddhist painting next became, in a time of great social change, more popularized in its expression, more monotonous and aesthetically tasteless. The grace and nobility of the past, no longer sustained by lofty spiritual ideals and polished artistic techniques, gradually faded under the impact of the popularization of the Buddhist faith.

Despite the decline of the art, even in this period excellent and noteworthy works were produced. In Esoterism, the aforementioned Twelve Devas on folding screens of Tō-ji were very strongly influenced by Sung Chinese painting; so also was the Buddhalocanī of Kōzan-ji, Kyoto. The Five Vidyārājas and the Ekākṣara-uṣṇīṣacakra of Daigo-ji were powerfully depicted with traditional techniques. In Exoterism, there are the classically beautiful panel painting for the miniature shrine of Śrīdevī in the Tokyo University of Arts, dating to 1212; the Mañjuśrī Crossing the Sea at Daigo-ji, which skilfully blended the old and new techniques, of somewhat later date; and the detailed illustrations of the *Saddharmapuṇḍarīka* scenes, complete in twenty-two scrolls, at Hompō-ji, Toyama Prefecture, dated to 1326–28.

Pure Land Buddhism, which prospered in this period, also produced many important paintings. Outstanding among them are the *raigō* scene at Kombu-in, Nara, which seems to depict the Buddha's descent as a rapid one, and also the one at Chion-in, Kyoto, which is known as the Haya (or 'Rapid') Raigō for it emphasizes a feeling of speed. Examples of a new style of *raigō* scene called Amitābha Appearing over the Mountains (Yama-goe Amida) are the famous one at Zenrin-ji, Kyoto (Pl. 310) and another in the Kyoto National Museum, formerly in the possession of Mr. Ueno.

The Last Phase of Buddhist Sculpture and Painting, and Zen Art

While the early Kamakura period saw a temporary prosperity of realistic Buddhist sculpture and of painting devoted to the worship of Amitābha, Buddhist art as a whole began

[16]In Japanese proper names, we retain the Japanese spelling of mandala: *mandara*.

to decline. In the latter part of the period, it showed every indication of having entered a last phase; and in the Muromachi period (1336–1573), under the second of the warrior régimes, there was marked degeneration in formative ideals and techniques.

Changes in the political and social order and a general vulgarization of culture may have contributed to this phenomenon, but the most direct cause must have been the rise of the Zen schools. Replacing the earlier types of Buddhism in the religious loyalties of the ruling families, Zen opposed the worship of holy images that played so central a role in the past. At the same time, several distinctive art-forms, especially painting in Chinese ink (Japanese: *suiboku-ga*), were fostered by Zen Buddhism. Within ink painting, traditional Buddhist themes like the White-robed Kannon (Pāṇḍaravāsinī Avalokiteśvara) or Mañjuśrī Riding on His Lion, greatly altered in style and rendered informal in spirit, were mingled with secular motifs, such as landscapes and birds and flowers. The trend to purely secular imagery had begun, and after the nation-wide civil wars that raged from the 1460's to the third quarter of the following century, Japanese art became largely secular in character. Mahāyāna Buddhist imagery never regained the prosperity, aesthetic levels, or cultural importance it had previously enjoyed. The last phase of traditional Japanese Buddhist art and the growth of the Zen sects were thus closely interrelated.

Zen Buddhism was introduced from Sung China in two separate forms, the Rinzai sect by Eisai in 1191 and the Sōtō sect by Dōgen in 1227. These two sects spread rapidly because of the support they received from their devotees among the warrior class then in power. China and Japan were in unusually close contact; Japanese Zen monks made frequent visits to the mainland to study in monastic centres especially in the region of Hang-chou, the capital of Southern Sung, and a number of prominent Sung and Yüan Chinese Zen masters came to Japan. Many new temple complexes, vast in scale, were built in Kamakura and Kyoto; in both cities, the five leading Zen monasteries were called the Five Mountains (*gozan*) in the Chinese fashion. Their new buildings gave rise to a new style of architecture and gardening, usually referred to as the Zen style; their monks produced a new genre of poetry and essays in Chinese, the so-called Gozan literature. This transplanting of Sung and Yüan culture by Zen monks gave particular prominence to an essentially new form of pictorial art in Japan, *suiboku-ga* ('water-ink-painting') in the Chinese style.

With its emphasis on mental discipline, Zen Buddhism did not actively promote the formative arts; but having absorbed pictorial styles widespread in Sung and Yüan China, Japanese Zen Buddhism added a new dimension to the last phase of Buddhist art. In addition to boldly transfigured forms of some of the Mahāyāna deities, it placed great emphasis upon imaginary depictions of the first patriarch Bodhidharma and also the legendary Arhats who came to be regarded as forerunners of Zen, having realized Enlightenment by their own exertions. Realistic portraits (*chinzō*) of Zen masters, which were presented to their direct disciples, were often accompanied by inscriptions in verse by the masters themselves. Produced actively in the late Kamakura and Muromachi periods, many of them are outstanding examples of sensitive, vivid portraiture.

Ink painting had been widely practised in Zen monasteries of the Hang-chou region, and the custom was brought to Japan and spread by the Zen clergy who had studied in that part of China. Unlike Buddhist devotional painting of the past, based ultimately on ancient Indian or T'ang Chinese precedents that stressed rich effects of colour and gilding, ink painting was limited to dark and light tones of ink on paper or silk. It was an art-form peculiar to East Asia, which succeeded in expressing a profound spirituality by subtleties of shading and composition, technical devices that made a virtue of simplicity. Its most remarkable achievements were in the field of landscape, yet regardless of whether the subject might be landscape, birds and flowers, or the human figure, its emphasis was always on capturing and expressing the so-called spirit (Chinese: *shên* or *shên-ch'i*; Japanese: *shinki*) immanent in the object, rather than closely describing its physical appearance. This feature of ink painting was welcomed not only by highly cultivated literati but also by well-read Zen monks, who saw how compatible it was with their spiritual goals. Among these men were many gifted painters, who served to create the golden age of Southern Sung and Yüan ink painting.

In Japan, ink painting developed in roughly the same way. Especially welcomed by the Japanese Zen monks were works in the so-called *i-p'in* ('untrammelled') style. This style of painting in ink wash alone was characterized by rough brushwork and highly simplified depiction of form, unrestrained in technique, yet rich in suggestions of spiritual insight. Works in this style by Chinese masters like Liang K'ai (early 13th century) and Mu-ch'i (mid-13th century) of the Southern Sung, and Yin-t'o-lo (Indra, mid-14th century) and other masters of the Yüan period were imported in large numbers and became models for Japanese ink painting. The simple, direct expression of the *i-p'in* style came close to suggesting the Zen conception of Enlightenment, to evoking many spiritual qualities cherished by Zen Buddhists. Although landscapes were a major pictorial theme, the monk painters also depicted anecdotes of Zen masters of the past and also the *kōan* ('precedents'), conundrums used by Zen teachers to challenge their students. Examples of this genre are: The Sixth Patriarch Chopping Bamboo and Tearing up a Sutra, by Liang K'ai, in a pair of scrolls; the Monk from Tan-hsia Burning a Wooden Image of the Buddha, by Yin-t'o-lo (Pl. 313); in Japan, the Four Sleepers, by Mokuan (first half of the 14th century); and Catching a Catfish with a Gourd, by Josetsu (early 15th century). Especially valued are the paintings that bear inscriptions by one or more Zen masters and thereby express by both visual and literary means the full range of intention in Zen thought. Yet many of the so-called *Zenga*, highly simplified 'one-stroke' paintings produced by amateur monk-painters, were not remarkably artistic. Much more professional and accomplished as works of art were the *suiboku* landscapes done by Zen monks and by laymen such as Shūbun, Sesshū, and Sōami, masters of the Muromachi period, but this is beyond the scope of the present work.

From a theological point of view, Zen Buddhism was at best indifferent, if not hostile, to the worship of holy images of the Buddhas and Bodhisattvas that had long been central to the Buddhist faith. Zen was a practical religion that also rejected elaborate rituals and scholastic analysis of texts so characteristic of earlier types of Buddhism; single-mindedly it pursued Enlightenment as the experience of absolute freedom of the mind. This stand of

Zen Buddhism was skilfully expressed in the Monk Tan-hsia Burning a Wooden Image of the Buddha (Pl. 313). In this painting, the monk Tan-hsia burns a statue to warm himself, contending that if the image is an embodiment of the Buddha, sacred ash relics (*śarīra*), will come from it. But if it is a mere wooden image, there is no reason not to burn it—a forceful expression of the Zen view of holy images. When Zen Buddhism spread in Japan, the record of the high achievements of traditional Buddhist sculpture and painting came to an end.

VI. THE SYMBOL AS THE ULTIMATE BUDDHA IMAGE

The practice of substituting symbols for personal images was by no means restricted to the early phase of Buddhist art, but continued to be valid as a general principle throughout the entire history of Buddhism within the Śrāvakayāna as well as the Māhayāna tradition, despite the rich growth of imagery described in the preceding chapters. The symbols were not displaced by the images but were used in conjunction with them, often even reaching into a higher spiritual sphere in that they transcended the realm of imagery altogether. Thus it may be said that in Buddhist art the symbols not only precede the images historically but also transcend them metaphysically.

For all Buddhists of all times and countries, the highest goal has been Nirvana, or Supreme Enlightenment. This is manifested and personified in the Buddha whose image, if really perfectly formed, transcends the categories and limitations of empirical reality by its highly idealized, almost abstract shape that makes it a symbol of highest truth and absolute essence. But even the most perfect, the most highly spiritualized Buddha figure is, to a radical Buddhist, nothing but an expedient, a 'means' (*upāya*), merely hinting at the absolute truth of Final Enlightenment, but unsuited for grasping its ultimate essence. The really effective image fulfils its purpose by transmuting itself into the sphere of non-phenomenality, thus making itself superfluous, at least for all those who strive for the highest spiritual objective. Images, it is true, have their undeniable value as 'supports' for meditation or as 'instruments' (*yantra*) evoking the intuition of sacred beings in the mind, or even conjuring them up for magical purposes, but on the highest levels of religious consciousness, images may become a hindrance rather than a help. The true adept can never content himself with taking an image as something final and ultimate; he has to transcend any possible mental and philosophical state in an infinite dialectical progress so that he is liberated from all empirical bonds, even from the bondage of imagery. In Buddhist terminology, an image (*pratimā*, *pratibimba*, *pratirūpa*) is a mere reflection (as in a mirror) or a shadow, a particular and ephemeral phenomenon incapable of revealing the ultimate reality, valuable only within certain limits as a starting point ('support'), and serving as a 'springboard to send the mind into purer realms of more abstract spiritual realization'.[1]

Thus compared with images, non-figurative or abstract signs or symbols are more efficient 'instruments' (*yantra*), opening the way to higher insight because they more easily allow the meditating mind to cross the borderline towards final elimination of phenomenal

[1]Heinrich Zimmer, *The Art of Indian Asia*, vol. 1 (New York, 1955), p. 232.

visualization by way of systematic destruction of corporeal or mental imagery. The symbols used in later Buddhism are in part identical with those of the early phase, but often take a geometrical shape or that of written characters, corresponding to the sacred words or syllables (*mantra*), which, according to an important and influential school of thought, the Mantrayāna, contain the very essence of the holy personages, such as Buddhas, Bodhisattvas, etc., whom they designate. In yet another symbolic medium, their essence and meaning is expressed by bodily signs, the hand-gestures (*mudrā*). Sacred word or written character (*akṣara*), symbolic gesture (*mudrā*) and image (*pratimā*) constitute, according to the *Mahāvairocana-sūtra*, the mystic 'Body' of a Buddha; they are ultimately identical and can substitute each other, but the abstract signs are thought to be of higher metaphysical rank, conveying in the purest manner the real essence of things and leading most directly to the final goal, the unimaginable state of Enlightenment.

Among the symbols of a fundamental and universal nature, signifying such central and basic ideas as that of Buddhahood and the Way to Buddhahood or Final Enlightenment, which have been in use at one period or another over most of the Buddhist world, we may distinguish two groups, one that comprises the ancient traditional symbols as described in Chapter 1 of this book, and the other where new symbols have been introduced, symbols that become increasingly abstract so that they may be mere geometrical signs, or stylized Sanskrit syllables, or Chinese/Japanese characters. Now these two groups correspond largely to the separate spheres of influence of the earlier forms of Buddhism, the Śrāvakayāna, on the one hand, and the later forms, the Mahāyāna and the Mantrayāna on the other. Since only the Theravādins have survived from all the early sects that made up the Śrāvakayāna, we can for practical purposes often identify the two groups as Theravāda and Mahāyāna.

The primary Buddhist symbol throughout all Buddhist lands is the stupa, and while it has undergone distinctive developments in almost every Buddhist land, its original significance in Theravādin lands has remained unchanged (Pls. 314–326).[2] It served as the ritual centre in the older known rock-hewn temples of western India, and in Sri Lanka and the other Buddhist lands of South-East Asia it became the ritual centre of the first monastic establishments; as such it has remained to this day. The more personal Buddha image has never replaced it, but image and stupa have remained in close association, mutually complementing one another. While it may seem easy for us nowadays to make clear distinctions between the Theravāda and the Mahāyāna, historically there was seldom any clearly drawn distinction between the symbols employed by the followers of the earlier sects (Śrāvakayāna) and the followers of the Mahāyāna. Thus many countries, whose traditions have been followed in this book and which are generally regarded as Mahāyānist, such as Nepal, Tibet, China and Japan, were open in the earlier period to the influences of early sects other than the Theravāda, and this influence has remained to this day, although seemingly overlaid with the richer Mahāyāna and Mantrayāna symbolism. Thus in the monastic

[2]On the architectural developments of the stupa, see Gisbert Combaz, 'L'évolution du stūpa en Asie', in *Mélanges Chinois et Bouddhiques*, Brussels, vol. 2 (1933), pp. 163–305; vol. 3 (1935), pp. 93–144; vol. 4 (1936), pp. 1–125.

314. Ruvanveliseya, Anurādhapura, Sri Lanka

Founded in the 2nd century B.C.

Founded by Duṭṭhagāmaṇī (161–137 B.C.), one of the most famous of the kings of Sri Lanka, this colossal stupa, which is also known as Mahāthūpa ('Great Stupa'), was the largest in the Buddhist world of its time, measuring slightly more than 100 metres both in height and base diameter. Its enshrined relic-chamber, the magnificence of which is celebrated in the Chronicles, contained relics of the Buddha. It was rebuilt several times. The last restoration was undertaken by a Sinhalese monk in 1893. The jewel surmounting the crowning umbrellas was a gift of Burma. The square base of the stupa was decorated with elephants' forequarters in high relief, no doubt during the Polonnaruwa period (ninth to twelfth century). The history of this edifice, which has always been an object of great veneration, is recounted in detail in the Chronicles, particularly the *Mahāvaṃsa* and the *Thūpavaṃsa*.

315. The Vatadāge of Medirigiriya, Sri Lanka

7th century A.D.

The Vatadāge ('circular religious building'), a stupa surrounded by concentric rings of stone pillars, is peculiar to Sinhalese architecture. The outermost row is surrounded, as in this case, by a railing, or by a wall (Polonnaruwa). The pillars bore a dome-shaped structure which protected the stupa. This type of stupa would seem to derive from Indian *caityagṛha*, smaller and less elaborate circular buildings also containing a stupa, examples of which can be seen at Guntupalli, while remains have also been unearthed at Nāgārjunakonda and Salihundam. The Vatadāge of Medirigiriya, which has been restored, was, according to the *Cūḷavaṃsa*, built in the seventh century to replace older structures. The external railing is thought to have been added later, blocking up the outermost ring of pillars, which were doubtless older.

316. The Shwesandaw Pagoda, Pagan, Burma

11th century A.D.

The first stupa built by King Anawrahta after the conquest of Thaton (1057), this is said to have enshrined the hair of the Buddha presented by the king of Pegu. The stupa is supported by a high-rising, square, pyramid-shaped base with five receding terraces served by four axial staircases. The lower terrace is protected by statues of guardian Brahmanic deities. The terracotta plaques showing the 550 *jātaka*s that adorned the terrace are now in the museum at Pagan. Shrines have been built into the surrounding wall and the line of the western wall is interrupted by a building that contains a colossal image of the Final Nirvana (*mahāparinirvāṇa*).

317. The Shwezigon Pagoda, Pagan, Burma

End of 11th–beginning of 12th century A.D.

A bell-shaped stupa, this is characteristic of Pagan architecture. The edifice may have been begun by King Anawrahta and was certainly completed by Kyanzittha (r. 1077–1113). It is said to have enshrined two relics of the Buddha, the forehead bone brought from Śrīkṣetra and a duplicate of the tooth relic given by the king of Sri Lanka, and it is therefore an object of great veneration. A series of enamelled earthenware plaques on plinths surrounding the three recessed terraces depict the *jātaka*s. At each of the four cardinal points, a small temple contains a colossal bronze standing image in Pāla style of the historical Buddha and the three previous Buddhas. To the north-east of the platform are representations of the 37 *nat*, guardian deities or spirits of Burma.

318. The Kyauktawgyi Pagoda, Mandalay, Burma

A.D. *1847–78.*

Built as a replica of the famous Ānanda Temple at Pagan by the Pagan king Min (1846–53), the Kyauktawgyi Pagoda bears witness to the fame of its model, although the influence of Mandalay art is to be seen in the extensive use of wood. This temple contains a large number of statues of the Buddha and of mythical personages accompanying the main figure, a bejewelled Buddha subduing Māra. The frescoes in the four porches, unfortunately unfinished, are of great interest for the light they throw on life in Burma in the last century; they show some traces of European influence.

319. The central structure, Wat Mahathat, Sukhothai, Thailand

End of 13th–first half of 14th century A.D.

Wat Mahathat is the great temple built in the centre of the town of Sukhothai by King Rām Kamheng at the end of the thirteenth century and rebuilt and improved by King Lo Thai (c. 1299, or 1316, to c. 1346). In an exceedingly complex overall design, the main stupa is treated as a high *caitya* surrounded by eight subsidiary *caitya*s at the corners and on the axes of the structure. The bulb-shaped summit of the main *caitya* in the so-called lotus-bud form is characteristic of the architecture of the kingdom of Sukhothai. The niches and their surmounting arches on the fronts of the eight *caitya*s were decorated with images of the Buddha and illustrations of the great miracles in stucco. These are all now unfortunately in very poor condition. The base was decorated in the same way with a frieze in high relief showing a procession of the 80 great disciples worshipping the holy reliquary; like all the main buildings at Wat Mahathat, it has been restored.

320. Wat Kukut, Lamphun, Thailand (see also Pl. 235)
12th–13th century A.D.

321. The *prang* of Wat Rājapūraṇa, Ayutthaya, Thailand
Founded in A.D. *1424.*

A monument built by King Paramarāja II over the site where his two elder brothers were cremated after their death in single combat. The *prang* is the most representative building of the religious architecture of the Ayutthaya and Bangkok periods. This sanctuary, standing on a very high base, derives from the Khmer sanctuary tower, adapted to the needs of Buddhism. The characteristically high base, which was to become even more pronounced in the course of the centuries, contains walled-up reliquary chambers. Those of the *prang* at Wat Rājapūraṇa were decorated with wall paintings and contained a large and valuable collection of cult-figures and precious objects that was discovered in 1957.

322. The Pra Chedi, Wat Ku Thao, Chieng Mai, Thailand

End of 16th century A.D.

This stupa, of which the elevation is unique, is said to have been built to contain the ashes of Prince Tharawadi Meng, whom his father, King Bureng Naung of Burma, had appointed as viceroy of Chieng Mai in 1578. Supported on a square tiered base with small *caitya*s at the corners and surmounted by the usual umbrella-pinnacle, this stupa consists of five bulbous domes of decreasing sizes. Each of the domes has been hollowed out into four niches originally containing images of the Buddha, most of which have now disappeared. The process of encrusting multicoloured porcelain was also very common in Bangkok art.

323. That Luong, near Vientiane, Laos

Founded in A.D. *1586.*

This stupa, known in Laos as *that* (a word derived from Sanskrit *dhātu*, understood with the meaning of 'relics'), with its baluster-shaped spire, produces a silhouette peculiar to Laotian architecture. Emerging from an enormous lotus the spire surmounts a hemispherical dome, which has been largely obscured by later transformations and additions. The whole is enclosed by a series of thirty slender *caitya*s arranged in a square and by a gallery of which the base is decorated with enormous petals of stylized lotus flowers. That Luong was restored in 1930–35.

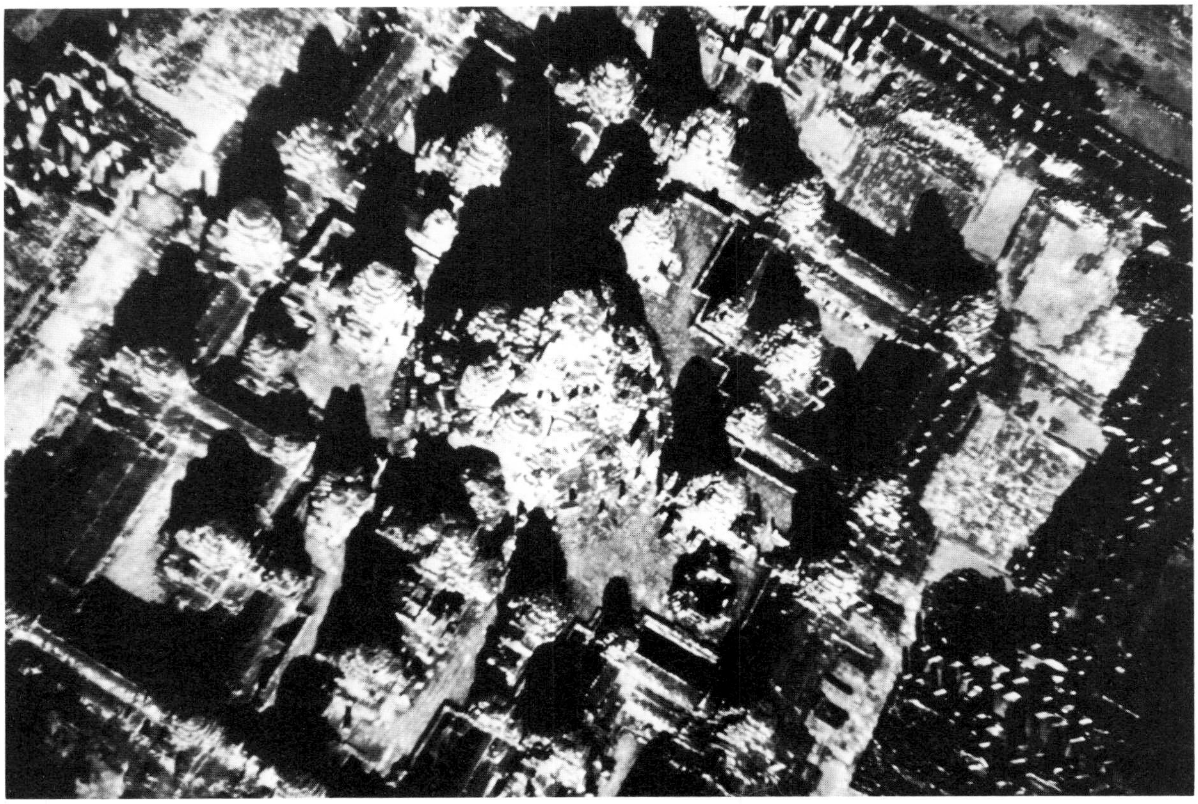

324. Aerial view of the Bayon (Angkor Thom), Cambodia

End of 12th century A.D.

This monument, which occupies the centre of the capital (Angkor Thom) rebuilt by Jayavarman VII (1181–c.1218), is unquestionably one of the most complex of Mahāyāna Buddhism. Despite some confusion, accentuated for the visitor by its present state of ruin, there can be no doubt but that this temple with its vast central sanctuary and smaller radiating chapels is an architectural adaptation of a mandala, the layout of which can be clearly seen from the air. The exceptional nature of the Bayon has given rise to a multitude of conjectures, some wilder than others, but, apart from the fact that it was obviously the centre of the country's religious life, an inscription at Angkor Thom (south-east Prasat Chrung) suggests that the Bayon was intended as a terrestrial image of the gods' assembly hall in Indra's city.

325. The Bayon, detail of a face-tower

The Bayon is famous for the colossal faces adorning its towers, and many are those who have sought to imagine whom they portray. These serenely smiling faces have been identified in turn as images of the Buddha, of the god Śiva, of the Bodhisattva Avalokiteśvara and of Jayavarman VII himself. Fascinating though these conjectures are, it would seem that the faces should be identified more simply, and on the basis of the indications contained in the inscriptions, as those of Brahmā appearing to the gods at their assemblies as the 'eternally young' Gandharva Pañcaśikha. It should be noted that this interpretation is in accordance with local Buddhist tradition.

326. General view of Borobudur, Indonesia

First quarter of 9th century (?) A.D.

This most famous of Javanese monuments, on account both of the beauty of its bas-reliefs covering five kilometres in all (Pls. 113, 114) and of its complexity, is basically a stupa with exceptionally large terraces and a mandala. The originality of Borobudur's structure has been analyzed, its symbolism explained and its bas-reliefs identified by many writers. The monument as a whole is to be seen as a product of the later Mahāyānist period and is no doubt intended as an illustration of a cosmic system centred on the 'Body of the Law' and governed by the various Jinas occupying the 72 perforated stupas on the upper platform and the 432 niches on the terraces. The reliefs depict heaven and hell, the life of the Buddha (in the *Lalitavistara* version) and his previous existences, and scenes relating to particular Mahāyānist cults.

327. The stupa of Cā-bāhī, near Kathmandu, Nepal

According to local legend the Cā-bāhī was founded by Aśoka's daughter (see p. 171fn.). Tibetans refer to this stupa as *Sa-lhag do-lhag*, meaning 'remains of earth and remains of stone', maintaining that it was built with spare materials after the building of Khāsti (Pl. 329). Both these stupas are built towards the end of the the ancient trade-route from Lhasa to the Nepal Valley. The all-seeing eyes of the stupa seem to be a Nepalese innovation.

328. The Great Stupa of Svayambhu (the Self-Existent One), near Kathmandu, Nepal

This is traditionally one of the oldest Buddhist sites in the Nepal Valley. It has often been reconstructed, and the central 'spire' was reset and the dome revetted in the late nineteenth century. Because of religious susceptibilities the core has never been investigated archaeologically, and just as in the case of the four great Pātan stupas, the inset shrines for the Five Buddhas (the fifth is included on this important stupa) can be seen in the illustration. The small stupas in the foreground are of various ages, the one right in the front of the picture being nineteenth century. The small two-roofed temple is dedicated to Ajima, the indigenous 'mother-goddess' of the Nepal Valley, but inside, the shrine is represented by the Hindu goddess Bhagavatī (the Lady).

329. The Great Stupa of Bauddha (Khāsti), supposed to contain the relics of Kāśyapa Buddha

Never having been investigated archeologically, the date of the foundation of this stupa is uncertain. It was certainly in existence in the thirteenth century and may be very much older. The present concrete revetment, with the 108 small shrines containing inset Buddha images (not visible in the photograph) around the main stupa, dates from the last century. Tibetan worshippers maintain the general décor. This stupa is known as 'Bauddha' by Nepāli speakers and by 'Khāsti' (a corruption of *Kāśyapa-caitya)* by Newārs.

330. Buddha footprint

From Wat Pra Rup, Suphanburi, Thailand; Ayutthaya style, c. 15th century A.D.*; wood relief; L. approximately 200 cm.; in situ.*

According to inscriptions at Sukhothai, the Buddha footprints (*buddhapāda*) carved there in the fourteenth century at the command of King Lo Tai are supposed to be copies of the earlier footprint on Adam's Peak in Sri Lanka. They were objects of veneration intended to ensure the prosperity of Buddhism in the kingdom. The Suphanburi footprint is appreciably later but similar in feeling. Guarded by four armed personages wearing ornaments, probably *dharmapālas*, it differs in composition from other examples but shows the same 108 signs of good omen, here assembled on the wheel, imprinted, according to the texts, on the soles of the Buddha's feet.

331. Buddha footprint

One of two relief slabs erected on the left and right of a seated Buddha statue in Preah Bat, Angkor Wat, Cambodia; c. 12th century A.D.*; sandstone decorated with black lacquer and gold leaf; H. 177 cm.; in situ.*

This is an example of footprints being used as independent cult-objects. Around the central wheel are arranged, in twelve horizontal rows with nine panels each, no less than 108 symbols of cosmological significance and of good omen, assembled into a representation of the world. Hymns were recited enumerating all the signs. A detailed explanation is given is Bizot's article listed in the Bibliography.

332. Buddha footprint from Gandhāra, now in the Peshawar Museum

It shows on the heel a *triśūla*, representing the Three Gems (*triratna*), which rests on a lotus. Above this is a Wheel of the Doctrine (*dharmacakra*) and on the toes are swastikas (signs of good fortune).

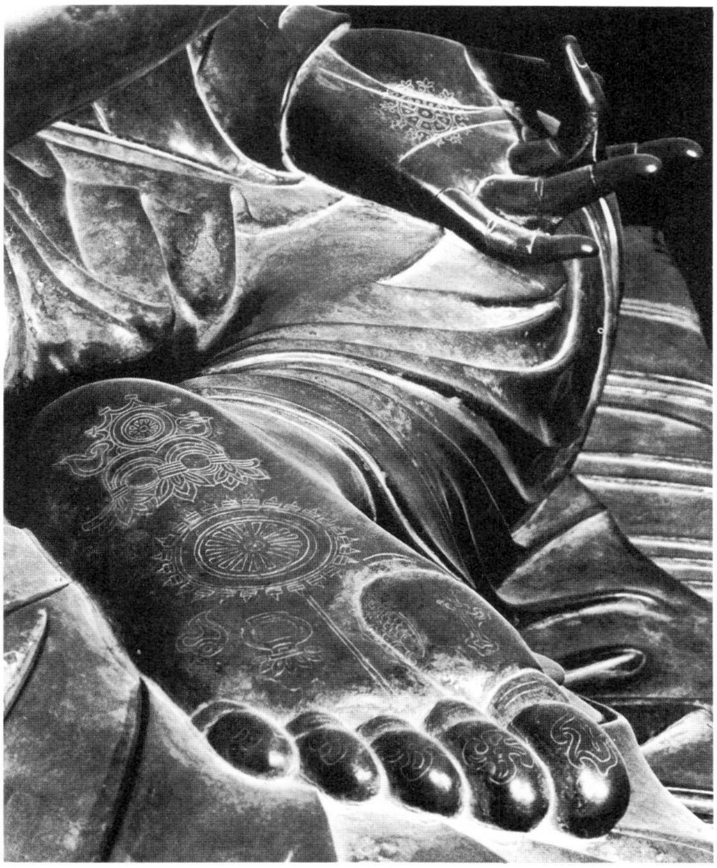

333. Foot of the Buddha Bhaiṣajyaguru (Yakushi) with symbols

Detail of the main icon, Kondō, Yakushi-ji, Nara, Japan; c. A.D. *720; cast bronze, originally gilt, with engraved symbols; H. of statue 254.7 cm.; in situ.*

The symbols engraved here represent a set of Auspicious Signs, namely, the *triśūla* (see Pl. 19) on the heel, the Wheel of the Doctrine in the centre, then in a row the *vajra*, a pair of fish, a vase of abundance (*pūrnaghaṭa*) and a conch shell; lastly, on the toes, is the swastika.

courtyards of Nepal the stupa has retained the place of honour as the central Buddhist symbol (Pl. 327), despite the fantastic iconographic changes that have affected a whole pantheon of Buddhas, Bodhisattvas, gods and goddesses, some terrifying in their horrific manifestations, and others symbolizing 'wisdom' and 'means', the two main co-efficients of Enlightenment, by a feminine partner (*prajñā*, 'wisdom') clinging to the male divinity (*upāya* 'means'). Nepal is important in our study, for in many respects it still represents the whole later phase of Indian Buddhism, which has disappeared for ever, and thus we have a clear indication how much, though not all, of the later more complex symbolism is Indian-inspired. In India the stupa underwent a long period of architectural and symbolic development, and the main change from the earlier interpretation of its significance to the later Mahāyāna one is marked by the presence of the four directional Buddhas inset into its four sides. Thus from being the symbol of the Buddha's Nirvana as explained in Chapter 1, it tends to become the symbol of Buddhahood as a kind of ineffable essence, manifest through the Five Buddhas or Jinas (see p. 135). The fifth all-comprehending Buddha is sometimes shown on the great stupas on Nepal inset east-south-east, that is to say on the southern side of Akṣobhya, the Buddha of the eastern direction, but there is really no need to show him, for the whole stupa is his symbol (Pls. 328, 329). Despite such complex developments in Mahāyāna lands, stupas of the simpler type have continually been produced in vast numbers at the request of the faithful, and thus one may say that while the stupa has changed in meaning for some, it has retained its original meaning for others. Whatever extra interpretation one gives it, it still remains the symbol of the Buddhist goal under whatever name it may be known.

Other important symbols of the first group of the old traditional style are the Buddha footprint and the Wheel of the Doctrine. Already at quite an early date, the second century A.D., the footprint (*buddhapāda*), symbol of the Buddha's personal presence, was separated from its narrative context and appears at Amarāvatī (South India) as an isolated cult-object. Another early example of very simple design is found at Gandhāra (Pl. 332). As such it became increasingly popular, and often these footprints are found in natural surroundings, impressed on rocks like the famous example on Samantakūta (Adam's Peak) in Sri Lanka, where it is associated with the legendary account of Śākyamuni's supposed visit to the island. Yet another rock-imprint at Pāṭaliputra (modern Patna) is supposedly related to his last presence in Magadha, where he had done most of his teaching before setting out northwards towards Kuśinagara (modern Kasia), where he finally passed into Nirvana. Rubbings of 'original' footprints such as these were taken to China and there transferred to new stone slabs, which in turn were copied still further afield in Japan. At the temple of Yakushi-ji, near Nara, a footprint stele of the eighth century is still to be seen. Also at the same temple the main image, a bronze statue of Bhaiṣajyaguru (Yakushi) of about A.D. 720 shows on the upturned soles of the feet some of the beautifully engraved signs usually seen on these footprints, such as the wheel, the vase of life, the trident (*triśūla*), the pair of fishes, and the swastika (Pl. 333). There are many examples from South-East Asia. After Burma and Thailand (Pl. 330), we may note especially the fine example from Angkor Wat that shows a complete set of 108 symbols (Pl. 331). As the last trace of the Buddha's earthly presence

334. The Wheel of the Doctrine
Carved face of a stone dome slab; from Amarāvatī, Andhra Pradesh, India; British Museum, London.

these footprints suggest in philosophical thought the boundary between his visibility and his invisibility, but to the simple believer they represent a magically powerful and auspicious sign, guaranteeing deliverance from the effects of evil *karma.*

The Wheel of the Doctrine (*dharmacakra*) is the most ubiquitous of Buddhist symbols, occurring in so many varied contexts, iconographic as well as ornamental, that it would be impossible to enumerate them all here. It occurs in its ancient, and, as we have seen, cosmologically significant form, surmounting a column (Pl. 334), and in this style it reappears in medieval East Asian iconography (Fig. D), especially in the esoteric schools of the Vajrayāna. Placed on a lotus pedestal and encircled by a halo, it symbolizes the essential Word of the Buddhas (Fig. E). Executed in gilt bronze, it also serves as one of the implements of Buddhist priests in East Asia. In Tibet it would probably be impossible to find any temple or gateway to a religious enclave where the Wheel of the Doctrine is absent. It is often shown with a deer on either side with reference to the Deer Park at Vārānasi, where the Buddha's first sermon was preached. Equally popular in Theravāda as in Mahāyāna lands, it is the most common of Buddhist symbols after the stupa (Pls. 335, 336).

As symbols of the actual event of the Enlightenment we must mention once more the tree, still growing at Bodhgayā, as well as its famous offshoot at Anurādhapura in Sri Lanka (Pl. 337). In a later period the main temple at Bodhgayā, which still survives in its nine-

Fig. E. Wheel over lotus and column

Iconographic drawing for a mandala (redrawn) from the Gobu-shinkan, a collection of iconographic drawings given in A.D. *855 to the Japanese priest Enchin by his Chinese master Fa-ch'üan and brought back to Japan in* A.D. *858; original: T'ang dynasty, 9th century* A.D.*; ink on paper; H. 30 cm.; Onjō-ji (Mii-dera), Shiga Prefecture.*

This is one of a large number of drawings showing the constituent elements to be assembled into a large and comprehensive mandala diagram of the Vajrayāna. Collections of such drawings were made, probably after Indian models, during the middle ages in China and Japan; in Japan, they are well preserved—some of them being Chinese originals—in several leading temples of the Tendai, Shingon and Kegon sects, mainly dating from the twelfth and thirteenth centuries. The Japanese terms for these iconographical compendia, which served the priests and the monastic artists as reference works, is *zuzō-shō*. The drawing reproduced here shows, from bottom to top: a lotus pedestal, an altar-like dais that by its shape resembles the mythical world-mountain Sumeru, a column embellished with a streamer, and a lotus flower as a 'seat' for the main element, the Wheel of the Doctrine (*dharmacakra*). The Sumeru and the column make it perfectly clear that this arrangement is meant to symbolize the central axis of the world; on it rests the sun-like wheel. At the same time the imaginary body of the Buddha is suggested, as in several other examples shown here. The two hand-gestures (*mudrā*) on the right and left are those ritually affiliated with this symbol and the holy being it represents.

Fig. D. The Wheel of the Doctrine, found at U Thong, Thailand; restored by the Fine Art Dept., Bangkok.

335. The Wheel of the Doctrine

From Nakhon Pathom, Thailand; Dvāravatī art, c. 7th–8th century A.D.*; limestone; H. 72 cm.; National Museum, Bangkok.*

Placed at the top of a pillar, the Wheel of the Doctrine is one of the most ancient symbols of Buddhism and one of its earliest objects of worship. In the present state of research, however, Thailand appears to be the only country in the whole of South-East Asia to have yielded examples—and there are many of them. Varying in size from about seventy centimetres to about two metres, the wheel was shown at the top of a pillar, as in the early Indian tradition. This one, supported by two small 'Atlas' figures, is decorated with an image of Sūrya (Sun God). The inscriptions carved on two of them, as also on a number of pillars or shafts, prove that these wheels were a Buddhist symbol.

336. The Wheel of the Doctrine

Flanked by two deer, this wheel surmounts the roof of the main temple in Lhasa, the Jo-khang ('House of the Lord'). This temple was founded in the seventh century A.D. and has been frequently reconstructed and re-decorated over the centuries.

teenth-century restored form, was copied elsewhere as a symbol of the Enlightenment, just as the tree had once been. Famous replica temples of this kind, simply known as Mahābodhi ('Great Enlightenment'), are found in places as far apart as Pagan in Burma, Chieng Mai in Thailand and Pātan in Nepal (Pls. 338, 339, 340) as well as in Peking.

We may now resume briefly the symbols of our second group, that which corresponds largely with Mahāyāna and Mantrayāna concepts. As has often been emphasized above, there was no clear break between the earlier sects and the Mahāyāna, and although there is certainly a vast difference between the use of the more limited fundamental symbols of the earlier period and the far greater variety of esoteric symbols in use in later periods, there is no rigid dividing line, and the first group merges into the second. We have already mentioned some of the later elaborations that affected the ancient symbol of the stupa, once the one and only symbol of Nirvana, Buddhahood, Final Enlightenment. The later cult of the Buddha icon, which we have followed in this book, resulted inevitably in a temple-cult, where a free-standing temple, as for example the famous temple at Bodhgayā, served ultimately the same symbolic function as the aniconic stupa had once done. The Buddha image is first inset into stupas or into wall shrines, and only later, like the great gods of Hinduism, does it come to occupy an imposing independent temple specially conceived as its sacred domain. Respect had earlier been shown to the stupa by crowning it with a series of royal parasols, which later coalesced into a spire. In an analogous way the temple was crowned with a series of roofs, resulting in what Europeans refer to as a pagoda.[3] Here we are not concerned with temple architecture, but with the image of Buddha as a kind of universal symbol, and this is precisely what the temple, like the stupa, came to represent. In their most elaborate forms they become one and the same (Fig. F). Representing the *axis mundi* as the Buddhists understand the world, the stupa may even be built as a temple with three or more storeys inside it, through which one moves ever higher amongst the gods and Buddhas of the impressive Mahāyāna pantheon. One passes protecting divinities, up to a storey where Buddhas appear as teachers in human guise, then one moves above to the sphere of the great Bodhisattvas and great tantric manifestations—Heruka, Saṃvara and the rest—and then still higher to the sphere of the Five Buddhas, and finally to a small chapel at the very summit, where the Supreme Buddha manifestation, Vairocana or Vajradhāra, presides alone. Temple-stupas such as this are found at Gyantse in Tibet (Pl. 341) and at Paro in Bhutan. Comprising the entire pantheon as elaborated in later Indian Buddhism, the whole complex is certainly of Indian inspiration, and Chinese pilgrims would certainly have seen impressive edifices such as these on their travels through Gandhāra and India. It is interesting to note that the Chinese called tiered-roof pagodas by the term *t'a*, a word certainly derived from local Indian pronunciation of *stūpa*, which in dialectical forms dropped its initial 's' (compare the Anglo-Indian word '*tope*').[4] Not only

[3]The origin of the term 'pagoda', as used by Westerners for tiered-roof temples, remains obscure. It may be simply a corruption of the Indo-Persian term *but-kada*, as picked up by the first Portuguese travellers in the early sixteenth century. See, for example, the narrative of Domingo Paes, as translated by Robert Sewell, *A Forgotten Empire* (London, 1900), pp. 236–90. For a review of the various etymological arguments, see S. R. Dalgado, *Contribuições para a lexicologia Luso-Oriental* (Lisbon, 1916), pp. 161–68.
[4]See also Turner, *Nepali-English Dictionary*, pp. 298–99, where various Indian forms are given.

337. Mahābodhi, the sacred bodhi tree

Planted in Anurādhapura, Sri Lanka, in the second half of 3rd century A.D.

The cutting of the sacred bodhi tree, brought from Bodhgayā to Sri Lanka by Aśoka's daughter (the nun Saṅghamittā) at the request of King Devānaṃpiya Tissa (247–207 B.C.), was transported to Anurādhapura with great pomp and planted in the Mahāmeghavana park. This and the Thūpārama, the stupa built by the monarch for the Buddha's collar-bone, thus introduced to the island the two major cults of primitive Buddhism, that of the stupa and that of the bodhi tree. This venerable tree has been the object of constant care and attention ever since it was planted. A surrounding wall was built to protect it in the eighteenth century, when the abandoned city was overgrown by jungle, and successive additions have further embellished the site. The railing surrounding the tree is a gift of Thailand.

338. Mahābodhi, Pagan, Burma

339. Mahābodhi, Chieng Mai, Thailand

340. Mahābodhi, Pātan, Nepal

This temple was built in the seventeenth century on the general model of the famous temple marking the site of Śākyamuni's Enlightenment at Bodhgayā. This particular version has five storeys with the following shrines in ascending order: Śākyamuni's image, an image of Amitābha, a stone stupa, a Garbhadhātu Mandala, and then a Vajradhātu Mandala, the latter two representing respectively the sphere of the Five Buddhas and their supreme tantric aspect.

341. The Great Stupa of Gyantse, Tibet

Built in the fifteenth century, the four storeys of this stupa contain symmetrically arranged shrines holding a vast number of Buddhas, divinities and sacred persons. The shrine is known locally as Kumbum (sKu-'bum) in Tibetan, which means 'one hundred thousand images'.

the term but the whole structure became one in East Asia. As a tower-like multi-storeyed 'pagoda', it could still retain its function as a shrine for bodily relics (*śarīra*) preserved in a receptacle usually in its base (Fig. G), and thus it still represents the absolute state of Buddhahood. In some mandalas, the central figure of the Absolute under whatever name he may be known may be represented by a stupa, shown as sacred by its lotus pedestal and halo. The link with the earliest stupas, which were both reliquaries and symbols of ineffable Buddhahood, remains constant. Stupa-shaped reliquaries or tombstones have remained popular in all Buddhist countries, but especially in Japan (Pls. 342, 343) and Tibet, where

Fig. F. Stupa representing Vairocana

Iconographic drawing for a mandala; from the Kongōkai Samaya Mandara, a collection of iconographic drawings; copied after a Chinese original brought to Japan in A.D. *806 by Kōbō Daishi on his return from T'ang China; Fujiwara period, 12th century* A.D.*; ink on paper; Ishiyama-dera, Shiga Prefecture.*

For iconographic drawings, see the explanation of Fig. E, p. 418. By this stupa, Vairocana, the Supreme Buddha of the Vajrayāna in Sino-Japanese tradition, is represented, as indicated by the Chinese-Japanese inscription on the lower right; in addition, his *siddhām* letter '*Vam*', signifying Vairocana in the 'Mandala of the Elemental Sphere' (Vajradhātu Mandala) is written on the front petal of the lotus seat. Before the stupa, which is an East-Asian type directly derived from the Indian dome-like stupa but provided with a roof (cf. Pl. 342), a *vajra* is placed in order to further emphasize the all-pervading power of this highest truth and wisdom. The whole symbolic ensemble is encircled by a flaming halo, thus 'identifying' it with the Buddha's person.

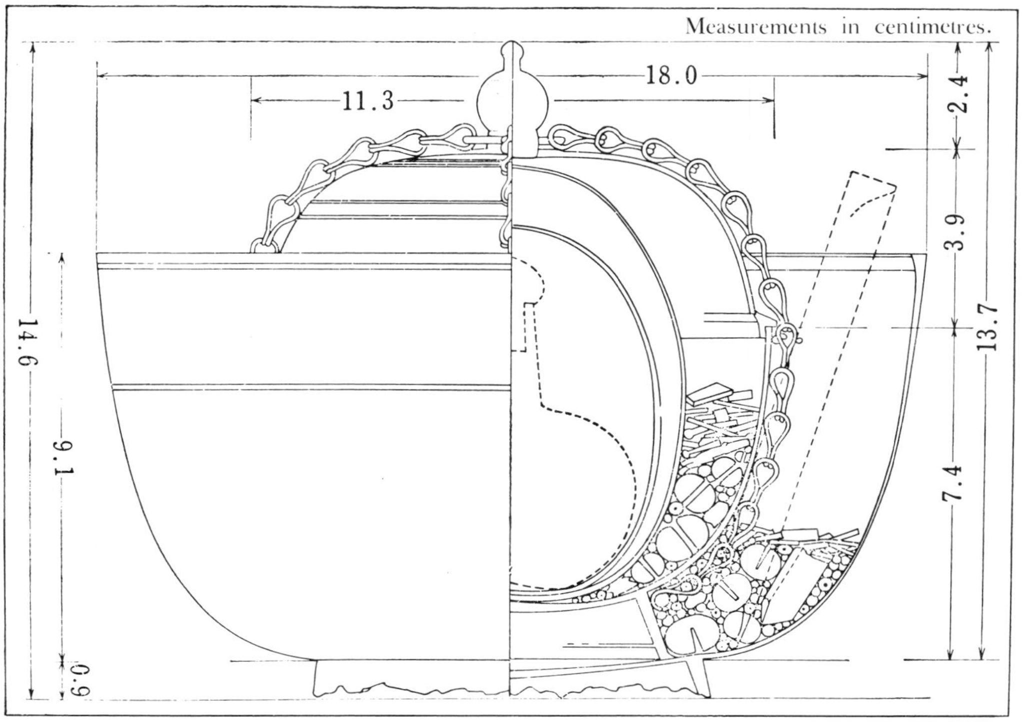

Fig. G. The drawing of the reliquary deposited in the foundation stone of the pagoda at Hōryu-ji, near Nara, Japan

In 1949, during restoration work, a reliquary was brought to light from the foundation stone, more than three metres below ground level, of the pagoda of Hōryū-ji, one of the oldest and most venerated temples in Japan, founded in 607. On this stone rests the central pillar of the pagoda (33.5 m. high), growing, as it were, out of this deeply hidden 'seed' of utmost sanctity, thought to contain the bodily relics (*śarīra*) of the Buddha. In a cavity of the stone block there was found a bronze bowl containing—besides various offerings such as a bronze mirror, gold leaf and innumerable precious stones—three receptacles one within the other. The outermost was of bronze and was secured by chains, the next was of silver and the last of gold, the latter two being oval-shaped and decorated with openwork ornaments. The increasing preciousness of the material reaches its climax in the—by contemporary standards—still more valuable flask of green glass, which contains the relics in the form of little beads of a crystalline substance such as those that are believed to remain when a Buddha's body is cremated.

it was quite normal for the relics of revered lamas to be enshrined in stupas.

The symbolism of stupa and temple coalesce in the special symbol of later Mahāyāna Buddhism, the *maṇḍala*, or mystic circle. This is essentially a stylized two-dimensional version of the stupa-temple in its elaborate form as just described above. Thus it represents the sacred domain of Buddhahood, as represented by a Supreme Buddha manifestation at its centre and directional manifestations to the four quarters or, in more complex versions, in eight or more directions. In accordance with Mahāyāna philosophic theory of the essential identity of *saṃsāra* (phenomenal existence) and Nirvana (its transcendence), these mystic circles symbolize both the world and release from it, and thus they serve the purpose of meditation and ritual, whereby the religious practiser is reintegrated into the absolute body of Buddhahood. The lay-out varies in accordance with the particular ritual that is followed, but most schools have placed either Vairocana or a manifestation of Akṣobhya at the centre. But in so far as any chosen divinity, such as Avalokiteśvara or Mañjuśrī or Tārā, is considered as consubstantiated in Buddhahood and also as a means through faith for the eventual consubstantiation of the worshipper, mandalas of great variety have been produced. But in all their variety they are but a means of expressing the final truth of Buddhahood in a form adapted to the faith and training of those who use them (Pl. 344).

Since the Buddha images are themselves but symbols, they can be replaced by other symbols, such as ritual implements or written signs, and a mandala composed of these is sometimes known as a *samaya-maṇḍala*, where *samaya* means 'convention' (literally, 'coming together') or conventional sign. Just like the images, these symbols can be used in their own right, as well as in the mandala in which they serve as component parts. Thus the more important ones require some brief consideration. The *vajra*, originally the thunderbolt of the Vedic god Indra, very much like Jove's thunderbolt in Greek tradition, was accepted in Buddhism as the symbol of Vajrapāṇi, the divinity who often appears on early Buddhist sculptures as Śākyamuni's special guardian. This is nothing more than a Buddhist adoption of Indra under another name. Vajrapāṇi, meaning literally 'Thunderbolt-in-Hand', rises in importance in the ever-increasing Buddhist pantheon as chief of all divine and powerful beings who are converted to the doctrine. Thus, as one of the great Bodhisattvas, he is paired with Avalokiteśvara, who is chief of the converted gods of the lotus family (since in Buddhist belief gods are normally born miraculously from lotus flowers), and who is therefore correspondingly known as 'Lotus-in-Hand'. The thunderbolt, as a symbol of indestructible essence and overwhelming power, destroying all the obstacles of ignorance, delusion and passion, has been interpreted in Far Eastern Buddhism and often, too, in Western translations of Buddhist works as 'diamond', and this term may be used so long as one bears in mind that it retains a transcendent significance for which there is no tradition in our Western use of the word. The later Mahāyāna defined two co-efficients that in union sparked off, as it were, the absolute truth of Buddhahood, namely 'wisdom', conceived as feminine (Sanskrit: *prajñā*) and 'means', conceived as masculine (Sanskrit: *upāya*), and we have already referred above to the sexual implications of this theory for Buddhist iconography. As pure symbols, the *vajra* represents the male element and the lotus the female. Since iconographically the male normally predominates, so too the *vajra* predomi-

342. Stupa-shaped reliquary

Made to enshrine relics brought back from China by Kōbō Daishi (774–835); c. A.D. *1140; gilt bronze; H. 49.5 cm.; Tō-ji, Kyoto.*

Stupas of this type are used as reliquaries and sometimes as grave monuments; in Japanese they are called *shari-tō* ('*śarīra* stupa'). In their cylindrical or dome-shaped body they contain relics of a Buddha or some other holy person in the form of beads or ashes. The more simple specimens, like this one, preserve a good deal of the austere grandeur of the primeval Indian stupa, while others are highly elaborate, richly decorated works of ritual art.

343. Reliquary in *gorintō* shape

Kamakura period, c. 13th century A.D.*; gilt bronze, rock crystal; H. approximately 10 cm.; Shitennō-ji, Osaka.*

This is another very popular type of *shari-tō* (cf. Pl. 342), used not only as reliquaries but also very frequently as tombstones for Buddhist believers who supposedly have entered Nirvana. The old Nirvana symbol, the stupa, is still retained in the circular body rising on a base and surmounted by a canopy; but at the same time the five parts—base (square or octagonal), circle, triangle, semi-circle and pearl—symbolize the Five Circles, or elemental realms constituting the world: earth, fire, water, air and void space. Thus this type of reliquary or tombstone is called *gorintō* ('stupa of the five elemental circles'). The relics are faintly visible in the receptacle made of crystal. By them, the holy person in his real essence is bodily or symbolically present in image-less form. At the same time, this Nirvana symbol represents the universe and is a sort of mandala, as is indicated by the seed-syllables on the eight sides of the base and of the 'roof', corresponding to the eight points of the compass as well as to the centre of the mandala (cf. Pl. 347). The letters on the base symbolize the *Garbhadhātu*, those on the roof the *Vajradhātu*, and the relics in between the non-duality of both the phenomenal and the spiritual worlds.

344. Mandala of Vairocana from Alchi, Ladakh

This mandala with a four-headed figure of Vairocana at the centre comprises the 37 main divinities of his circle according to the *Durgatipariśodhana Tantra*. In the inner set of nine squares there are, apart from Vairocana himself, the other four Buddhas of the Supreme Pentad (see p. 135) and the four great goddesses, Locanā, Māmakī, Paṇḍuravāsinī and Tāra. The remainder are eight goddesses of offerings, a set of sixteen Bodhisattvas, and four door-guardians. It is on the upper storey of the 'Three-tier' (*gSum-brtsegs*) Temple, one of several that go to make up this old monastic site, founded probably in the late eleventh century. The walls of the 'Three-tier' Temple were repainted in the sixteenth century, but efforts were made to preserve earlier styles. This fairly simple design shows up quite clearly the structure of a mandala. It is essentially the sphere of Buddhahood represented as a four-sided temple, as seen from above, with four doors, facing the four directions, and the whole enclosed in a protective circle of *vajra*s and flames. One may also note the Wheel of the Doctrine with a deer on either side surmounting the *toraṇa* over each of the doorways, exactly as they often appear over the entrances to temples.

Fig. H. Two *vajras* set in the form of a cross, a sign of the centre of existence

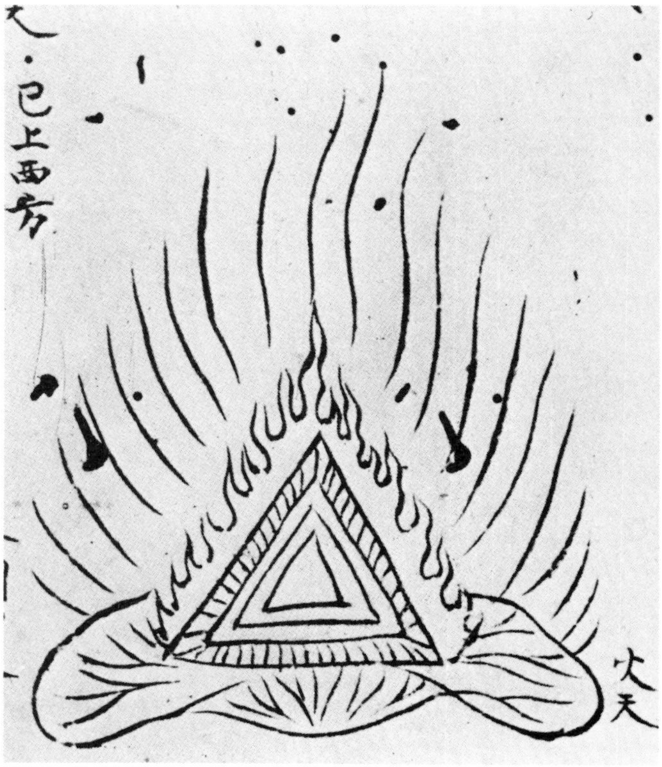

Fig. I. The *vajra* as the axis of the universe, identical with the Perfection of Wisdom.

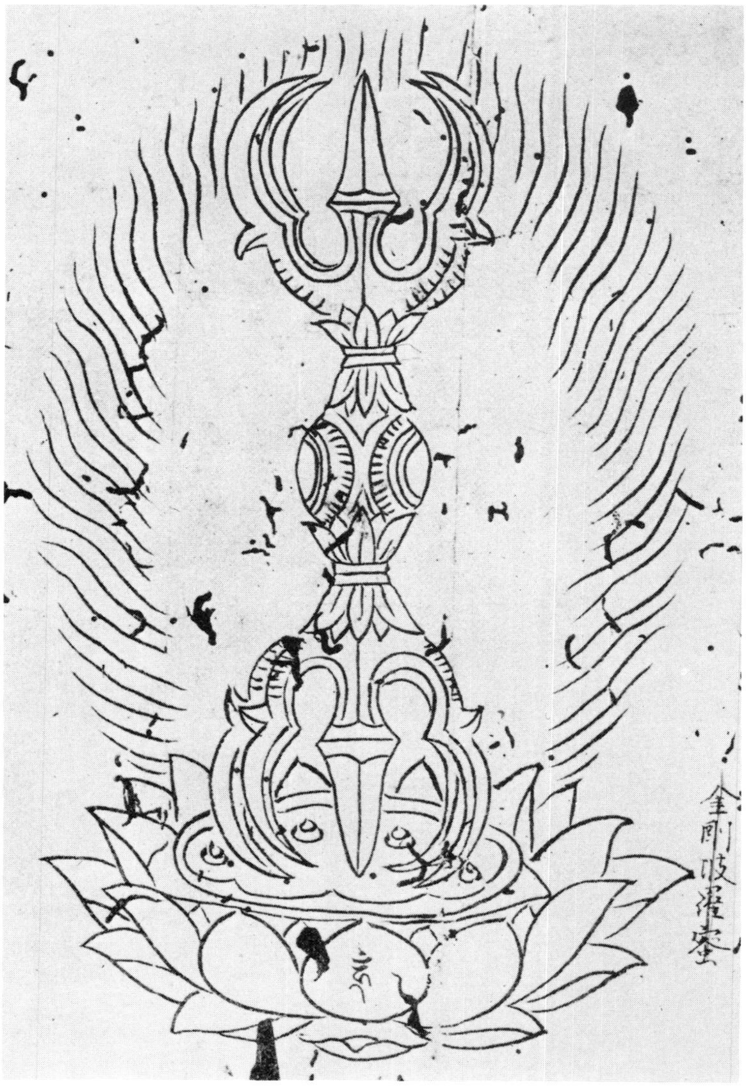

Fig. J. Triangle representing the fire-god Agni (Kamakura period, Japan)

nates as the primary symbol of the later Mahāyāna, which in its more elaborate form is known precisely as the Vajrayāna (Fig. H). Thus the *vajra* is often shown iconographically with a lotus pedestal and halo (Pl. 345) as the supreme Buddha image. Placed vertically, it emphasizes its central significance as the *axis mundi* (Fig. I). Tantric texts often refer to the supreme truth as the union of *vajra* and lotus.[5]

Certain other implements used for Buddhist rituals, which were all originally of Indian origin at a time when Hinduism and Buddhism progressed side by side, have become symbols of the ultimate. Foremost of these is the ritual vase (*ghaṭa, kalaśa*), whose sacred rotundity is thought of as comprehending all the Buddhas and attendant divinities, and thus it can replace all other symbols at the centre of an entirely diagrammatical mandala. In late Indian Buddhism the bell (*ghaṇṭa*) often replaces the lotus as a symbol of wisdom, and thus with the pair of the *vajra* and lotus we have the corresponding pair of the *vajra* and bell. These are manipulated together in Tibetan and Japanese Buddhist rituals up to the present day (Pl. 346). While the symbols mentioned above belong to the sphere of tangible objects, another category of symbol is provided by purely geometrical signs. Thus the triangle was early associated with Agni, the Vedic god of fire, later accepted by Buddhists quite as much as by Hindus as the god of sacrifice or more specifically of burnt offerings. The corresponding ceremony, known as *homa* in Sanskrit, was adopted by Buddhists, and to the accompaniment of burnt offerings, mainly butter and various forms of grain, invocations were offered to Buddhist divinities through the medium of Agni for the success of one's undertakings, whether this-worldly or other-worldly. The sacrificial hearth is always triangular in shape, and thus the triangle of fire represents access to supreme reality (Fig. J). In East Asian tradition, it comes to represent the fierce manifestation Acala ('Immovable'), better known under his Japanese name, Fudō. Acala belongs to the class of Vidyādhara, 'holders of secret spells (*vidyā*)', and in East Asian tradition he is considered as their king (Vidyārāja).[6] Through Acala, symbolized by the triangle, one gains access to Vairocana, the Supreme Buddha. Thus this triangle is called the 'triangular wisdom-fire' or 'seal of all the Buddhas' wisdom'. Like other symbols the triangle may appear as a Buddha image, elevated on a lotus pedestal and surrounded by a halo.

The most conspicuous and self-evident geometric symbol of the Buddha's universality is the circle. We have already met it throughout this book in the form of the Wheel of the Doctrine and as that of the halo (Sanskrit: *prabhāmaṇḍala*, 'circle of light'), and we have referred to it in its highly symbolic form of the circle of divinities, or mystic circle (*maṇḍala*). As much in its simple as in its elaborate form, it represents the totality and the primordial non-duality of the phenomenal and the Buddha spheres. In the terminology of East Asian Buddhism we constantly encounter the term 'circle' or 'round', signifying something absolutely perfect and unsurpassable, as in 'round Enlightenment or wisdom', symbolized

[5]The most popular of Tibetan Buddhist spells is *Oṃ Maṇipadme Hūṃ*, often translated in travellers' books as 'Hail to the Jewel in the Lotus'. Although such a meaning makes sense in the context we have just described, in origin *Maṇipadme* is probably a feminine vocative, meaning 'O thou with jewelled lotus', and it is the spell (*vidyā*), feminine in form as pointed out elsewhere (p. 431), of Avalokiteśvara.

[6]Concerning this category of divine being, see J. Przyluski, 'Les Vidyārāja', *Bulletin de l'École Française d' Extrême-Orient* (Hanoi, 1923), p. 301 ff.

345. Reliquary

Cult implement; Kamakura period, 13th century A.D.*; gilt bronze; H. 53 cm.; Tokyo National Museum.*

The reliquary is a combination of the *vajra* and the stupa symbols; all elements found separately in other examples are assembled here: the lotus pedestal, *vajra*, halo, and a stupa 'dome', which at the same time resembles the *cintāmaṇi* (wish-fulfilling gem). However, it is primarily to be interpreted as a form of stupa since it contains relics.

346. Pasang Khambache, a Nepalese layman of distinction, manipulating *vajra* and bell

by the mirror, or 'round truth' or 'round stillness' for Nirvana, or 'round emptiness' for the absolute emptiness of all concepts (*śūnyatā*), and even 'round Buddha'.

Another highly abstract form of symbol used already in the earlier Mahāyāna period is represented by the mystic syllable, known as *bīja*, literally 'seed', the enunciation of which not only invokes but also represents a Buddha manifestation or divinity in the formless realm of pure sound. Thus the Five Buddhas have their separate 'seeds', such as *Hūṃ* (Akṣobhya), *Buṃ* (Vairocana), *Jrīṃ* (Amitābha), *Aṃ* (Ratnasambhava) and *Khaṃ* (Amoghasiddhi), although variations are possible in different traditions. In such syllables as these, the holy beings conceal themselves from the impious, but reveal themselves to those who know. These syllables are linked with others that often preserve a trace of their original meaning to produce spells, or *mantras*. Thus for example '*Oṃ Trailokyākṣepa Hūṃ Hūṃ Hūṃ Phaṭ Svāhā*' is a *mantra* of Akṣobhya is his fierce form of Heruka as 'overcomer of the three-fold world' (*trailokyākṣepa*). Again, '*Oṃ Vāgīśvarī Hūṃ*' is the spell of Mañjuśrī, and the spell (*vidyā*) is thought of as feminine and thus has a feminine form. All these enunciated symbolic sounds, known generally as *mantra*, played such an important part in the later Mahāyāna that the term Mantrayāna is used as equivalent for Vajrayāna.

When these non-phenomenal word-symbols assume visual shape, they are written preferably in a stylized form, but usually the form of writing currently in use has been employed. Thus in India the earlier form of the *devanāgarī* script, still in use, might be employed, but also the older Brāhmī script. The Tibetans used their own script as developed from Indian models, but they also used stylized versions of Brāhmī letters (p. 432). These 'seed-syllables' may be referred to in East Asian tradition by the Sanskrit term *siddha*, that is, 'successfully accomplished', or 'supernaturally efficacious'. Thus in the mandala these syllables may replace the images (Pl. 347) or other symbols, and similarly they may be shown in isolated pictures, painted scrolls, metal plaques, etc., as cult-objects with lotus and halo (Pl. 348), thus functioning as 'supports' for meditation. Since they make possible an immediate intuition of the real essence of the holy beings represented by them, they occupy, by their very abstractness, a high metaphysical level and therefore possess an enormous religious efficacy. The efficacy of an image, on the other hand, can be considerably enhanced by the *mantra* or other sacred texts deposited in its interior; they animate it by representing the spiritual body of the Buddha, as enshrined in his doctrine. The hierarchy of image/symbol/abstract sign is clearly demonstrated by certain Japanese scrolls showing an image of a holy being at the bottom, a symbolic object above it and the corresponding seed-syllable in the highest place—all three of them signifying one and the same entity.

Not only in the highly involved, scholastic and mystic system of the Vajrayāna but also in more popular and simple forms of Buddhism, the abstract symbolism of written characters figures prominently as embodying central tenets of the faith. The Japanese Lotus Sect (Hokke-kyō), founded by Nichiren (1222–82) and exclusively based on the *Lotus Sutra* (*Saddharmapuṇḍarīka-sūtra*) uses as its most sacred cult-object the holy title of this book, taken as the concentrated embodiment of the Buddha's essence as concealed in the believer's heart. The invocation formula in Japanese, *Namu Myōhō Renge-kyō* ('Homage to the *Lotus Sutra* of the Wonderful Law'), is written in a special calligraphic style and recited innumerable times by individual believers as well as by huge crowds in trance-like rapture.

The most consistent aniconists have been the followers of Ch'an (or Zen) Buddhism. Although they were not on principle against images—Buddhism never knew dogmatic and intolerant iconoclasm—they considered them simply as irrelevant. The famous anecdote of the monk Tan-hsia (728–824) burning a Buddha statue does not contradict this statement because the seemingly sacrilegious act was meant to demonstrate the absurdity

347. Seed-syllables representing Buddhas and Bodhisattvas

Central field of a mandala relief; Kamakura period, 13th century A.D.*; gilt bronze; H. approximately 36 cm.; Daigo-ji, Kyoto.*

Most mandalas in Central and East Asian Buddhism were executed in painting but not infrequently they took the form of metal plaques; both kinds were used in temple halls for meditation and ritual. This plate shows the central field of a much larger mandala (the Garbhadhātu, or 'Womb', Mandala) containing the seed-syllables of the central group of five Buddhas (in the centre and the four main points of the compass) and four Bodhisattvas in the intermediate directions. The central position is occupied by the *Garbhadhātu* form of Vairocana seated on the seed-pod of a lotus flower, while the other holy beings occupy its eight petals extending in the eight main directions of the universe. Correspondingly eight *vajras* issue radially from the centre like the spokes of a wheel. In the corners of the panel are placed four identical specimens of the old fertility symbol, the vase of abundance (*pūrṇaghaṭa*) (cf. Pl. 4).

Fig. K. Tibetan monogram consisting of combined mystic syllables

348. Seed-syllable '*A*' representing Vairocana

Japanese painted scroll used for ritual purposes; Muromachi period, c. 15th century A.D.*; colours and gold on silk; Museum of Fine Arts, Boston.*

This is an example of how a single large seed-syllable can take the place of a sacred figure. It can be easily replaced by an image of Vairocana in his Garbhadhātu Mandala form, seated on the lotus and encircled by a halo. The *vajra* supporting the lotus not only emphasizes the absolute essence of Vairocana's Buddhahood, but at the same time symbolizes the axis of the universe.

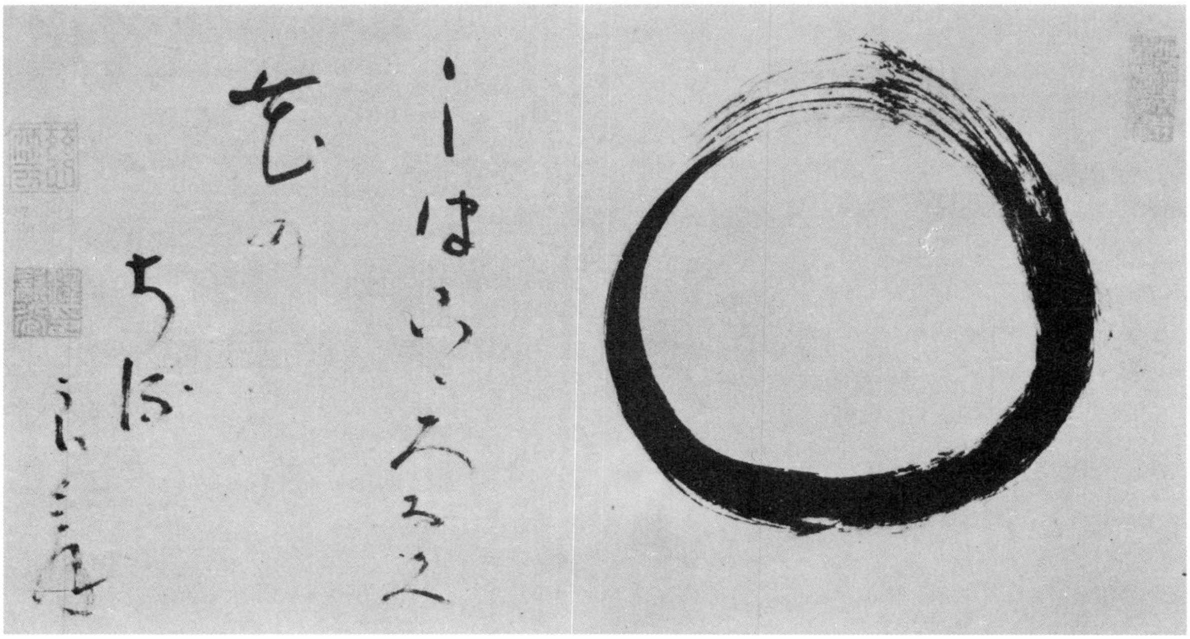

349. Circle

Ink drawing by Jiun (1718–1804); H. 31.5 cm., W. 52.9; private collection, Tokyo.

Calligraphic works of this type were often presented by a Zen master to a pupil as a concentrated statement of basic experience and insights expressed in a form that is a highly personal one but at the same time of universal validity. The writer of this piece, however, was originally a priest of the Shingon sect, a branch of Vajrayāna Buddhism, and a great authority on Sanskrit studies and the use of seed-syllables. Having embraced Zen Buddhism he could create impressive symbols using these syllables and Zen calligraphy, testifying to the intrinsic unity and common tradition of diverging types of aniconic symbolism in Mahāyāna art.

of image-worship. On the other hand, the Ch'an Buddhists shunned the use of symbolic objects or signs as 'supports' for meditation because they knew more direct methods to reach Enlightenment (Chinese: *wu*; Japanese: *satori*). It is true that early Chinese Ch'an masters of the ninth century developed systems of symbolic circles to be used in the spiritual training of monks under the guidance of their master, but these were soon discarded as being more of an obstacle than a help in reaching the goal of Enlightenment. In Ch'an Buddhism, abstract symbols are nothing but hints without any of the metaphysical reality or ritual efficacy, as ascribed to many of the Vajrayāna symbols, and in most cases they express, often in a highly individual and unconventional manner, the personal experience of one who, having already attained Enlightenment, wishes to stimulate it in others. Circles, drawn by Ch'an masters with powerful calligraphic expressiveness (Pl. 349), are taken as signifying complete perfection without beginning or end, and at the same time the emptiness of the absolute nought, both perfection and emptiness being identical with the Buddha essence as well as the real nature of the individual self. The circle is also likened to a spotless mirror reflecting everything, but in itself completely empty and undefiled. The full moon with its perfect roundness and brightness is another symbol of ultimate reality and perfect knowledge of it. The enlightened person points to the real moon (Pl. 350), but the unenlightened mind—in Ch'an paintings often exemplified by the monkey—tries instead to catch its wavering and evanescent reflection in the water.

In order to facilitate direct attainment of true reality—that is, the emptiness and non-diversity—of all existing things, Ch'an masters liked to paint, with powerful, utterly concentrat-

350. The Ch'an (Zen) saint Pu-tai (Hotei) pointing to the full moon

By Mokuan Reien (c. 1300–45); c. A.D. *1333–45; hanging scroll, ink on paper; H. 80.3 cm., W. 31.3 cm.; Atami Museum.*

Pu-tai (Japanese: Hotei) was a legendary mendicant monk who is said to have lived around A.D. 900, roaming through China carrying a knapsack, always carefree and in a good humour out of true wisdom and profound detachment from the worries of the suffering world. He was thought to be an incarnation of Maitreya, the Buddha of the future, and in Japan he became one of the Seven Gods of Good Luck. Mokuan Reien was a Japanese monk trained in Zen monasteries at Kamakura who later went on a pilgrimage to South China. There he spent the rest of his life in some of the leading Ch'an (Zen) monasteries under the guidance of great masters, studying ink painting. In this medium he created works similar to Mu-ch'i and other Ch'an painters and somehow this painting was brought to Japan. It is based on Chinese painting on the same theme, one of which, however, does show the full moon as a symbol of the Perfect Truth. Mokuan, in a more radical Ch'an interpretation, omitted this in order to show that even a symbol like this is incapable of conveying the inconceivable and that true understanding has to transcend the language of images and symbols.

351. Six Persimmons

By Mu-ch'i (died after 1269); 13th century A.D.*; ink on paper; H. 35.1 cm., W. 29.0 cm.; Ryūkō-in, Daitoku-ji, Kyoto.*

Mu-ch'i was a Chinese Ch'an (Zen) monk living in a monastery near Hangchou, one of the Ch'an centres of South China. His works or those attributed to him—exclusively ink paintings of Buddhist figures, of objects like flowers, fruit, vegetables, of animals like monkeys, tigers or dragons, and of landscapes—have been eagerly appreciated and collected by the Japanese since the fourteenth and fifteenth centuries, while in China they were neglected. Thus all these works entered Japanese collections in old Zen temples and of aristocratic families such as the Ashikaga. They are thought to be among the most successful artistic realizations of the Zen spirit because they give a radically concentrated quintessence of the inner nature of things and of true reality by grasping it with utter simplicity and directness and making it transparent by penetrating contemplation.

352. Nought (Chinese: *wu;* Japanese: *mu*)
'Ink vestige' (bokuseki) *by Shidō Bunan (1603–76); H. 33 cm., W. 46 cm.; Takekoshi Collection, Japan.*

353. 'Ink vestige' (*bokuseki*)
By Mujaku Dōchū (1653–1744), who after 1707 was abbot of the large Zen monastery of Myōshin-ji, Kyoto, Japan; ink on paper; H. 129.5 cm., W. 27.4 cm.; collection of Dietrich Seckel, Heidelberg.

ed brush-strokes, simple objects taken from everyday life and experience—flowers, fruits (Pl. 351), vegetables, stones—or highly abbreviated landscapes, because they all can, if seen with right understanding, convey the real essence in its concreteness and immediate evidence, unimpaired by theoretical reasoning or by the complicated system of imagery and symbolism. Thus it may be said that Ch'an Buddhism, in transcending traditional symbolism, raised to a higher degree of symbolism the most commonplace things, freely chosen from the sphere of daily experience. Usually, such objects are shown on an empty background, or rather 'ground', signifying the ultimate basis or true nature of all things; this may be called the most radical, most directly expressive aniconic symbol of the Buddha essence and of the 'emptiness' of Nirvana inherent in and even identical with the infinitely diversified phenomenal world. Japanese Zen masters sometimes went so far as to hang up a white sheet of paper mounted as a scroll: an empty image as an image of emptiness.

The basic ideas of Ch'an Buddhism are most impressively coined in written characters like 'Buddha', 'Enlightenment', 'Nought' (Pl. 352), 'Emptiness', 'True Reality', and in famous sayings of old masters as collected in Ch'an literature. Written with the powerful brush-strokes of enlightened personalities, they belong to the greatest works of East Asian art and represent an important type of aniconic symbolism—totally opposed to the metaphysically significant, ritually efficacious seed-syllables which, contrary to the expressive, often informal and irregular Ch'an writings, are executed with utmost precision, correctness and even cool perfection. One of the Ch'an sayings (Pi-yen-lu, Chapter 90) very clearly expresses the fundamental tendency, inherent in Buddhist thought from the very beginning, to transcend the image: 'The Universal Body has no reflection (or shadow-image)'. We reproduce it (Pl. 353) from a scroll written by the Japanese master Mujaku Dōchū (1653–1744). 'Universal Body' means the essential nature of the Buddha and of any living being; it is pervaded by an all-embracing, all-penetrating, perfectly clear and bright knowledge of the ultimate truth. Since for the enlightened mind all determinations and dualities of the phenomenal world disappear, there does not exist any longer the opposition of a body and its reflection, nor of the light and an obstacle causing a shadowy image. The negation or non-image implies a strong affirmation: what is without shadow, reflection, appearance or image, is truly real and partakes of the state of Nirvana. But it would still be an over-simplification to say that the image is the opposite of the 'Universal Body'; the word 'no' in the translation of the sentence is actually the word 'nought' (Chinese: *wu*; Japanese: *mu*), which does not express a simple negation but rather a non-statement beyond 'yes' and 'no', transcending any conceivable alternatives and expressing an insight that cannot be transmitted unless by a silent sign or an imageless image. Now we realize that between the principle, quoted at the beginning in Chapter 1 (p. 23), concerning the impossibility of conceiving and depicting the Buddha in his true nature, and the seemingly contradictory principle of making images as the only means of rendering manifest the reality of Buddhahood, there is no fundamental opposition. The relationship is a dialectical one, and between this paradoxical dialectic of image and non-image, Buddhist art has always been suspended.

APPENDICES

NOTE ON NAMES AND TECHNICAL TERMS

The original language of Buddhism as taught by Śākyamuni and first recorded by his followers is presumed to have been the local Indian dialect of the land of Magadha in the central Ganges Valley, where he spent nearly all his life. As Buddhism spread to other regions of India, local dialectical peculiarities were introduced. The earliest complete set of canonical writings is one that was produced in Sri Lanka probably in the first century B.C. This is written in an Indian dialect that has undergone various transformations in its slow progress from Magadha to the far south. This language is known as Pāli (*pāli*), the language of the sacred books, and is still the Buddhist canonical language of South-East Asian lands.

In India itself, where Buddhism has all but disappeared, various local dialects were in use during the early Buddhist centuries. However, from the first century A.D. onwards, Sanskrit, the classical language of India, came increasingly into use, and many early works were turned into Sanskrit, while new works, as typified by the enormous Mahāyāna literature, were often in this language from the start. Thus for Buddhists of northern India, of Kashmir and Nepal, of Central Asia, of Tibet, China, Korea and Japan, Sanskrit has always been the sacred Buddhist language *par excellence*, even when they translated the texts themselves into their own particular languages.

It is thus convenient in a work such as this to use Sanskrit names throughout. Many of these may be unfamiliar to our readers, but this is far simpler than using the various Tibetan, Chinese or Japanese names in the different chapters.

The Sanskrit alphabet is a simple one, scientifically arranged according to the mode of articulation of consonants, thus:

	surds		*sonants*	
	non-aspirate	*aspirate*	*non-aspirate*	*aspirate*
gutturals	k	kh	g	gh
palatals	c	ch	j	jh
dentals	t	th	d	dh
cerebrals	ṭ	ṭh	ḍ	ḍh
labials	p	ph	b	bh

	nasals	*sibilants*
gutturals	ṅ(ng)	—
palatals	ñ	ś
dentals	n	s
cerebrals	ṇ	ṣ
labials	m	—

There remain the semi-vowels: y, r, l, v; and the aspirate: h. Vowels are either long or short in the case of: a ā, i ī, u ū, e ai, o au. The semi-vowels r and l, when fully vocalized, are written ṛ and ḷ; in this work ṛ appears very rarely.

For all practical purposes the consonants may be pronounced much as in English, except that (i) c is a light 'ch' sound as in 'cheese', with which one may compare the more forceful 'ch' in 'church', and (ii) th is aspirated t-h, and ph is aspirated p-h, and in 'hot-house' and 'top-heavy'. Vowels should be pronounced pure as in German.

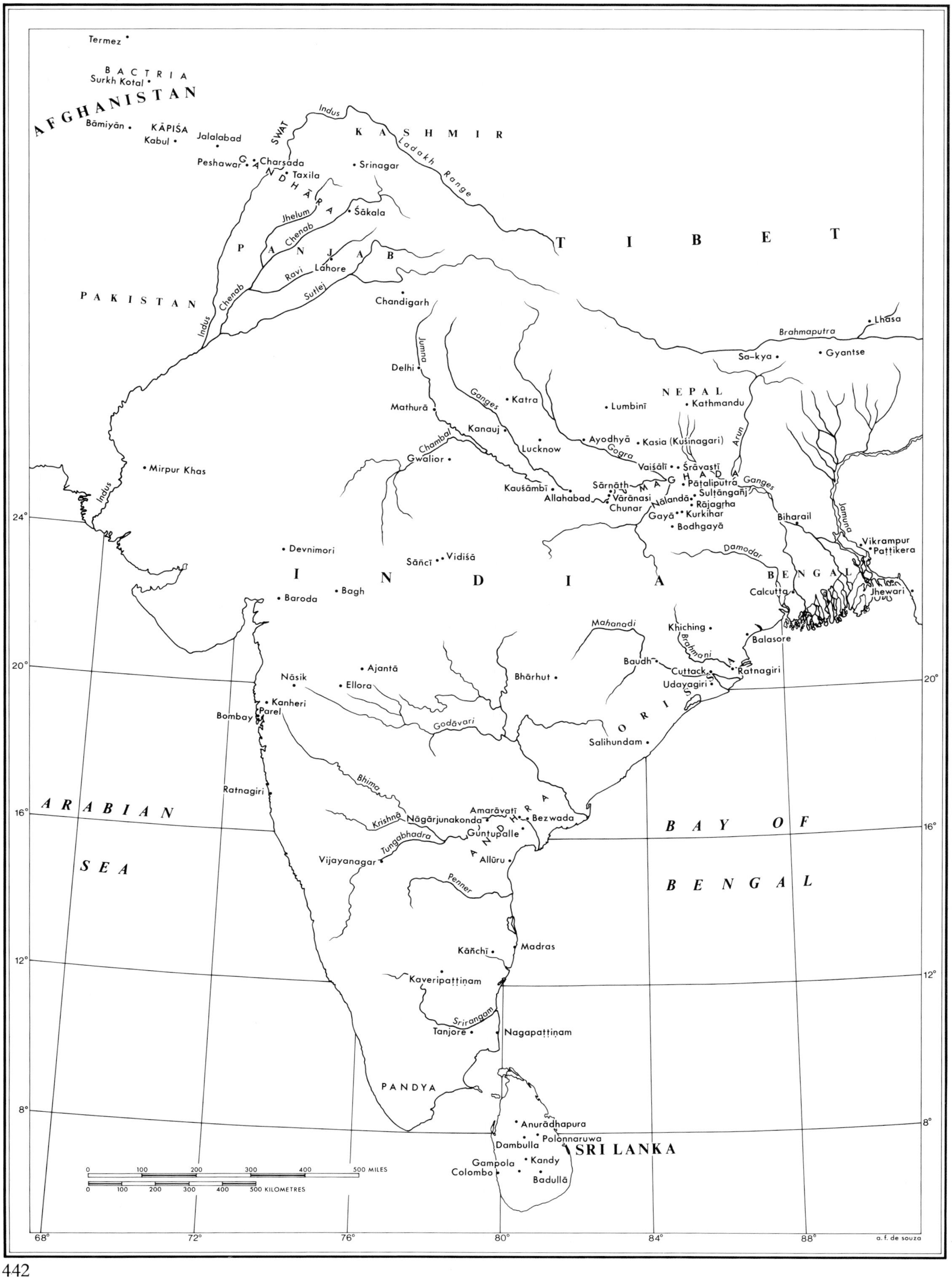
Termez
BACTRIA
Surkh Kotal
AFGHANISTAN
Bāmiyān
KĀPIŚA
Kabul
Jalalabad
SWAT
Indus
KASHMIR
Ladakh Range
Peshawar
Charsada
GANDHĀRA
Taxila
Srinagar
Jhelum
Chenab
Śākala
PANJAB
Lahore
Ravi
Sutlej
TIBET
PAKISTAN
Indus
Chenab
Chandigarh
Lhasa
Brahmaputra
Sa-kya
Gyantse
Jumna
Delhi
NEPAL
Ganges
Katra
Lumbinī
Kathmandu
Mathurā
Kanauj
Lucknow
Ayodhyā
Kasia (Kuśinagari)
Arun
Chambal
Gogra
Gwalior
Vaiśālī
Śrāvastī
Mirpur Khas
Sārnāth
MAGADHA
Pāṭaliputra
Ganges
Kauśāmbī
Vārānasi
Nālandā
Sultānganj
Allahabad
Chunar
Rājagṛha
Gayā
Kurkihar
Bodhgayā
Biharail
Jamuna
Indus
Vikrampur
Paṭṭikera
Devnimori
Damodar
Sāñcī
Vidiśā
INDIA
BENGAL
Baroda
Bagh
Calcutta
Jhewari
Mahanadi
Khiching
Balasore
Brahmani
Ajantā
Baudh
Nāsik
Ellora
Bhārhut
Cuttack
Ratnagiri
Udayagiri
Kanheri
Parel
Bombay
Godāvari
ORISSA
Salihundam
Bhima
Ratnagiri
ARABIAN
SEA
Amarāvatī
Krishnā
Nāgārjunakonda
ANDHRA
Bezwada
Guntupalle
Tungabhadra
Vijayanagar
Allūru
BAY OF
BENGAL
Penner
Kāñchī
Madras
Kaveripaṭṭinam
Srirangam
Tanjore
Nagapaṭṭinam
PANDYA
Anurādhapura
Polonnaruwa
Dambulla
SRI LANKA
Gampola
Kandy
Colombo
Badullā
0 100 200 300 400 500 MILES
0 100 200 300 400 500 KILOMETRES
24°
20°
16°
12°
8°
20°
16°
12°
8°
68°
72°
76°
80°
84°
88°
a. f. de souza

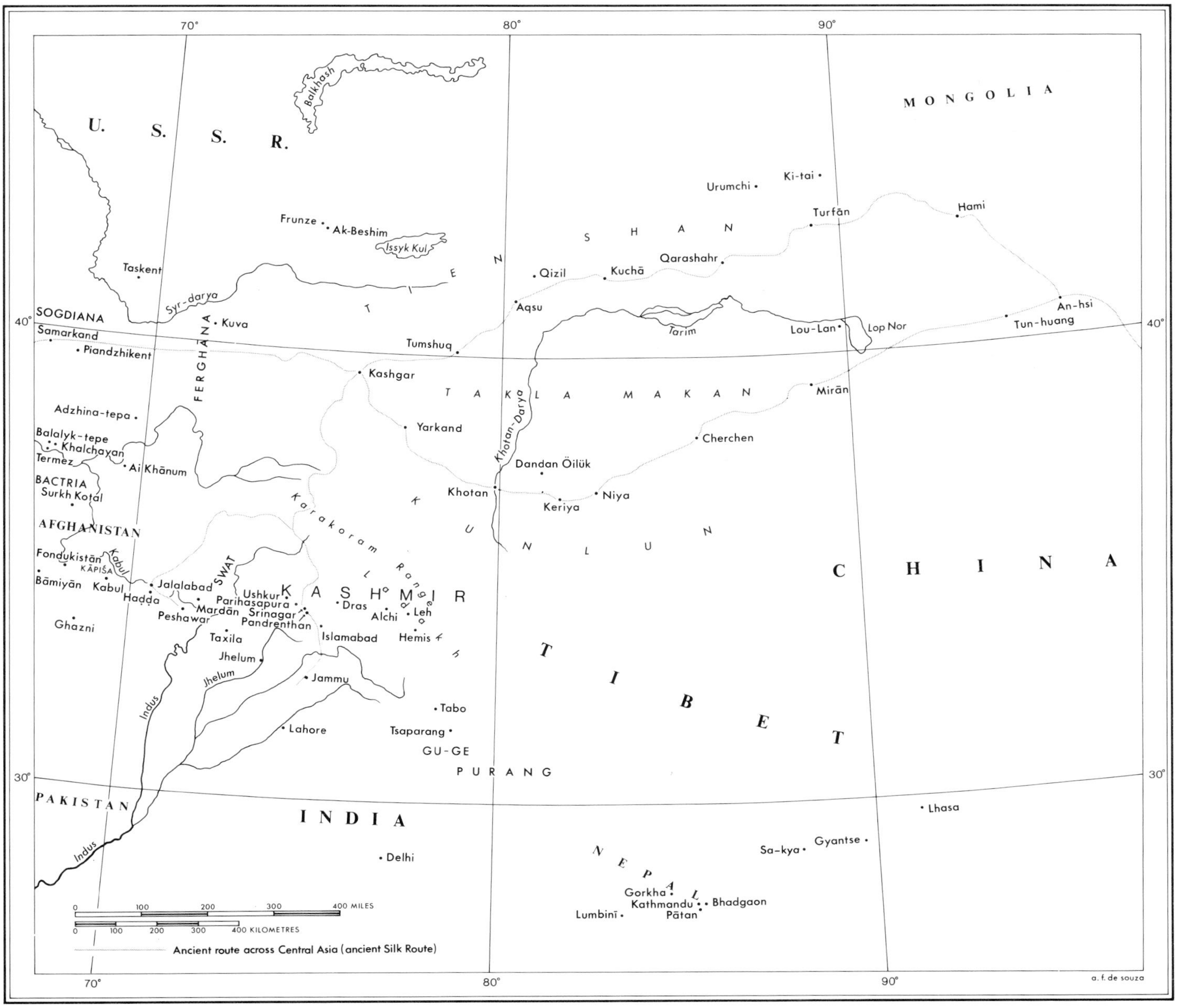

70°
80°
90°
U. S. S. R.
Balkhash
MONGOLIA
Urumchi
Ki-tai
Turfān
Hami
Frunze
Ak-Beshim
Issyk Kul
SHAN
TIEN
Qarashahr
Taskent
Qizil
Kuchā
Syr-darya
Aqsu
An-hsi
SOGDIANA
Kuva
Tarim
Lou-Lan
Lop Nor
Tun-huang
40°
Samarkand
Piandzhikent
FERGHĀNA
Tumshuq
Kashgar
TAKLA MAKAN
Mirān
Adzhina-tepa
Yarkand
Cherchen
Balalyk-tepe
Khalchayan
Termez
Ai Khānum
Khotan-Darya
Dandan Öilük
BACTRIA
Surkh Kotal
Khotan
Keriya
Niya
AFGHANISTAN
Karakoram Range
KUNLUN
Fondukistān
Kabul
KĀPIŚA
Bāmiyān
Kabul
Jalalabad
SWAT
CHINA
Hadda
Ushkur
Parihasapura
KASHMIR
Dras
Alchi
Leh
Mardān
Peshawar
Srinagar
Pandrenthan
Ghazni
Taxila
Islamabad
Hemis
Ladakh
Jhelum
Jhelum
TIBET
Jammu
Indus
Tabo
Lahore
Tsaparang
GU-GE
PURANG
30°
PAKISTAN
INDIA
Lhasa
Gyantse
Sa-kya
Indus
Delhi
NEPAL
Gorkha
Kathmandu
Bhadgaon
Lumbinī
Pātan
0 100 200 300 400 MILES
0 100 200 300 400 KILOMETRES
Ancient route across Central Asia (ancient Silk Route)
a. f. de souza

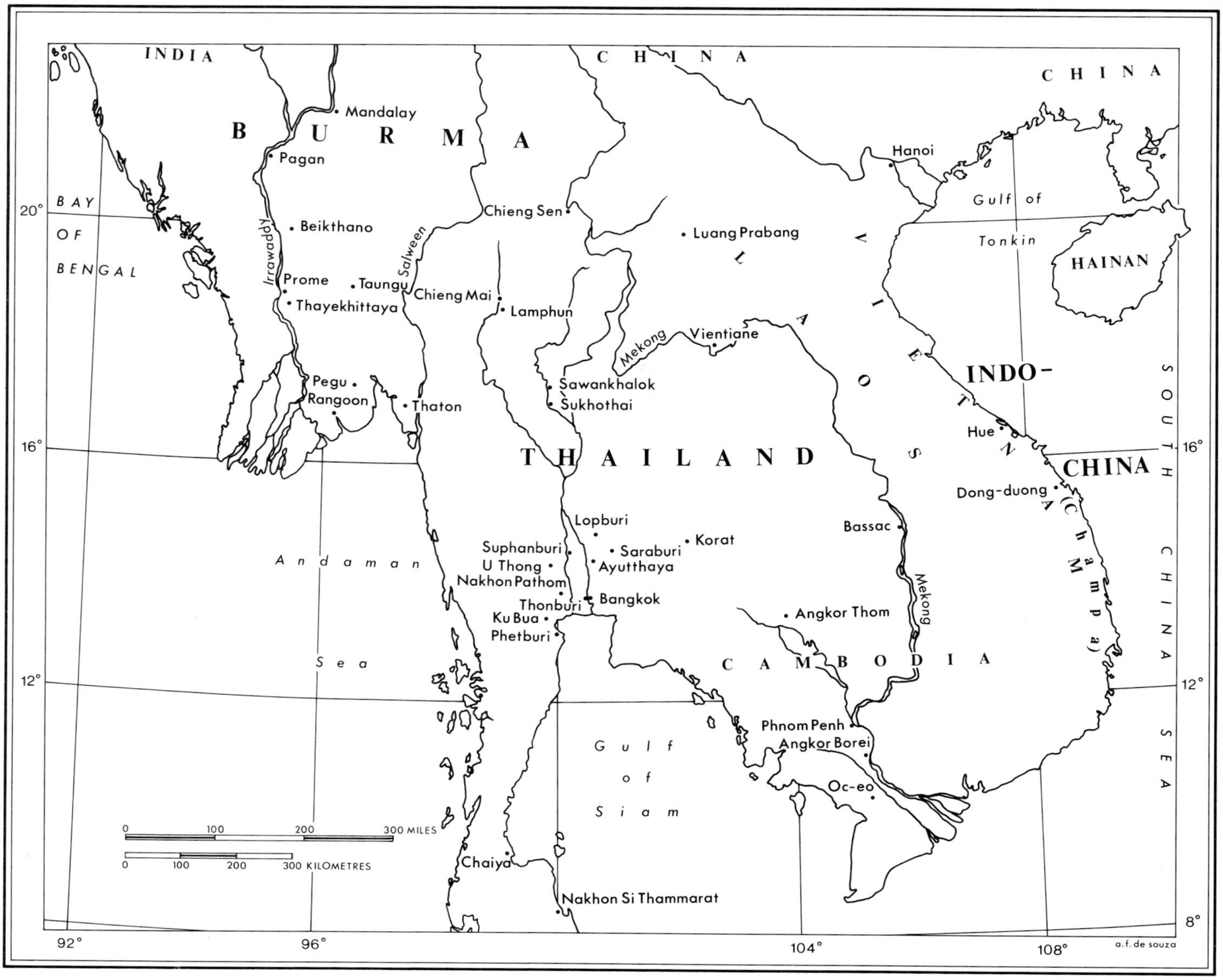
INDIA
CHINA
CHINA
BURMA
Mandalay
Pagan
Hanoi
Gulf of Tonkin
HAINAN
BAY OF BENGAL
20°
Chieng Sen
Luang Prabang
Beikthano
Irrawaddy
Salween
Prome
Taungu
Thayekhittaya
Chieng Mai
Lamphun
LAOS
VIETNAM (Champa)
Mekong
Vientiane
INDO-CHINA
SOUTH CHINA SEA
Pegu
Rangoon
Thaton
Sawankhalok
Sukhothai
Hue
16°
THAILAND
Dong-duong
Lopburi
Korat
Bassac
Suphanburi
Saraburi
U Thong
Ayutthaya
Andaman Sea
Nakhon Pathom
Thonburi
Bangkok
Angkor Thom
Ku Bua
Phetburi
CAMBODIA
12°
Phnom Penh
Angkor Borei
Gulf of Siam
Oc-eo
0
100
200
300 MILES
0
100
200
300 KILOMETRES
Chaiya
Nakhon Si Thammarat
8°
92°
96°
104°
108°
a.f. de souza

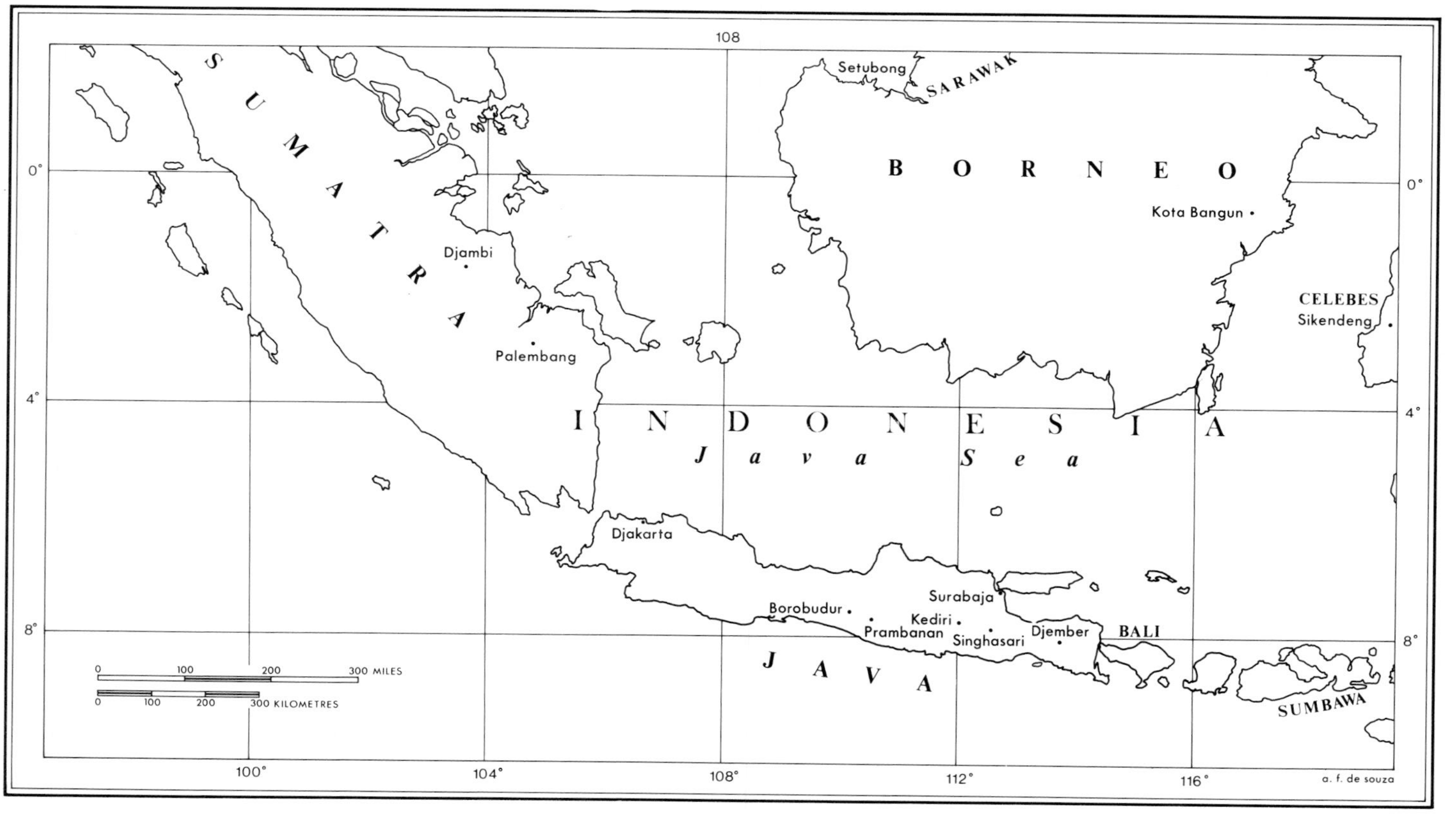
108
Setubong
SARAWAK
SUMATRA
BORNEO
0°
Kota Bangun
Djambi
CELEBES
Sikendeng
Palembang
4°
INDONESIA
Java Sea
Djakarta
Surabaja
Borobudur
Kediri
Prambanan
Singhasari
Djember
BALI
8°
JAVA
SUMBAWA
0
100
200
300 MILES
0
100
200
300 KILOMETRES
100°
104°
108°
112°
116°
a. f. de souza

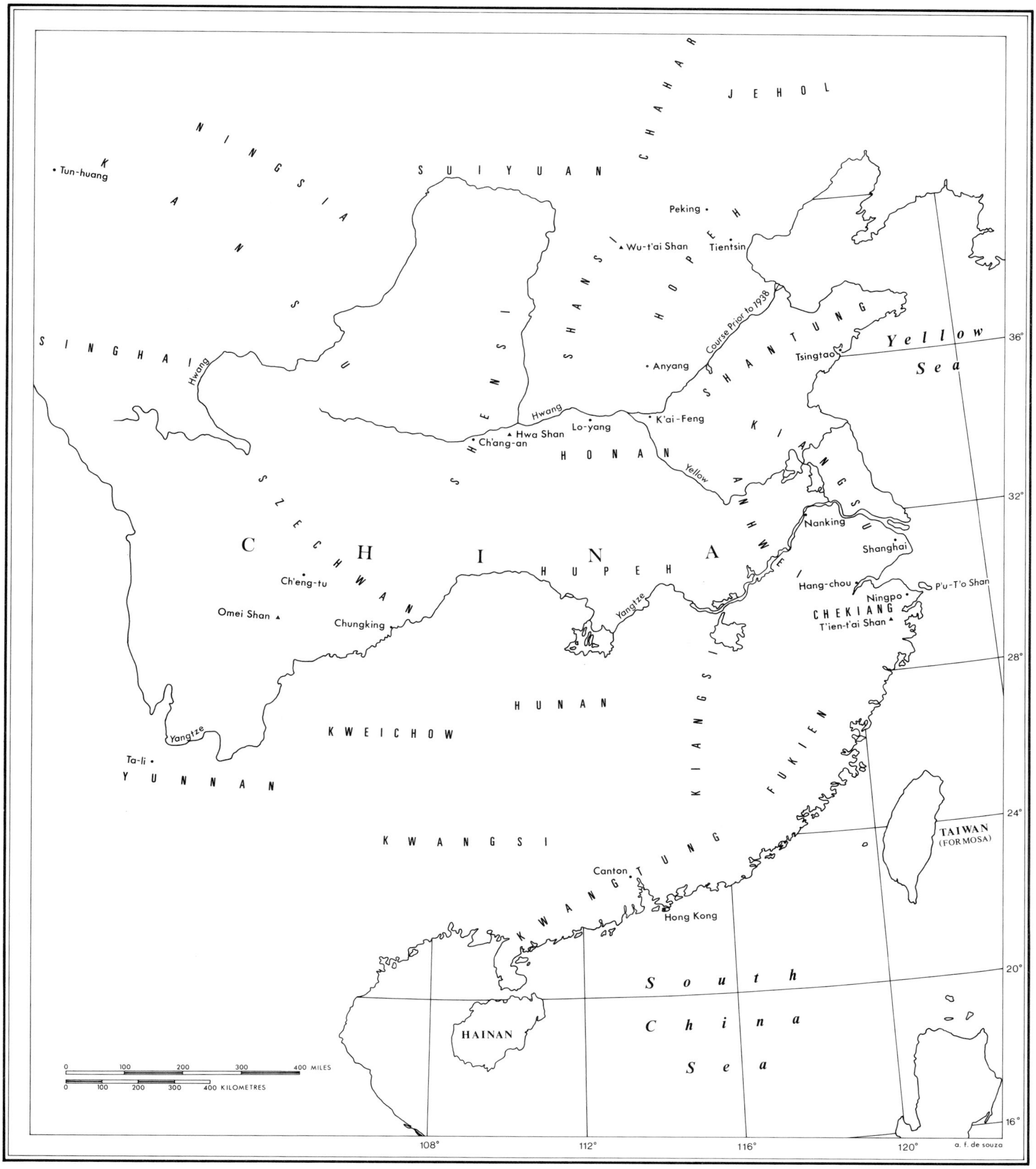
JEHOL
CHAHAR
SUIYUAN
NINGSIA
KANSU
Tun-huang
TSINGHAI
Hwang
SHENSI
SHANSI
HOPEH
Peking
Wu-t'ai Shan
Tientsin
Course Prior to 1938
SHANTUNG
Tsingtao
Yellow Sea
Anyang
K'ai-Feng
Hwang
Lo-yang
Hwa Shan
Ch'ang-an
HONAN
Yellow
KIANGSU
ANHWEI
Nanking
Shanghai
SZECHWAN
CHINA
Ch'eng-tu
HUPEH
Omei Shan
Chungking
Yangtze
Hang-chou
P'u-T'o Shan
Ningpo
CHEKIANG
T'ien-t'ai Shan
HUNAN
KWEICHOW
Yangtze
Ta-li
YUNNAN
KIANGSI
FUKIEN
KWANGSI
TAIWAN
(FORMOSA)
Canton
KWANGTUNG
Hong Kong
South China Sea
HAINAN
0 100 200 300 400 MILES
0 100 200 300 400 KILOMETRES
36°
32°
28°
24°
20°
16°
108°
112°
116°
120°
a. f. de souza

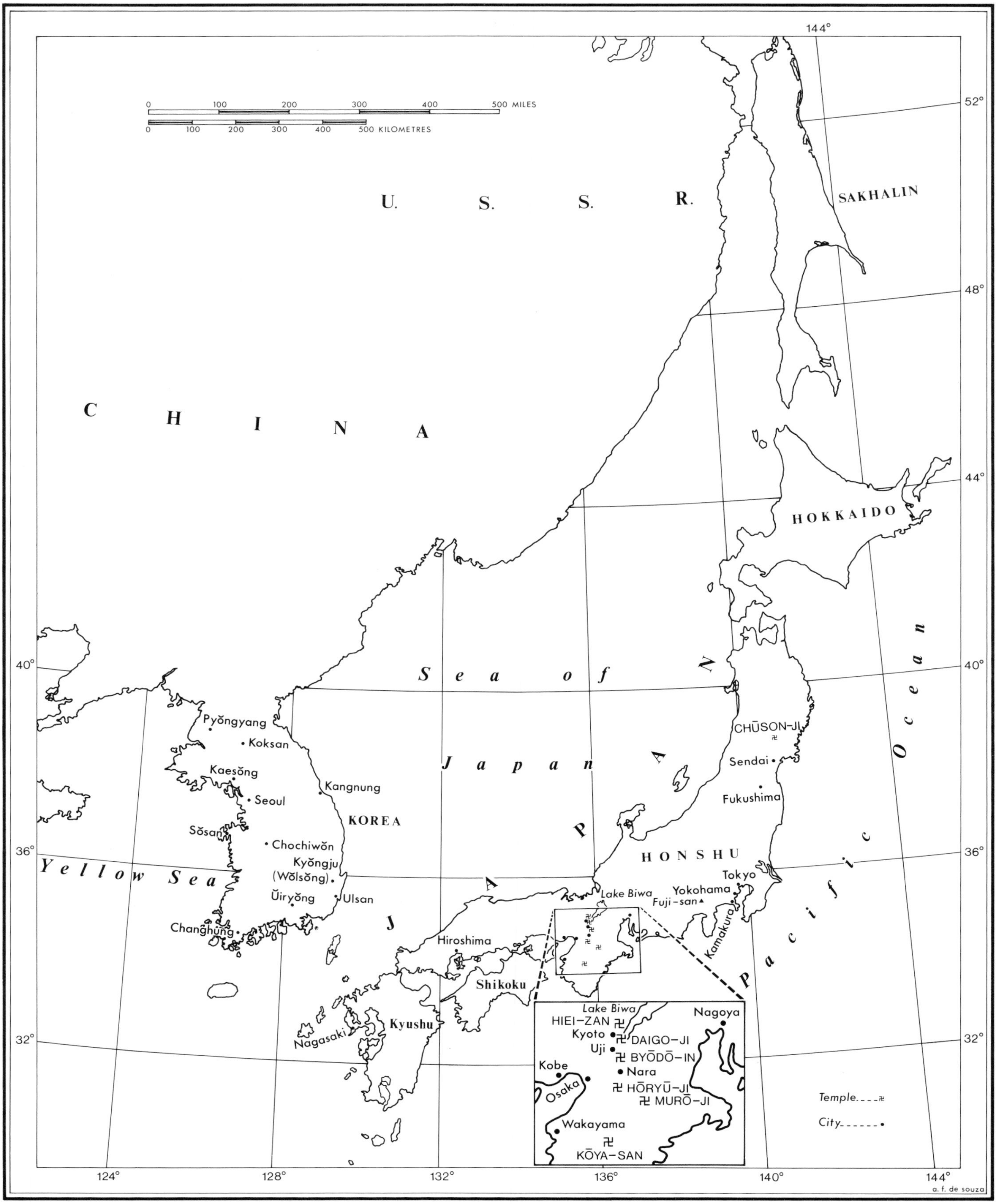

0 100 200 300 400 500 MILES
0 100 200 300 400 500 KILOMETRES
U. S. S. R.
SAKHALIN
C H I N A
HOKKAIDO
Sea of Japan
JAPAN
Pacific Ocean
Pyŏngyang
Koksan
Kaesŏng
Seoul
Kangnung
KOREA
Sŏsan
Chochiwŏn
Kyŏngju
(Wŏlsŏng)
Ŭiryŏng
Ulsan
Changhŭng
Yellow Sea
CHŪSON-JI
Sendai
Fukushima
HONSHU
Tokyo
Yokohama
Fuji-san
Kamakura
Lake Biwa
Hiroshima
Shikoku
Kyushu
Nagasaki
Lake Biwa
HIEI-ZAN
Kyoto
DAIGO-JI
Uji
BYŌDŌ-IN
Nara
Kobe
Osaka
HŌRYŪ-JI
MURŌ-JI
Wakayama
KŌYA-SAN
Nagoya
Temple
City
124° 128° 132° 136° 140° 144°
32° 36° 40° 44° 48° 52°
a. f. de souza

GLOSSARY

The terms occurring here are Sanskrit, since Pāli names and terms have usually been given throughout the book in their corresponding Sanskrit form.

abhaya
'Fearlessness'; see *mudrā*, where it refers to a hand-gesture suggesting the act of blessing.

abhiṣeka
Sprinkling water on the head of a person as a purificatory or initiating ritual act, thus connected with birth rites (compare Christian baptism) and with regal consecrations, etc. In later Buddhism, it refers to a complex rite of initiation into esoteric teachings and mystic identification with the essence of Buddhahood.

akṣara
A syllable (of the Sanskrit 'alphabet', which is really a syllabary, since every consonant sign includes the inherent vowel *a*, unless the appropriate vowel sign above or below the 'letter' indicates another inherent vowel, e.g., *i*, *u*, *e*, *o*).

ālaya-vijñāna
'Fundamental consciousness', understood as a kind of psychological basis for the ever-fluctuating personality of living beings. This is a comparatively late Buddhist concept, propagated mainly by the school known as Cittamātra ('Thought Only'), or as Vijñānavāda ('Consciousness School') (q.v.).

ambuja-pīṭha
A lotus flower base

aṇḍa
An egg, or egg-shaped, hence a dome (of a stupa).

antaravāsaka (for a Buddhist monk and so also for a Buddha)
Lower garment.

arhat (Arhat)
Literally 'worthy', used as a title of Śākyamuni and of the foremost of his monks who reached the state of Nirvana. The state of 'Arhatship' in this way represents the goal of the first disciples (*śrāvaka*).

āsana
a) seat, throne, base; e.g., *simhāsana*, a lion throne; *padmāsana*, a lotus throne or one with a lotus flower base; *vajrāsana*, the Diamond or Adamantine Seat under the Tree of Enlightenment at Bodhgayā, where all Buddhas gain Enlightenment.
b) sitting posture; e.g., *bhadrāsana*, sitting in the 'European' fashion; *lalitāsana*, sitting with one leg hanging down; *vajrāsana* (see also just above), sitting as a Buddha sits under the Tree of Enlightenment, i.e., in meditation, cross-legged with the soles of the feet turned upwards; *vīrāsana* (q.v.), the same posture.

aṣṭadhātu
An alloy composed of 'eight elements', of which the chief are copper, lead and tin, compounded with iron, zinc, antimony, silver and gold.

āśīsa-mudrā
A gesture of benediction and the term chosen to describe the hand-gesture peculiar to standing images in Sri Lanka (see Pl. 95) (Sanskrit: *āśis*, 'blessing'). The term *mudrā* (Pāli: *muddā*) is not in current usage in Theravāda Buddhism.

aśvatta
The pipal tree (*Ficus religiosa*) under which Buddhas gain Enlightenment, especially the famous example at Bodhgayā.

avadāna
'Heroic exploit', used of Buddhist stories about the 'lives' of Bodhisattvas, as they progress through a whole series of existences towards Buddhahood. Compare *jātaka* (q.v.).

āyāgapaṭa
A dedicatory plaque; see p. 54.

bāhā, bāhī
Newār form of *vihāra* (q.v.).

bhadrāsana
See *āsana*.

bhagavat
Nominative singular: *bhagavān*. Both forms appear in European works. The term literally means 'possessing a good share of things', thus 'blessed'. Used as an honorific title of address, it corresponds to our term 'Lord' in classical and religious usage. Kings, gods, and thus the Buddha are also so addressed.

bhakti
'Devotion', especially here religious devotion as directed towards the person of a particular Buddha or Bodhisattva.

bhikṣu
'Religious mendicant'. In so far as the Buddhists gradually established themselves in settled monastic communities, 'monk' becomes an appropriate translation.

bhūmisparśa-mudrā
The gesture of touching the earth. See also *mudrā* and Māravijaya for the rationale of this particular gesture.

bīja
'Seed', here meant in the sense of a mystic syllable (*akṣara*, q.v.), hence 'seed-syllable', the enunciation of which gives birth to a particular divine being; see p. 431.

bodhi
'Enlightenment', found in many compounds, e.g., *bodhivṛkṣa*, the Tree of Enlightenment, often written as Bo tree (or bodhi tree) in European works; *bodhimaṇḍa*, the place of the Enlightenment; *bodhighara*, an enshrined tree, see p. 43.

bodhisattva (Bodhisattva)
A living being (*sattva*) who has made the vow to achieve Enlightenment (*bodhi*), hence a being who is on the way towards Buddhahood, or who, being already worthy of Buddhahood, manifests himself in one of the worlds for the sake of helping other living beings. Śākyamuni is called '*bodhisattva*' under both these aspects. Stories of Bodhisattvas under the first aspect are told in the *jātaka* and *avadāna* (q.v.), while the second aspect is typical of the Mahāyāna (see pp. 85–86).

bodhyagrī-mudrā
See *mudrā*.

buddha (Buddha)
Grammatically the perfect participle of the verb '*budh*', 'to wake up'; *buddha*, meaning the A-woken One, the Enlightened One, can be used of any enlightened sage. In Buddhism, however, the term is reserved for the supreme state of transcendence as achieved by the great teachers of the past and of the present, of this world and of other worlds in the various quarters of the universe. The use of the term to refer exclusively to Śākyamuni as though he were the one and only Buddha is largely a recent Western habit. See pp. 14–19.

buddhapāda
Buddha footprints, usually of Śākyamuni.

caitya

The Sanskrit 'c' is pronounced rather as the English 'ch' in such a word as 'pitcher'. Thus this term is sometimes written in English works as 'chaitya', and in any case it should be pronounced more or less in this way. It means primarily a shrine, including sacred objects such as special trees or heaps of stones (cairns) and also stupas. Thus, in later Buddhist usage, it is often used as a synonym for stupa. The rock-cut shrines with a stupa within them are often referred to as '*caitya* halls'. In Nepal, the term is regularly used with the meaning of stupa, usually in the Newār form of *cībā*. In Thailand *caitya* has been corrupted to *cedi* (see Pl. 322).

cakra

'Wheel'; see *dharmacakra.*

cakrastambha

A pillar topped with the symbol of a wheel.

cakravartin

Literally, 'a turner of the wheel', i.e., a world-emperor, who is maybe thought of as revolving everywhere like the sun. It has been suggested that the idea entered India with the 'myth' of Alexander the Great. The concept was taken up in Buddhism in so far as a Buddha who is a world-teacher is thought of as the equivalent of a *cakravartin* in the religious sphere.

caṅkrama

A path for walking; see p. 33.

Cūḷavaṃsa

A sequel to the *Mahāvaṃsa* (q.v.), it is an historical chronicle of Sri Lanka in three parts, beginning at the end of the twelfth century (the reign of Parākramabāhu I) and continuing up to the annexation of the kingdom by England.

deva (*devī*) (Deva)

A god (goddess).

devatā

A divine being, male or female.

dhāraṇī

An Indian sacred formula composed of mystic syllables, which holds or comprehends (*dhāranī* derives from a verbal root '*dhṛ*', 'to hold') the essence of a teaching or of a particular Buddha or Bodhisattva, when the term may become identical in meaning with *mantra* (q.v.). Their use has been widespread in Mahāyāna and Vajrayāna. The Tibetans usually preserve these 'spells' in their original Sanskrit form. In Far Eastern Buddhism, they are written in *siddhām* script or in Chinese characters.

dharma

A real or true thing or state of affairs. In Buddhist usage the term is used of a Buddha's teaching, conceived of as the final and absolute truth, or in philosophical language in the sense of the real elemental particles that make up the sum total of ephemeral existence (*saṃsāra*, q.v.).

dharmacakra

The 'Wheel of the Dharma (q.v.)', a Buddhist adaptation of the imperial wheel symbol (see *cakravartin*), expressing the absolute universality of Buddhist doctrine and the Buddha's dominion.

dharmacakra-(pravartana-)mudrā

'Turning the Wheel of the Doctrine', a Buddhist expression of his universal power through his preaching of the doctrine. This is represented in iconography by a particular hand-gesture; see *mudrā* and Pls. 257, 280.

dharmadhātu

'The Elemental Sphere', the sum total of existence as represented by the sphere (*dhātu*) of all the elements (*dharma*). Since, in Mahāyāna teaching, the whole *saṃsāra* is essentially immersed in Nirvana, *dharmadhātu* becomes yet another term for the absolute.

dharmakāya

'Dharma Body', where 'Body' must be understood rather in the platonic sense of 'form'. This is the transcendental 'form' of Buddhahood into which a Buddha 'disappears' when he abandons a physical body (see *nirmāṇakāya*).

dharmapāla

'Guardian of the Doctrine', as referring to local fierce divinities of various kinds who have been taken into the Buddhist fold as powerful protectors. *Dvārapāla* (q.v.) are just such 'guardians' who are placed at the entrance of temples, mandalas, etc. *Lokapāla* (q.v.) is a more elevated title for much the same function.

dhātu

In Buddhist usage this term has the meaning of 'essence' or of 'sphere of operation'. In the former meaning it comes to mean 'holy relics' and occurs in the corrupted form of *dāgaba*, derived from *dhātu-garbha* (see *garbha*). In its other more widely applied meaning it occurs in *dharmadhātu* (q.v.) and in *Vajradhātu* (the Vajra Sphere) and *Garbhadhātu* (the Embryonic Sphere), especially as referring to sets of mandalas, well known in Japanese and Tibetan tradition, which centre on Vairocana. See Pl. 202.

dhyāna

Meditation, or concentration of thought, as part of religious discipline (Chin.: *ch'an*; Jap.: *zen*).

dhyānāsana

The manner of sitting cross-legged and composed for the practice of *dhyāna* (q.v.). See also *āsana*.

dhyāni-buddha (Dyāni-buddha)

See *jina* and *tathāgata*.

dvārapāla

Door-guardian.

garbha

'Womb', or in a more philosophical sense 'embryonic sphere'. In this sense the term is applied to the stupa (see p. 33) and is found in the popular Sinhalese name for a stupa, viz. *dāgaba*, which can be interpreted as 'the embryonic sphere of the holy person as represented by his sacred relics' (see *dhātu*). For *garbhadhātu*, see also *dhātu*.

garuḍa

The king of the birds, an Indian mythological creature.

hīnayāna (Hīnayāna)

'Inferior Way'. The term used by the followers of the Mahāyāna in order to deprecate the earlier teachings as expressed in the 'Way of the Disciples' (Śrāvakayāna). There were several such sects, but only the Theravāda survives to this day.

jātaka

'Birth story' in the special sense of a story of Śākyamuni's actions in previous lives, with special reference to the law of *karma* and hence to rebirth.

jina (Jina)

'Conqueror', used also as the title of leading religious figures, especially by the Jains, who refer to Mahāvīra, the Jina of the present age, and his predecessors by this title. Jain (Sanskrit: *jaina*) is in fact an adjectival form derived from *jina*. However, just as the term '*buddha*', although appropriated especially by the followers of Śākyamuni as his primary title, may be used in its usual sense of 'enlightened' by any other religious group, so the term '*jina*', while appropriated by the Jains, may be used in its usual sense of 'conqueror' by non-Jains. Thus Śākyamuni and other Buddhas are referred to as 'conquerors', and the term is used for the five cosmic Buddhas, who may be known as the Five Tathāgatas (q.v.) or the Five Jinas. In European works, this set is sometimes referred to as the Five Dyāni-buddhas, but this terms seems to lack traditional authority and is of some doubtfully late Nepalese origin. Brian Hodgson, British Resident in Nepal during the first part of the nineteenth century, brought it into currency.

kalpa

An enormous period of time covering the age of one universe, and conceived of as following one after another in an endless series of conflagration and re-manifestation.

kaparda
'Snail-shell', used to describe twisting curls and sometimes a type of top-knot on a Buddha head; see Pl. 29. The adjective *kapardin* may be used to describe such an iconographical type.

karma
'Act', in the special sense of a moral act that influences the course of one's life and one's eventual state of rebirth in accordance with its moral or immoral quality.

karuṇā
'Compassion', a primary quality of a Bodhisattva; see p. 54.

kinnara
A heavenly being, half bird and half man.

lakṣaṇa
A 'mark' or 'sign', specifically the 32 primary marks of a *mahāpuruṣa* (q.v.) as applied to a Buddha; see p. 48.

lalitāsana
An easy and graceful sitting posture, with the body slightly inclined with one leg drawn in and the other resting on some base such as a lotus flower or a cushion; see Pl. 222.

lokapāla
'Guardian of the Regions', the name of a guardian divinity usually of one of the four quarters of the compass. Local divinities, such as *yakṣa* (q.v.), were often co-opted by the early Buddhists to serve this function. Cf. *dharmapāla* and *dvārapāla*.

mādhyamika (Mādhyamika)
A Mahāyāna philosophical school; see pp. 86–87.

mahāpuruṣa
A pre-Buddhist religious concept of a kind of 'heavenly man', literally meaning 'Great Man'. The early followers of Śākyamuni conceived of him and by implication of all previous Buddhas as pre-eminent examples of *mahāpuruṣa*. The concepts relating to this term, especially the 32 primary marks (*lakṣaṇa*, q.v.) and the 80 secondary marks, greatly enriched early Buddhological notions, which were not without influence on iconography. See pp. 48, 54.

mahāyāna (Mahāyāna)
The 'Great Vehicle', which offers the Bodhisattva path towards ultimate Buddhahood to all living beings who are disposed to raise their aspirations so high, as opposed to the Hīnayāna (q.v.), which limits Buddhist aspirations to the goal of *arhat* (q.v.). It is usually assumed that the Mahāyāna is a comparatively late development (approximately the beginning of the Christian era), but its main concepts relate to the earliest Buddhological conceptions of the Buddha idea as applied to Śākyamuni himself. See pp. 15–17.

Mahāvaṃsa
A religious, quasi-historical chronicle produced in the Pāli language in Sri Lanka probably in the sixth century, describing the fortunes of Buddhism in India from the Theravādin standpoint up to the time of its entry into Sri Lanka and from then on its subsequent history there.

makara
A mythological sea-monster.

maṇḍala (mandala)
'A circle', specifically a circular diagram incorporating divinities or sacred symbols, arranged symmetrically in accordance with instructions given in religious texts known as *tantra* (q.v.) or in the liturgies based upon them. See p. 137.

mandara
The Japanese form of *maṇḍala*.

mantra
A spell consisting of mystic syllables or short invocations; see p. 431.

mantrayāna (Mantrayāna)
'Mantra Way', a synonym for Vajrayāna (q.v.).

māravijaya (Māravijaya)

'Victory over Māra', used especially in Thailand to describe the scene of Śākyamuni's victory over the Evil One immediately before his Enlightenment. Śākyamuni called the earth-goddess to witness by touching the ground, thus making the *bhūmisparśa-mudrā* (q.v.), the 'earth-touching' gesture, which more than any other iconographic type represents the moment of his Enlightenment at Gayā. As such he came to be known as *akṣobhya*, 'Imperturbable', despite the attacks of Māra, and as a proper name, Akṣobhya came to signify the Buddha of the eastern quarter. See p. 135.

mucilinda/mucalinda (Mucilinda/Mucalinda)

The name of a tree, or of a pond, and especially of a *nāga* king who is supposed to have sheltered Śākyamuni from a heavy rainstorm during his meditation in the sixth week following his Enlightenment.

mudrā

A gesture, especially used here in the sense of a hand-gesture suggesting a particular activity of a Buddha or Bodhisattva, e.g., *abhaya-mudrā,* the gesture of bestowing fearlessness or confidence (see Pl. 29); *bodhyagrī-mudrā*, the gesture of the 'peak of Enlightenment' (e.g., Pl. 180); *bhūmisparśa-mudrā*, the gesture of touching the earth (e.g., Pls. 203–208 and see also *māravijaya* above); *dharmacakra-(pravartana-)mudrā*, the gesture of (turning) the Wheel of the Doctrine (e.g., Pl. 42 and see also *dharmacakra* above); *dhyāna-mudrā*, the gesture of meditation (e.g., Pl. 59); *varada-* or *dāna-mudrā,* the gesture of giving or generosity (e.g., Pl. 87); *vitarka*-or *vyākhāna-mudrā*, the gesture of elucidation or explanation.

mūlasarvāstivāda (Mūlasarvāstivāda)

A branch of the Sarvāstivāda (q.v.).

nāga

A serpent, especially a serpent divinity.

nirmāṇakāya

'Manifest Body' or 'Phenomenal Body', as displayed by Śākyamuni or any other Buddha who appears in our world or in any other world as imagined by the Buddhists. The translation 'human form' would do, were it not for the fact that the Buddhas can appear in other forms to suit other forms of existence, especially as gods, titans and animals. Compare *dharmakāya* and *sambhogakāya.* See especially pp. 22, 138.

nirvāṇa (Nirvana)

See *samsāra.*

padmāsana

See *āsana.*

pagoda

The European term for a tall temple of several tiered roofs, such as are still found in Kerala (South India) and the Kangra Valley (North-West India) and are still flourishing especially in Nepal, which has preserved so much else of earlier Indian cultural forms. The style was taken from North-West India to China and Japan, where it was much transformed. For the origin of the term itself, see p. 420, note 3. In Burma, the same term has been used by Europeans to refer to the Burmese type of stupa.

pāli (Pāli)

An early Indian language; see Theravāda.

pañcāṅgagulika

'Five-fingered'; see p. 44.

paribhogika

'Serving a purpose'; see p. 44.

paridhāna

A garment, especially covering the lower part of the body, as worn by layfolk and also by Bodhisattvas (see Pls. 90, 135). Cf. *antaravāsaka.*

parinirvāṇa
Complete or Final Nirvana, specifically the Great Decease of Śākyamuni at Kuśinagara (Kasia). See p. 18.

prabhāmaṇḍala
'Circle of light', hence 'halo'.

pradakṣiṇā
The clockwise walking around or circumambulation by a devotee of a shrine, holy person, or holy image in order to show respect.

prajnā
'Wisdom', often pairing with *upaya*, 'means', as the feminine co-efficient of Enlightenment (*bodhi*). See pp. 273, 416, 425.

Prajñāpāramitā
'Perfection of Wisdom', referring especially to the ten perfections (*pāramitā*) which a Bodhisattva must achieve, and of which the 'Perfection of Wisdom' is all important. This name also refers to a whole class of philosophical dogmatics (see pp. 86–87, and for more information Conze in the Bibliography) and also to the goddess 'Perfection of Wisdom', who symbolizes the supreme wisdom of the Buddhas.

pratyeka-buddha (Pratyeka-buddha)
A Buddha who gains Enlightenment for himself, and who therefore does not teach.

pūjā
'Worship'.

pūrṇaghaṭa
'Vase of abundance'; see p. 27.

sādhana
Literally, 'the act of accomplishment', it refers in religious terms to a rite that renders the divinity of one's choice present to one with the result that one's aspirations are fulfilled through the intermediacy of one's chosen divinity and those of his entourage. A mandala is drawn and the appropriate spells (*mantra*) and gestures (*mudrā*) performed with precisely such an intention.

śakti
'Potency', referring in Hindu *tantras* to the feminine partner as active principle of the main divinities. The term is often used wrongly by modern writers for the feminine partner of the great tantric divinities in Buddhism. Here, however, the correct term is *prajñā* (q.v.), regarded as the quiescent principle, while the male divinity, referred to in this context as 'means' (*upaya*), represents the active principle. The mutual relationship of the pair is thus the reverse of the Hindu divinities.

samādhi
'Composure' or concentration of the mind in meditation, as represented iconographically by the *dhyāna-mudrā* (see *mudrā*).

sambhogakāya
Literally 'Body of Enjoyment', the glorified form of Buddha manifestation; see p. 138.

saṃsāra
Worldly existence conceived in the Buddhist sense of a perpetual series of rebirths and re-evolving universes, from which only *nirvāṇa* (the 'extinction' of the whole miserable process) offers final release (*mokṣa*).

saṅgha
'Community', specifically the Buddhist religious order. Buddha, *dharma* (q.v.) and *saṅgha* make up the *triratna*, the 'Three Gems' or 'Three Treasures'.

saṅghārāma
A Buddhist monastery.

saṅghāṭi
The outer monastic cloak.

sarvāstivāda (Sarvāstivāda)

An early Buddhist school, no longer surviving, but well known from early Buddhist literature and especially from the works of the great fourth-century exponent, Vasubandhu. Compare Theravāda;-*vādin* (-vādin), a follower of that school.

satori

The Japanese word for Enlightenment, a term popularized in the West by Zen teachings.

śūnyatā

'The void', emptiness of all characteristic marks, refering to the absolutely ineffable nature of the Buddha state and concurrently of all phenomenal appearances. A concept particularly pleasing to the Mādhyamikas (q.v.).

siraspota

The name given in Sri Lanka to the ornament in the form of a flame that surrounds the *uṣṇīṣa* (q.v.), thus representing the light of supreme knowledge.

śrāvakayāna (Śrāvakayāna)

'The Way of the Early Disciples', contrasted with the Pratyeka-buddhayāna (Way of the Lone Buddhas) and the Bodhisattvayāna or Mahāyāna (q.v.).

stūpa (stupa)

A tumulus, funeral mound, and especially a royal grave-mound, as was raised over Śākyamuni's relics. Hence it becomes the symbol of his *dharmakāya* (q.v.) and the primary Buddhist monument.

sūtra (sutra)

A religious discourse. In Buddhism the term is used for discourses that are attributed to Śākyamuni or some other Buddha.

tantra

A religious discourse. The term is adopted in later Buddhism to differentiate the discourses that are attributed to a single preaching Buddha from those that emanate from a circle (*maṇḍala*, q.v.) of divinities of whom a tantric-style Buddha emanation (e.g., Vairocana in his fivefold form, Heruka as the fierce manifestation of Akṣobhya, etc.) is the chief. There can be no clear dividing line, and thus some texts such as the *Sarvatathāgatatattvasaṃgraha* (see p. 135) are classed in different traditions as either *sūtra* or *tantra*. The term *tantra* has recently come to be used in Western circles in the sense of Vajrayāna but in the vague sense of such largely incomprehending Westernizations.

tathāgata (Tathāgata)

'He who has reached such a state (of perfection)', i.e., a Buddha. This is a very early title for a Buddha, and in the early canonical literature Śākyamuni uses it of himself, speaking in the third person. The term becomes a synonym for a Buddha, and is used especially in the later Buddhist concept, *pañcatathāgata*, the Five Buddhas or Tathāgatas. See pp. 16–17, 135–37.

theravāda (Theravāda)

The only surviving one of a number of early Buddhist schools, conventionally listed as eighteen; -*vādin* (-vādin), a follower of this school. Reaching Sri Lanka probably as early as the third century B.C., its followers took the 'scriptures' with them mainly in oral form. They were committed systematically to writing in the first century B.C., still in the Indian dialectical form in which they had been transmitted orally. Known then as the 'book' (*pāli*) just as the Greek *byblos* ('book') came to mean exclusively 'Bible', the term *pāli* came to be applied to the actual language in which they are written.

toraṇa

A decorative top-piece, made either of wood or of worked metal or stone, placed over a gateway or doorway, especially over the entrances to shrines. It can also mean the gateway itself.

tribhaṅga

Literally, 'triply bent', i.e., at the neck, the waist and one knee, a particular stance, see Pl. 215.

Tripiṭaka

'Three Baskets', a general term for the canonical collection of Buddhist scriptures.

triratna
See *saṅgha*.
triśūla
Trident.
uddeśika
'Indicating', as a stupa indicates or commemorates a particular event at a particular place; see p. 44.
upāya
'Means'; see *prajñā*.
ūrṇā
'Beauty-spot'; see p. 54.
uṣṇīṣa
'Wisdom-bump'; see pp. 75–76.
uttarāsaṅga (of a monk, so also of a Buddha) and *uttarīya* (of a layman or Bodhisattva)
Upper garment.
vajra
Divine weapon indicating overwhelming power, as attributed in pre-Buddhist tradition to Indra's thunderbolt. In early Buddhist tradition it is the attribute of a kind of personal guardian of Śākyamuni, known as Vajrapāṇi, 'Thunderbolt-in-Hand', who appears on many sculptures. In later Buddhist tradition the *vajra* becomes the symbol of the supreme 'adamantine' truth, essentially indestructible as a 'diamond'. *Vajra* is thus translated in Chinese and Japanese tradition.
vajrāsana
See *āsana*.
Vajrayāna (Vajrayāna)
'The *Vajra* Way', or the tantric form (see *tantra*) of Buddhism, also referred to as Esoteric Buddhism in the sections of the book dealing with Far Eastern Buddhism. It bases its liturgies, evocations and states of trance on the use of *maṇḍala, mantra, mudrā* (q.v.) and a transmutation of the sexual act (*maithuna*). A synonym is Mantrayāna, the 'Way of Spells'.
vidyārāja
'King of the Spell', a class of fierce divinities who were incorporated into Mahāyāna Buddhism. For more information, see J. Przyluski, 'Les Vidyārāja', *Bulletin de l'École Française d'Extrême-Orient* (1923), p. 301 ff.
vihāra
A Buddhist monastery.
Vijñānavāda (Vijñānavāda)
The Buddhist philosophical school of 'Consciousness Only', that is to say, of consciousness as the primary reality, the foundation of which is ascribed to Asaṅga and his teacher Maitreya (? the Bodhisattva Maitreya) who lived and taught in the fourth century A.D. The school had great success in India and spread not only across Central Asia to the Far East, but also to Tibet, where it has survived until recent times, and also to Cambodia, where it is known to have existed at the end of the tenth century and seems to have played an important role up to the thirteenth century.
vīrāsana
'Heroic posture', used to define the seated cross-legged position, the right leg resting with the sole of the foot upwards on the left leg, the most common attitude in the art of South-East Asia. See Pls. 96–98.
vitarka-mudrā
See *mudrā*.
vyākhyāna-mudrā
See *mudrā*.
yakṣa
A tree-spirit; see pp. 47–48.

	INDIA	SRI LANKA (CEYLON)	BURMA	THAILAND
B.C. 500	563?–483? Śākyamuni, the Buddha. c. 480. First Buddhist council (Rājagṛha).	c. 500. Beginning of historic period (according to the Chronicles).		c. 500. Painted ceramics of Ban Chieng. Latest Bronze Age.
400	c. 380. Second Buddhist council (Vaiśālī). c. 324–187. Maurya dynasty.			
300	c. 273–232. Aśoka. Sāñcī, Stupa 1 (core). c. 256. Missionaries sent by Aśoka to teach Buddhist doctrine. 250. Third Buddhist council (Pāṭaliputra).	c. 250. Beginning of the Anurādhapura period. 247–207. Reign of Devānampiya Tissa. Introduction of Buddhism by Mahinda. The cutting of the Bodhi Tree arrives. Mahāvihāra Monastery founded.	c. 240. The missionaries Soṇa and Uttara at Suvaṇṇabhumi (according to Buddhist tradition).	
200		199. Death of Mahinda. 161–137. Reign of Duṭṭhagāmaṇī. Buddhist establishments at Anurādhapura and Mihintale.		
100	Bhārhut; Sāñcī, enlargement of Stupa 1; Ajantā Caves Nos. 9–10. c. 50. *Caitya* hall at Bhājā. c. 25 B.C.–A.D. 320. Late Āndhra.	35–32. Pāli canon produced. First disagreements in the Buddhist community.		
0	From 1st cent. A.D. Mahāyāna develops. Sāñcī, Stupa 1, *toraṇa* reliefs; *caitya* hall at Bedsā. c. 50–5th/7th cent. Kuṣāṇa dynasty.			
A.D. 100	c. 120. *Caitya* hall at Kārlī. 128? 144? Kaniṣka. 1st?/2nd cent. Earliest Buddha images in Mathurā and Gandhāra. 2nd cent. Nāgārjuna (Mādhyamika doctrine). 2nd/3rd cent. Mathurā art (early phase); Amarāvatī, Nāgārjunakonda. 2nd–5th cent. Gandhāran art.			
200	c. 200. First dharanis (magical formulas). 249. Sassanid invasion of Gandhāra.	214–36. Mahāyāna spreads.	c. 3rd cent. Pyu kingdom (Indianized, according to Chinese sources).	c. 3rd cent. Indianized kingdoms in the peninsula (according to Chinese sources). First evidence of contacts with India and the West.
300	320–c. 550/650. Gupta period. Mathurā; Sārnāth; Bodhgayā. 4th cent. Asaṅga and Vasubandu (Yogācāra school). c. 399–413. Fa-hsien's pilgrimage.	4th–5th cent. Height of the Anurādhapura period. c. 362. Arrival of the tooth relic.		c. 4th cent. Influence of Āndhra art (U Thong).
400	From 5th cent. Theravāda Buddhism at Kāñcī, Kāveripaṭṭiṇam, Madura. c. 440. Nalandā founded (Mahāyāna). 5th/6th cent. Classical Gupta style in Mathurā and Sārnāth. Mahābodhi Temple at Bodhgayā.	412–13. Fa-hsien stays at Anurādhapura. 432–59. Tamil domination 459–77. Reign of Dhātusena, new Buddhist establishments and additions to old ones. 477–95. Reign of Kassapa I, construction of Sīgiriya.	Remains (walls and monuments) at Prome, Beikthano, Halin. 5th–11th cent. Ramaññadesa (Thaton), the centre of Mon and Buddhist culture.	c. 5th cent. Bronze Buddha of Sungai Kolok, Korat, etc. (Amarāvatī style).
500	c. 500 Gandhāran art, Bāmiyān. Rock-cut art: Ajantā, Ellora, Aurangābād, Bādāmi, etc. Tantric Buddhism, Mahāyāna flourishes.		6th–7th cent. South Indian influence on Buddhist sculpture.	c. 6th cent. Gupta influence in Buddhist statuary.
600	606–47. Harṣa (capital: Kanauj). c. 640. Hsüan-tsang at Nālandā. 7th/8th cent. Late Gupta art; Ellora, Ajantā, etc. 675–85. I-tsing stays at Nālandā.	618–84. Pallava domination. 7th cent. Construction and restoration of monasteries.	7th–8th cent. Walls of Śrīkṣetra (Prome) and of Sudhammavatī (Thaton), temples and stupas, some Mahāyāna images.	Kingdom of Dvāravatī, Buddhism (especially using Pāli). Buddhist establishments at Nakhon Pathom, Ku Bua, U Thong, etc. Dvāravatī Buddhist art spreads. Mon kingdom of Haripuñjaya (Lamphun) founded (according to the Chronicles).

LAOS	CAMBODIA	INDONESIA	VIETNAM AND CHAMPA	
From c. 5th cent. Megaliths in the province of Hua Phan (Later Bronze Age) and the Plain of Jars in the province of Xieng Khouang (Iron Age).		c. 5th–3rd cent. Bronzes in the Dong-son style.	2nd–1st mill. Kingdom of Van-lang (Bronze Age). c. 500–c. 257. Dong-son civilization (end of Bronze, beginning of Iron Age).	B.C. 500
				400
				300
			257–207. Kingdom of Au Lac.	
			207–111. Kingdom of Nam Viet.	
			111. Invasion and start of domination by Chinese (Former Han).	200
				100
	c. 1st cent. Kingdom of Fu-nan (according to Chinese sources).			0
			40. Revolt of the Trung sisters. 43. Ma Yuan's expedition, end of independence, sinicization. Introduction of Confucianism, Taoism, and Buddhism.	A.D. 100
	c. 3rd–5th cent. Evidence of relations with India and the West (Oc-eo).		Hīnayāna Buddhism arrives from India via the sea route. Construction of pagodas at Luy-lau. Han-type brick vaulted tombs.	200
4th–5th cent. Chams in the area of Champassak, Śaivism.		c. 4th–5th cent. Bronze Buddha (statues in the Amarāvatī style).	Increasing trade with East and West Asia. c. 375. Sanskrit inscriptions in Champa (Brahmanism).	300
	c. 5th–6th cent. Buddha statues (South Indian style).	First Sanskrit (Brahmanical) inscriptions.	Bronze Buddha of Dong-duong (Amarāvatī art).	400
From 6th cent. Khmers in the area of Champassak, Wat Phu centre of the Kambuja, Śaivism, Khmer art.	484. The monk Nāgasena's embassy to China. 537. Last reference to Fu-nan. c. 550. Beginnings of Chen-la (future Cambodia).		c. 550. Mahāyāna makes headway in Vietnam. Foundation of the Thien sect, construction of temples and monasteries, influence of Six Dynasties art.	500
	7th–8th cent. Many Brahmanical establishments. Statues of the Buddha, often similar to Dvāravatī art.	Buddhist communities (Lesser Vehicle, Sanskrit). Beginnings of Śrīvijaya kingdom (Sumatra). Mahāyāna makes headway (according to I-tsing).	From c. 650. Brahmanical art in Champa (Mi-son E.1).	600

	INDIA	SRI LANKA (CEYLON)	BURMA	THAILAND
700	c. 750. Pāla dynasty established in eastern India. Late classical Buddhist art and spread of Vajrayāna. Odantapurī founded. 8th cent. Islam penetrates N.-W. India. 8th–9th cent. Mahāyāna Buddhist bronzes at Nāgapaṭṭiṇam.	777–97. Buddhist establishments at Anurādhapura and Polonnaruwa. Mahāyāna predominant.		775. Evidence of Śrīvijaya presence in the peninsula.
800	c. 800. Vikramaśila (tantric Buddhist monastery) founded. 9th cent. Mahābodhi Temple at Bodhgayā restored. Bhauma-Karas dynasty in Orissa (favourable to Buddhism).	c. 840. Pāṇḍya invasion, sack of Anurādhapura.	825. Pegu founded. 849. Pagan fortified.	Śrīvijaya expands into the Maenam Basin. Surge of Mahāyāna Buddhism, Buddhist and Brahmanical art influenced by Indonesia.
900	Moslem pressure moves steadily eastwards. Pāla and Bhauma-Karas still protect Hindu/Buddhist culture in eastern India. 985–1310. Cōla empire	959. Cōla invasion. 985–1070. Cōla domination, annexed to Cōla empire. 993. Capture and sack of Anurādhapura by the Cōlas.		Decline of Mahāyāna in the Maenam Basin.
1000	Kanauj falls to Mahmud of Ghazni, but Hindu rule re-established.	1017. Polonnaruwa made capital of the Cōla vice-roy. 1055–1110. Reign of Vijayabāhu, who liberated Sri Lanka from the Cōlas. 1073. Capital moved to Polonnaruwa.	1044–1287. Kingdom of Pagan. 1044–77. Reign of Aniruddha. 1077–1113. Reign of Kyanzittha. Pagan art flourishes: 'Mon' period, Theravādin Buddhism, Pala-Sena influence on sculpture.	1022–25. Khmer expansion to Lopburi and towards the west of the Maenam Basin. Influence of Khmer art in Lopburi. 1063. Foundation of the Great Relic Monastery at Lamphun.
1100	Sena dynasty (favourable to Hindu/Buddhist culture) in Orissa. c. 1100. Mahābodhi Temple restored by Burmese. 1197. Nālandā destroyed by Moslems. 1198/99. Fall of Kanauj to Moslems.	1153–86. Reign of Parākramabāhu I. Religious buildings, great irrigation works. Unification of the Buddhist sects within the Mahāvihāra (Theravāda). 1187–96. Reign of Nissamkamalla, Buddhist establishments at Polonnaruwa.	1113–1287. 'Burmese' period, decline of Mon influence, introduction of Sinhalese Buddhism.	c. 1113–45. Khmer expansion in the north-east and at Sukhothai, Khmer buildings (Mahāyāna and Brahmanism). 1181–c. 1220. Khmer Bayon style at Lopburi, Pimai, Phetburi, Muang Sing, Sukhothai, etc. (Mahāyāna).
1200	Final collapse in eastern India of all Hindu/Buddhist dynasties before advance of Islam. Theravāda Buddhism persists in the south (Kāñcī, etc.). 1295–96. Second restoration of the Mahābodhi by the Burmese.	1236–70. Reign of Parākramabāhu II. Polonnaruwa abandoned. Period of various capitals. Beginning of the Dambedeniya period. 1293–1341. Capital at Kuruṇegala.	1287. Pagan captured by the Mongols.	c. 1220–50. Thai kingdom of Sukhothai founded (Theravāda). 1289. Lopburi freed from Khmer occupation. 1292. End of the Mon kingdom of Haripuñjaya. 1296. Chieng Mai founded as capital of western Thai kingdom (Lan Na). Sukhothai and Lan Na (or Chieng Sen) Buddhist art schools, traces of Khmer art in Lopburi art.
1300	1336. Vijayanagar founded. Buddhism survives in the south in an ever-weakened form until perhaps even the 17th cent.	c. 1320. Burmese religious embassy. 1331–1408. Period of Gampola, Buddhist buildings in the area of Kandy. Sukhothai religious embassy.	1315. Sagaing founded, Sinhalese influence. 1347. Taungu made capital of the Burmese kingdom. 1364. Ava founded.	c. 1316–46. Reign of Lo Thai at Sukhothai. Influence of Sinhalese Buddhism. 1350. Kingdom of Ayutthaya founded; political expansion and great artistic activity in Ayutthaya (national style formed) and in Lan Na in the 14th and 15th cent.

LAOS	CAMBODIA	INDONESIA	VIETNAM AND CHAMPA	
c. 8th cent. Some Buddhist statues related to Dvāravatī art near Vientiane.	Mahāyāna makes headway.	c. 750–930. Art of Central Java. c. 768. Śailendra dynasty established in Java, patronage of Buddhism (Mahāyāna). Buddhist establishments (Kedu plain: Caṇḍi Mendut, C. Kalasan, Borobudur, etc.), influence of Nālandā art in statuary. Brahmanical establishments (Dieng plateau, then Kedu plain: Lara Janggrang).	End of 8th cent. Indonesian raids in Champa, influence of Indonesian statuary, Mahāyāna spreads.	700
	802–50. Reign of Jayavarman II, institution of royal Angkorian ritual (Śaivite). 889–c. 900. Reign of Yaśovarman I, foundation of Yaśodharapura (the first Angkor, centred around Phnom Bakheng). Brahmanical cults predominant.		875. Great Mahayana temple of Dong-duong built in Champa. National hero cult develops in Vietnam.	800
	From 2nd half of 10th cent. Buddhist renaissance (Mahāyāna).	c. 930. Beginnings of the art of eastern Java (Mataram kingdom). Decline of Buddhism.	939. Independence of Vietnam (capital: Co-loa). 968. Unification of Vietnam (Dai Co Viet; capital: Hoa-lu). Buddhism becomes state religion. Golden age of Cham art (Mi-son, Tra-kieu), especially Brahmanical art. 982. Vietnam victorious over Champa. Influence of Cham art in Vietnam.	900
	1002–49. Reign of Sūryavarman I; after dynastic wars, conquest of Lopburi region. Prah Vihear founded (Śaivite type).	1016–49. Reign of Airlanga, syncretism of Buddhism and Brahmanism. 1078–1222. Kingdom of Kediri. Relations between Sumatra and South India.	1000. The Chams abandon Indrapura and make Vijaya their capital. 1009–1225. Ly dynasty, monarchical centralization. 1010. Capital of Vietnam moved to Dai-la, renamed Thang-long.	1000
1118–c. 1220. Khmer expansion into the Vientiane area, Bayon style. Mahāyānist and Brahmanical movement towards Luang Prabang.	1113–c. 1145. Reign of Sūryavarman II, Angkor Wat founded (Vaiṣṇavite). Buddhism makes headway (Mahāyāna). 1177. Angkor captured by Champa troops. 1181–c. 1218 Reign of Jayavarman VII, Mahāyāna and syncretism predominant. Territorial expansion (Champa, modern Thailand and Laos). Many large Buddhist establishments throughout the kingdom. Construction of the new Yaśodharapura (Angkor Thom, centred around the Bayon); Avalokiteśvara cult becomes strong.		c. 1113–45. Khmer attacks on Champa and Vietnam. Mahāyāna spreads in Champa, dynastic struggles, Vietnam intervenes, the influence of Khmer art in Champa. 1177. Champa attacks Angkor by river. 1191. The Khmers capture Vijaya, Champa is divided into two kingdoms.	1100
		1222–93. Kingdom of Singhasari. Religious syncretism, art becomes more Indonesian.	1203–20. Champa annexed by Cambodia, the Khmer Bayon style in Champa. 1225–1400. Tran dynasty in Vietnam, Buddhist art.	1200
c. 1279–1316. Sukhothai kingdom expands into the Vientiane region.	1296. Visit of the Chinese envoy Chou Ta-kuan. Buddhism makes headway (Theravāda).	1275. Javan expedition against Sumatra. 1268–92. Reign of Kṛtanagara (Śiva-buddha). Tantric Buddhism (Kālacakra), syncretism. 1293–1528. Kingdom of Majapahit.	1283–85. Mongol attacks on Vietnam and Champa. Decline of Cham art.	
1350. Kingdom of Lan Chang (modern Laos) founded, cultural and material assistance of Cambodia, Sinhalese Buddhism. Capital: Xieng Dong-Xieng Thong (site of Luang Prabang). The Prabang (Buddha) image is the protector of the kingdom.	1352. Angkor besieged by the Ayutthaya armies. 1393–94. Angkor captured.	Buddhist-Śaivite syncretism in Sumatra. Islam spreads.	1353–90. Cham attacks on Vietnam.	1300

	INDIA	SRI LANKA (CEYLON)	BURMA	THAILAND
1400	Buddhist sculpture in the Tanjore district.	1412–67. Reign of Parākramabāhu VI, great literary and artistic activity. 1415–1597. Kingdom of Kōṭṭe.	15th–16th cent. Buddhist establishments at Pegu (Mon kingdom).	1475. Buddhist council at Chieng Mai.
1500 | 1900	1565. Fall of the Vijayanagar empire.	1505. The Portuguese arrive in Colombo. Kingdom of Kōṭṭe occupied, persecution of Buddhism. 1658. End of Portuguese domination. From 1687. Temple of the Tooth at Kandy built and expanded.	1541. Pegu annexed by Taungu. 1636. Ava made capital, artistic renaissance. 1783–1885. Amarapura and Mandalay art.	16th–17th cent. Relations with Europe and Japan (embassies, treaties). 1569. Ayutthaya captured by the Burmese. 1592. Nong Saray's victory over the Burmese. 1632. Chieng Mai captured by the Burmese. 1728–62. Chieng Mai regains independence. 1750. Sinhalese religious mission to Ayutthaya. 1767. Capture and sack of Ayutthaya by the Burmese. 1767–76. Liberation of the nation. 1782. Chakri dynasty founded (capital: Bangkok), great artistic activity (Bangkok, Thonburi, etc.). Cult of the 'Emerald' Buddha installed in Bangkok in 1785.

	CENTRAL ASIA	KASHMIR	NEPAL	TIBET
B.C. 300 | 0	Hellenistic influences attested in Bactria (northern Afghanistan). Buddhism reaches Kāpiśa (S.-W. Afghanistan). Aśoka's inscription at Kandahar.	First city of Śrīnagarī (modern Pandrenthan) said to have been founded by Aśoka.		
0 A.D.	Chinese campaigns westwards.			
100	Kuṣāṇa dynasty becomes established in Gandhāra.			
200	Chinese influence pervades the Takla Makan. Gandhāran influences begin to pervade the Takla Makan city states (Khotan, Qarashahr, Kuchā, Turfān all flourishing). 3rd/4th cent. Paintings at Mirān. 3rd–5th cent. Colossal Buddhas at Bāmiyān.	City of Ushkur founded by Huviṣka, successor of Kaniṣka.		
300	4th–5th cent. Haḍḍa sculpture. 4th/5th cent.? Khotan, sculpture on Rawak Stupa. 366–700. Tun-huang (latter half of 5th cent.; earliest surviving paintings).		c. 360. First historical reference to the existence of Nepal—on Samudragupta's pillar at Allahabad.	
400	Ephthalite Huns cause havoc in Gandhāra.	Pravapura founded on site of present capital Srinagar.	Licchavī dynasty established for the next three centuries with capital at Pātan.	
500	c. 500–700. Paintings at Qizil (Kuchā area). c. 500. 1st Indo-Iranian style.			

LAOS	CAMBODIA	INDONESIA	VIETNAM AND CHAMPA	
1478. Vietnamese invasions. 1480–1520. New Buddhist building and reconstruction. Relations established with Lan Na.	1431. Angkor captured, the capital abandoned. 1434. Capital moved to "Four-arms" (modern Phnom Penh). Theravāda predominant.	c. 1406. Decline of Majapahit kingdom. 1499. Last embassy from Java to China.	1405–7. Chinese attacks on Vietnam. 1418–28. Victorious resistance of Le Loi, a national hero, founder of the later Le dynasty. 1471. Vijaya captured by Vietnam, provinces north of Cape Varella annexed. Islam makes headway in Champa.	1400
1548–56. Expansion into Lan Na. Vientiane made capital. Wat Pra Keo and That Luang built. 1563–74. Burmese invasions, Vientiane occupied and under Burmese suzerainty. 1591. Kingdom liberated, dynastic struggles. 1641–47. Visits by Dutch and Italian travellers. c. 1711–31. Lan Xang divided into three kingdoms: Luang Prabang, Vientiane and Champassak.	c. 1507–56. Reign of Ang Chan (capital: Lovek). c. 1550. Brief reoccupation of Angkor. 1594. Lovek captured by Ayutthaya armies; king flees to Laos. Portuguese and Spanish involvement in affairs. From 1620. Vietnam expands in the Mekong delta. Dynastic struggles. Many wooden statues of the Buddha (often decorated).	1526. Islam is predominant. Brahmanism persists in Bali.	1527. Start of the rivalries between the Mac, the Trinh and the Nguyen in Vietnam. 1543. Last Cham embassy to China. 1611–35. Champa becomes an enclave of Phan-rang. 1620. Vietnam divided into two kingdoms, under the Trinh and the Nguyen. 1687. Hue made capital of Vietnam.	1500 – 1900

MONGOLIA	CHINA	KOREA	JAPAN	
	481–221. Warring States (Late Chou period). 221–206. Ch'in dynasty. 206 B.C.–A.D. 220. Han dynasty.	108 B.C.–A.D. 313. Nang-ang (Lolang, Rakurō): Han colony. 37 B.C.?–668. Koguryŏ. 37 B.C.?–661. Paekje. 57 B.C.?–668. Silla.	to c. 200 B.C. Jōmon period. c. 200 B.C.–A.D. 550. Yayoi (Tumulus) period.	B.C. 300 – 0
	65. First evidence of Buddhist communities.			0 A.D. 100
	220–65. Three Empires. 265–581. Six Dynasties period. 265–420. Western and Eastern Ch'in dynasty.			200
	3rd/4th cent. Spread of Buddhism in North and South China. Earliest surviving Buddha images, some under Gandhāran influence. 386–535. Northern Wei dynasty (T'o-pa).	372. Koguryŏ becomes Buddhist. 384. Paekje becomes Buddhist.	Earliest cultural influences from Korea and China (including writing).	300
	399–414. Fa-hsien's pilgrimage. 402. Kumārajīva's journey to China. 4th–7th cent. Maitreya cult. From c. 400. Amitābha cult. 444. Buddhists persecuted. 5th–6th cent. Buddhist art in North China; cave temples (Yün-kang, Lung-men, etc.).	424/524. Silla becomes Buddhist.	Probable earliest sporadic contact with Buddhism.	400
	From c. 500. Ch'an Buddhism brought to China (Bodhidharma). 550–81. Northern Ch'i/Northern Chou dynasty. Caves of Hsiang-t'ang Shan. From late 6th cent. T'ien-t'ai school. 581–618. Sui dynasty.	6th/7th cent. Flowering of early Buddhist art in Koguryŏ, Paekje and Silla.	Closer contact with Buddhism. 552 (official date). Buddhism adopted from Paekje. 552–648. Asuka (Suiko) era. 574–622. Crown Prince Shōtoku. Art under Korean influence.	500

	CENTRAL ASIA	KASHMIR	NEPAL	TIBET
600	c. 600,700. 2nd Indo-Iranian style. 7th cent.? Sculpture at Fondukistān. Hsüan-tsang describes Buddhist civilization in Takla Makan and Gandhāra. 655. The Tibetans attack Khotan and gradually take control of the whole Takla Makan.			c. 625. Buddhism reaches Tibet through agency of King Srong-tsen-gam-po's Nepalese wife. First temples built.
700	In Gandhāra Buddhism begins to succumb before Islam. The Tibetans, now fast converting to Buddhism, extend their control as far as Tun-huang. 751. Arab victory over T'ang army on the Talas; thereafter Islam makes headway. 755–840. Uighur empire in eastern Turkestan (Manichaean and Buddhist).	Kashimir's greatest period under King Lalitāditya-Muktāpīḍa(727–56).	Thākurī dynasty replaces Licchavi.	
800	Civilization flourishes in the city-states around the Takla Makan with combination of Indian (as inherited via Gandhāra), Iranian, Tibetan and Chinese influences. 842. End of Tibetan domination, although cultural influence remains (as at Karakhoto, Turfān area). Chinese power reasserted. 850–c. 1300. Artistic work continues at Tun-huang. 868. Diamond Sutra print from Tun-huang.			842. Break-up of the old Tibetan kingdom based on Lhasa.
900	9th/10th century. Paintings in Chinese style in southern Turkestan and Turfān (Bezeklik). From 10th cent. Almost all Chinese Turkestan becomes Islamic.		Bhadgaon begins to become a rival city to neighbouring Pātan.	Kingdoms of Gu-ge and Purang in western Tibet already thriving. The 'Great Translator' Rin-chen bZang-po (958–1055) active in Kashmir and Tibet.
1000	The Takla Makan area succumbs to Islam. End of Buddhist civilization there. Buddhism continues to flourish at Tun-huang.			1042. Atiša arrives in Tibet from eastern India. 1073. Sa-kya Monastery founded. Lama Mar-pa (1012–96), from whom derive ultimately the various *bKa-rgyud-pa* religious orders.
1100				
1200	c. 1215/20. Chinese Turkestan conquered by Mongols. Mongol invasion. Final destruction of Buddhist civilization in the whole area.			1204. The 'Great Kashmir Scholar' Śākya Śrī goes to Tibet. 1207. The Tibetans submit to Genghiz Khan.
1300–1900		1337. Kashimir finally taken over by Moslems.	c. 1480. The Nepal Valley divided between three Malla kings with capital cities at Pātan, Bhadgaon and Kathmandu. 1768/69. The three kingdoms of the Nepal Valley conquered by the Gorkhas.	1368. Fall of the Yüan (Mongol) dynasty in China leaves Tibet independent once more. Tsong-kha-pa (1357–1419), founder of the reformed Tibetan religious order, the *dGe-lugs-pa*('Way of Virtue'). 1642. Tibet reunified under the authority of the 5th Dalai Lama with the aid of Gu-shri Khan, leader of the Qošot Mongols. 1721. Emperor K'ang Hsi establishes Chinese authority in Lhasa through the 7th Dalai Lama. 1792. Gorkha invasion of Tibet repulsed by Chinese troops. Policy of excluding foreigners adopted. Tibet and Mongolia included within a Chinese sphere of influence.

MONGOLIA	CHINA	KOREA	JAPAN	
	618–906. T'ang dynasty (capital: Ch'ang-an). 629–45. Hsüan-tsang's pilgrimage. 671–95. I-tsing's pilgrimage. 7th/8th cent. Classical flowering of Buddhist art. Painters: Wu Tao-tse (c. 690–760) and others. Until mid-8th cent. Late phase of caves at T'ien-lung Shan.	668–935. Kingdoms united in United Silla empire (capital: Kyŏngju). 7th–9th cent. Classical Buddhist art under T'ang influence. 7th/8th cent. Pulguk-sa. 8th cent. Sŏkkur-am.	607. Hōryū-ji founded. 645–710. Early Nara (Hakuhō) era. Art under Sui and early T'ang influence.	600
			710–94. Late Nara (Tempyō) period. Buddhist art on T'ang model. Wall paintings at Hōryū-ji. Temples built at Nara, the capital: Yakushi-ji, Tōdai-ji, etc. (Great Buddha, 752). 756. Shōsō-in built.	700
	8th/9th cent. Vajrayāna art (Mi-tsung/Chen-yen school). 842–46. Persecution of Buddhists. Japanese monk Ennin in China.		794–897. Jōgan period (capital: Heian, modern Kyoto). Vajrayāna from China: Saichō, Kūkai (beginning of 9th cent.). Monasteries built on Hiei-zan (Tendai school) and Kōya-san (Shingon school); syncretism of Buddhism and Shinto. 897–1185. Fujiwara period (capital: Heian). Flowering of courtly culture, largely independent of Korea. Architecture, sculpture and painting of Tendai and Shingon schools.	800
	906–60. Five Dynasties period. 960–1278. Sung dynasty. 960–1127. Northern Sung. 907–1125. Liao dynasty. 985. Copy of Udāyana Buddha produced for Chōnen (Seiryō-ji, Kyoto).	918–1392. Koryŏ period (capital: Kaesŏng). Continuation of Silla art; some Sung influence.		900
		1097. Ch'an (Son) Buddhism transmitted to Korea.	1053. Hōō-dō (Phoenix Hall) of Byōdō-in, near Uji, built (Amitābha statue by Jōchō).	1000
	1127–1278. Southern Sung. Ch'an Buddhist ink painting (esp. 13th cent.). Neo-Confucianism.		Flowering of belief in Amitābha (Hōnen and others) and art associated with it. 1185–1336. Kamakura period. Kamakura headquarters of the military rulers; feudal warrior culture; introduction of Zen Buddhism (monasteries at Kamakura and Kyoto). Fresh Chinese influence (Sung). Sculpture: Unkei and his school; colossal Buddha at Kamakura (1252).	1100
The Mongols appoint the Sa-kya Pandit as their Tibetan vice-roy. Beginning of Tibetan missionary activities in Mongolia.	1278–1368. Yüan (Mongol) dynasty. Tibetan Buddhism makes headway, esp. in North China.	1206–36. Mongol invasions.		1200 1300 1900
Beginning of *dGe-lugs-pa* (Yellow Hat) political and religious activites in Mongolia. 1578. Altan Khan gives title of 'Dalai' to the 3rd grand lama of the Tibetan *dGe-lugs-pa* order.	1368–1644. Ming dynasty. Late Buddhist art (imitative); predominance of literary men's non-Buddhist painting (*wen-jen-hua*). 1644–1912. Ch'ing dynasty. Buddhist art chiefly Tibetan.	1392–1910. Yi dynasty. Confucianism. Decline of Buddhism and Buddhist art.	1336–1572. Ashikaga (Muromachi) period. 15th/16th cent. Flowering of Zen art (ink painting, tea cult, etc.) in Kyoto under strong Chinese influence. 1420–1506. Sesshū (Zen monk, ink painter) and many followers. 1573–1603. Momoyama period. 1603–1868. Tokugawa period. Residence of the rulers (shoguns) at Edo (modern Tokyo). Renaissance of Confucianism and Shintō; late phase of Zen painting (Hakuin and others).	

BIBLIOGRAPHY

The Indian Subcontinent

Agrawala, V. S. *Handbook of the Sculptures in the Curzon Museum of Archaeology, Mattra.* Allahabad, n.d.

———. 'Buddha and Bodhisattva images in the Mathura Museum'. *Journal of the United Provinces Historical Society*, vol. 21, pts. 1 and 2 (1948), pp. 43–98.

Ahmed, Nazimuddin. *Mahasthan.* Karachi, 1964.

Aiyappan, A., and Srinivasan, P. R. *Guide to the Buddhist Antiquities.* Madras, 1952.

———. *The Story of Buddhism with Special Reference to South India.* Madras, 1960.

———. 'Indian archaeology: A review'. *Archaeological Survey of India (1953–54, 1967–68)*, New Delhi.

Auboyer, Jeannine. *Le trône et son symbolisme dans l'Inde ancienne.* Annales du Musée Guimet: Bibliothèque d'études 55. Paris, 1949.

Bachhofer, Ludwig. *Early Indian Sculpture*, 2 vols. Pegasus Press, New York, n.d.

Banerji, R. D. 'Eastern Indian school of mediaeval sculpture'. *Archaeological Survey of India*, Imperial series, vol. 47. Delhi, 1933.

———. *History of Orissa*, vols. 1 and 2. Calcutta, 1932.

Banerji-Sastri, A. 'Ninety-three inscriptions on the Kurkihar bronzes'. *Journal of the Bihar and Orissa Research Society*, vol. 26 (1940), pp. 236–51, 299–308.

Bareau, André. *Les premiers conciles bouddhiques.* Paris, 1955.

———. *Recherches sur la biographie du Buddha dans les sūtrapiṭaka et les vinayapiṭaka anciens: De la quête de l'éveil à la conversion de Śāriputra et Maudgalyāyana* (Publications de l'École Française d'Extrême-Orient, vol. 53), Paris, 1963; *Les derniers mois, le parinirvāṇa et les funérailles* (id., vol. 77), in two parts, Paris, 1970 and 1971.

Barrett, Douglas. *Sculptures from Amaravati in the British Museum.* London, 1954.

———. 'Bronzes from North-West India and Western Pakistan'. *Lalit Kalā*, no. 11 (April 1962), pp. 35–44.

Barua, Benimadhab. *Gayā and Bodhgayā.* 2 vols. Calcutta, 1931 and 1934.

———. *Bhārhut.* Calcutta, 1934–37.

Bernett-Kempers, A. J. *The Bronzes of Nalanda and Hindu-Javanese Art.* Leiden, 1933.

Bhandarkar, D. R. 'Excavations near Mirpur Khas'. *Progress Report of the Archaeological Suvey of India, western circle* (year ending 31/3/1917), pp. 47–48.

Bhattacaryya, B. *The Indian Buddhist Iconography.* London, 1924. 2nd rev. ed., Calcutta, 1958.

Bhattasali, N. K. *Iconography of the Buddhist and Brahmanical Sculptures in the Dacca Museum.* Dacca, 1929.

Bourda, M. G. 'Quelques réflections sur la pose assise à l'européenne dans l'art bouddhique'. *Arts Asiatiques*, 12 (1949), pp. 302–13.

Buchthal, H. 'The western aspects of Gandhara sculpture'. *Proceedings of the British Academy*, vol. 31 (1945).

Burgess, James. *The Buddhist Stūpas of Amarāvatī and Jaggayyapeta.* London, 1887.

Bussagli, M., and Sivaramamurti, C. *5000 Years of the Art of India.* New York, n.d.

Chanda, R. P. 'The Mathura School of sculpture'. *Annual Report of the Archaeological Survey of India (1922–23)*, pp. 164–70.

———. 'Mayurbhanj and Khiching'. *Annual Report of the Archaeological Survey of India (1922–23)*, pp. 124–28; *(1923–24)*, p. 87.

Chandra, Moti. 'A study of the terracottas from Mirpur Khas'. *Bulletin of the Prince of Wales Museum*, Bombay, no. 7 (1959–62), pp. 1–22.

Chandra, Pramod. *Stone Sculptures in the Allahabad Museum: A descriptive catalogue.* American Institute of Indian Studies, Varanasi, 1971.
Combaz, Gisbert. 'L'évolution du stūpa en Asie'. *Mélanges Chinois et Bouddhiques*, Brussels, vol. 2 (1933), pp. 163–305; contd. in vol. 3 (1935), pp. 93–144, and in vol. 4 (1936), pp. 1–25.
Conze, Edward. *Buddhist Texts through the Ages*, in collaboration with I. B. Horner, D. L. Snellgrove, A. Waley. Cassirer, Oxford, 1954; Harper Torchbooks, 1964.
———. *Buddhist Scriptures.* Penguin Classics, 1959; reprinted 1960, 1966, 1968, 1969, 1971, 1973.
———. *The Prajñāpāramitā Literature.* Indo-Iranian Monographs, 6. Mouton & Co., 's-Gravenhage, 1960.
Coomaraswamy, A. K. 'The origins of the Buddha image'. *Art Bulletin*, vol. 9, no. 4 (1926–27). Reprinted in book form, New Delhi, 1972.
———. *History of Indian and Indonesian Art.* London, 1972.
———. *Elements of Buddhist Iconography.* Cambridge, Mass., 1935; 2nd ed., New Delhi, 1972.
———. 'La sculpture de Bodhgayā'. *Ars Asiatica*, 18. Paris and Brussels, 1935.
———. *La sculpture de Bhārhut.* Annales du Musée Guimet: Bibliothèque d'art, nouvelle série 6. Paris, 1956.
———. *Yakṣas*, pts. 1 and 2. Smithsonian Institute, Washington, 1928 and 1931.
Cousens, Henry. 'Buddhist *stūpa* at Mirpur Khas'. *Annual Report of the Archaeological Survey of India (1909–10)* (Calcutta, 1914), pp. 80–92.
Cunningham, C. *Mahābodhi or the Great Buddhist Temple at Buddhagaya.* London, 1892.
Dani, A. H. 'Shaikhan Dheri excavations'. *Ancient Pakistan: Bulletin of the Department of Archaeology*, vol. 2 (1965–66), University of Peshawar.
———. 'Excavation at Andan Dheri'. *Ancient Pakistan: Bulletin of the Department of Archaeology*, vol. 4 (1968–69), University of Peshawar.
Dikshit, K. N. 'Excavations at Paharpur, Bengal'. *Memoirs of the Archaeological Survey of India*, no. 55. Delhi, 1938.
Dikshit, M. G. 'Some Buddhist bronzes from Sirpur, Madhya Pradesh'. *Bulletin of the Prince of Wales Museum*, Bombay, no. 5 (1955–57), pp. 1–11.
Fabri, Charles. *History of the Art of Orissa.* Calcutta, 1974
Foucher, A. *L'art gréco-bouddhique du Gandhāra.* Paris, 1922.
———. *The Beginnings of Buddhist Art and Other Essays in Indian and Central Asian Archaeology.* London, 1917.
———. *La vie du Bouddha d'après les textes et les monuments de l'Inde.* Paris, 1949.
Franz, H. G. *Buddhistische Kunst Indiens.* Leipzig, 1965.
Frédéric, Louis. *L'Inde, ses temples, ses sculptures.* Paris, 1959.
Gangoly, O. C. 'The antiquity of the Buddha image: The cult of the Buddha'. *Ostasiatische Zeitschrift*, neue Folge, vol. 14, Heft 2/3 (1938), pp. 41–53.
Goetz, H. *Studies in the History and Art of Kashmir and the Indian Himalaya.* Wiesbaden, 1969.
Grünwedel, Albert. *Buddhist Art in India.* Translated by A. C. Gibson, revised and enlarged by J. Burgess. London, 1901.
Gupta, P. L. *Patna Museum Catalogue of Antiquities.* Patna, 1965.
Gupta, R. S. *The Iconography of the Buddhist Sculptures (Caves) of Ellora.* Aurangabad, 1964.
Gupta, R. S., and Mahajan, B. D. *Ajanta, Ellora and Aurangabad Caves.* Bombay, 1962.
Hallade, Madelaine. *The Gandhāra Style.* London, 1968.
Hargreaves, H. 'Excavations at Shah-ji-ki Dheri'. *Annual Report of the Archaeological Survey of India (1910–11)* (Calcutta, 1914), pp. 25–32.
———. 'Excavations at Takht-i-Bahi'. *Annual Report of the Archaeological Survey of India (1910–11)* (Calcutta, 1914), pp. 33–39.
———. 'Excavations at Jamalgarhi'. *Annual Report of the Archaeological Survey of India (1921–22)* (Simla, 1924), pp. 54–62.
Härtel, H., and Auboyer, Jeannine. *Indien und Sudostasien.* Propyläen-Kunstgeschichte 16. Berlin,

1971.
Heeramanech, Nasli and Alice (Collection). *The Arts of India and Nepal.* Museum of Fine Arts, Boston.
Hsüan-tsang. *Si-yu-ki, Buddhist Records of the Western World, translated from the Chinese of Hiuen Tsiang (A.D. 629).* Translated by Samuel Beal. London, 1884; reprinted Delhi, 1969.
———. Watters, Th. *On Yuan Chwang's Travels in India.* 2 vols. London, 1904 and 1905.
Ingholt, H. *Gandhāran Art in Pakistan.* New York, 1957.
Istituto del Medio ed Estremo Oriente, Rome. *Reports on the Campaigns in Swat (Pakistan) 1956–58.* Ed. by D. Faccenna, vol. 1 (1962), vol. 2, no. 2 (1962), and vol. 2, no. 3 (1964).
I-tsing. *A Record of the Buddhist Religion, as practised in India and the Malay Archipelago (A.D. 671–695).* Translated by J. Takakusu. Oxford, 1896.
Jayaswal, K. P. 'Metal images of Kurkihar Monastery'. *Journal of the Indian Society of Oriental Art,* vol. 2, no. 2 (Calcutta, 1934), pp. 70–82.
Kak, Ram Chandra, *Ancient Monuments of Kashmir.* London, 1933.
———. *Handbook of the Archaeological and Numismatic Sections of the Sri Pratap Singh Museum, Srinagar.* Calcutta, 1923.
Khan, F. A. *Mainamati: Recent archaeological discoveries in East Pakistan.* Karachi, 1955.
———. *Mainamati: Further excavations in East Pakistan.* Karachi, n.d.
———. *Third Phase of Archaeological Excavations in East Pakistan.* Dacca, 1957.
Khan, M. Ishtiaq. 'Mathura objects in Taxila Museum'. *Journal of the Asiatic Society of Pakistan,* Dacca, vol. 11, no. 1 (1966), pp. 44–49.
Kramrisch, Stella. *The Art of Nepal.* Asia Society, New York, 1964.
———. 'Pāla and Sena sculptures'. *Rupam,* Calcutta, 1928.
Lamotte, Étienne. *Histoire du Bouddhisme indien des origines à l'ère śaka.* Louvain, 1958; reprinted 1967.
———. 'Vajrapāṇi en Inde'. *Bibliothèque de l'Institut des hautes ètudes chinoises,* 20 (Paris, 1966), pp. 113–59.
Law, B. C. *Geography of Early Buddhism.* London, 1932.
Lévi, Sylvain. *Le Népal, étude historique d'un royaume hindou.* 3 vols. Paris, 1905–8.
van Lohuizen-de Leeuw, J. E. *The 'Scythian' Period.* Leiden, 1949.
Longhurst. A. H. 'The Buddhist monuments at Guntupalle, Krishna District'. *Annual Report of the Archaeological Survey of India, southern circle* (Madras, 1917), pp. 30–36.
———. 'The Buddhist antiquities of Nagarjunakonda, Madras Presidency'. *Memoirs of the Archaeological Survey of India,* no. 54. Delhi, 1938.
Marshall, Sir J. *The Buddhist Art of Gandhara.* Cambridge, 1960.
———. *Taxila.* 3 vols. Cambridge, 1951.
Marshall, Sir J., and Foucher, A. *The Monuments of Sāñcī.* 3 vols. Calcutta, 1940.
McCrindle, J. W. *Ancient India as described by Ptolemy.* Calcutta, 1927.
Misra, Binayak. *Orissa under the Bhauma Kings.* Calcutta, 1934.
Mitra, Debala. 'Three Kushāna sculptures from Ahicchatrā'. *Journal of the Asiatic Society,* letters, vol. 21, no. 1 (1957), pp. 19–22.
———. 'Ratnagiri: Unearthing of a new Buddhist site in Orissa'. *Indo-Asian Culture,* vol. 9, no. 2 (1960), pp. 160–75.
———. *Buddhist Monuments.* Sahitya Samsad, Calcutta, 1971.
Mukherjee, B. N. 'Shah-ji-ki Dheri Casket inscription'. *British Museum Quarterly,* vol. 28, no. 1–2, pp. 39–47.
Naudou, J. *Les bouddhistes kaśmīriens au moyen âge.* Paris, 1968.
Oldfield, H. A. *Sketches from Nepal.* 2 vols. London, 1880.
Patil, D. R. *The Antiquarian Remains in Bihar.* Patna, 1963.
Plaeschke, H. *Buddhistische Kunst: Das Erbe Indiens.* Leipzig, 1972.
Ramachandran, T. N. 'Nagarjunakonda 1938'. *Memoirs of the Archaeological Survey of India,* no. 71. Delhi, 1953.
———. 'The Nagapattinam and other Buddhist bronzes in the Madras Museum'. *Bulletin of the Mad-*

ras Government Museum. Madras, 1954.
Rao, P. R. Ramachandar. *The Art of Nagarjunakonda*. Madras, 1956.
Rao, T. A. Gopinatha. 'Buddha vestiges in Kanchipura'. *Indian Antiquary* (1915), pp. 127–29.
Rosenfield, John M. *The Dynastic Arts of the Kushans*. Berkeley and Los Angeles, 1967.
Rowland, Benjamin. *The Art and Architecture of India*. 2nd ed. London, 1956.
———. *The Evolution of the Buddha Image*. Asia Society, New York, 1968.
———. 'A note on the invention of the Buddha image'. *Harvard Journal of Asiatic Studies*, vol. 2 (1948), pp. 181–86.
Sahni, Daya Ram. *Catalogue of the Museum of Archaeology at Sarnath*. Government of India, Calcutta, 1914.
———. 'Pre-Muhammadan monuments of Kashmir'. *Annual Report of the Archaeological Survey of India (1915–16)* (Calcutta, 1918), pp. 49–78.
Sahu, N. K. *Buddhism in Orissa*. Utkal University, Bhuvanesvar, 1958.
Seckel, D. *The Art of Buddhism*. Art of the World Series, London, 1964. Original German edition, *Kunst des Buddhismus*. 2nd ed. Baden-Baden, 1964.
———. *Buddhistische Kunst Ostasiens*. Stuttgart, 1957.
———. 'Sechs Kaki-Früchte (von Mu Ch'i)'. *Einführung in die Kunst Ostasiens* (Munich, 1960), pp. 345–65.
Sharma, G. R. 'Excavations at Kausambi, 1949–55'. *Annual Bibliography of Indian Archaeology* (for years 1948–53), Kern Institute (Leiden, 1958), pp. xxxvi-xlv.
Sivaramamurti, C. 'Amaravati sculptures in the Madras Government Museum'. *Bulletin of the Madras Government Museum*. Madras, 1942.
Snellgrove, D. L. 'Shrines and temples of Nepal'. *Arts Asiatiques*, 8 (1961), pp. 3–10, 93–120.
Subramanian, K. R. *Buddhist Remains in Andhra and the History of Andhra between 225 and 610 A.D.* Madras, 1932.
Subrahmanyam, R. *Salihundan: A Buddhist Site in Andhra Pradesh*. Andhra Pradesh Government Archaeological Series, no. 17. Hyderabad, 1964.
Taddei, Maurizio. *India*. London, 1970.
Thomas, E. J. *The Life of the Buddha as Legend and History*. London, 1949.
Tucci, Giuseppe. *The Theory and Practice of the Mandala*. London, 1961.
Viennot, Odette. *Le culte de l'arcre dans l'Inde ancienne*. Annales du Musée Guimet: Bibliothèque d'études 59. Paris, 1954.
Vogel, J. P. *Catalogue of the Archaeological Museum at Mathurā*. Government of U. P., Allahabad, 1910.
———. 'Inscribed Gandhara sculptures'. *Annual Report of the Archaeological Survey of India (1903–4)* (Calcutta, 1906), pp. 244–60.
———. 'La sculpture de Mathura'. *Ars Asiatica*, 15. Paris, 1930.
Waldschmidt, Ernst. *Grünwedels Buddhistische Kunst in Indien*. Berlin (Lankwitz), 1932.
Waldschmidt, Ernst, and Waldschmidt, Rose Leonore. *Nepal: Art Treasures of the Himalayas*. London, 1967.
Ward, W. F. 'The Lotus symbol: Its meaning in Buddhist art and philisophy'. *Journal of Aesthetics and Art Criticism*, vol. 11, no. 2 (December 1952).
Wayman, Alex. 'The mirror-like knowledge in Mahāyāna Buddhist litterature'. *Asiatische Studien/ Études Asiatiques*, 25 (1971), pp. 353–63.
Wiesner, Ulrich. *Nepal, Königreich im Himalaya, Geschichte, Kunst und Kultur im Kathmandu-Tal*. Cologne, 1976.
———. 'Zur Frage der vier sogenannten Aśoka-Stūpas in Patan, Nepal'. *Zur Kunstgeschichte Asiens, 50 Jahre Lehre und Forschung an der Universität Köln*, ed. by Roger Goepper (Wiesbaden, 1977), pp. 189–98.
Yazdani, G. *Ajanta*, pts. 1–4. London, 1930, 1933, 1946, 1955.
Zimmer, Heinrich. *The Art of Indian Asia*. 2 vols. Pantheon Books, New York, 1955.
———. *Kunstform und Yoga im indischen Kultbild*. Berlin, 1926.

South-East Asia

Aung Thaw, *Historical Sites in Burma*. Rangoon, 1972.

Bernet Kempers, A. J. *The Bronzes of Nālandā and Hindu-Javanese Art*. Leiden, 1933.

———. *Ancient Indonesian Art*. Amsterdam, 1950.

Bizot, François. 'La figuration des pieds du Bouddha au Cambodge'. *Asiatische Studien/Études Asiatiques*, 25 (1971), pp. 407–38.

Boisselier, J. *La statuaire Khmère et son évolution*. Publications de l'École Française d'Extrême-Orient. Paris and Saigon, 1955.

———. *La statuaire de Champa*. Publications de l'École Française d'Extrême-Orient. Paris and Saigon, 1963.

———. *Manuel d'archéologie, Asie du Sud-Est: Le Cambodge*, vol. 1. Paris, 1966.

———. 'Le Bouddha de Tuol Ta Hoy et l'art bouddhique du Sud-Est asiatique'. *Annales de l'Université des Beaux-Arts*. Phnom-Penh, 1967.

Chand, M. C., and Yimsiri, Khien. *Thai Monumental Bronzes*. Bangkok, 1957.

Coedès, G. 'Les collections archéologiques du Musée national de Bangkok'. *Ars Asiatica*. Paris and Brussels, 1928.

———. 'Une Roue de la Loi avec insciption en pāli . . .'. *Artibus Asiae*, 19. Ascona, 1956.

Devendra, D. T. *The Buddha Image and Ceylon*. Colombo, 1957.

Dhanapala, D. B. *Peintures de temples et de sanctuaires à Ceylan*. Coll. UNESCO, 1964.

Diskul, M. C. Subhadradis. *Ayuthya Art*. Bangkok, 1956.

———. *Art in Thailand*. Bangkok, 1970.

Dupont, P. 'La statuaire pré-angkorienne'. *Artibus Asiae*, suppl. Ascona, 1955.

———. *L'archéologie mône de Dvāravatī*. Publication de l'École Française d'Extrême-Orient. Paris, 1959.

Frédéric, Louis. *Sud-Est Asiatique*. Paris, 1964.

Giteau, M. 'Pièces d'art bouddhique de la Coll. S. M. le Roi du Laos'. *Arts Asiatiques*, 25. Paris, 1972.

Godakumbura, C. E. *Tivaṅka Pilimage Frescoes*. Art Series 4. Colombo, n.d.

———. *Buddha Statues*. Art Series 6. Colombo, n.d.

Griswold, A. B. 'The Buddha of Sukhodaya'. *Archives of the Chinese Art Society of America*, 7 (1953).

———. 'Dated Buddha images of Northern Siam'. *Artibus Asiae*, suppl. Ascona, 1957.

———. 'Imported images and the nature of copying in the art of Siam: Essays off. to G. H. Luce . . .'. *Artibus Asiae*. Ascona, 1966.

———. *Towards a History of Sukhodaya Art*. Bangkok, 1967.

Griswold, A. B., and Buribhand, Luang Boribal. 'Thai images of the Buddha'. *Thai Cultural Series*, 18. Bangkok, 1958.

Krom, N. J. *The Life of Buddha on the Stupa of Barabudur, According to the Lalitavistara Text*. The Hague, 1926.

Lalita Vistara. Translated by Ph. Ed. Foucaux, Annales du Musée Guimet. Paris, 1884.

Le May, R. *Buddhist Art in Siam*. Cambridge, 1938.

Lingat, R. 'Le culte du Buddha d'Émeraude'. *Journal of the Siam Society*, 27. Bangkok.

Luce, G. H. *Old Burma: Early Pagan*. 3 vols. *Artibus Asiae*. New York, 1969.

Malakul, M. L. Pin, and Diskul, R. C. Subhadradis et al. *In Commemoration of the Year 2500 of the Buddhist era in Thailand*. Bangkok, 1957.

Paranavitana, S. *Art and Architecture of Ceylon: Polonnaruwa Period*. Art Council of Ceylon, 1954.

Rajanubhab, H.R.H. Prince Damrong. 'Wat Benchamabopit and its collection of images of Buddha'. *Journal of the Siam Society*, 22. Bangkok.

Sang hyang Kamahāyānikan. Ed., translated, and commentaries by J. Kats. La Haye, 1910.

Schnitger, F. M. *The Archaeology of Hindoo-Sumatra*. Leiden, 1939.

Shorto, H. 'The stupa as Buddha icon in South East Asia'. *Mahāyānist Art after A.D. 900*. Ed. by William Watson. Colloquies on Art and Archaeology in Asia, No. 2 (London, 1971), pp. 75–81.

Souk, Thao Boun. *L'image du Bouddha dans l'art lao*. Vientiane, 1971.

Wijesekera, N. *Early Sinhalese Sculpture*. Colombo, 1962.

Yupho, Dhanit. *Dharmacakra or the Wheel of the Law*. Bangkok, 1965.
———. *Quartzite Buddha Images of the Dvāravāti Period*. Bangkok, 1967.

TIBET

Bhattacharyya, B. *The Indian Buddhist Iconography*. Calcutta, 1958.
Chandra, Lokesh, and Ragu Vira. *A New Tibeto-Mongol Pantheon*. 20 vols. New Delhi, 1961–72.
Clark, W. E. *Two Lamaist Pantheons*. 2 vols. Cambridge, Mass., 1937.
Francke, A. H. *Antiquities of Indian Tibet*. 2 vols. Calcutta, 1914 and 1926.
Getty, Alice. *The Gods of Northern Buddhism*. Oxford, 1928; reprint, 1963.
Hummel, Siegbert. *Geschichte der tibetischen Kunst*. Leipzig, 1953.
Karmay, Heather. *Ancient Sino-Tibetan Art*. Warminster, 1975.
Lowry, John. *Tibetan Art*. Her Majesty's Stationary Office, London, 1973; reprinted 1976.
———. 'Tibet, Nepal or China?—an early group of dated thang-kas'. *Oriental Art*, 19 (1973), pp. 306–15.
Macdonald, Ariane, and Imaeda, Yoshiro, in collaboration with Dvags-po Rinpoche, Yon-tan rGya-mtsho, Anne Marie Blondeau, Heather Karmay, John Lowry, H. E. Richardson, R. A. Stein. *Essais sur l'art du Tibet*. Paris, 1977.
Pott, P. H. *Introduction to the Tibetan Collection of the National Museum of Ethnology, Leiden*. Leiden, 1951.
Olschak, Blanche C., in collaboration with Geshé Thupten Wangyal. *Mystic Art in Ancient Tibet*. London, 1973.
Roerich, G. *Tibetan Paintings*. Paris, 1925.
Snellgrove, D. L. *Buddhist Himālaya*. Cassirer, Oxford, 1957.
Snellgrove, D. L., and Richardson, H. E. *A Cultural History of Tibet*. London, 1968.
Snellgrove, D. L., and Skorupski, T. *The Cultural Heritage of Ladakh*, vol. 1. Warminster, 1977.
Tucci, Giuseppe. *Indo-Tibetica*. 4 vols. Rome, 1932–41.
———. *Tibetan Painted Scrolls*. 3 vols. Rome, 1949.
———. *The Ancient Civilization of Transhimalaya*. Lonnod, 1973.

AFGHANISTAN AND CENTRAL ASIA

Albaum, L. I., and Brentjes, B. *Wächter des Goldes*. Berlin, 1972.
Andrews, Fred H. *Wall Paintings from Ancient Shrines in Central Asia Recovered by Sir Aurel Stein*. London, 1948.
Auboyer, Jeannine. *The Art of Afghanistan*. Feltham, Middlesex, 1968.
Barthoux, Jules. 'Les fouilles de Haḍḍa: 1. Stupas and sites'. *Mémoires de la Délégation Archéologique Française en Afghanistan*, 4. Paris, 1933.
———. 'Les fouilles de Haḍḍa: 3. Figures et figurines—Album photographique'. *Mémoires de la Délégation Archéologique Française en Afghanistan*, 6. Paris and Bussels, 1930.
Belenitsky, Alexander. *Asie Centrale*. Geneva, 1968.
Bussagli, Mario. 'Osservazioni sulla persistenza delle forme ellenistiche nell'arte del Gandhāra'. *Rivista dell'Istituto Nazionale d'Archeologia e Storia dell'Arte*, n.s., nos. 5 and 6 (1956 and 1957), pp. 149–247.
———. *L'arte del Gandhāra in Pakistan e i suoi incontri con l'arte dell'Asia Centrale. Catalogo della mostra, Roma-Turino 1958*. Rome, 1958.
———. 'L'influsso classico ed iranico sull'arte dell'Asia Centrale'. *Rivista dell'Istituto Nazionale d'Archeologia e Storia dell'Arte*, n.s., no. 2 (1953), pp. 171–262.
———. *Painting of Central Asia*. Geneva, 1963.
Dagens, Bruno et al. 'Monuments préislamiques d'Afghanistan'. *Mémoires de la Délégation Archéologique Française en Afghanistan*, 19. Paris, 1964.
Fischer, Klaus. 'Gandharan sculptures from Kunduz and environs'. *Artibus Asiae*, 21 (1958), pp.

231–53.
Gaulier, Simone, and Jera-Bézard, Robert, and Maillard, Monique. *Buddhism in Afghanistan and Central Asia*, pts. 1 and 2. Iconography of Religions, Section 13, Indian Religions, fascicles 14 and 15. Brill, Leiden, 1976.
Godard, André et al. 'Les antiquités bouddhiques de Bāmiyān'. *Mémoires de la Délégation Archéologique Française en Afghanistan*, 2. Paris, 1928.
Gray, Basil. *Buddhist Cave Paintings at Tun-huang*. London, 1959.
Grünwedel, Albert. *Altbuddhistische Kultstätten in Chinesisch-Turkistan*. Berlin, 1912.
———. *Alt-Kutscha*. Berlin, 1920.
Gullini, Giorgio, ed. *L'Afghanistan dalla preistoria all'Islam: Capolavori del Museo di Kabul*. Turin, 1961.
Hackin, Joseph. 'Sculptures gréco-bouddiques du Kapiśa'. *Monuments Piot*, 28 (1925–26), pp. 35–44.
Hackin, Joseph, and Carl, Jean. 'Nouvelles recherches archéologiques à Bāmiyān'. *Mémoires de la Délégation Archéologique Française en Afghanistan*, 3. Paris, 1933.
Hackin, Joseph, and Hackin, Ria. 'The colossal Buddhas at Bāmiyān: Their influence on Buddhist sculpture'. *Eastern Art*, vol. 1, no. 2 (1928), pp. 109–16.
Hackin, Joseph et al. 'Diverses recherches archéologiques en Afghanistan (1933–1940)'. *Mémoires de la Délégation Archéologique Française en Afghanistan*, 8. Paris, 1959.
Hallade, Madelaine. *Inde: Un millénaire d'art bouddique*. Paris, 1968.
Hallade, Madelaine et al. *Toumchouq; Mission Paul Pelliot*, 1–2 (Plates and text). Paris, 1961–64.
Hambis, Louis, ed. *Douldour-Aqour et Soubachi; Mission Paul Pelliot*, 3 (Plates). Paris, 1967.
Kyzlasov, L. R. 'Arkheologicheskie issledovanija na gorodishche Ak-Beshim v 1953–1954 gg.'. *Trudy Kirgizskoj arkheologo-étnograficheskoj ékspeditsii*, 2. Moscow, 1959.
Le Coq, Albert von. *Chotscho; Königlich-Preussische Turfan-Expedition*. Berlin, 1913.
———. *Bilderatlas zur Kunst und Kulturgeschichte Mittelasiens*. Berlin, 1925.
———. *Auf Hellas Spuren in Ost-Turkestan*. Leipzig, 1926.
———. *Von Land und Leuten in Ostturkistan*. Leipzig, 1928.
Le Coq, Albert von, and Waldschmidt, E. *Die Buddhistische Spätantike in Mittelasien*. 7 vols. Berlin, 1922–33.
Litvinskij, B. A., and Zejmal, T. I. *Adhzhina-tepa: Arkhitektura, Zhivopis. Skul'ptura*. Moscow, 1971.
Meunié, Jacques. 'Shotorak'. *Mémoires de la Délégation Archéologique Française en Afghanistan*, 10. Paris, 1942.
Mizuno, Seiichi, ed. *Durman Tepe and Lalma: Buddhist Sites in Afghanistan Surveyed in 1963–1965*. Kyoto, 1968.
Mustamandi, Shahebye. 'Preliminary report on Hadda's fifth excavation period'. *Afghanistan*, vol. 24, no. 2–3 (1971), pp. 128–37.
Mustamandi, Shahebye (Moustamindy, Ch.). 'Preliminary report of the sixth and seventh excavations expeditions in Tapa-Shutur, Hadda'. *Afghanistan*, vol. 26, no. 1 (1973), pp. 52–62.
Mustamandi, Shahebye, and Mustamandi, Mari. 'The excavation of the Afghan Archaeological Mission in Kapisa'. *Afghanistan*, vol. 20, no. 4 (1968), pp. 67–79.
Mustamandi, Shahebye, and Mustamandi, Mari (Mostamindi, Shaïbaï, and Mostamindi, Mariella). 'Nouvelles fouilles à Haḍḍa (1966–1967) par l'Institut Afghan d'Archéologie'. *Arts Asiatiques*, 19 (1969), pp. 15–36.
Ol'denburg, S. Th. *Russkaja turkestanskaja ékspeditsija 1909–1910 goda*. Sanktpeterburg, 1914.
Ōtani, K. *Shin Saiiki ki*. 2 vols. Tokyo-Yūkōshan, 1937.
Pelliot, Paul. *Les Grottes de Touen-houang*. 6 vols. Paris, 1920–24.
Riboud, Krishna, and Vial, Gabriel. 'Tissus de Touen-houang conservés au Musée Guimet et à la Bibliothèque Nationale'. *Mission Paul Pelliot*, 13. Paris, 1970.
Rosenfield, John M. *The Dynastic Arts of the Kushans*. Berkeley and Los Angeles, 1967.
Rowland, Benjamin. *The Wall-Paintings of India, Central Asia and Ceylon*. Boston, 1938.
———. 'The bejewelled Buddha in Afghanistan'. *Artibus Asiae*, 24 (1961), pp. 20–24.

———. *The Evolution of the Buddha Image.* Asia Society, New York, 1963.
———. *The Art and Architecture of India.* 3rd ed. Harmondsworth, 1967.
———. *Ancient Art from Afghanistan.* Asia Society, New York, 1966.
Rowland Benjamin, and Rice, M. F. *Art in Afghanistan (Objects from the Kabul Museum).* London, 1971.
Scerrato, Umberto. 'A short note on some recently discovered Buddhist grottoes near Bāmiyān, Afghanistan'. *East and West*, 11 (1960), pp. 94–120.
Schlumberger, Daniel. 'Descendants non-méditerranéens de l'art grec'. *Syria*, 37 (1960), pp. 131–66, 253–319.
Soper, Alexander C. 'Aspects of light symbolism in Gandhāran sculpture'. *Artibus Asiae*, 12 (1949), pp. 252–83, 314–30; 13 (1950), pp. 63–85.
Staviskij, Boris Ja., ed. *Materialy Sovmestnoj arkheologicheskoj ékspeditsii na Kara-tepe.* 3 vols. Moscow, 1964–72.
Stein, Sir Aurel. *Ancient Khotan.* Oxford, 1907.
———. *Ruins of Desert Cathay.* London, 1912.
———. *Serindia.* Oxford, 1921.
———. *Innermost Asia.* Oxford, 1928.
Taddei, Maurizio. 'Tapa Sardār': first preliminary report'. *East and West*, 18 (1968), pp. 109–24.
———. *India antica.* Milano, 1972.
———. 'Appunti sull'iconografia di alcune manifestazioni luminose dei Buddha'. *Gururājamañjarikā: Studi in onore di Giuseppe Tucci*, 2 (Naples, 1974), pp. 435–49.
———. 'A note on the Parinirvāṇa Buddha at Tapa Sardār (Ghazni, Afghanistan)'. *South Asian Archaeology 1973* (Leiden, 1974), pp. 111–15.
Waldschmidt, E. *Gandhara Kutscha Turfan: Eine Einführung in die frühmittelalterliche Kunst Zentralasiens.* Leipzig, 1925.
Williams, Joanne. 'The iconography of Khotanese painting'. *East and West*, 23 (1973), pp. 109–54.

China

Akiyama, T., and Matsubara, S. *Buddhist Cave Temples: New Researches.* Arts of China, vol. 2. Tokyo and Palo Alto, 1969.
Chavannes, E. *Mission archéologique dans la Chine septentrionale*, vol. 1:2 (text on Lung-men caves and their inscriptions). Paris, 1915.
Cheng Chen-to. *Mai-chi-shan Chü-k'u; Rock Grottos of Mai-chi-shan, Kansu.* Peking, 1954.
Davidson, J. Leroy. *The Lotus Sūtra in Chinese Art.* New Haven and Oxford, 1954.
Liu Chih-yüan and Liu T'ing-pi. *Ch'eng-tu Wan-fo-ssŭ shih-k'ê i-shu* [The sculptures of Wan-fo temple, Ch'eng-tu]. Shanghai, 1958.
Mizuno, S., and Nagahiro, T. *Yün-kang, the Buddhist Cave-temples of the Fifth Century in North China*; contains general essays on the evolution of cave temples, figure style and iconography, as well as descriptions of the Yün-kang sculpture; full English translations. Kyoto, 1952–56.
Møller, J. Prip. *Chinese Buddhist Monasteries.* Copenhagen, 1937 and Hong Kong, 1967.
Omura, S. *Chōsōhen: History of Chinese Art Sculpture.* Shina Bijutsu, 2 vols. Tokyo, 1922.
Sickman, Lawrence, and Soper, Alexander C. *The Art and Architecture of China. Artibus Asiae*, suppl. 19. Ascona, 1959.
Priest, Alan. *Chinese Sculpture in the Metropolitan Museum of Art.* New York, 1944.
Rowland, Benjamin. 'Indian Images in Chinese Sculpture'. *Artibus Asiae*, 10 (1947).
Sirén, Osvald. *Chinese Sculpture from the Fifth to the Fourteenth Centuries.* 4 vols. London, 1925.
Watson, William. *Style in the Arts of China.* Penguin Books, 1974; Universe Books, New York, 1975.
———. 'A dated Buddhist image of the northern Wei period'. *The British Museum Quarterly*, 22 (1960), p. 86 ff.
de Visser, M. W. *Ancient Buddhism in Japan*; 2 vols. on 7th and 8th centuries (material all from Chinese practises). Leiden, 1935.

Korea

Art Historical Association of Korea. *A Short History of Korean Art.* Seoul, 1970.

Bureau of Cultural Properties, Ministry of Culture and Public Information. *Mun Hwa Jae Tae Kwan* (National Treasures). Seoul, 1967.

Chosun Kojoktobo; an illustrated catalogue of Korean antiquities, vols. 3 (1916), 5 (1917) and 7 (1920).

Hwang, Su-young. 'On the stone Maitreya Buddha of the Silla dynasty from Samhwaryong, Namsan Kyŏnju'. Special publication commemorating the 60th birthday of Dr. Chewon Kim. Seoul, 1961.

Hwang, Su-young. *Study on Korean Sculpture.* Seoul, 1972.

Hwang, Su-young. 'Study on the meditative image of Paekje'. *Yoksa Hakbo* (The Korean Historical Review), no. 13 (October, 1960), Seoul.

Hwang, Su-young. 'Two newly discovered bronze images of the Koryŏ dynasty'. Commemorative publication for the 60th birthday of Dr. Sang Beck Lee. Seoul, 1964.

Kim, Che-won, and Kim, Won-yong. *The Arts of Korea.* London, 1966.

Kim, Won-yong. 'On the Buddhist image excavated at Dok-do, Seoul'. *Yoksa Kyoyuk* (The Korean Historical Education Review), no. 5 (March, 1961), Seoul.

Matsubara, Saburō. 'A systematic study on the stone Buddhas of the Silla kingdom'. *Bijutsu Kenkyū*, no. 250. Tokyo, 1966.

Nakagiri, I. *Sculpture of the Silla and Koryŏ Dynasties.* Tokyo, 1971.

Watson, William. 'The earliest Buddhist images of Korea'. *Transactions of the Oriental Ceramic Society*, 31 (1957), pp. 83–94.

Yi Wangka Bakmulkwan Sajinchop; an illustrated catalogue of the Buddhist images in the Yi Household Art Gallery. Seoul, 1929.

Japan

Note: The present bibliography covers only publications in book form. Titles marked by an asterisk are works in western languages; English renderings of Japanese titles are given and sometimes brief annotations have been added.

*Adachi, Kō. *Studies on the History of Japanese Sculpture.* Tokyo, 1944.

Akiyama, Terukazu, ed. *Japan (5): The Heian (1).* Kadokawa's Art of the World, 5. Tokyo, 1962.

———. *Emakimono* (Hand-scroll Paintings); with 111 plates. Shōgakukan's Art of Japan in Colour, vol. 8. Tokyo, 1968.

Asano, Kiyoshi, and Mōri, H. *The Buddhist Temple, Architecture of Nara and Tempyō Sculpture*; with 106 plates. Shōgakukan's Art of Japan in Colour, vol. 3. Tokyo, 1966.

———. *Studies on the Buddhist Temple Architecture of the Tempyō Period.* Tokyo, 1969.

*Brasch, Kurt. *Zenga: Zen Malerei.* Tokyo, 1961.

———. *Zenga.* Tokyo, 1962.

Buddhist Arts, an Illustrated Catalogue of the Exhibition at the Fukuoka-ken Culture Hall Gallery. Fukuoka, 1969.

Chikuma-shobō. *History of Japanese Culture.* 8 vols. Tokyo, 1965–66. 1. *Ancient* (1966); 2. *The Heian* (1965); 3. *The Kamakura* (1966); 4. *The Muromachi* (1966); and so on, with many illustrations.

Commission for Protection of Cultural Properties. *Wall-paintings of the Hōō-dō (Phoenix Hall), Byōdō-in*; with 74 plates. Tokyo, 1958.

———. *Wall-paintings of the Five-storeyed Pagoda, Daigo-ji*; with 86 colour and monochrome plates. Tokyo, 1961.

*Fontain, Jan, and Hickman, Money L. *Zen Painting and Calligraphy*; with a catalogue of the Zen art exhibition at the Museum of Fine Arts, Boston. Boston, 1970.

Fujita, Tsuneyo, ed. *A General History of Japanese Arts.* 2 vols. Tokyo, 1959–60. Revised popular edition, 6 vols. Tokyo, 1968–69.

Fukuyama, Toshio. *Byōdō-in and Chūson-ji: Buddhist Art and Architecture of the Late Heian Period.*

Heibonsha's Arts of Japan, vol. 9. Tokyo, 1964.
———. *Studies on the History of Japanese Architecture*. Tokyo, 1968.
———, ed. *Japan (2): The Asuka-Hakuhō*. Kadokawa's Art of the World, 2. Tokyo, 1961.
Fukuyama, Toshio, and Kuno, Takeshi. *Yakushi-ji*; its history, architecture and sculpture. Tokyo, 1958.
Fukuyama, Toshio et al. *Buddhist Temples in Japan* (bound volume). Tokyo, 1969.
Gangō-ji Buddhist Folklore Materials Publishing Society. *Chikō Mandara, a Representation of the Amitābha's Pure Land*. Tokyo, 1969.
van Gulik, Robert Hans. *Siddham*. Nagpur, 1956.
Hamada, Takashi. *Zuzō or Buddhist Iconography*. Shibundō's Arts of Japan, vol. 55. Tokyo, 1970.
———. *The World of the Mandala*. Tokyo, 1971.
Haruyama, Takematsu. *A History of Ancient Japanese Paintings*. Tokyo, 1949.
———. *A History of Paintings in the Heian Period*. Tokyo, 1950.
———. *A History of Medieval Japanese Paintings*. Tokyo, 1953.
Hayashiya, Tatsusaburō. *Japan: History and Culture*; with many colour and monochrome illustrations. 2 vols. Tokyo, 1966.
Hemmi, Baiyei. *Images of Kannon (Avalokiteśvara)*. Tokyo, 1960.
Henderson, Gregory, and Hurvitz, Leon. 'The Buddha of Seiryō-ji'. *Artibus Asiae*, 19/1 (1956).
Hisamatsu, Shin'ichi. *Zen Buddhism and Its Art*; with 290 plates. Kyoto, 1958.
*———. *Zen and the Fine Arts*. Translated by Gishin Tokiwa. Tokyo, 1971.
Hummel, Siegbert. 'Die Fubspur des Gautama Buddha auf dem Wu-t'ai-shan'. *Asiatische Studien/Études Asiatiques*, 25 (1971), pp. 389–406.
Ienaga, Saburō. *Studies on the History of Buddhist Thought in Japan*. 2nd rev. ed. Kyoto, 1966.
Inoue, Yasushi, and Nakano, Genzō. *Buddhist Images in Nara*. Kyoto, 1969.
Ishida, Hisatoyo. *Esoteric Buddhist Paintings*. Shibundō's Arts of Japan, vol. 33. Tokyo, 1969.
Ishida, Ichirō. *The Pure Land Buddhist Art in Japan*. Kyoto, 1956.
Ishida, Mosaku. *Buddhist Art Objects* (classified and illustrated). Tokyo, 1967.
———. *Mikkyō Hōgu* (Ritual Implements of Esoteric Buddhism). Tokyo, 1965.
Ishida, Mosaku, and Okazaki, Jōji. *Instruments (in metal) for Esoteric Buddhist Rituals*; with 12 colour plates and 623 figures. Tokyo, 1965.
Itō, Nobuo, and Kobayashi, Takeshi. *Medieval Buddhist Temple Architecture and Kamakura Sculpture*; with 158 plates. Shōgakukan's Art of Japan in Colour, vol. 9. Tokyo, 1968.
Kageyama, Haruki. *Studies on Shinto Arts*. Kyoto, 1962.
———. *Arts of Shintoism*. Shibundō's Arts of Japan, vol. 18. Tokyo, 1967.
Kameda, Tsutomu. *Studies on the Buddhist Art History of Japan*. Tokyo, 1970.
———, ed. *Japan (4): The Heian (1)*. Kadokawa's Art of the World, 4. Tokyo, 1961.
Kanamori, Jun. *Studies on the History of Japanese Sculpture*. Tokyo, 1949.
*Kidder, J. Edward. *Masterpieces of Japanese Sculpture*. Tokyo, 1961.
*———. *Japanese Temples*. Tokyo, 1964.
Kobayashi, Takeshi. *The Daibutsu (Colossal Buddha) of Tōdai-ji*; and sculpture of the Nara period. Heibonsha's Arts of Japan, vol. 5. Tokyo, 1964.
Kudō, Yoshiaki, and Nishikawa, Shinji. *The Amida-dō (Amitābha Hall) and Fujiwara Sculpture*; with 124 plates. Shōgakukan's Art of Japan in Colour, vol. 6. Tokyo, 1969.
Kuno, Takeshi. *Studies on the Early Sculpture in the Tōhoku Region*. Tokyo, 1971.
Kuno, Takeshi, and Suzuki, Kakichi. *Hōryū-ji*; its architecture and arts, with 126 plates. Shōgakukan's Art of Japan in Colour, vol. 2. Tokyo, 1966.
Kurata, Bunsaku. *Appreciation of Buddhist Images: Their Techniques and Expression*. Tokyo, 1965.
———. *Esoteric Buddhist Temples and Jōgan Sculpture*; with 122 plates. Shōgakukan's Art of Japan in Colour, vol. 5. Tokyo, 1967.
Kurata, Osamu. *Buddhist Ritual Instruments*. Shibundō's Arts of Japan, vol. 16. Tokyo, 1967.
Kyoto National Museum, ed. *Narrative Paintings of Japan*; with 78 plates. Kyoto, 1961.

Machida, Kōichi. *Yakushi-ji*. Tokyo, 1960.
The Mainichi Newspapers, ed. *Kokuhō* (National Treasures); with colour plates. 6 vols. Tokyo, 1963–67.
———, ed. *Kokuhō (National Treasures) in Colour*; popular edition, 11 vols. with 1,125 plates and an index volume. Tokyo, 1967–69.
Matsushita, Takaaki. *Suibokuga* (Ink painting). Shibundō's Arts of Japan, vol. 13. Tokyo, 1967.
Mizuno, Seiichi. *Hōryū-ji*; and Asuka-Hakuhō sculpture. Heibonsha's Arts of Japan, vol. 4. Tokyo, 1965.
Mōri, Hisashi. *Studies on the History of Buddhist Sculpture in Japan*. Kyoto, 1970.
———. *Sculptor Unkei and Kamakura Sculpture*. Heibonsha's Arts of Japan, vol. 11. Tokyo, 1964.
Murata, Jirō. *Historical Review of Researchers on Hōryū-ji*. Tokyo, 1949.
———. *Hōryū-ji*; its architecture and sculpture, with 141 plates. Tokyo, 1960.
Maruyama, Shūichi. *Arts of Pure Land Buddhism in Japan and the Amitābha Cult*. Tokyo, 1966.
Nakano, Genzō. *Sculpture of the Fujiwara Period*. Shibundō's Arts of Japan, vol. 50. Tokyo, 1970.
Nara National Museum, ed. *Buddhist Arts in the Hokkaidō and Tōhoku Regions*. Tokyo, 1972.
———. *Suijaku Arts* (Shintoistic arts); with 3 colour plates and 239 figures. Tokyo, 1964.
Nishikawa, Shinji. *Kamakura Sculpture*. Shibundō's Arts of Japan, vol. 40. Tokyo, 1969.
Noma, Seiroku, ed. *Japan (3): The Nara*. Kadokawa's Art of the World, 3. Tokyo, 1961.
*———. *The Arts of Japan*. 2 vols., with 198 colour plates. Tokyo, 1966.
Oka, Naomi. *Studies on the Sculpture of Shintō Gods*. Tokyo, 1966.
Okazaki, Jōji. *Paintings of Pure Land Buddhism in Japan*. Shibundō's Arts of Japan, vol. 43. Tokyo, 1969.
*Ōmura, Seigai. *History of Esoteric Buddhism*; in Chinese. 5 vols. Tokyo, 1918.
Ono, Genmyō. *Introduction to Buddhist Art*. Tokyo, 1917.
———. *Art and History of Buddhism in Japan*; with 32 colour plates and 113 figures. Tokyo, 1937.
Ōoka, Minoru. *Temples of Nara*. Heibonsha's Arts of Japan, vol. 7. Tokyo, 1965.
———. *Studies on the Seven Great Temples of Nara*. Tokyo, 1966.
Ōta, Hirotarō. *Introduction to the History of Japanese Architecture*. Tokyo, 1962.
Ōta, Hirotarō et al. *History of Japanese Architecture*. Shōkokusha's Outline of World Architecture, vol. 4, no. 1. Rev. ed. Tokyo, 1968.
Ōta, Koboku. *Techniques of Carving Wooden Buddhist Statues*. Kyoto, 1965.
*Paine, R. T., and Soper, Alexander C. *Art and Architecture of Japan*. Pelican History of Art. Harmondsworth, 1955.
*Sansom, George, B. *Japan: A Short Cultural History*. London, 1931; rev. 2d ed., 1964. Japanese translation by Rikichirō Fukui. 3 vols. Tokyo, 1951–52.
*Saunders, E. Dale. *Mudrā: A Study of Symbolic Gestures in Japanese Buddhist Sculpture*. New York, 1960.
Sawa, Ryūken. *Studies on Esoteric Buddhist Art*. Kyoto, 1955.
———. *Esoteric Buddhist Art in Japan*. Kyoto, 1961.
———. *Art of Esoteric Buddhism*. Heibonsha's Arts of Japan, vol. 8. Tokyo, 1964.
———, ed. *Illustrated Dictionary of Buddhist Iconography*. Tokyo, 1962.
*Scherman, Lucian. 'Siddha'. *Art and Thought*, ed. by K. Bharatha Iyer (London, 1947), pp. 52–62.
Shibue, Saburō, and Miyama, Susumu. *Buddhist Images in Kamakura*. Kamakura, 1965.
Shimada, Shūjirō, ed. *Buddhist Paintings, Yamato-e and Suibokuga*; 106 colour and 15 gravure plates, with an explanatory text with 126 figures. Japanese Paintings in Western Collections, vol. 1. Tokyo, 1969.
Shōgakukan, ed. *Illustrated History of Japanese Culture*. Rev. ed., 13 vols. and index vol. Tokyo, 1956–68. Vol. 2: *The Asuka*; with 28 colour plates and 490 figures. Vol. 3: *The Nara*; with 32 colour plates and 505 figures. Vol. 4: *The Heian* (1); with 28 colour plates and 469 figures. Vol 5: *The Heian* (2); with 28 colour plates and 459 figures. Vol. 6: *The Kamakura*; with 24 colour plates and 489 figures. Vol. 7: *The Muromachi*; with 28 colour plates and 655 figures.
Suzuki, Daisetz, T. *Sengai the Zen Master*. London, 1971.

*Tajima, Ryūjun. *Les deux grands mandalas et la doctrine de l'ésotérisme Shingon*. Tokyo and Paris, 1959.
Takakusu, Junjiro, ed. *Taishō Shinshū Daizō-kyō Zuzō* (The Tripiṭaka in Chinese, Picture Supplement). 12 vols. Tokyo, 1932–.(Corpus of Japanese Iconographic Drawings, Supplement of the Taishō Tripiṭaka Edition.)
Takasaki, Fujio. *History of Buddhist Paintings in Japan*; with 6 colour and 125 monochrome plates. Tokyo, 1966.
Takata, Osamu. *Studies on Buddhist Art History*. Tokyo, 1969.
———, ed. *Wall-paintings in Daigo-ji Pagoda*; joint researches, with 7 colour and 75 monochrome plates. Tokyo, 1959.
Takata, Osamu, and Akiyama, Terukazu, and Yanagisawa, Taka. *Takao Mandara, the Ryōkai Mandara* (Mandalas of the Two Principles of the Jingo-ji, Kyoto); with 100 plates. Tokyo, 1967.
Tanaka, Ichimatsu. *Studies on the History of Japanese Paintings*. Tokyo, 1966.
———, ed. *Japan (6): The Kamakura*. Kadokawa's Art of the World, 6. Tokyo, 1962.
Tanaka, Ichimatsu, and Yonezawa, Yoshiho. *Suibokuga* (Ink painting); with 118 plates. Shōgakukan's Art of Japan in Colour, vol. 11. Tokyo, 1970.
Tanaka, Toyozō. *Studies on Japanese Art*. Tokyo, 1960.
Tani, Shin'ichi. *The Muromachi Period in the History of Japanese Art*. Tokyo, 1942.
———, ed. *Japan (7): The Muromachi*. Kadokawa's Art of the World, 7. Tokyo, 1962.
Tazawa, Hiroshi, and Ōoka Minoru. *Illustrated History of Japanese Art*, with 830 figures and 601 text figures. 2nd ed., 2 vols. Tokyo, 1957; student edition, 1964.
Toganoo, Shōun. *A Study of Mandalas*; with 151 figures. Kōya-san, 1927; 2nd ed. 1932; reprint, 1958.
———. *A History of Esoteric Buddhism*. Kōyasan, 1933.
Tokyo National Museum, ed. *Catalogue of the Treasures Dedicated by Hōryū-ji*; with 313 figures. Tokyo, 1964.
Tsuji, Zennosuke. *History of Buddhism in Japan*. 10 vols. Vol. 1: *Early Age* (from Asuka to the Heian), 1944. Vols. 2–6: *Medieval Age* (from the Kamakura to the Yoshino-Muromachi), 1955. 2nd edition. Tokyo, 1960.
Tsukamoto, Zenryū, and Nakano, Genzō. *Buddhist Images in Kyoto*. Kyoto, 1968.
Ueno, Naoaki. *Sculpture of the Early Periods*. Tokyo, 1942.
Umezu, Jirō. *Studies on Emakimono* (Hand-scroll paintings). Tokyo, 1968.
The Wall-Paintings in the Kondō, Hōryū-ji. Portfolio. Kyoto, 1951.
*Warner, Landon. *Japanese Sculpture of the Suiko Period*. New Haven, 1923.
*———. *Japanese Sculpture of the Tempyō Period*; with 217 plates. Ed. and arranged by James M. Plumer. Cambridge, Mass., 1959.
Watson, William. *Sculpture of Japan from the Fifth to the Fifteenth Century*. London, 1959.
Yanagisawa, Taka, and Takata, Osamu. *Buddhist Paintings*; with 246 plates. Shōgakukan's Art of Japan in Colour, vol. 7. Tokyo, 1969.
Yashiro, Yukio. *Characteristics of Japanese Art*. Tokyo, 1943. Rev. 2nd ed. with 210 plates (separatum), 1967.
*Yashiro, Yukio, and Paine, P. C. *2000 Years of Japanese Art*. London, 1958.
Yoshikawa, Itsuji. *An Introduction to Japanese Art*. Heibonsha's Arts of Japan, vol. 1. Tokyo, 1966.

INDEX

All references refer to pages numbers. When special reference to an illustration is intended, the corresponding page number is shown in italics.
Terms which appear in the Glossary are marked (G).

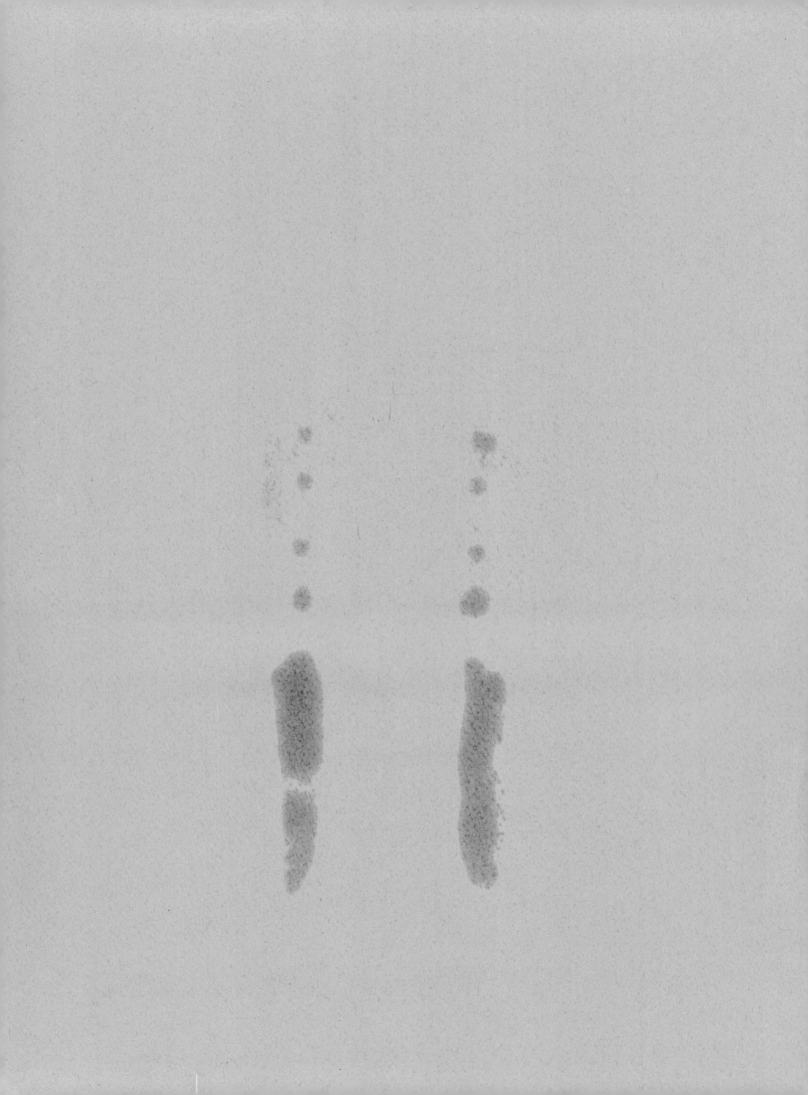